American Bar Exam Review

미국 변호사법

CEE 편

백
희
영

박영사

머 리 말

본 서는 미국변호사 캘리포니아 에세이 시험(CEE) 대비를 위한 책이다. CEE 시험대비 강의 요청이 있어 준비를 하던 중에 제대로 된 수험서를 내야겠다고 생각되어 본 서를 집필하게 되었다. MEE시험(DC Bar 에세이 시험)과 CEE시험(캘리포니아 바 시험)은 공통과목이 있으나, 양 시험의 성격 및 요구되는 답안 포맷이 전혀 다르다. 한 문제당 30분이 주어지는 MEE 시험에서는 질문과 직결되는 꼭 필요한 rule 및 단어를 작성하는 것이 중요한 반면, 1시간이 주어지는 CEE 시험에서는 주어진 사안에 대해 arguable points를 짚어내어 답안을 풍부하게 작성하는 것이 키포인트이다. 따라서 기존에 출판된 졸저「미국변호사법—Essay편」과는 전혀 다른, CEE만을 위한 수험서가 별도로 필요하여 이 책을 또 집필하게 되었다.

집필 과정에서 CEE 시험을 치르는 수험생과 동일한 감각으로 7개년치의 기출문제를 모두 풀었고, 관련 원서를 모두 읽으며 개념을 분석하였다. 그리고 나의 노하우와 답안요령 등을 모두 고스란히 담아 두었으므로, 수험자들은 본 서를 통해 단기간에 CEE 에세이 시험을 보다 쉽게 준비할 수 있을 것이다.

CEE 시험범위는 총 12개 과목으로, 그중 7개는 객관식 시험(MBE)과 동일한 과목이고, 나머지 5개는 에세이 시험에서만 다루는 과목이다. 다만, 7개 과목이 객관식 시험과 동일하다 하더라도 '캘리포니아 주' 시험이라는 특성상 MBE에서 요구되는 rule에 반드시 캘리포니아 룰을 추가적으로 익혀야 한다. 따라서 필자는 캘리포니아 룰과 common law 및 federal rule을 구분하는 데 중점을 두었다. 한편, 에세이 시험에서만 다루는 5개 과목에 대해서는 최대한 한글 설명을 덧붙여 수험자들이 이해하기 쉽도록 하였다.

본 서의 구체적인 특징과 구성은 다음과 같다.

1. 본 서의 '답안요령'은 실제 답안지에 반드시 써야 할 키워드들이다.

2. 본 서의 '모범답안'은 합격답안 포맷과 질이 어느 정도인지 보여준다.

3. 본 서의 '글쓰기 Tips'는 각 과목의 출제경향 및 전형적인 문제유형을 보여준다.

4. 본 서의 'TIP'은 고득점 포인트들과 자주 출제되는 arguable point들이다.

5. 본 서의 '별표(★)'는 반드시 암기해야 할 중요 핵심단어와 문장들이다.

6. 본 서의 '네모박스'는 암기노하우 및 복잡한 내용을 간략화한 것이다.

7. 본 서의 'Case'는 출제빈도가 높고 난해한 문제를 간략하게 한글로 설명하여 이해가 쉽게 하였고, 결론(답)까지의 과정을 logic하게 보여준다.

8. 본 서는 최근 기출문제 7년치의 논점을 모두 분석하여, 압축·정리해서 실었다.

9. 본 서의 '그림'과 '도표'는 복잡한 내용을 간결하게 정리하여 한눈에 파악되게 하였다.

10 본 서는 한글과 영문을 적절히 혼용하여 비유학파나 초심자라도 쉽게 이해되도록 하였다.

11. 본 서의 후반부 '부록'은 CEE 실제 기출문제 및 백변 answer이다.

끝으로, 이 책이 나올 수 있도록 도와주신 부모님과 출판에 고생하신 박영사 여러분께 감사드리며, 본 서와 함께 박학(薄學)인 나의 강의가 여러분들께 조금이라도 도움이 된다면 매우 기쁘겠다. 아무쪼록 머지않아 여러분들의 합격 소식을 듣게 되길 기대한다.

2021년 4월 20일
백희영 씀

Contents

제1편 CEE

1장 Professional Responsibility

2장 Business Associations

4장 Wills and Trusts

5장 Remedies

제2편 CEE/MBE

6장 Real Property

7장 Contracts

8장 Civil Procedure

9장 Torts

11장 Evidence

12장 Criminal Law and Criminal Procedure

Appendix

제 1 편

CEE

//

1장
Professional Responsibility

//

본 장은 '변호사 윤리'에 관해 논하는 바, 그 내용은 크게 변호사와 의뢰인간 수임 관계(attorney-client relationship) 형성, 변호사가 의뢰인·상대방 측·법원에 대해 지는 의무(duty), 변호사 사퇴(withdrawal) 그리고 변호사 및 비변호사간 협업 관계로 구분된다. 모든 주(州)는 각자의 변호사 윤리규정을 제정할 수 있으나, 대체로 미국변호사 협회(American Bar Association)가 규정한 ABA Model Rules of Professional Responsibility를 그대로 채택하고 있으나, 캘리포니아는 ABA Model Rules를 채택하지 않고 California Rules of Professional Conduct에서 별도로 변호사 윤리에 관해 규정하고 있다. CEE에서는 ABA Model Rules와 캘리포니아 변호사협회(State Bar of California)가 규정한 California Rules of Professional Conduct 두 규정에 대해 모두 출제되고 있는 바, 각 규정의 차이점에 유의하여야 한다. 본 서에서는 ABA Model Rules와 California Rules간 차이점이 있는 논점의 경우 각 rules의 내용을 구분하여 논하였다.

- ABA Model Rules of Professional Responsibility
- California Rules of Professional Conduct

☑ 글쓰기 Tips

1. Professional Responsibility는 최근 7년간 CEE 기출문제 중 출제 빈도수가 가장 높은 과목으로서, 주로 Evidence, Contracts, 그리고 Business Associations와 연계되어 출제되었다. Evidence와 연계되어 출제된 경우, 주로 attorney-client privilege와 work-product doctrine 논점이 출제되었다. Business Associations와 연계되어 출제된 경우, 변호사가 타 변호사 및 비변호사인 자와 함께 법무사업을 운영하는 과정에서의 윤리문제에 대해 논하도록 요구되었다.

2. 최근 7년간 출제되었던 Professional Responsibility 문제는 California rules와 ABA rules 모두에 대해 논하도록 요구되었다.

3. 문제 본문을 읽으면서 '윤리규정을 위반한 행위'에 표시하는 것이 좋다.

4. 변호사의 행위 중 윤리규정을 위반한 행위가 어떤 것이 있는지 수험자에게 판단토록 요구하는 포괄적인 문제가 자주 출제된다.

   Q: <u>What ethical violations, if any, has 갑 committed? Answer according to California and ABA authorities.</u>

   ⇒ 대체로 '변호사의 행위'를 title화하여 작성하는 것이 쉬우나, 그렇지 않은 경우에는 변호사의 행위와 변호사가 위반한 duty를 함께 title화하여 작성한다.

5. 변호사의 특정행위에 대한 윤리규정 위반 여부를 묻는 문제가 출제되기도 한다.

   Q: <u>What are 갑's ethical violations with regard to [representation against 을]?</u>

   Q: <u>May 갑 ethically [ignore the court order]?</u>

   ⇒ 변호사가 '위반한 duty'를 title화하여 작성한다.

6. 본 장에 관한 모든 답안은 '변호사와 의뢰인간 수임관계 형성여부'를 가장 먼저 서술한다.

[Attorney-Client Relationship]

If a client reasonably believes he was being represented by the lawyer, an attorney-client relationship is formed. The duty begins when the relationship is formed or, at very least, at the execution of a retainer agreement.

Ⅰ. Attorney-Client Relationship

변호사가 의뢰인에게 지는 의무는 변호사와 의뢰인간 수임관계가 형성되어야만 인정된다. 따라서 변호사의 윤리위반 여부 판단을 하기 위해서는 수임관계 형성 여부에 대한 판단이 선제적으로 이루어져야 한다. 수임관계는 '의뢰인'이 자신의 사건이 변호사에게 수임되었다는 것을 합리적으로 예상할 수 있는 경우 형성되었다고 본다. 즉, 변호사와 의뢰인간 별도의 수임계약서를 작성하지 않았다 하더라도 의뢰인에 대한 변호사의 비밀유지의무, 성실의무 등의 의무가 인정될 수 있다. 한편, 수임료에 대한 계약(fee agreement)은 수임계약과는 다른 유형의 계약으로서 일정 요건을 만족해야만 그 유효성이 인정되는 바, fee agreement의 유형은 일반 수임료(regular fee)인 경우와 성공보수(contingent fee)인 경우로 구분되고 각 경우에 대한 요건은 ABA와 California에서 다르게 규정한다.

> | TIP | 특정 행위의 ethical violation 여부는 ① attorney-client relationship 존재여부 ② retainer agreement 유효성 여부에 대해 우선 판단하고, 그 이후 변호사의 다양한 duty에 대해 analysis한다.

A. General Rule

★If a **client reasonably believes** he was being represented by the lawyer, an attorney-client relationship is formed.

An attorney-client relationship can be formed even without any fee changing and without a signed agreement.

B. Attorney-Client Contract (Fee Agreement) (16Feb, 18July)

• Fee agreement = Retainer agreement

1. Regular Fee Agreement

a. General Rule

A fee agreement for non-contingent fee must state:

ⅰ. How the lawyer's fee is calculated;

ⅱ. Expenses that will be paid out of the fee; and

ⅲ. Duties of the clients and the lawyer.

b. Reasonability Requirement

ⅰ. ABA Rules

★Under the ABA rules, retainer fee should be **reasonable.**

Reasonability is determined in considering several factors such as:

① The **experience and ability of the lawyer;**

② The **nature and length of the professional relationship** between the lawyer and the client; and

③ The **fee** charged for **similar** legal services.

ii. California Rules

★In California, retainer fee should **not be illegal or unconscionable.**

c. Writing Requirement

i. ABA Rules

Under the ABA rules, writing is **not required** for a valid retainment agreement.

ii. California Rules

★In California, fee agreement should be in writing, **unless:**

① **The client waives** the writing;

② The client is a **corporation;**

③ The fee is **less than $1,000;**

④ The fee is for **routine work** for a regular client; or

⑤ There is an **emergency.**

2. Contingent Fee Agreement

A contingent fee is a fee where payment depends on the outcome.

a. General Rule

★Under the both ABA and California rules, contingent fees are **prohibited** in both **criminal and domestic cases.** Domestic cases are cases regarding a divorce, alimony or support, or property settlement.

b. Requirements

A contingent fee agreement should:

① Be **in a writing;**

② Be **signed by the client;**

③ Include the **method** how the fee is to calculated (e.g., percentage);

④ Include **litigation and other expenses** to be deducted from the recovery; and

⑤ Include whether such expenses are to be deducted **before or after** the contingent fee is calculated.

ⅰ. California Rules

California rules further require the contingent fee agreement should:

① Be signed by the lawyer (**both lawyer and client**); and

② State that the fee is **negotiable.**

3. Malpractice Liability (16Feb)

Malpractice는 부정행위 및 위법행위를 뜻하는 바, malpractice liability는 변호사가 자신의 직무수행 중의 malpractice에 대해 지는 책임을 의미한다. 의뢰인은 변호사의 malpractice에 대해 조사하고 그에 대한 책임을 묻는 소송(disciplinary^{징계의} action)을 제기할 수 있는 권리를 가지는 바, 본 권리에 대한 제한은 원칙적으로 금지된다. 예컨대, 변호사가 의뢰인은 변호사의 malpractice에 대해 소송을 제기하지 않겠다는 조항이 있는 수임계약을 체결할 경우, 해당 변호사의 ethical violation이 인정된다. 다만, ABA에서는 의뢰인이 수임계약을 체결할 당시 다른 변호인을 선임하였을 경우에 한해 의뢰인의 권리가 제한되는 것을 허용한다.

> TIP   Malpractice liability 논점은 ① 사안에 변호사와 의뢰인간의 수임계약서 내용이 자세히 명시되어 있는 경우, ② 수임료가 보통의 경우보다 적게 책정된 경우, ③ 변호사가 경험이 적은 분야의 소송을 수임하는 경우 자주 출제된다.

a. ABA Rules

Under the ABA rules, a lawyer may **not limit** a client's right to seek disciplinary action or to participate in an investigation.

However, if the client is represented by an **independent counsel** in making the agreement, limitation of malpractice liability is allowed.

b. California Rules

In California, **any limitation** of malpractice liability is forbidden.

4. Fee Disputes (16Feb)

변호사 갑이 의뢰인 을을 대리하여 병을 상대로 소송을 제기하였고, 이에 대해 병이 을에게 100만원의 손해배상액을 지급해야 한다는 법원의 판결이 내려진 경우, 병은 일반적으로 100만원을 갑에게 지급하고, 갑이 100만원 중 을이 자신에게 지불해야 하는 수임보수를 제한 나머지 금액을 을에게 송금한다. 즉, 변호사가 의뢰인을 대리하여 손해배상액 등 자금을 받은 경우 변호사는 이를 의뢰인에게 notify하고 해당 자금을 시기적절하게 지급해야 한다. 만일 변호사와 의뢰인간 수임보수에 있어 분쟁이 있는 경우라면, 변호사는 전체 금액(100만원) 중 분쟁이 없는 부분만을 을에게 전달하고 분쟁이 있는 금액은 을의 trust account에 예치하여야 한다. 분쟁이 해결될 때까지 trust account는 변호사가 관리한다. 예컨대, 갑·을간 수임보수 40만원에 대해 분쟁이 있다면, 갑은 병으로부터 지급받은 100만원 중 60만원을 을에게 송금하고 분쟁이 있는 40만원은 을의 trust account에 예치하여야 한다. 만일 갑이 수임보수 70만원을 주장하고 을은 40만원을 주장하는 경우, 30만원에 대해 분쟁이 있으므로 30만원은 trust account에 예치하고 갑에게는 분쟁이 없는 수임보수 40만원이 지급되며 나머지 30만원(100만원−30만원−40만원)은 을에게 지급된다.

When the lawyer received the funds on the client's behalf, a lawyer has the **duty to notify** the client and **distribute client funds promptly.** However, when there is a **dispute** between a lawyer and a client regarding the fees owed, the lawyer must send the **undisputed portion** to the client.

The disputed portion should be **kept by the lawyer** in the **client trust account** until the dispute has been resolved.

C. Attorney-Client Privilege (17July)

Attorney-client privilege는 변호사와 의뢰인간 이루어졌던 confidential communication에 대한 진술거부권으로서, 이는 의뢰인 및 변호사가 그러한 communication에 대한 증언을 거부하기 위해 행사하는 특권이다. 즉, 의뢰인과 변호사 모두 본 특권을 행사함으로써 confidential communication에 대한 증언을 거부할 수 있다. 한편, 본 특권은 "'의뢰인'이 hold하고 있다"고 표현되는데, 이는 의뢰인이 본 권리를 행사하여 의뢰인 스스로 진술을 거부할 수 있을 뿐만 아니라 수임관계에 있는 상대방(변호사)에게 진술거부를 강요할 수도 있다는 의미이다. 따라서 변호사 스스로 본 특권을 행사하지 않았다하더라도 의뢰인이 행사하였다면, 변호사는 confidential communication에 대해 증언할 수 없다. 반면, 변호사는 의뢰인이 attorney-client privilege를 행사하지 않더라도 본 권리를 행사하여 진술을 거부할 수 있으나, 자신이 본 권리를 행사하였다하여 본 권리를 행사하지 않은 의뢰인에게 이를 강요할 수는 없다. 여기서 'confidential communication'은 의뢰인 및 그의 대리인이 법적 조언을 얻기 위해 변호사에게 언급한 비밀 대화를 뜻하는 바, 대화 내용을 적은 memorendum은 본 특권으로부터 보호받지 못한다. 즉, 상대방 측 및 법원이 범행에 사용된 knife, gun 또는 memorendum의 제출을 요구하였을 때 의뢰인 또는 변호사는 이를 거부할 수 없다. 한편, attorney-client privilege는 변호사가 업무상 알게 된 의뢰인의 비밀을 공개하여서는 아니 된다는 '변호사'의 duty of confidentiality와 변호사가 소송준비를 위해 작성한 문서에 대해 제출을 거부할 수 있다는 내용의 work-product doctrine과 연관성이 깊다. 변호사가 attorney-client privilege를 행사하지 않고 의뢰인간 나누었던 confidential communication에 대한 증언을 한다면, 이는 duty of confidentiality를 위반하는 행위이다. 하지만 attorney-client privilege는 대화만을 보호하는 반면, duty of confidentiality는 변호사가 업무상 알게 된 의뢰인에 대한 모든 것을 보호한다는 점에서 차이가 있다.

그렇다면 attorney-client privilege는 언제까지 지속되는가. 수임관계가 종료된 이후에도 본 특권이 지속되는지 그 여부가 주된 논점이다. ABA rules에 따르면, 본 특권은 변호사가 해당 사건으로부터 remove되었다 하더라도 지속되고 일반적으로 의뢰인이 사망 시까지 지속된다고 본다. 즉, 의뢰인이 이를 행사하는 시점에서의 attorney-client 관계 형성여부는 본 특권 행사여부와 무관하다. 다만, 캘리포니아에서는 의뢰인이 사망하였고 그의 유산(estate)이 모두 정리(settle)된 후에는 본 특권이 종료된다고 본다. 예컨대, 갑이 변호사 을을 수임하는 동안 법적 조언을 위한 confidential communication이 이루어졌고 그 이후 갑이 을을 fire한 경우, 을이 fire된 이후에도 갑·을 간의 confidential communication은 보호된다. 반면, 만약 상기 예시에서 갑이 을을 fire한 후 사망하였고 그의 유산이 모두 정리되었다면 ABA rules와 CA rules 모두 해당 대화를 보호하지 않는다.

1. General Rule

★Attorney-client privilege protects **confidential** communications made **by the client or the client's agents to facilitate legal relationship. Client** holds the privilege.

a. End Point

i. ABA Rules

The privilege **applies** even if a lawyer is subsequently removed from a case.

ii. California Rules

★In California, the privilege **ends** when the client **dies and his estate is entirely disposed of.**

2. Exceptions

a. ABA Rules

However, there are some exceptions:

i. When such communications are related to **client's future commission** of a crime or fraud; and

    ii. When there are **disputes between the attorney and the client, or between the clients.**

  b. California Rules

    In California, there are some exceptions:

    i. When such communications are related to the **future commission of a crime or fraud** (committed by anyone);

    ii. When there are **disputes between the attorney and the client, or between the clients**; and

    iii. <u>When the lawyer **reasonably believes** that disclosure would be necessary to prevent serious bodily harm to others.</u>

✔ Client의 친인척과 변호사간의 대화 내용 → 친인척은 client's agent 가 아님 → privilege 적용 ✕

✔ Client의 의사(physician) → client's agent ○ → privilege 적용 ○
A physician who is hired to examine the client is recognized as a client's agent, and the attorney-client privilege is applicable.

✔ 회사가 client인 경우 employee speaking on behalf of the corporation → client's agent ○ → privilege 적용 ○

✔ 공동피고인(co-defendants)의 변호인이 되는 경우 → privilege 적용 ✕(The privilege is waived between the defendants.)

D. Sexual Relationship (16Feb)

변호사는 의뢰인과 성관계를 가질 수 있는가. 이에 대해 ABA rules와 캘리포니아 rule은 각각 다르게 규정하고 있으며, 변호사와 의뢰인과의 관계 및 관계형성 시점을 기준으로 다른 기준을 적용하고 있다. ABA rules에 따르면 수임관계가 형성되기 이전부터 변호사와 성관계를 가져왔던 자가 도중에 의뢰인이 된 경우(pre-existing sexual relationship)에는 수임관계 형성된 이후의 성관계가 허용되는 반면, 수임관계가 형성된 이후 의뢰인과의 성관계(sexual relationship with current client)는 금지된다. 캘리포니아 rules의 경우, ABA rules와 마찬가지로 pre-existing sexual relationship이 허용되나 current client는 변호사의 배우자와 배우자가 아닌 자로 구분하여 배우자인 경우에 한해 허용하고 있다. 즉, 배우자가 아닌 current client와의 성관계는 금지된다. 본 캘리포니아 rules는 2018년 11월 1일부터 시행된 개정안 내용이다. 개정되기 이전의 rule은 current client와의 조건부 관계와 강요에 의한 관계는 금지하였으나 그렇지 않은 sexual relationship with current client는 허용하였다. 개정안에서는 변호사의 배우자를 제외한 나머지 current client와의 성관계를 모두 금하고 있는 바, 개정되기 이전의 rule과 비교하여 변호사와 의뢰인간 sexual relationship에 대해 더 엄격히 금하고 있다고 할 수 있다.

한편, 변호사가 sexual relationship을 가지고 있는 의뢰인의 사건을 수임하는 것은 duty of loyalty에 위배되는 행위이다. 이는 sexual relationship을 가지고 있는 의뢰인의 이익이 변호사 개인의 이익과 충돌하기 때문이다. 의뢰인은 변호사로부터 능숙한 변론을 받아야 할 interest가 있으나, 변호사는 개인적으로 그러한 의뢰인의 부탁을 들어주고자 하는 personal interest가 있다. 하지만 의뢰인의 부탁을 들어주는데 있어 그가 능숙한 변론을 제공해야 하는 의무가 제한된다면, conflict of interest가 발생하는 것이다. 예컨대, 이혼 전문 변호사 갑이 sexual relationship을 가지고 있는 을의 부탁으로 을의 계약 관련 소송을 수임한 경우, 변호사 갑이 을의 부탁을 들어주고자 하는 personal interest는 을이 갑으로부터 능숙한 변론을 받을 interest와 충돌한다. 따라서 갑의 수임은 duty of loyalty에 위배된다.

[표 1-1]

	ABA	California (개정안)	
Pre-existing 관계	○	○	
With current client	×	Lawyer's spouse or registered domestic partner	○
		그 외	×

1. General Rule

a. ABA Rules

Representing a client with whom an attorney has a sexual relationship **before is allowed.** Attorneys should **not** have sexual relationships with clients **after** they take on the clients.

b. California Rules

In California, **pre-existing** sexual relationships **are allowed.**

Sexual relationships with a **current client** who is not he lawyer's spouse or registered domestic partner are **not** allowed.

[California Rules of Professional Conduct §1.8.10]

Effective November 1, 2018

(a) A lawyer shall not engage in sexual relations with a current client who is not he lawyer's spouse or registered domestic partner, unless a consensual sexual relationship existed between them when the lawyer-client relationship commenced.

(b) For purposes of this rule, "sexual relations" means sexual intercourse or the touching of an intimate part of another person for the purpose of sexual arousal, gratification, or abuse.

2. Conflicts of Interest (Duty of Loyalty)

When a lawyer has sexual relationships with his client, there is a **conflict of interest** and the lawyer violates the **duty of loyalty.**

The **lawyer's personal interest** in attempting to appease^{요청을 들어주다} his lover would materially limit his competent representation.

1. Sexual relationship 허용여부 (ABA v. Cal)
   + analysis
2. Conflicts of interest
   + analysis

TIP1 변호사가 의뢰인과 sexual relationship을 가지고 있는 사안에서는
      ① ABA rules와 California rules에 따른 sexual relationship 허용여
      부와 ② conflicts of interest 존부를 모두 analysis한다.

TIP2 사안에 따라 duty of competence, duty of fairness 등 다양한 duty
      와 관련이 있을 수 있다.

모범답안 001

1. Sexual relationship

General rule

Under the ABA rules, attorneys should not have sexual relationships with clients after they take on the clients. Representing a client with whom an attorney has a sexual relationship before is allowed. In California, both pre-existing sexual relationships are allowed. Sexual relationships with a current client who is not he lawyer's spouse or registered domestic partner are not allowed.

(ANALYSIS: In this case, attorney 갑 had sexual relationship with 을 after 갑 represented 을. Thus, the sexual relationship between 갑 and 을 is not allowed under the ABA rules. Moreover, in California, the sexual relationship is not allowed since 을 is not 갑's spouse or registered domestic partner.) In conclusion, the sexual relationship between 갑 and 을 is not allowed under the both ABA rules and California rules.

Conflicts of interest

A lawyer owes duty to avoid all conflicts of interest with his client. Duty of loyalty is breached when a lawyer represents a client with interests adverse to the interest of the lawyer, other clients, or third party. There are three types of conflicts of interest: conflicts between the client and the lawyer's own interest, conflicts between the clients, and conflicts between the client and the third party.

When a lawyer has sexual relationships with his client, there is a conflict of interest and the lawyer violates the duty of loyalty. The lawyer's personal interest in attempting to appease his lover would materially limit his competent representation.

(ANALYSIS: In this case, 갑 has no experience in contract cases but 을 wanted him to represent her contract suit. There is a conflict between the client and the lawyer's own interest. 갑 has personal interest in attempting to appease 을, but it would materially limit his competent representation for 을.)

Conclusion

In conclusion, there is a conflict between the client and the lawyer's own interest and 갑 violated the duty of loyalty.

E. Lawyer as Witness

1. ABA Rules

Under the ABA rules, a lawyer may not represent a client if he is likely to have to testify at trial.

However, a lawyer may stand at trial as a witness when:

ⅰ. The matter is related to his services;

ⅱ. The matter is related to the breach of duty; or

ⅲ. The testimony is necessary to prevent undue hardship.

2. California Rules

In California, a lawyer may stand at trial as a witness at bench trial, or at jury trial with a consent of a client.

Bench trial은 판사가 최종 판결을 내리는 재판을 뜻하고, jury trial은 배심원이 최종 판결을 내리는 재판, 즉 국민참여 재판을 뜻한다.

3. Lawyer as Witness and Duty of Confidentiality

When a lawyer's testimony is necessary, the lawyer must consider the conflicts of interest issue.

If there is a conflict of interest, the lawyer must have client's informed consent, confirmed in writing (informed written consent in California).

II. Duty to avoid Conflicts of Interest (Duty of Loyalty)
(16Feb, 16July, 17Feb, 18July, 19July, 20Feb)

- Concurrent conflict of interest: 모든 유형의 conflicts of interest를 통틀어 일컫는 용어
- Current conflict = Actual conflict
- Potential conflict = Future conflict

[ABA §1.7]

A concurrent conflict of interest exists if:

(1) The representation of one client will be directly adverse to another client; or

(2) There is a significant risk that the representation of one or more clients will be materially limited by the lawyer's responsibilities to another client, a former client or a third person or by a personal interest of the lawyer.

변호사는 변호사 자신 및 타인과의 이익(interest)이 서로 충돌되는 자를 대리하거나 변론할 수 없다. 즉, 변호사는 conflicts of interest가 존재하는 사건은 수임할 수 없다. 이는 변호사는 의뢰인의 최대 이권을 위해 업무해야 한다는 duty of loyalty로부터 파생된 의무이다. 여기서 "conflicts of interest가 존재한

다"는 의미는 ABA rules와 California rules에서 다르게 해석된다. ABA rules에 따르면 사건을 수임하면 바로 발생할 이익충돌(actual conflict)이 존재하는 경우 conflicts가 존재하는 바, 변호사는 해당 사건을 수임하여서는 아니 된다. 한편, California rules는 actual conflict뿐만 아니라 미래에 발생할 가능성이 높은 이익충돌(potential conflict)도 conflict로 보고, 이 중 어느 하나라도 존재한다면 변호사는 해당 사건을 수임 할 수 없다. 예컨대, 공동피고인 2명이 변호사 갑에게 사건을 수임하기를 원하는 경우 양 피고인간 당장의 이익충돌 (actual conflict)은 존재하지는 않으나 미래에 변론하는 과정에서 피고인이 다른 피고인에게 불리한 진술을 하고자 하는 경우와 같이 이익충돌(potential conflict)이 존재할 가능성이 높다. 따라서 ABA rules에 따르면 변호사는 본 사건을 수임할 수 있는 반면, California rules에 따르면 수임할 수 없다.

Conflicts of interest의 유형은 충돌하는 이익간 관계를 기준으로 ① 수임하고자 하는 의뢰인의 이익과 변호사의 이익(lawyer's personal interest)이 서로 충돌하는 경우, ② 수임하고자 하는 의뢰인의 이익과 변호사가 현재 수임하고 있는 의뢰인(current client)의 이익이 충돌하는 경우 그리고 ③ 수임하고자 하는 의뢰인의 이익과 제3자의 이익이 충돌하는 경우, 이렇게 세 유형으로 구분된다. Conflicts of interest가 존재한다 하더라도 일정 요건을 만족하면 예외적으로 변호사가 대리 및 변론할 수 있는데, 상기 ①, ②, ③ 유형에 대해 동일한 예외 요건이 적용되나, ABA rules와 California rules가 규정하는 예외 요건에는 다소 차이가 있다.

ABA Model Rules는 예외 요건 세 가지를 다음과 같이 규정하고 있다. Conflicts of interest가 존재함에도 자신이 능숙한 변호를 수행할 수 있을 것이라고 변호사가 '합리적'으로 판단할 것, 이익이 충돌하는 의뢰인에게 '동의'를 구할 것, 해당 수임이 법적으로 금지되지 않을 것이 그것이다. 그중 변호사의 합리적 판단 요건을 reasonability standard라 일컬으며, California rules는 본 요건을 제외한 나머지 두 요건만을 예외요건으로 규정하고 있다. 즉, 의뢰인의 동의가 있고 법적으로 금지된 수임이 아니라면 conflicts of interest가 존재하더라도 예외적으로 수임가능하다. ABA rules와 California rules의 가장 큰 차이점은 예외 요건 중 의뢰인의 '동의' 의미를 해석하는 데 있다. ABA rules에 따르면 client의 동의가 반드시 서면으로 이루어져야 하는 것은 아니고, 구두상으로 동의했다

하더라도 이후에 동의한 내용을 서면으로 작성하였다면 인정된다. 반면, California rules는 client가 동의할 당시 해당 내용이 서면으로 작성되어야만 유효한 동의로 인정하고, 이후에 서면으로 작성하였다 하더라도 인정하지 않는다. 즉, California rules가 ABA rules에 비해 더 엄격한 기준을 가지고 있다. 한편, ABA rules는 상기 예외 요건(3개)을 ①, ②, ③ 유형에 공통적용하나, California rules는 ②, ③ 유형에 대해 상기 예외 요건(2개)을 적용하고 ① 유형에 대해서는 별도의 예외 요건을 적용한다. 즉, 수임하고자 하는 의뢰인(갑)의 이익과 lawyer(을)'s personal interest가 서로 충돌하는 경우, 이익이 충돌하는 의뢰인(갑)에게 변호사(을)가 해당 conflict에 대해 서면으로 disclose해야 한다. 별도의 written consent는 요구되지 않는다.

[표 1-2]

	ABA	California
'conflict of interest' 의미	actual conflict (potential conflict는 무관)	actual conflict 또는 potential conflict
	⇒ actual conflict가 존재하는 경우 수임불가	⇒ actual conflict와 potential conflict 중 어느 하나라도 존재하는 경우 수임불가
예외 요건 (수임할 수 있는 경우) 유형 ① 유형 ② 유형 ③	i. lawyer's reasonable belief ii. client's consent iii. not prohibited by law	written disclosure i. client's consent ii. not prohibited by law
Consent 내용	actual conflict	actual + potential conflict
Consent 방식	informed consent, confirmed in writing	informed written consent = informed consent in writing
	⇒ 최종적으로 의뢰인이 양해(consent)한 내용이 서면 작성이면 OK	⇒ 의뢰인이 양해할 당시 양해할 내용이 서면으로 작성되어 있어야만 함

A. General Rule

★A lawyer owes duty to avoid all conflicts of interest with his client. Duty of loyalty is breached when a lawyer represents a client with interests adverse to the interest of the lawyer, other clients, or third party. There are three types of conflicts of interest: conflicts between the client and the lawyer's own interest, conflicts between the clients, and conflicts between the client and the third party.

1. ABA Rules

Under the ABA rules, a lawyer should not represent a client when there is **actual** conflict.

★However, a lawyer **can** represent a client when:

ⅰ. He **reasonably believes** that he can provide competent and diligent representation to affected client;

ⅱ. Affected client gives **informed consent, confirmed in writing;** and

ⅲ. The representation is not prohibited by law.

2. California Rules

In California, a lawyer should not represent a client when there is **actual conflict or potential** conflict.

However, a lawyer **can** represent a client when:

ⅰ. Affected client gives **informed consent in writing;** and

ⅱ. The representation is not prohibited by law.

✔ Co-defendants를 변론하는 경우 — potential conflict
✔ 변호사의 개인적인 생각과 의뢰인의 주장이 충돌하는 경우 — potential conflict
✔ 회사의 director(member of BOD)이면서 동시에 사내변호사인 경우 — potential conflict
   갑 would not act in the best interest of the corporation, but for his

own personal financial benefit as a director.

✔ 회사와 회사의 owner를 동시 수임하는 경우 — potential conflict

B. Lawyer – Client Conflicts (16Feb, 16July, 17Feb)

1. General Rule

★Duty of loyalty is breached when a lawyer represents **a client** with interests adverse **to his own personal interests.**

In California, the lawyer can represent the client when the lawyer provides written disclosure.

✔ 친인척 관계의 사람을 against하는 자를 변호해야 하는 경우 → conflict between attorney and his client (personal conflict of interest) 인정

✔ 두 명의 co-defendants를 모두 변호해야 하는데, 그중 한명이 친인척 관계인 경우 → conflict 인정

✔ Former fiancee(前 부인)가 상대편 변호사인 경우(특히 former fiancee 와 여전히 사이가 좋은 경우) → Former fiancee와 좋은 사이를 유지 하고자 하는 변호사 개인의 interest와 complete representation을 받을 의뢰인의 interest가 충돌한다. → conflict 가능성 有

✔ Current fiancee가 상대편 변호사인 경우 → conflict 인정

✔ Sexual relationship을 형성하고 있는 client를 수임하는 경우 → conflict 가능성 有

✔ Client가 변호사가 속한 단체를 상대로 소송하고자 하는 경우 → conflict 인정

2. Personal Belief

When a lawyer disagrees with the client's objective, **potential** conflict of interest is recognized. Thus, the lawyer commits ethical violation by representing such client under the California rules.

✔ 변호사의 개인적인 생각과 의뢰인의 주장이 충돌하는 경우 → potential

conflict가 존재함. → 본 사건을 수임하는 경우 ABA rules상 no violation 이나, California rules상 violation이 인정된다.

3. Lawyer's Personal Relationship

When opposing lawyer is **closely related by blood or marriage**, a lawyer must obtain **informed consent** before representing.

California rules further require written disclosures when:

ⅰ. One lawyer is **the client of the other lawyer;**

ⅱ. Two lawyers **cohabitate;** or

ⅲ. Two lawyers personally have a **close relationship.**

C. **Conflicts Between Clients** (18July, 19July)

변호사는 자신의 의뢰인과 이익(interest)이 서로 충돌되는 자를 대리하거나 변론할 수 없다. 여기서 변호사의 '의뢰인'은 현재 대리 및 변론하고 있는 의뢰인(current client)뿐만 아니라 위임사무가 종료된 종전 의뢰인(former client)도 포함한다. 이러한 conflicts of interest는 변호사가 co-defendants 모두를 변론하는 경우 또는 변호사가 타 로펌으로 이직하는 경우 자주 발생하는 유형이다. 전자(前者)의 경우는 current client의 이익이 충돌되는 경우이며, 후자(後者)의 경우는 변호사가 이직한 새로운 로펌에서 종전 의뢰인(former client)과 이익이 충돌되는 자를 대리함으로써 발생한다. 예컨대, 변호사 갑이 을이 병을 상대로 제기한 소송을 수임하고 있던 중 병을 대리했던 로펌으로 이직하여 그 새로운 로펌에서 을을 상대로 하는 소송을 수임한다면, 변호사 갑의 former client 을에 관한 conflict of interest가 발생하는 바, duty of loyalty에 위배된다. Duty of loyalty에 따르면, 변호사 갑은 former client 을을 상대로 하는 소송에 참여해서는 아니 되며, 종전 의뢰인의 정보를 사용하는 것도 금지된다. 그런데 변호사 갑이 을을 상대로 하는 소송에 참여하면 duty of loyalty뿐만 아니라 duty of confidentiality에도 위배된다. 한편, 변호사 갑이 병이 을을 상대로 하는 소송을 수임하여 duty of loyalty를 위반한 것에 대한 책임은 새로운 로펌이 지며, 그 로펌에 속한 모든 변호사는 해당 소송을 수임해서는 아니 된다. 다만, 일정 요건을 만족하는 경우에는 변호사 갑이 아닌 새로운 로펌 내의 다른 변호사는 수임가능하다.

1. General Rule

★Duty of loyalty is breached when a lawyer represents **a current client** with interests adverse to **one another** (another client) or represents a current client whose interests are adverse to a **former client.**

2. Conflicts with Former Clients

a. Duty to avoid Conflicts of Interest and Duty of Confidentiality

★An attorney may not:

ⅰ. Participate in an action against former client; or

ⅱ. Use information relating to the representation of former client.

When a lawyer uses information relating to the former representation, the duty of confidentiality is violated.

b. Switching Law Firm

ⅰ. **Lawyer**

When a lawyer moved to new firm, the lawyer should not knowingly represent a person in the same or a substantially related matter when the lawyer's previous firm represented a client whose interests are materially adverse to that person.

If the lawyer represents the person, a conflict of interest exists unless the former client makes an **informed consent confirmed in writing** (informed written consent in California).

ⅱ. **New Firm**

The new firm is disqualified as the conflicts of interest are imputed to^{책임을 지우다} the entire new firm, **unless:**

① The disqualified lawyer is **timely screened** from any participation in the matter;

② The disqualified lawyer **shares no fees** from the case;

③ **Written notice** is given to the former client; and

④ **Certification** of compliance with ethical rules is given to the former client when the client requested it.

답안요령

Q: What ethical obligations must 갑 respect with regard to ABC firm's job offer?

1. Duty of loyalty 기본 rule
   + analysis(수임관계 형성여부)★
2. Conflicts of interest of former client & Duty of confidentiality★
   + analysis
4. New firm으로 move한 변호사의 책임
   + analysis
5. New firm의 책임 (imputation)
   + analysis

TIP1 변호사가 타 로펌으로 이직한 사안의 경우 ① duty of loyalty, ② duty of confidentiality 그리고 ③ conflicts of interest에 대한 imputation on new firm 모두를 analysis하여 판단하는 것이 고득점 포인트다.

TIP2 Duty of loyalty에 관한 analysis(위 1번)는 수임관계 형성여부를 판단하여 변호사에게 duty of loyalty가 있음을 서술한다.

모범답안 002

1. ABC's job offer

Duty of loyalty

A lawyer owes a duty of loyalty to his clients to zealously advocate on their behalf. Thus, a lawyer is required to avoid any conflicts of interest that could materially affect their ability. That duty begins when an attorney-client relationship is formed or, at very least, at the execution of a retainer agreement.

(ANALYSIS: 갑 and 을 properly executed a retainer agrement, and thus the attorney-client relationship was formed. Thus, 갑 owed 을 all of the duties, including duty to avoid conflicts of interest.)

Conflicts of interest and Duty of confidentiality

Duty of loyalty is breached when a lawyer represents a client whose interests are adverse to a former client. An attorney may not: (1) participate in an action against former client; or (2) use information relating to the representation of former client. When a lawyer uses information relating to the former representation, the duty of confidentiality is violated.

(ANALYSIS: In this case, 갑 was representing 을 in a suit between 을 and 병. 갑 moves to new firm, ABC firm, and ABC firm is representing 병. 을 is a former client and 갑 should not participate in the suit between 을 and 병 and should not use information as to the representation.)

Moving to a new firm

When a lawyer moved to new firm, the lawyer should not knowingly represent a person in the same or a substantially related matter when the lawyer's previous firm represented a client whose interests are materially adverse to that person. If the lawyer represents the person, a conflict of interest exists unless the former client makes an informed consent confirmed in writing (informed written consent in California).

(ANALYSIS: In this case, 갑 is going to represent 병 whose interests are materially adverse to 을, a former client of 갑. There is no fact indicating that 을 made a consent. Thus, under the both ABA and California rules, 갑 will violate the duty of loyalty.)

Imputation in the new firm

The conflict of interest is imputed in the new firm, unless: (1) the disqualified lawyer is timely screened from any participation in the matter; (2) the disqualified lawyer shares no fees from the case; (3) written notice is given to the former client; and (4) certification of compliance with ethical rules is given to the former client when the client requested it. (ANALYSIS: In this case, there is no fact indicating that 갑 was properly screened. Thus, the conflict of interest is imputed in ABC firm.)

Conclusion

In conclusion, 갑 moved to a new firm and 을 is a former client. 갑 should not participate in the suit between 을 and 병 and should not use information as to the representation. Under the both ABA and California rules, 갑 will violate the duty of loyalty since there is no consent of 을. Moreover, the conflict of interest is imputed in ABC firm since there was no proper screened procedure.

D. Client-Third Party Conflicts

변호사는 타인(third party)과 이익(interest)이 서로 충돌되는 자를 대리하거나 변론할 수 없다. 여기서 '타인과 이익이 충돌되는 경우'란, 타인(third party)이 변호사가 의뢰인을 대리하는데 제약을 가할 수 있는 경우를 뜻한다. 보통 제3자가 변호사에게 수임비용을 지불하는 경우를 말하는데, 이러한 경우 변호사가 사건을 수임하는데 있어 제3자의 영향을 받을 수밖에 없기 때문이다. 즉, '타인(third party)'은 일반적으로 변호사에게 수임료를 지급하는 제3자를 의미한다. 다만, 의뢰인의 양해가 있고, 수임료를 지불하는 제3자로부터의 변호사의 독립성이 보장되며, 의뢰인의 비밀유지가 보장되는 경우에는 제3자로부터 수임료를 받더라도 변호사는 예외적으로 사건을 수임할 수 있다.

1. General Rule

★Duty of loyalty is breached when interest of a third person materially limit the lawyer's ability to represent the client.

2. Exception

a. ABA Rules

★A lawyer must not accept compensation from a third person for representing a client, **unless:**

    ⅰ. Client makes informed **consent;**

    ⅱ. **Lawyer's independence** is not interfered by the third person; and

    ⅲ. Client's information remains **confidential.**

  b. California Rules

    In California, exception rule for compensation from a third person further requires **consent in writing.**

| case 1 |

회사 ABC의 bylaw에는 다음과 같은 내용이 명시되어 있다. "회사 직원을 상대로 그의 회사업무에 관해 제기된 소송비용은 일체로 회사가 부담하며, 회사는 해당 직원을 상대로 indemnify하지 않는다." 변호사 갑은 회사 ABC로부터 변호사비용을 지급받는다. 갑이 ABC 직원 을을 변호하는데 있어 ethical violation이 있는가?

⇒ Yes. 갑이 변호하고자 하는 client는 을이고, 회사 ABC는 갑의 수임료를 지불하는 third party이다. 만일 갑이 을의 변호를 맡게 된다면, 이에 대한 모든 비용을 회사 ABC, 즉 갑의 수임료를 지불하는 회사(third party)가 지불해야 하므로 갑이 을을 대리하는데 있어 상당한 제약이 있을 것으로 예상된다. 따라서 을과 회사 ABC간 conflict가 존재한다.

| case 2 |

갑이 ABC 자선단체에 1,000불 이상 기부하는 자의 will을 작성하는 경우 해당 자선단체가 그에게 수임료를 지불하기로 하였다. 갑이 을의 will을 작성하는 업무를 수임한다면, ethical violation을 하는가?

⇒ Yes. 자선단체는 third party, 을은 갑이 수임하고자 하는 client이다. 갑이 자선단체로부터 조건부 수임료를 받고 있기 때문에, 을의 will을 작성하는데 있어 ABC 자선단체로부터 자유롭다고 보기 어렵다.

> 1. Duty of loyalty & Duty to avoid conflicts of interest
>   + analysis — 수임관계 형성여부★
> 2. Conflict of interest 유형
>   + analysis
> 3. Exceptions (ABA v. Cal)
>   + analysis

TIP1 Ethical violation에 관한 문제는 '수임관계 형성여부'를 먼저 판단한 후, 변호사의 윤리위반에 대해 판단한다.

TIP2 이익충돌이 존재하더라도 수임할 수 있는 예외요건, 특히 consent 요건에 관해 ABA rules와 California rules가 다르게 규정하고 있다는 점을 명시하는 것이 좋다.

TIP3 주어진 사안에 retainer agreement의 내용이 명시되어 있는 경우, 그 내용은 consent 요건과 관련이 있을 가능성이 높다.

모범답안 003

1. Duty to avoid conflicts of interest

Duty of loyalty

A lawyer owes a duty of loyalty to his clients to zealously advocate on their behalf. Thus, a lawyer is required to avoid any conflicts of interest that could materially affect their ability. That duty begins when an attorney-client relationship is formed or, at very least, at the execution of a retainer agreement.

(ANALYSIS: In this case, 갑 and 을 properly executed a retainer agrement, and thus the attorney-client relationship was formed. Thus, 갑 owed 을 all of the duties, including duty to avoid conflicts of interest.)

Conflicts between the client and the lawyer's own interest

There are three types of conflicts of interest: conflicts between the client and the lawyer's own interest, conflicts between the clients, and conflicts between the client and the third party.

(ANALYSIS: In this case, 갑 has no experience in contract cases but 을 wanted him to represent her contract suit. There is a conflict between the client and the lawyer's own interest. 갑 has personal interest in attempting to appcase 을, but it would materially limit his competent representation for 을. Thus, there is a conflict between the client and the 갑's own interest.)

In conclusion, there is a conflict between the client and the 갑's own interest and 갑 will violate his duty of loyalty if he represents 을.

Exception

Under the ABA rules, a lawyer may represent a client with actual conflicts of interest if: (1) the lawyer reasonably believes that he can provide competent and diligent representation to affected client; (2) affected client is given an informed consent; and (3) the representation is not prohibited by law. The reasonability standard uses subjective test and an informed consent which is confirmed in writing is enough. Under the CA rules, a lawyer may represent a client with actual or potential conflicts of interest when written disclosure is made. Written consent is not required in the case with conflicts between the client and lawyer's own interest.

(ANALYSIS: In this case, 갑 informed the client 을 that there is an actual conflict between his and 을's conflict. 을 made written consent for 갑 to represent him. Thus, there is no ethical violation under the ABA rules. However, 갑 did not give 을 a written information about the conflict of interest. Thus, 갑 will violate the duty of loyalty if he represents 을 under the California rules.)

Conclusion

In conclusion, there is an actual conflict of interest between 갑's personal interest and 을's interest, but, under the ABA rules, 을 gave an informed consent and there is no breach of duty of loyalty. However, under the

California rules, 갑's representation will violate the duty of loyalty.

Duty to avoid conflicts of interest (potential interest)

1. Duty of loyalty & Duty to avoid conflicts of interest
   + analysis — 수임관계 형성여부★
2. Potential conflict of interest 고려여부(ABA v. Cal)
   + analysis — potential interest 고려여부
3. Conflict of interest 유형
   + analysis
4. Exceptions (ABA v. Cal)
   + analysis

모범답안 004

1. Duty to avoid conflicts of interest

Duty of loyalty

A lawyer owes a duty of loyalty to his clients to zealously advocate on their behalf. Thus, a lawyer is required to avoid any conflicts of interest that could materially affect their ability. That duty begins when an attorney-client relationship is formed or, at very least, at the execution of a retainer agreement.

(ANALYSIS: In this case, 갑, 을, and 병 properly executed a retainer agrement, and thus the attorney-client relationship was formed. Thus, 갑 owed 을 and 병 all of the duties, including duty to avoid conflicts of interest.)

Potential conflict of interest

Under the ABA rules, a lawyer should not represent a client when there is actual conflict. In California, a lawyer should not represent a client when there is actual conflict or potential conflict.

(ANALYSIS: In this case, there is a potential conflict of interest because 갑 represents co-defendants, 을 and 병. Both 을 and 병 decided to hire 갑

as their lawyer, but there is a high possibility that one might want to testify against the other. There are no actual conflicts of interest and, therefore, 갑 can represent 을 and 병 under the ABA rules. However, 갑 cannot under the California rules.

Types of conflicts

There are three types of conflicts of interest: conflicts between the client and the lawyer's own interest, conflicts between the clients, and conflicts between the clients and the third party.

(ANALYSIS: In this case, 을 and 병 are 갑's clients and there is a potential conflict between the clients.)

Exception

Under the ABA rules, lawyer may represent a client with actual conflicts of interest if: (1) the lawyer reasonably believes that he can provide competent and diligent representation to affected client; (2) affected client is given an informed consent; and (3) the representation is not prohibited by law. The reasonability standard uses subjective test and an informed consent which is confirmed in writing is enough. Under the CA rules, reasonability is not required and the consent must be informed in writing. (ANALYSIS: In this case, the representation is proper under the ABA rules and exception rule is inapplicable. Under the CA rules,······.)

Conclusion

In conclusion, there is a potential conflict of interest between 을 and 병. Thus, under the ABA rules, the representation will not violate the duty of loyalty but violate the duty under the California rules. However, 을 and 병 were given written disclosure and 갑's representation will not violate the duty of loyalty.

III. Lawyer's Duties

A. Duty of Competence and Duty of Diligence (16Feb, 16July, 18Feb, 19Feb, 19July)

Duty of competence는 client를 변호하는데 필요한 지식과 스킬을 모두 활용해야 할 변호사의 의무를 뜻한다. 이는 client의 이권을 위해 헌신할 의무인 duty of diligence와 유사한 의무로서, duty of competence가 위반된 행위는 duty of diligence를 위반하는 경우가 많다. Duty of competence와 duty of diligence의 위반여부를 판단하는 기준은 ABA와 California에서 다르게 규정하고 있다. ABA rules는 '합리성(reasonableness)'을 기준으로 한다. 즉, 합리적인 변호사가 동일한 상황에서 활용했을 지식과 스킬 수준을 요구하는 바, 그 수준에 미치지 못한 변호사의 행위는 duty of competence와 duty of diligence를 위반했다고 판단한다. 한편, California rules는 'recklessness'를 기준으로 한다. 즉, 변호사가 고의적인 부주의 또는 중과실(gross negligence)로 필요한 지식과 스킬을 활용하지 않은 경우 두 의무를 위반했다고 판단한다.

1. General Rule

★A lawyer has a **duty of competence,** requiring a lawyer to act with the **legal knowledge and skill necessary to represent** the client.

A lawyer has a **duty of diligence,** requiring a lawyer to act with diligence^{근면성실} in representing a client. A lawyer should act with dedication^{헌신} to the client's interests.

2. Standards

a. ABA Rules

★ABA uses reasonable lawyer standard, requiring a lawyer to act with the knowledge and skill **reasonably necessary** to provide competent and diligent legal services.

✔ 변호사가 마음속으로 client의 패소를 바라는 경우 — ABA rules상

breach(breach of the duty of competence는 인정되나, conflicts of interest는 인정되지 않는다.)

✔ Court order를 거부하라고 조언한 경우 — ABA rules상 breach → breach the duty to competence & duty to the court

✔ Fail to appear in front of court — ABA rules상 breach → breach the duty of competence & duty to the court

✔ Frivolous claim을 file한 경우 — ABA rules상 breach → breach the duty of competence & duty to the court

✔ 변호사가 경험이 없는 또는 경험이 많지 않은 분야의 소송을 수임하는 경우 — ABA rules상 breach → breach the duty of competence

b. California Rules

★In California, reckless standard is used, requiring a lawyer not to act **intentionally, recklessly, or with gross negligence.**

✔ File a claim한다면 법원에서 impose sanction할 것이라고 '예상했음에도 불구하고' file a claim하는 경우 — ABA와 CA (reckless) rules상 breach

✔ '상습적으로' frivolous claim을 file하는 변호사 — ABA와 CA (intentionally) rules상 breach

✔ 증인의 증언이 false statement인지 '알면서도' 아무 조치를 취하지 않은 경우 — ABA와 CA (reckless) rules상 breach → breach of duty of competence & breach of duty to court

✔ 변호사가 자신의 전문 분야가 아닌 분야를 수임하였고, 해당 분야에 대해 철저한 준비가 없었던 경우 — ABA와 CA (reckless) rules상 breach
⇒ 문제 본문에서 '특정 업무에 대한 변호사의 경험' 유무에 대해 명시되어있는 경우, duty of competence에 대해 analysis한다.

✔ 변호사의 employee가 의뢰인의 계약서를 작성하였고, 이를 변호사가 검토한 경우 — ABA와 CA rules상 모두 breach 없음(so long as the lawyer exercises competent and diligent review and independent legal judgment in rendering advice).

3. Duty to avoid Frivolous Claims (16July, 19July)

변호사는 소송(claim)을 제기하는데 있어 반드시 법적 근거(basis in law)와 good-faith가 있어야 한다. 법적 근거 및 good-faith 없이 제기하는 claim은 frivolous^{경솔한} claim으로서, 이를 제기하는 변호사는 duty to avoid frivolous claims, duty of competence 그리고 duty of fairness 모두 breach하게 된다. Duty of competence는 상기 언급한 바와 같이 client를 변호하는데 있어 적절한 지식과 스킬을 활용해야 하는 의무로서, frivolous claim을 제기할 경우 본 의무를 위반하게 된다. 한편, duty of fairness는 상대방 및 법원을 상대로 공정하게 행동할 의무이다.

When a lawyer files a legal claim, the claim must be warranted **by existing law or by a good-faith argument.**
If a lawyer raises a frivolous claim, he breaches the duty to avoid frivolous claims.

- ✔ To pursue a legal right — not a frivolous claim
- ✔ To threat/harass the opposing party — frivolous claim
- ✔ To get the attention of the opposing party — frivolous claim
- ✔ 상대방의 요청에 대해 overbreadth objection을 하는 경우(interpose^{덧붙이다} reasons) — frivolous claim
- ✔ 변호사 본인의 생각과 반대되는 소송을 제기했다는 사실만으로는 breach of the duty to avoid frivolous claims를 주장하기 어렵다.
  The fact that the lawyer 갑 personally disagree with the filing of the complaint does not ensure a frivolous claim.

B. Duty to Communicate (17Feb, 20Feb)

Duty to communicate에 따르면, 변호사는 그의 client와 원활한 소통을 해야 한다. 본 의무는 변호사가 수임하고 있는 사건의 중요한 사안(material facts)들을 client에게 전달해야 하는 의무와 client가 해당 사건에 대해 요청하는 바에 대해 즉시(promptly) 답해야 하는 의무를 모두 포함한다. 만일 client가 회사인 경우에는 변호사는 회사의 책임자(higher authority), 즉 board of directors(BOD)와 원활한 소통을 해야 한다고 해석된다. 특히 회사 사원의 행동이 회사에 막대한 영향을 끼칠 우려가 있는 경우 변호사는 이를 회사 내부의 higher authority에 전달해야 하는데, 이렇게 회사에 관한 정보를 누군가에게 전달하는 행위를 "reporting out"라 표현한다. 만일 회사 내부의 higher authority가 변호사로부터 해당 사안에 대해 전달받았음에도 불구하고 이에 대해 어떠한 조치도 취하지 않는 경우라면 변호사가 취해야 하는 행동이 있는데, 이에 대해 ABA와 California는 다르게 규정하고 있다. ABA는 외부에 reporting out를 하도록 요구하며, 이를 변호사의 duty of confidentiality의 예외로 인정한다. 반면 California rules는 변호사가 사임할 수 있도록(MAY withdraw) 허용하고, 외부에 reporting out를 하는 것을 원칙적으로 금한다.

1. General Rule

A lawyer must promptly and diligently communicate with his client. The duty to communicate requires a lawyer **to disclose all material facts** to the representation and **to respond promptly** to the client's requests.

- ✔ Client가 변호사에게 무언가를 요구한 경우, 해당 요구사항이 client에게 어떤 불이익이 있을지에 대해 알려줄 의무
- ✔ 변호사가 유능하게 representation을 하기 위해 요구되는 client의 행위가 있는 경우, 변호사는 이를 client에게 알려줄 의무가 있다. (예: 변호사가 client에게 email을 보낼 때 "답장을 해달라"는 내용을 언급해야 한다.)
- ✔ 회사를 대표하는 lawyer: owe **to board** of directors (not to employees)
- ✔ 회사 직원이 personally hire the corporation's lawyer하려는 경우, the lawyer is required to **disclose the scope** of representation more clearly.

2. Report to Higher Authority (16July, 20Feb)

When a lawyer is representing **a corporation** and he discovers corporate misconduct, he **must report it up to a higher authority in the corporation.**

a. ABA Rules

If the higher authority fails to remedy the reported problem, the lawyer **may report out** the information to an outside agency as an exception to the duty of confidentiality.

b. California Rules

If the higher authority fails to remedy the reported problem, the lawyer **may not report out** the information, but **may resign (withdraw)** from the representation.

Reporting out is permitted only when the lawyer believes that:

ⅰ. He has **remonstrated**^{항의하다} the client not to take this action; or

ⅱ. The disclosure is **reasonably necessary to prevent the harm.**

C. Duty of Confidentiality (16July, 17July, 19July)

변호사는 client 정보에 대해 비밀유지의무가 있다. 따라서 변호사는 자신이 수임했었던 client의 정보를 이용해서는 아니 되며, 그 client의 반대측을 변호해서도 안 된다. 본 의무는 변호사가 다른 로펌으로 이직할 경우 violate될 확률이 매우 높다. 다만, client의 서면동의가 있거나 client를 변호하는데 있어 공개가 필요한 경우라면 예외적으로 client 정보를 공개할 수 있다. Client의 서면 동의에 관해 ABA rules는 informed consent confirmed in writing을, California rules는 informed written consent를 요건으로 규정하고 있다. 한편, 법원에서 client 정보 공개를 요구하거나 discovery 단계에서 상대방의 client 정보공개 요청이 있는 경우 변호사는 client 정보를 공개할 수 있다.

✔ 회사의 unlawful conduct에 대해 report out하는 행위 → duty of confidentiality 위배되지 않음(duty of confidentiality의 예외에 해당)

✔ 변호사 갑이 close relationship을 가지고 있는 회사 A를 상대로 회사 B가

소송을 제기하였고, 갑이 회사 B를 대리하는 경우 → 변호사 갑이 회사 B
의 정보를 회사 A에 줄 가능성이 높다.

There is a high possibility that 갑 provides B's confidential information
to A.

✔ 변호사가 현재 의뢰인 갑을 수임하고 있는데, 상대방 을을 수임하고 있는
로펌에서 job offer를 받아 이직한 경우 — duty of confidentiality 위배될
확률이 매우 높다.

1. General Rule

★A lawyer should not disclose any information relating to the
representation.

Under the duty of confidentiality, an attorney may not:

ⅰ. Participate in an action against a client; or

ⅱ. Use information relating to the representation of a client.

a. Exceptions

However, a lawyer may disclose confidential information when:

ⅰ. There is an **express written consent** by a client;

ⅱ. There is an **implied authorization** (requirement by a statute or
court order);

ⅲ. It is necessary to prevent death or serious bodily injury;

ⅳ. A lawyer **reasonably believes** that disclosure is **necessary to
avoid imminent bodily harm to a third party**; or

ⅴ. The fact has become **generally known to the world**.

✔ Discovery 단계에서 증거에 대한 상대방측의 합법적 요청이 있는
경우 → 위 ⅱ 경우에 해당 → 상대방측의 implied authorization이
인정되는 바, 변호사는 수임한 의뢰인에 관한 정보를 상대방측에게
disclose해야 하며, 본 행위는 duty of confidentiality에 위배되지
않는다.

TIP1 생각 route: Duty of confidentiality ⇒ implied authorization ⇒ duty of competence & duty of fairness

상대방이 권리에 입각하여 client 정보 공개를 요청한 경우, 이는 duty of confidentiality와 관련이 있으나 상대방에게 implied authorization이 있는 경우에 해당한다. 따라서 정보를 공개하지 않는 경우 변호사는 client에 대한 duty of competence와 상대방에 대한 duty of fairness를 모두 위반하게 된다.

TIP2 주어진 사안이 co-defendants의 사건 수임에 관한 경우, 양 피고 (인)의 attorney-client privilege가 waive되나 변호사가 의뢰인들로부터 서면동의를 받지 못한다면 duty of confidentiality에 위배된다는 점을 명시해야 한다.

2. Co-Defendants (18July)

When an attorney represents co-defendants, duty of confidentiality and attorney-client privilege are waived between the defendants.

An attorney must tell the defendants as to the risk of losing confidentiality and get **written consent**.

D. Duty to Safeguard

★A lawyer owes a duty to safeguard possessions of the client, including evidence and property.

When a lawyer keep the client's property, he **should not commingle** funds with his own property. Usually, a lawyer deposits the client's property in bank accounts labeled "Trust Account," or "Client's Funds Account."

E. Duty to the Court (17Feb, 18Feb, 19July)

변호사가 법원에 대해 지는 의무에는 duty of fairness to the court, duty to candor to the court 그리고 duty of decorum to the tribunal이 있다. Duty of fairness to the court는 잘못된 사실관계 및 법적 관계를 발설하는 행위

또는 잘못된 증거임을 인지했음에도 불구하고 법원에 제출하는 행위 등을 금한다. Duty to candor^{솔직} to the court는 법적근거 없는 소송을 제기하는 행위를 금한다. Duty of decorum^{예의} to the tribunal는 변호사가 재판 진행 과정을 방해하는 행위 또는 재판관(judges) 및 배심원(jurors)에 영향을 끼치는 행위를 금한다.

1. Duty of Fairness to the Court

A lawyer should not **knowingly:**

ⅰ. Make a false statement of fact or law;

ⅱ. Offer evidence that he knows to be false; and

ⅲ. Fail to disclose adverse legal authority.

An attorney is required **to investigate** legal positions and pleadings representing before he stands before the court.

✔ 상대방의 요청에 대해 overbreadth objection을 하는 경우 (interpose^{덧붙이다} reasons) — 위 ⅰ 경우에 해당

2. Duty of Candor to the Court

A lawyer owes a duty of **candor**^{솔직} **to the court,** and the duty requires the lawyer not knowingly put forward a claim that is unsupported by the law.

3. Duty of Decorum to the Tribunal

A lawyer has duty of decorum^{예의} to the tribunal not to:

ⅰ. Influence jurors or judges; and

ⅱ. Disrupt proceedings.

✔ Lack of preparation for a trial

F. Duty of Fairness (19July)

A lawyer has duty of fairness to the court and opposing counsel.

An attorney should not knowingly and intentionally obstruct another party's access to evidence. Altering, concealing, or destroying evidence is violation of duty of fairness.

An attorney should not make a false statement or offer evidence that he knows its falsity.

Ⅳ. Withdrawal (17Feb)

Withdrawal은 변호사 '사퇴'를 뜻하는 바, 변호사가 반드시 사퇴해야 하는 경우의 mandatory withdrawal과 사퇴할 수 있는 경우의 permissive withdrawal로 구분된다. 변호사는 어떤 사건을 수임할지 또는 수임을 거부할지 선택할수 있으나, 일단 수임하기로 하면 변호사 윤리규정에 의거하여 임의적 사퇴가 불가능하다. 따라서 withdrawal의 유형과 무관하게 변호사가 withdrawal을 하고자 하는 경우에는 반드시 그에 따른 피해를 최소화하기 위해 노력해야 하는 바(duty to mitigate), 의뢰인이 새로운 변호사를 선임할 수 있도록 의뢰인에게 일정 기간 이전에 자신의 withdrawal에 대해 notify해야 한다. 또한 withdrawal을 함과 동시에 변호사는 해당 의뢰인의 사건과 관련된 모든자료를 의뢰인에게 return해야 하고, 미리 선입금된 attorney fee를 refund해야 한다. 적합한 withdrawal을 하지 않은 변호사 행위는 duty of continued representation에 위배된다.

Although a lawyer is free to take or not to take a case, ethical rules regarding withdrawal apply once the lawyer decides to take a case.

When a lawyer makes an withdrawal that violates ethical rules, the lawyer will violate **the duty of continued representation**.

A. Mandatory Withdrawal

1. ABA Rules

Under the ABA rules, a lawyer **must** withdraw if:

ⅰ. Representation necessarily causes a violation **of any rules;**

ⅱ. The mental or physical condition of the lawyer materially impairs the representation; and

ⅲ. The lawyer is discharged.

2. California Rules

In California, a lawyer **must** withdraw if:

ⅰ. Representation necessarily causes a violation **of ethical rules;**

ⅱ. The mental or physical condition of the lawyer materially impairs the representation;

ⅲ. The lawyer is discharged; and

ⅳ. The lawyer knows or should know that a client is bringing a frivolous claim.

✔ Client가 상대방을 상대로 잦은 소송(vexatious claim)을 제기한 경우 → 반드시 frivolous claim인 것은 아니다. 따라서 변호사는 자신이 수임한 소송이 frivolous한지 그 여부를 판단하기 위해 reasonable precautions를 취할 필요가 있다.

A reasonable lawyer would take reasonable precautions to ensure whether the claim is frivolous.

B. Permissive Withdrawal

1. ABA Rules

A lawyer **may** withdraw if:

ⅰ. A client insists on pursuing an **illegal conduct or fraud;**

ⅱ. A client insists the lawyer take actions **against the attorney's judgment;**

ⅲ. A client makes representation **unreasonably difficult;** or

iv. A client does not pay her fees (The lawyer has an **unreasonable financial burden** from the representation).

✔ 변호사가 로펌에 속해 있지 않고 sole practitioner인 경우 — 위 iv경우에 해당할 가능성이 높다.

2. California Rules

A lawyer **may** withdraw if:

i. A client insists on pursuing an **illegal conduct or fraud**;

ii. A client insists the lawyer take actions **against the attorney's judgment**;

iii. A client makes representation **unreasonably difficult**;

iv. The lawyer is unable to work **with co-counsel**; or

v. The client's claims or defenses cannot be supported **by good faith**.

C. Duty to Mitigate

When a lawyer withdraws, he owes client **duty to mitigate the harm from withdrawal.**

A lawyer must **inform the client** of the withdrawal timely and provide the client **reasonable time** to seek new representation.

When litigation is pending, a lawyer must obtain **court approval** for either mandatory or permissive withdrawal.

A lawyer must **return all papers or possessions** to the client which are reasonably necessary for the representation, regardless of the client's payment for representation.

A lawyer must refund any advanced fees.

TIP 본 논점은 lawyer가 client의 증거를 보관하고 있는 사안과 관련이 높다.

V. Lawyer and Others

A. Unauthorized Practice of Law (19Feb)

변호인은 수임한 업무를 처리하는데 있어 많은 사람들과 협업할 수 있다. 변호사가 변호사가 아닌 사람들(non-lawyer)과 함께 협업하는 것은 가능하나, 그들이 '전적으로' 변호 업무를 처리(practice)하는 것은 허용되지 않는다. 여기서 'practice'가 협업한다는 의미보다는 변호 업무를 전적으로 처리한다는 의미로 사용된다는 점에 유의해야 한다. 만일 non-lawyer가 변호 업무를 전적으로 처리(practice)한다면 해당 행위는 unauthorized practice of law로서, 그를 고용한 변호인 갑에게 ethical violation에 대한 책임이 주어진다. 예컨대, 변호사 갑이 고용한 non-lawyer 을이 갑을 대신하여 소장을 작성하고 갑이 이를 검수하였다면 문제가 없지만, 을이 소장을 작성하고 갑의 검수가 없었다면 이는 unauthorized practice of law로서 duty to supervise에 위배된다.

A lawyer should not practice with a non-lawyer or disbarred attorney.
★A lawyer must take care to prevent a non-lawyer from conducting activities that constitute the **unauthorized practice of law.**
★A lawyer must **supervise** the nonlawyer's work and **the lawyer** should be **primarily responsible** for the work product. A lawyer is responsible for other non-lawyer's unauthorized practice of law, since he violated **duty to supervise.**

✔ Hire a nonlawyer — 가능
✔ Hire a disbarred lawyer as a clerk or paralegal — 가능
✔ Form a partnership or association with a non-lawyer — unauthorized practice of law
✔ Draft a claim/deposition primarily by nonlawyer/disbarred lawyer — unauthorized practice of law
✔ Draft a claim/deposition by nonlawyer/disbarred lawyer and the claim

is reviewed/supervised by a lawyer — 가능

✔ A conduct research by nonlawyer — 가능

✔ Administrative tasks done by nonlawyer — 가능

✔ Communicating with client concerning billing — 가능 (= administrative task)

✔ Nonlawyer attends a deposition with a lawyer — unauthorized practice of law(Deposition에는 lawyer, witness, court report만이 참석 가능. 그 외의 사람은 참석 불가)

B. Lawyer-Other Partner (Duty to Report Ethical Violations) (19July)

변호사는 사건을 함께 수임하고 있는 다른 변호사의 ethical violation에 대해 고지할 의무를 진다. 또한 ABA rules에 따르면, 변호사는 다른 변호사의 ethical violation을 윤리위원회 등과 같이 적합한 곳에 고지할 의무를 가진다. 이를 영어로 "duty to report ethical violations"라 한다. 반면, California rules에서는 타인의 ethical violation을 고지할 의무는 인정하지 않고, 변호사 스스로 자신의 ethical violation에 대한 고지(self-report)의무를 인정하고 있다. 변호사는 자신의 ethical violation을 발견한 날을 기준으로 30일 이내로 고지해야 한다.

A lawyer is responsible for other lawyer's ethical violation.

1. ABA Rules

a. General Rule

Under the ABA rules, a lawyer is required to report misconduct **by another lawyer** when he has actual knowledge of the misconduct. Misconduct as to **material matters of clear and weighty importance** should be reported.

b. Duty to Report and Duty of Confidentiality

When a lawyer knew misconduct by another lawyer through communication which is protected under the duty of confidentiality, the lawyer is **not** required to report it, unless the future crime exception is applicable.

c. Sanctions

Under the ABA rules, there are no particular sanctions for misconduct.

2. California Rules

a. General Rule

In California, a lawyer is required to **self-report** as to misconduct committed by himself. A lawyer should self-report **in writing within 30 days from the date he has knowledge** of the commission of misconduct.

A lawyer is **not** required to report misconduct by another lawyer.

b. Sanctions

In California, sanctions for misconduct are ranged from permanent disbarment^{자격박탈} to suspension^{정직}.

C. Lawyer-Supervising Partner (19July)

변호사는 상사(supervising partner)의 order를 따라야 하는 의무와 동시에 윤리적 위반을 하지 않을 의무를 동시에 진다. 만약 상사의 order가 윤리적 위반을 동반한다는 사실이 명백한(clearly) 경우에는 변호사는 상사의 order를 따르지 않고 자신의 독립적인 판단에 따라 행동해야 한다. 반면 상사의 order의 윤리적 위반여부 및 사실관계에 있어 논란의 여지가 있는 경우에는 상사의 order를 따라야 하며, 그 결과 윤리적 위반을 하게 되더라도 상사의 order에 따라 행동한 변호사에게는 윤리적 위반에 대한 책임이 없다. 다시 말해, 변호사는 상사의 order가 명백히 윤리적으로 위반한 경우에 한해 독립적인 판단 및 행동을 취할 수 있다.

A lawyer who is supervised by other lawyer has a duty to follow the supervising partner, as well as a duty not to violate ethical obligation.

If there is a **clear ethical violation** by supervising partner, a lawyer **should refuse** the supervising partner's order and should maintain independent professional judgment.

If there is a **reasonable question of law or fact**, a lawyer should follow the supervising partner's order.

✔ 상사의 지시가 윤리적으로 옳지 못하다고 생각되나, less experience인 경우 — 有 question of law or fact
✔ Further search를 한 경우 — No question of law or fact

| 답안요령 |

```
1. 기본 rule
   + analysis
2. If no question of law or fact★
   + analysis
4. 결론
```

| TIP1 | Lawyer-supervising partner에 관한 답안은 아래 두 논점을 모두 논해야 한다.

　① 변호사 갑이 supervising partner 을의 지시에 따르지 않은 것이 변호사 윤리법에 위배되는지 그 여부를 판단한다.

　② Supervising partner 을의 지시에 questionable issue of fact or law가 있는지 그 여부를 판단한다.

| TIP2 | Questionable issue of fact or law의 존부는 명백히 판단할 수 없는 경우가 많아, 존재하는 경우와 존재하지 않는 경우를 '가정(if)'하여 서술하는 것이 고득점 포인트다.

| TIP3 | 위 2번 analysis: "만일 해당 업무에 관해 no question of law or fact이라면, 갑은 ~ duty를 위반하게 된다."

1. Filing a claim against 병
Supervising partner's order

A lawyer who is supervised by other lawyer has a duty to follow the supervising partner and a duty not to violate ethical obligation. If there is a clear ethical violation by supervising partner, a lawyer should refuse the supervising partner's order and should maintain independent professional judgment. If there is a reasonable question of law or fact, a lawyer should follow the supervising partner's order.

(ANALYSIS: In this case, 을 has instructed him to file a claim against 병. However, 갑 believes the claim is frivolous and the filing may rise to sanctions. 갑 has less experience compared to 을 and, therefore, there is a questionable issue of law. Thus, 갑 should follow the supervising partner's order.)

If no question of law or fact

If 갑 made further search and knew that the claim against 병 should not be filed, there is no questionable issue of law. Thus, 갑 should not follow 을's order and should maintain independent professional judgment.

(ANALYSIS: If there is no questionable issue of law but 갑 filed the claim, 갑 will violate the duty of competence, duty of fairness, and duty of candor to the court. The duty of competence requires a lawyer ……. In this case, 갑 ……. The duty of fairness requires a lawyer ……. In this case, 갑 ……. The duty of candor to the court requires a lawyer ……. In this case, 갑 …….)

Conclusion

In conclusion, there likely is questionable issue of law and 갑's relying on 을 is proper. However, if there is no questionable issue of law, 갑 will violate duty of competence, duty of fairness, and duty of candor to the court.)

[표 1-3]

	ABA	California
Written fee agreements	**not** require (예외: contingency fees성공 사례금인 경우 require)	require when more than $1,000 (예외: corporation인 경우는 **not** require)
Duty of competence 판단 기준	reasonable lawyer standard	reckless standard
Duty of competence 기준	reasonableness	intentionally, recklessly, or with gross negligence.
Fee 적합성 판단기준	reasonableness	conscionable
Personal conflicts of interest(유형 ①)	예외 요건(×3) 만족 시, 수임가능	written disclosure가 있는 경우, 수임가능
Limitation of malpractice liability	금지, unless independent counsel	일체 금지
Attorney-client privilege 적용기간	일반적으로 의뢰인 사망 시까지 인정	의뢰인이 사망한 후 estate is entirely disposed of된 시기까지 인정
Sexual relationship with clients	pre-existing	가능	가능
	with current client	불가	변호사의 배우자를 제외한 자와의 성관계 불가
Lawyer as witness 예외	when 변호사 증언이 necessary한 경우	① bench trial; or ② at jury trial with a consent of a client
'Consent' 의미	informed consent, confirmed in writing	informed written consent
'Conflicts of interest' 의미	actual conflicts	actual conflicts 또는 potential conflicts
Duty to report ethical violations	misconduct of another lawyer	self-report
After higher authority fails to remedy	report out	resign (withdraw)
Sanction for misconduct	규정된 바 없음	규정 有

[표 1-4]

Case	관련 논점
상대방 측이 특정 증거제출을 요구하는 경우	• attorney-client privilege • duty of confidentiality • work-product doctrine
변호사가 court order를 disobey하라고 조언한 경우	• duty of competence • duty of diligence • duty of candor to the court
소송을 악의로 제기하는 경우	• duty to avoid a frivolous claim • duty of competence • duty of fairness
변호사가 자신의 client 정보를 타인에게 제공한 경우	• duty of confidentiality • duty of competence • duty of fairness
변호사가 withdrawal하는 경우	• mandatory/permissive withdrawal • return • duty to mitigate
변호사가 moves to new firm	• conflicts of interest (former client) • duty of confidentiality • imputation on new firm
Report out 문제	• duty of confidentiality • duty of communication
Corporation client 문제	• corporation ≠ employee • fee agreement exception • reporting out (duty to communicate)
Co-defendants 문제	• conflicts of interest (duty of loyalty) • duty of confidentiality • attorney-client privilege

2장
Business Associations

//

본 장은 한국법상 회사법에 해당하며, 대리(agency)·합명회사(general partnership, GP)·합자회사(limited partnership, LP)·유한책임회사(limited liability partnership, LLP)·유한회사(limited liability corporation, LLC)·주식회사(corporation)의 6개 부분으로 되어 있다. 미국법에서는 합명회사(GP), 합자회사(LP), 유한책임회사(LLP)를 통틀어 partnerships라 칭하며, 각 partnership의 유형은 회사 채무에 대한 '사원의 책임 정도'를 기준으로 구분한다. 본 장에서는 각 회사 유형의 설립 및 해산, 사원과 회사 관계, 사원의 권리 및 의무 등에 관해 논하기로 한다. 그중 사원과 회사 관계에서의 법적 논점은 기본적으로 대리에 관한 규정(agency law)을 근거로 판단된다. 회사의 사원은 회사의 업무를 대리하는 대리인으로서, 사원의 unlawful acts에 대한 책임, 사원의 권리 및 의무 등에 모두 적용된다.

본 장에 관한 기출문제는 지난 7년간 가장 적은 빈도로 출제되었으나, 출제범위가 타 과목에 비해 매우 방대하다. 회사 유형의 성격과 그 사원이 회사 채무에 대해 지는 책임의 정도 등 각 회사마다 다른 특징을 가지고 있으나, agency rule과 personal liability 및 limited liability 등과 같이 공통적으로 적용되는 rule이 많아 기본적인 rule을 정확히 익히는 것이 중요하다.

[미국 법인의 유형 정리]
한국법상 법인은 '합명, 합자, 유한책임, 유한, 주식회사'로 나누어지며 이 분류의 기준은 기본적으로 유한책임사원과 무한책임사원의 존재로 구분된다. 미국도 이와 유사하게 GP, LP, LLP, LLC, corporation으로 나뉜다.

- GP: 무한책임사원(partners)으로 구성되며, 한국의 합명회사에 해당함.
- LP: 무한책임사원(partners) 및 유한책임사원(partners)으로 구성되며, 한국의

합자회사에 해당함.

- LLP: 유한책임사원(partners)으로 구성되며, 한국의 유한책임회사에 해당함.
- LLC: 유한책임사원(members)으로 구성되며, 한국의 유한회사에 해당함.
- Corporation: 유한책임사원(shareholders and directors)으로 구성되며, 한국의 주식회사에 해당함.

[도표 2-1]

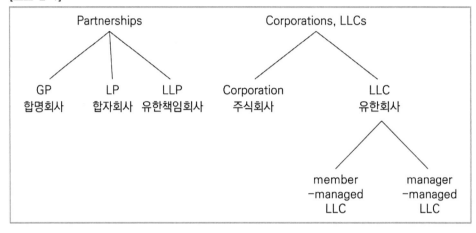

☑ 글쓰기 Tips

1. 두 명 이상의 변호사가 함께 회사를 설립하여 운영하는 case가 자주 출제되며, 이러한 case는 「2장 Business Associations」와 「1장 Professional Responsibility」가 연계되어 출제되기도 한다.
2. 본 장에 관한 문제는 회사의 '유형'을 가장 먼저 파악하는 것이 중요하다.
3. 회사와 사원의 책임문제에 관한 문제가 주를 이룬다.
   Q: What claims, if any, does 갑 have against 을, 병, and 회사 ABC? Discuss.
   Q: On what legal theory, if any, can 갑 reasonably seek to recover against 을 on its claim against 회사 ABC?
   ⇒ 피고가 여러 명인 경우 '각 피고'를 title화하여 agency rule을 적용한다.
4. 회사의 유형을 파악하는 문제가 출제되기도 한다.
   Q: What type of business entity is the firm using to conduct business? Discuss.
   ⇒ 본 장에서 논하는 '다섯 유형의 회사'를 title화하여 작성한다.

TIP1 GP인 경우, partner 갑's torts에 대한 소송
   ① partnership? ⇒ vicarious liability

② 본인 당사자(갑)? ⇒ (a) vicarious liability가 인정되는 경우 갑의 책임이 GP에 귀속되는 바, personally liable하나 그 책임은 부종성(附從性)을 띤다. (b) 인정되지 않는 경우, 갑 is personally liable for his own torts. 따라서 torts 요건에 대해 analysis를 한다.

③ 타 partner? ⇒ 갑's liability가 partnership에 귀속되는 경우, jointly and severally liable. 다만, 그 책임은 부종성(附從性)을 띤다.

TIP2 GP인 경우, partner 갑's contract에 대한 소송

① partnership? ⇒ Agency rule에 따라 갑의 authority 및 ratification이 인정되는 경우 partnership이 책임을 진다.

② 타 partner? ⇒ 갑's liability가 partnership에 귀속되는 경우, jointly and severally liable. 다만, 그 책임은 부종성(附從性)을 띤다.

③ 본인 당사자(갑)? ⇒ 갑은 GP의 partner이므로, partnership의 liability에 대해 타 partner와 마찬가지로 jointly and severally liable. 다만, 그 책임은 부종성(附從性)을 띤다.

TIP3 Corporation인 경우

① S/H가 director를 상대로 제기한 소송
   - direct v. derivative suit 구별문제
   - fiduciary duty 문제
   - BJR, fairness (duty of loyalty) 문제

② Corporation인 경우, 제3자가 director를 상대로 제기한 소송
   - authority
   - pierce the veil 문제

[General Partnership (GP)]

A general partnership is formed when two or more persons carry on a business for profits, as co-owners. No written agreement or formalities are required. When a person receives a share of the profits, the person is presumed as a general partner, unless the profits are for rent or for debt repayment. General partners are each personally and jointly and severally liable for the debts of a GP. There is no limited liability for the partners of a GP.

[Limited Partnership (LP)]

A limited partnership is a partnership that has at least one general partner and one limited partner. All limited partners have limited liability, while all general partners are personally liable for the debts of a LP. A limited partnership is formed when the partners file the Certificate of Limited Partnership which is signed by all of the general partners. The Certificate of Limited Partnership must state name of the partnership including the words "limited partnership" and name and address of general partners.

[Limited Liability Partnership (LLP)]

A limited liability partnership (LLP) is a partnership where all partners are not personally liable for the partnership obligations. To form a limited liability partnership, the Statement of Qualification should be filed with the Secretary of State.

[Corporation]

A corporation is formed by filing Articles of Incorporation with the Secretary of State. All of owners and directors are limited liability for the corporation's liability.

[Limited Liability Companies (LLC)]

A limited liability company (LLC) is a hybrid company. A LLC is a form of business association that combines the features of corporations and partnerships. Like general partnerships, LLCs have tax advantages. Like corporations, a LLC generally provides its investors (members) limited liability for firm debts. To form a LLC, the Articles of Organization with the state must be filed.

Part One. Agency

본 장은 대리관계(agency)에서 발생하는 contracts상의 문제와 torts상의 법률문제에 대해 다룬다. Agent는 수임인 또는 대리인을 뜻하고 principal은 위임인을 뜻하는 바, 양자간 성립된 관계, 즉 대리관계는 agency라 표현한다. Agency는 회사와 사원간의 관계, 근로자와 고용주간의 관계, testator 및 beneficiary와 trustee간의 관계 등에 모두 적용될 정도로 그 적용범위가 매우 넓은 개념으로서, 이에 관한 문제는 크게 세 유형으로 나누어진다. ① Agent가 principal(위임인)을 대리하여 3rd party와 체결한 계약에 대해 agent와 principal 중 누가 3rd party에게 책임을 지는가 하는 문제, ② 근로자와 고용주간 근로계약을 체결한 후 근로자가 3rd party에게 위법행위(torts)를 한 경우 agent와 principal 중 누가 3rd party에게 책임을 지는가 하는 문제, ③ 회사에 소속된 사원의 유형을 파악하는 문제, 이렇게 세 유형이다. 본래 ③ 유형은 agency뿐만 아니라 본 2장의 내용을 전체적으로 논하는 문제이나, 대부분의 사원이 회사와 agency 관계를 맺고 있는 바, 본 파트에서 논하였다. 본 파트에서는 각 회사유형의 사원을 구분하는 기준에 중점을 두어 논하고 각 사원의 구체적인 책임 범위 등에 대해서는 이후 각 파트에서 자세히 논하도록 한다.

[도표 2-2]

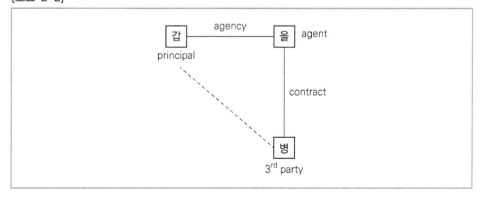

Ⅰ. Agency and Contracts

A. Agency Creation

Agent is a person or entity that acts on behalf of another, the principal.
Agency is a **fiduciary relationship** and it is established if there is:

ⅰ. **Agreement** (a formal or informal agreement between the principal and the agent);

ⅱ. **Benefit** (the agent's conduct on behalf of the principal primarily benefits the principal); and

ⅲ. **Control** (the principal has the right to control the agent by supervising the agent's performance).

B. Principal's Liability

Agent가 principal을 대리하여 제3자와 체결한 계약에 대해 principal은 책임이 있는가. 이는 agent가 계약 체결 당시 authority를 가지고 있었는가를 기준으로 판단한다. 만약 agent가 제3자와 계약을 체결할 당시 authority를 가지고 있었다면, principal은 그 계약에 대해 책임을 진다.

Authority는 크게 actual authority와 apparent authority로 구분되는데, actual authority와 apparent authority 중 어느 하나라도 존재하면 agent가 맺은 계약에 대한 책임은 principal에게 귀속된다. "Actual and apparent authority"라고 표현하는 경우가 많은데, 이는 두 개념을 설명하기 위해 actual authority와 apparent authority라는 뜻으로 표현된 것일 뿐, agent가 actual authority와 apparent authority 모두 가지고 있는 경우에만 그 계약에 대한 책임이 principal에게 귀속된다는 의미가 아니다. 한편, implied actual authority는 'agent'의 합리적인 믿음을 기준으로 agent's authority 유무를 판단하고, apparent authority는 '3rd party'의 합리적인 믿음을 기준으로 agent's authority 유무를 판단한다.

1. General Agency Rule

★An agent who acts on behalf of a principal **can bind the principal** to contracts if the **agent has either actual or apparent authority.**

2. Actual Authority

An agent has **actual** authority if he reasonably believes that the principal wishes the agent so to act based on the **principal's manifestations** to the agent.

a. Actual Express Authority

Actual express authority is granted when the principal has expressly given to the agent whether orally or in writing if statute of frauds (SOF) requires.

b. Actual Implied Authority

Actual implied authority is granted when the **agent** reasonably believes because of **necessity, custom, or prior dealings.**

3. Apparent Authority

a. General Rule

★An agent has apparent authority when:

ⅰ. A **third party reasonably believes** that the person has authority to act on behalf of the principal;

ⅱ. That belief is traceable to the **principal's manifestation;** and

ⅲ. The third party had **no notice** the agent was exceeding his authority.

b. Lingering Authority

If a principal does not provide a notice to a third party that an agent's actual authority has been terminated, the agent has **apparent lingering authority.**

✔ Agent가 incompetent인 상태가 되었으나 principal이 이에 대해 notice를 주지 않은 경우, 해당 agent의 apparent lingering authority 가 인정된다.

✔ Principal이 사망하는 경우, 기존의 authority는 유지되므로(the authority does not terminate) apparent lingering authority가 인정될 수 없다.

C. Agent's Liability

Agent가 principal을 대리하여 제3자와 계약을 체결한 경우, agent는 그 계약에 대해 책임(agent's liability on 3rd party)이 있는가. 이는 ① 계약체결 당시 agent에게 그 계약을 체결할 authority가 존재했는가에 대한 여부 그리고 ② 계약체결 당시의 principal 상태, 이 두 요소를 기준으로 판단한다. Agent가 제3자와 계약을 체결할 당시 authority가 있었고 fully disclosed principal인 경우에 한해 agent's liability on 3rd party가 없으며, 그 외의 모든 경우에는 agent가 계약의 상대방인 제3자에게 계약 불이행에 대한 책임을 진다.

① Agent의 authority 유무여부는 상기 express authority 및 implied authority 내용을 기준으로 판단하며, ② principal 상태는 agent가 제3자와 계약을 체결할 당시 그 제3자가 principal에 대해 인지하고 있었던 정도를 기준으로 판단한다. 원칙적으로 agent는 제3자에게 principal에 대해 명확히 언급을 하여 제3자가 principal의 '존재'를 알고 있을 뿐만 아니라, principal이 '누구인지' 정확히 특정할 수 있어야 한다. 이 경우의 principal을 fully disclosed principal이라 칭하며, principal이 해당 계약에 대해 책임을 지고 agent는 책임이 없다. 반면, fully disclosed principal이 아닌 경우, 즉 제3자가 principal의 존재는 알고 있었으나 누구인지 정확히 특정할 수 없었거나 제3자가 principal의 존재를 알지 못했고 누구인지 정확히 특정할 수도 없었던 경우에는 principal이 아닌 agent가 해당 계약에 대해 책임을 진다. 전자(前者) 경우의 principal을 partially disclosed principal, 후자(後者) 경우의 principal을 undisclosed principal이라 칭한다.

1. General Rule

The agent is personally liable for contracts with third parties when:

i. The agent had no authority;

ii. Principal was partially disclosed (identity of principal was not disclosed); or

iii. Principal was undisclosed (identity and existence of principal was not disclosed).

[도표 2-3]

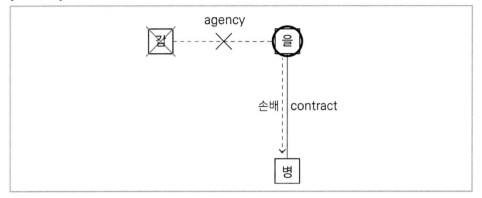

2. Principal Status

a. Fully Disclosed Principal

existence of principal + identity of principal

Fully disclosed principal이란, agent가 제3자와 계약을 체결할 당시, principal에 대해 명확히 언급을 하여 제3자가 principal의 '존재'를 알고 있을 뿐만 아니라, principal이 '누구인지' 정확히 특정할 수 있었던 상태의 principal을 의미한다. 이 경우, agent에게 authority가 있는 한 agent는 해당 계약에 관해 제3자에게 책임이 없고 principal은 책임을 진다.

When a third party contracts with a person that the third party knows is acting in an agency capacity for another and the third party is aware of the identity of the principal, the principal is called a "fully identified principal."

b. Partially Disclosed Principal

existence of principal + ~~identity of principal~~

Partially disclosed principal(unidentified principal)은 agent와 제3자가 계약할 당시, 제3자가 principal의 존재는 알고 있었으나 누구인지 정확히 특정할 수 없었던 상태의 principal을 의미한다. 이 경우, agent는 제3자에게 책임이 있다.

When a third party contracts with a person that the third party knows is acting in an agency capacity for another, but the third party is unaware of the identity of the principal, the principal is called a "partially disclosed principal."

c. Undisclosed Principal

~~existence of principal~~ + ~~identity of principal~~

Agent가 제3자와 계약을 체결할 당시, 제3자가 principal의 존재를 알지 못했고 누구인지 정확히 특정할 수 없었던 경우의 principal을 undisclosed principal이라고 한다. 이 경우, agent는 그 계약에 대해 제3자에게 책임을 진다.

When a third party contracts with a person that the third party did not know is acting in an agency capacity for another and is unaware of the identity of the principal, the principal is called an "undisclosed principal."

D. Ratification

Ratification이란, agent가 authority 없는 상태에서 계약을 체결했고 그 이후에도 authority가 생기지 않았지만 principal이 그 계약의 존재를 인지한 후 agent의 권한유무와 관계없이 계약을 승인 및 재가(裁可)하는 것을 뜻한다. Principal이 ratify하면 agent는 더 이상 해당 계약에 대한 책임이 없다. 다만, principal이 ratify할 당시 그에게 capacity가 있고 해당 계약의 주된 내용(material facts)에 대해 모두 인지하고 있어야만 유효한 ratification으로 인정된다.

[도표 2-4]

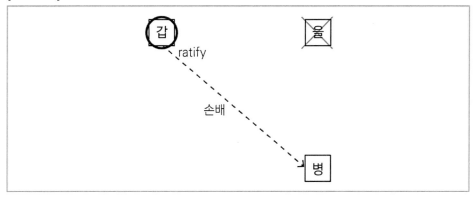

★Ratification occurs when an agent took action without authority, and the principal **subsequently approves** the action **with capacity and full knowledge of material terms.**

Agent is **no longer liable** once ratification occurs.

TIP Agent의 authority 유무는 ① actual 및 apparent authority 뿐만 아니라 ② principal의 ratification이 있었는지 그 여부를 통해 판단한다.

E. Duties of Principal and Agent

Principal과 agent는 서로에 대한 의무를 지고 있는데, principal은 계약상 채무(contractual duty)를, agent는 신의칙 의무(fiduciary duty)를 진다. Principal이 agent에 대해 지는 contractual duty는 대리비용(compensation) 지불, 협조(cooperation) 등 principal과 agent간 체결한 agency contract에 의해 발생하는 의무를 뜻한다. Agent가 principal에 대해 지는 fiduciary duty에는 합리적인 주의를 기울일 의무(duty of care), principal의 최대 이익을 위해 행위할 의무(duty of loyalty), principal의 합리적인 지시에 따라 행위 할 의무(duty of obedience) 그리고 principal과 소통할 의무(duty to communicate)

가 포함된다.

1. Principal Duties

a. Contractual Duties

A principal owes the agent all duties imposed by their agency contract.

b. Remedies

When the principal breaches those duties, the agent may:

ⅰ. Terminate the agency (refuse to perform);

ⅱ. Seek **contractual** damages; or

ⅲ. Seek a **possessory lien** for money due.

[Possessory Lien]

When a possessory lien is created, the creditor has a legal claim on the item until the debt is satisfied.

2. Agent Duties

a. Fiduciary Duties

An agent owes the principal the following fiduciary duties:

ⅰ. Duty of care (to use reasonable care when performing the agent's duties);

ⅱ. Duty of loyalty (no conflicts of interest and no commingling of funds);

ⅲ. Duty of obedience (to obey all reasonable directions given by the principal); and

ⅳ. Duty to communicate (to communicate information that would affect principal).

b. Remedies

When the agent breaches fiduciary duties, the principal may:

ⅰ. Discharge the agent;

ⅱ. Withhold compensation from the agent;

ⅲ. Seek **contract** remedies (e.g., rescission) **with duty to mitigate;**

ⅳ. Seek **tort** damages for agent's **intentional or negligent performance;** or

ⅴ. Seek **indemnity** for the agent's actions beyond the agency scope.

Ⅱ. Agency and Torts (15Feb)

Agent가 제3자에게 위법행위(torts)를 한 경우 principal은 이에 대해 vicarious liability가 인정되는 경우에 한해 책임을 진다. Vicarious liability는 위법행위를 한 자와 특별한 관계를 맺고 있는 자가 해당 위법행위에 대해 배상해야 하는 책임을 뜻하는 바, 한국법상 사용자책임에 해당한다. 여기서 '특별한 관계'란 대리관계(agency)를 뜻하며, 위법행위를 한 자가 agent, 위법행위를 한 자와 특별한 관계를 맺고 있는 자가 principal에 대응된다. 따라서 본 개념은 사용자와 근로자의 관계, partnerships(합명회사, 합자회사 또는 유한책임회사) 및 joint venture와 사원(partners)의 관계 등에 모두 적용가능하나 편의를 위해 이하 내용은 사용자와 근로자의 관계로 설명하였다. Vicarious liability가 인정되려면 두 요건이 만족되어야 하는데, ① 근로자의 위법행위가 고용업무 수행 과정(within the scope of employment) 중 발생할 것 ② 사용자가 근로자를 통제(control)할 수 있을 것이 두 요건이다. "사용자가 근로자를 통제(control)할 수 있다"는 것은 근로자가 independent contractor가 아닌 employee로 고용되어 있다는 것을 의미하는 바, 그 여부는 업무상 전문적인 skill이 필요한 정도, 급여 지급 방식, 고용기간 등 다양한 요소들을 종합적으로 판단하여 결정된다.

한편, vicarious liability는 agent가 범한 intentional torts와 criminal acts에 적용불가하다. 즉, 상기 두 요건이 만족된다 할지라도 사용자는 근로자의 고의에 의한 위법행위와 형법상 위법행위에 대해 책임이 없다. 다만, 사용자가 근로자에게 해당 행위에 대한 권한을 명시적으로 위임하였거나 해당 행위가 고용업무를 수행하는 과정에서 자연스럽게 발생하는 행위이거나 근로자가 사용자를 위해 해당 행위를 범하였다면, 예외적으로 고의에 의한 위법행위에 대해 vicarious liability가 인정된다.

The principal is **not** vicariously liable for the agent's **intentional torts or criminal acts.**

1. Within the Scope of Employment

★A principal will be liable for the agent's **tortious conduct** only if it occurred **within the scope of his employment.**

2. Employee v. Independent Contractor

a. General Rule

★**Principal is liable** for torts committed by the agent, when the agent's manner and method is **under the control** of the principal. In other words, principal is liable for **vicarious liability** when principal employed the agent **as an employee,** rather than an independent contractor.

[도표 2-5]

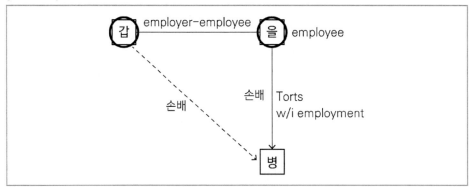

[도표 2-6]

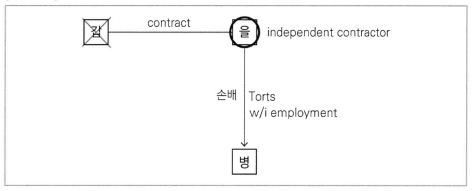

b. Considering Factors

A court will consider several factors in determining the degree of the principal's control over the agent, such as:

ⅰ. Level of skills required;

(Skill을 많이 요하지 않는 업무라면, employee로 본다.)

ⅱ. Whether work is part or whole of principal's business;

(근로자의 업무가 고용자 사업의 일부라면, employee로 본다.)

ⅲ. Payment for regular work; and

(시급이라면 employee로, 프로젝트 별로 급여를 지급한다면 independent contractor로 본다.)

ⅳ. The length of the relationship.

(지속되는 관계라면 employee로, 특정 프로젝트 동안에만 유지되는 관계라면 independent contractor로 본다.)

c. Exceptions

A principal is vicariously liable for an independent contractor's torts when:

ⅰ. The conduct is **ultra-hazardous**;

ⅱ. The conduct involves **non-delegable duties**;

ⅲ. The principal **negligently** select the independent contractor; or

ⅳ. **Estoppel doctrine** applies.

Arguable point: 사용자는 근로자가 independent contractor라고 주장하며 자신에게 vicarious liability가 없음을 주장할 것이다. 반면, 사용자를 상대로 소송을 제기한 피해자(원고)는 근로자가 employee라는 점 또는 independent contractor를 인정한다 하더라도 그의 행위가 exception에 해당한다는 점을 주장할 것이다.

The principal may argue that the agent is an independent contractor. In response, the agent may argue that he is an employee.

If the principal pursues that the agent is hired as an independent contractor, the agent may argue that principal's [conduct involves non-delegable duty].

3. For Intentional Torts

A principal is not vicariously liable for the agent's **intentional torts, unless:**

ⅰ. The principal specifically authorized the conduct;

ⅱ. The conduct was natural result from the nature of the employment; or

ⅲ. The agent was motivated to serve the principal.

Ⅲ. Agents and Firms

각 회사유형의 사원을 지칭하는 용어는 employee, partner, member, shareholder 등 다양하다. 사원이 회사를 운영할 수 있는 권리는 회사의 유형에 따라 다르며, 대부분의 경우 회사 운영권을 가진 사원들은 회사 이익을 나누어가진다. 따라서 사원의 유형을 구분하는데 있어 사원이 회사 이익에 대해 권리를 가지고 있는지 그 여부가 가장 중요한 기준이다.

1. Employees

An employee is a person who works for a firm. Employees have no right to manage and do not share profits of the firm. Employees are paid a fixed salary or wages.

2. Partners

A partner has right to manage and share profits of a firm.

3. Members

Members are owners of a LLC. Members have right to manage depending on the type of LLC.

4. Shareholders

Shareholders are owners of a corporation who own stock or equity. Shareholders have no right to manage.

Part Two. Partnerships (15Feb, 20Feb)

본 파트는 partnerships에 대해 논하며, 그 유형에는 GP, LP, LLP 이렇게 3가지가 있다. General partnership(GP)은 한국적 개념으로 합명회사, limited partnership(LP)은 합자회사, limited liability partnership(LLP)은 유한책임회사에 해당한다. 이하각 partnership의 설립 및 해산, partnership과 partner간의 관계, partner의 책임문제 등에 관해 논하기로 한다.

Ⅰ. General Partnership

General partnership(GP)은 "partnership"이라고도 하며, 한국적 개념으로 합명회사에 해당한다. GP 설립에는 형식적 요건이 요구되지 않기 때문에 단순히 두 명 이상의 사람들이 함께 경영을 하더라도 GP가 설립될 수 있다. 따라서 '함께 경영'하고자 하는 사원들의 의도가 GP 설립유무를 판단하는데 있어 가장 중요한 요소이며, 사원들이 'general partnership을 설립'하고자 하는 의도를 가지고 있어야 하는 것은 아니다. 한편, 사원들의 '함께 경영'하고자 하는 의도는 이익분배, 두 명 이상이 공유하고 있는 자산 등을 통해 인정된다. 여기서 '이익분배'는 매출액(gross profit)이 아닌 순이익(net profit)을 뜻하며, 고정된 임금(fixed salary)을 받는 자는 partner로 보지 않는다.

A. General Rule

★A general partnership is formed when two or more persons carry on a business for profits, as co-owners.

1. Formalities

★No written agreement or formalities are required.

When a person receives a share of the **net profits**, the person is **presumed** as a general partner, unless the profits are for rent or for debt repayment.

- ✔ A person participating in management or control of the business — partner 인정 ○
- ✔ A person receiving gross profits for new clients he brings to the firm — partner 인정 ×(is an employee)
- ✔ A person who is paid a fixed salary — partner 인정 ×(is an employee)
- ✔ A person who is paid a salary based on working hours (= fixed salary) — partner 인정 ×(is an employee)
- ✔ A person who is paid annual bonus if he works more than 2,000 hours a year (= fixed salary) — partner 인정 ×(is an employee) 본 annual bonus는 근무시간 2,000시간을 기준으로 지급되는 fixed salary로 볼 수 있다. 또한 일하는 모든 자에게 annual bonus가 동등하게

지급되는 것이 아니므로, 회사의 net profit을 동등하게 share하는 partner와는 다르다.

The annual bonus can be recognized as a fixed salary based on number of hours. Additionally, it is shared only between the qualifying workers and is different from the net profits which are shared equally between partners.

B. Partnership and Partners

General partnership은 사원과는 별개의 개체로서 회사 업무의 처리를 사원에게 위임하는 주체이다. 따라서 모든 사원은 회사 경영권을 동등하게 가진다. 즉, general partnership은 회사 업무의 처리에 대한 위임인(principal)에 대응되고 사원은 수임인(agent)에 대응되는 바, 사원들의 권한은 agency law의 원칙을 근거로 판단된다. 한편, 회사의 자산은 반드시 사원의 개인 자산과 구별되어 운영되어야 한다. 따라서 사원은 회사 자산(partnership asset)을 회사를 위한 목적으로 사용해야 하며 그 소유권은 사원이 아닌 회사에 있다.

1. General Rule

The partnership is a **legal entity** distinct from its partners.

Each partner has **equal rights** in the management and conduct of the partnership's business. Thus, the scope of a partner's authority is **governed by agency law principle.** In other words, partners are agents of the partnership.

2. Partnership Assets

ⅰ. Partnership property is owned by the partnership and a partner is not a co-owner of such property. Partners can use it **only for partnership purposes.**

ⅱ. A property is a partnership asset if:

① It is titled in partnership; or

② It is titled in a partner's name, but the person's capacity as a partner or the existence of the partnership is identified.

iii. A property is presumed as a partnership property if the partnership funds are used.

iv. A property is presumed as a separate property if:

① It is titled in a partner's name but the person's capacity is not identified; or

② The partnership is identified but the partnership funds are not used.

3. Fiduciary Duty

Partners owe fiduciary duties **each other and partnership.**

4. Partnership's Liability

★A partnership is bound by the contracts made by its partners when the partnership is **vicariously liable** and when such partners had actual **authority,** apparent authority, or the partnership **ratifies** the contracts.

5. Compensation

Partners have **no right to compensation** and they are not entitled to payment for their work, unless there is an agreement stating otherwise.

Partners are **not** entitled to **payment** for their work, but are entitled to an equal portion of **profits and losses** of the partnership.

C. Personal Liability

Personal liability란, 직접·무한·연대책임을 뜻하며, personal liability를 가지고 있는 partner는 무한책임사원이다. GP의 모든 partner는 personal liability 를 가지고 있다. 즉, GP의 모든 partner는 회사채권에 대해 직접·무한·연대 책임을 진다.

무한책임사원은 회사의 채무가 완제될 때까지 자기의 전 재산으로서 변제할 책임을 진다. 그러나 무한책임사원의 책임은 보증적 의미가 있고 부종성(附從性)을 띤다. 따라서 회사의 채무는 partnership 자산으로 우선 변제되고, partnership 자산이 부족한 경우에 한해 partner들이 회사 채무에 대해 직접·무한·연대책임을 진다. 회사의 자산이 회사의 채무를 변제하기에 부족한 경우, 회사의 채권자는 회사와 무한책임사원에 대하여 각각 소송을 제기하여야 한다. 회사와 사원은 별개의 개체이기 때문이다. 회사채권자가 GP partner를 상대로 제기한 소송에 대해 무한책임사원은 jointly and severally liable하다. 즉, 회사 채권자는 GP사원들 중 한 명을 임의로 선정하여 소송을 제기하더라도 recover full damage 할 수 있다.

다만, 모든 무한책임사원이 회사채권에 대해 동일한 책임을 지는 것은 아니다. 만약 Partnership Agreement 체결 등의 방법으로 각 무한책임사원의 책임범위가 별도로 규정되어 있다면, 해당 내용에 따라 각 사원의 책임범위가 결정된다. 만약 각 무한책임사원의 책임에 대해 정해진 바가 없다면, 모든 무한책임사원은 책임을 동일하게 나눠 갖는다.

1. General Rule

A partner has right to manage and share profits of a firm. ★A partner has **personal liability** for the partnership debt as a result of his status as a partner.

2. Jointly and Severally Liable

★Partners are **jointly and severally liable** for the partnership debts. A partnership creditor can collect the **full amount** of the debt from any one of the partners.

When the creditor recovered full amount from a partner, a partner may seek **contribution.**

3. As Guarantor

A partnership creditor must **first exhaust partnership's assets** before seeking payment on partner's individual property.

It places partners in the position of **guarantor,** rather than principal debtor on the partnership obligation.

D. Relationship between Partners

GP의 모든 partner(사원)는 회사를 경영하고 관리할 수 있는 권한을 가진다. 본 권한은 모든 partner가 동등한 위치에서 동등한 정도로 가지고 있는 바, 각 partner가 회사 경영을 위한 행위를 할 경우 타 partner의 동의는 필요하지 않다. 다만, 회사 경영에 관한 보편적인 업무(matter of ordinary course of business)에 있어 partner간 이견(異見)이 있는 경우에는 다수결로 결정하며 그렇지 않은 업무에 관해서는 모든 partner의 동의를 요한다. 그렇다면 GP의 partner 갑이 partnership 운영을 위한 행위를 하는 과정에서 torts가 발생한 경우, 다른 partner인 을에게 이에 대한 책임을 지울 수 있는가. Partner 갑의 행위는 GP(principal)를 위한 agent로서의 행위이므로, 그 torts에 대한 책임은 GP에게 귀속된다. 또한 GP의 모든 partner는 회사채권에 대해 jointly and severally liable하므로, 을은 그 torts에 대해 personal liability가 있다. 만약 이후 GP에 새로운 partner 병이 입사한다면, 병(incoming partner)은 어떤 책임을 지는가. 병의 personal liability는 병이 GP에 입사 한 '이후'에 발생하는 회사채권에 대해서만 존재하고, 입사하기 '이전'에 이미 존재했던 회사채권에 대해서는 personal liability가 없다. 즉, 병은 갑의 torts에 의한 회사채권(책임)에 대해서는 personal liability가 없다. 다만, 병이 GP에 투자한 금액이 이를 위해 사용될 수는 있다. 한편, 병이 입사하기 '이전'에 이미 존재했던 회사채권이더라도, 병이 회사채권자에게 personal liability를 지겠다는 계약을 직접 체결하거나 그러한 내용이 담긴 partnership agreement가 존재하는 경우에는 병의 personal liability가 인정된다.

1. Equal Rights

Each partner has **equal rights** in the management and conduct of the partnership's business.

When a difference arises regarding a matter in the **ordinary** course of business of a partnership, it may be decided by a **majority** of the partners.

When a difference arises regarding a matter **in the extraordinary** course of business of a partnership, it may be decided by **all consents** of the partners.

2. Fiduciary Duty

Partners owe **each other and partnership** following fiduciary duties:

ⅰ. Duty of care requires partners to use **reasonable care** when they performs the agent's duties;

ⅱ. Duty of loyalty requires partners to act solely for the principal's benefit and requires them not to make **conflicts of interest;**

ⅲ. Duty to communicate requires partners to disclose any **material** fact regarding partnership business; and

ⅳ. Duty of obedience requires partners to act in accordance with the express or implied terms of the relationship.

3. New partner (Incoming Partner)

a. General Rule

A new person who is admitted to an existing partnership is not personally liable for any partnership obligations incurred before his admission.

However, she will lose her investment in the partnership as a result of the creditor's claim. Her contribution is at risk for the satisfaction of existing partnership debt.

b. Exception

When a new partner **assumes liability** to third parties through private contractual guarantees or modifications to the partnership agreement, the partner **is personally liable.**

4. Dissociated Partner (Outgoing Partner)

a. Personal Liability

A dissociating partner is **personally liable** for partnership obligation which is incurred **prior to** the dissociation.

b. Partnership Obligation

A partnership is bound by an act of a dissociated partner which is undertaken **within two months after dissociation** if:

　ⅰ. The act **would have bound** the partnership **before dissociation;**

　ⅱ. The other party had **reasonable belief** that the dissociated partner was still a partner; and

　ⅲ. The other party had **no notice** of dissociation.

답안요령 | GP와 사원간 책임문제

Q: <u>What claims, if any, does 갑 have against ABC and 병? Discuss.</u>
<u>General partnership ABC의 사원 을이 갑과 계약을 체결하였으나, 본 계약을 이행하지 않았다. 이에 대해 갑이 회사 ABC와 ABC의 또 다른 사원인 병을 상대로 소송을 제기한 경우, 갑이 승소할 가능성을 논하라.</u>

---

1. GP 회사 특징
2. ABC 회사가 피고인 경우
　① Agency rule
　② Authority 존부 파악
　③ Ratification★
3. ABC 회사의 사원인 병이 피고인 경우
　① Agency rule
　② Jointly and severally liable (personal liability)

TIP1 ‘회사의 특징’에 관한 문제가 별도로 출제되지 않았다 하더라도 답안의 첫 문장에 작성하는 것이 고득점 포인트다.

TIP2 문제에서의 각 ‘피고’를 title화하여 작성한다.

General partnership

A general partnership is formed when two or more persons carry on a business for profits, as co-owners. No written agreement or formalities are required. When a person receives a share of the profits, the person is presumed as a general partner, unless the profits are for rent or for debt repayment. General partners are each personally and jointly and severally liable for the debts of a GP. There is no limited liability for the partners of a GP.

1. 갑 against ABC

Agency rule

A partnership is bound by the contracts made by its partners when the partnership is vicariously liable and when such partners had actual authority, apparent authority, or the partnership ratifies the contracts.

Actual authority

A partner has actual authority if he reasonably believes that the corporation wishes the agent so to act based on the corporation's manifestations to the partner.

(ANALYSIS: In this case, there is no fact indicating that a partner of ABC has actual authority to buy land. Thus, 을 had no actual authority.)

Apparent authority

A partner has apparent authority when: (1) a third party reasonably believes that the partner has authority to act on behalf of the corporation; (2) that belief is traceable to the corporation's manifestation; and (3) the third party had no notice that the partner was exceeding his authority.

(ANALYSIS: ⋯⋯ Thus, 을 had no apparent authority.)

Ratification

Even though an agent made a contract without authority, the corporation

can be bound by the contract by ratification. Ratification occurs when the corporation approves the action with full knowledge of material terms.
(ANALYSIS: Although 을 had no authority to make the contract with 갑, ABC is bound by the contract. This is because ABC ratified the contract. Thus, ABC is liable for the contract.)

Conclusion

In conclusion, 갑 can raise claim against ABC since there was ratification.

2. 갑 against 병

Agency rule

As mentioned above, the corporation ABC has liability for the contract under the agency rule.

Jointly and severally liable

A partner has personal liability for the partnership and partners are jointly and severally liable for the partnership obligations.
(ANALYSIS: In this case, the obligation under the contract is the partnership obligations. Even though 병 did not make the contract, he is jointly and severally liable for the partnership obligations. Thus, 갑 could raise claim against 병 for the contract.)

Conclusion

In conclusion, 갑 could raise claim against 병 for the contract.

Conclusion

In conclusion, 갑 could raise claim against ABC and 병. ABC ratified the contract and the corporation is bound by it. 병 is also liable for the contract since he is jointly and severally liable for the corporation debt.

E. Dissociation and Dissolution

Dissociation은 partner의 탈퇴를 뜻하며, dissolution은 회사의 해체를 뜻한다. Dissociation은 회사가 해체된 사유를 기준으로 voluntary dissociation과

involuntary dissociation으로 구분된다. Voluntary dissociation에는 partnership 이 설립될 당시 해당 partnership의 목적 또는 종료날짜가 정해졌고 해당 목적이 달성되거나 해당 날짜에 도달한 경우, 모든 partner가 회사의 해체에 동의한 경우, at-will partnership의 partner가 탈퇴하는 경우, 이렇게 세 유형이 있다. 한편, partnership이 불법적인 행위를 하였거나 partner의 신청으로 법원의 명령(decree)가 있는 경우에는 involuntary dissolution이 발생한다.

회사가 해체될 때 회사의 채무 및 자산을 정리하기 위한 일정 기간이 필요한데, 이 기간을 "winding up"이라 한다. Winding up 기간 동안 발생하는 liability는 partnership에 귀속되며 탈퇴한 partner를 포함한 모든 partner가 이에 대해 jointly and severally 책임진다.

1. Dissociation

a. General Rule

A partner can dissociate from the partnership **at any time** when the partner **expressed his will** to withdraw as a partner.

b. Liability of Dissociating Partner

A dissociating partner is personally liable for partnership obligation which is incurred prior to the dissociation.

2. Dissolution

a. General Rule

There are two types of dissolution: voluntary dissolution and involuntary dissolution.

ⅰ. Voluntary Dissolution

Voluntary dissolution occurs when:

① Specific purpose is achieved or specified end date is approached;

② All partners agree with the dissolution; or

③ One party dissociates in at-will partnership.

ii. Involuntary Dissolution

Involuntary dissolution occurs when:

① The partnership involved in an unlawful activity; or

② There is a court decree^{판결}.

b. Winding Up

Winding up is the period between the dissolution and termination of the partnership.

The **partnership** is bound by a partner's act after dissolution if the act was appropriate to the winding up of the partnership.

All partners, including the dissociating partner, are **jointly and severally liable** for partnership's obligation incurred **during the winding up process.**

II. Limited Partnership

Limited partnership(LP)이란, 합자회사를 뜻한다. Limited partnership은 "Certificate of Limited Partnership" 서류를 제출해야만 설립되며, 최소 한 명 이상의 무한책임사원이 존재해야 한다. 만약 이 두 요건을 갖추지 못한 채로 사업이 운영되면, 그 회사는 general partnership(GP)으로 인정된다. GP의 설립은 별도의 설립절차 없이 두 명 이상의 사람들이 함께 경영을 하면 인정되기 때문이다.

LP의 partner는 한 명 이상의 무한책임사원(general partners)과 한 명 이상의 유한책임사원(limited partners)으로 구성되어 있다. General partner는 GP의 partner와 동일한 역할을 한다. 즉, partnership의 경영을 맡고 회사의 채무에 대해 무한책임(personal liability)을 진다. 한편, limited partner는 유한책임, 즉 partnership의 경영에 일체 관여하지 않고 출자액에 한한 책임을 진다.

A. Creation and Formation

1. Definition

★A limited partnership is a partnership that has at least one general partner and one limited partner.

2. Formalities

★A limited partnership is formed when the partners file the Certificate of Limited Partnership which is signed by all of the general partners. The Certificate of Limited Partnership must state:

ⅰ. Name (including the words "limited partnership") of the partnership; and

ⅱ. Name and address of general partners.

3. General Partners v. Limited Partners

a. Right to Manage

A **general** partner shares the **right to manage and control** the partnership business equally between general partners.

A limited partner has **no** right to manage.

b. Liability

A general partner in a limited partnership has same duties and liability as in a general partnership. A general partner is **personally liable** (jointly and severally liable) and owes both partners and partnership **fiduciary duties.**

A limited partner is liable for the obligations of the partnership only to the extent of his capital contribution (is limited liable).

c. Common Characters

All partners in a limited partnership have right to distribution^{이익} in proportion to the value of each partner's contribution. The right is transferable.

All partners have contribution obligation. However, it can be excused by the unanimous consent, death, or disability.

All partners have right to apply for dissolution.

[표 2-1]

	General Partner	Limited Partner
Right to manage/control	○	×
Liability	personal liability	limited liability
Fiduciary duty to partnership	○	×
Common character (공통점)	① right to distribution which is transferable ② contribution obligation ③ right to dissolve ④ right to inspect (=right to information)	

답안요령 | LP와 사원간 책임문제

Q: What claims, if any, does 갑 have against ABC, 병, and 정? Discuss.

LP ABC 회사의 사원 을(general partner)이 갑과 계약을 체결하였으나 본 계약을 이행하지 않았다. 이에 대해 갑이 회사 ABC, 또 다른 general partner 병 그리고 limited partner 정을 상대로 소송을 제기하였다. 갑이 승소할 가능성을 논하라.

1. LP 회사 특징
2. ABC 회사가 피고인 경우
   ① Agency rule
   ② Authority 존부 파악
   ③ Ratification★
3. ABC 회사의 general partner인 병이 피고인 경우
   ① Agency rule
   ② Jointly and severally liable (personal liability)
4. ABC 회사의 limited partner인 정이 피고인 경우
   ① Agency rule
   ② Limited liability

TIP1 '회사의 특징'에 관한 문제가 별도로 출제되지 않았다 하더라도 답안의 첫 문장에 작성하는 것이 고득점 포인트다.

TIP2 문제에서의 각 '피고'를 title화하여 작성한다.

Limited partnership

A limited partnership is a partnership that has at least one general partner and one limited partner. All limited partners have limited liability, while all general partners are personally liable for the debts of a LP. A limited partnership is formed when the partners file the Certificate of Limited Partnership which is signed by all of the general partners. The Certificate of Limited Partnership must state name of the partnership including the words "limited partnership" and name and address of general partners.

1. 갑 against ABC

……

2. 갑 against 병

……

3. 갑 against 정

Agency rule

As mentioned above, ABC is bound by the contract made by 을 and ABC has liability for the contract under the agency rule.

Limited liability

A limited partner in LP has limited liability for the partnership.
(ANALYSIS: In this case, the obligation under the contract is ABC obligations. 정 is a limited partner and he has limited liability for ABC obligation. Thus, 갑 could not raise claim against 정 for the contract.)

Conclusion

In conclusion, 갑 could not raise claim against 정 for the contract.

Conclusion

In conclusion, 갑 has claims against ABC and 병. However, 갑 has no claim against 정 for the contract, since 정 has limited liability for ABC debt.

B. Dissolution

Limited partnership(LP)이 해체(dissolve)되는 상황에는 여러 가지가 있다. 첫째, LP를 설립할 당시 LP가 해체되는 상황에 대해 협의한 바가 있는 경우 해당 상황에서 LP는 해체된다. 둘째, 모든 general partner와 회사이익 (distribution)에 대해 많은 권한을 가지는 limited partner들의 서면동의가 있는 경우 LP는 해체된다. 셋째, general partner가 탈퇴를 하는 경우 LP가 해체될 수 있다. 다만, 해당 general partner가 탈퇴 후 LP에 다른 general partner가 존재하는지, 즉 탈퇴하는 general partner가 LP의 마지막 general partner인지 그 여부에 따라 적용되는 rule에 차이가 있다. LP의 마지막 general partner가 탈퇴하는 경우, 해당 general partner가 탈퇴한 날짜를 기준으로 90일 후에 LP는 해체된다. 만약 타 general partner가 LP에 존재한다면 general partner의 탈퇴 후 90일 이내로 partner들의 동의가 있는 경우에 한해 LP가 해체된다. 여기서 'partner들'은 distribution에 대해 많은 권한을 가지는 partner를 뜻한다. 넷째, LP의 마지막 limited partner가 dissociate한 후 90일 후에 LP는 해체된다. Limited partner는 스스로 탈퇴할 수 있는 권한이 없으나 계약상 탈퇴할 수 있는 요건을 만족한 경우 등과 같은 이유로 dissociate될 수 있다. 다섯째, 법원의 명령에 의해 LP가 해체될 수 있다.

1. General Rule

A limited partnership is dissolved upon the occurrence of:

ⅰ. The happening of an event specified in the limited partnership certificate;

ⅱ. When all general partners and limited partners who hold majority of distribution make **written consent;**

ⅲ. After the **dissociation of a general partner;**

ⅳ. After 90 days after the dissociation of the **last** limited partner; or

ⅴ. Upon **judicial decree.**

2. Priority of Distribution

In winding up process, assets are distributed in the following order:

i. Creditors;

ii. Partners (based on the partnership agreement); and

iii. Capital contributions by partners.

Ⅲ. Limited Liability Partnership (14July)

Limited liability partnership(LLP)는 한국법상 유한책임회사에 해당하는 바, 모든 사원이 회사의 채무에 대해 limited liability를 지는 유한책임사원이다. LLP의 사원은 회사(LLP)에 대해 fiduciary duty를 가진다는 점에서 LP의 limited partner와 차이가 있으나, 사원의 탈퇴(dissociation) 및 LLP의 해체 (dissolution)는 LP의 경우와 유사하다. 한편, LLP를 설립하기 위해서는 기업의 "LLP" 표현이 포함된 이름과 주소가 명시되어 있는 "Statement of Qualification" 서류를 제출해야 한다.

A. General Rule

1. Definition

★A limited liability partnership (LLP) is a partnership where all partners are not personally liable for the partnership obligations.

2. Formalities

To form a limited liability partnership,

i. The **Statement of Qualification** should be filed **with the Secretary of State**;

ii. Which includes the name (including the words "LLP") of the partnership; and

iii. The address of the partnership.

B. Partners

All partners have limited liability for partnership obligations, but they are personally liable for their own wrongful conducts.

All partners owe LLP fiduciary duties, including duty of care and duty of loyalty.

C. Dissociation and Dissolution

Dissociation and dissolution are similar to a limited partnership.

| 답안요령 | LLP와 사원간 책임문제 |

Q: <u>What claims, if any, does 갑 have against ABC and 병? Discuss.</u>
<u>LLP ABC 회사의 사원 을이 갑과 계약을 체결하였으나, 해당 계약을 이행하지 않았다. 이에 대해 갑이 회사 ABC와 또 다른 사원 병을 상대로 소송을 제기한 경우, 갑이 승소할 가능성을 논하라.</u>

> 1. LLP 회사 특징
> 2. ABC 회사가 피고인 경우
>   ① Agency rule
>   ② Authority 존부 파악
>   ③ Ratification★
> 3. ABC 회사의 사원이면서 또 다른 사원 병이 피고인 경우
>   ① Agency rule
>   ② Limited liability

| TIP1 | '회사의 특징'에 관한 문제가 별도로 출제되지 않았다 하더라도 답안의 첫 문장에 작성하는 것이 고득점 포인트다.

| TIP2 | 각 '피고'를 title화하여 작성한다.

| 모범답안 008 |

<u>Limited liability partnership</u>

A limited liability partnership (LLP) is a partnership where all partners are not personally liable for the partnership obligations. To form a limited liability partnership, the Statement of Qualification should be filed with the Secretary of State.

1. 갑 against ABC

……

2. 갑 against 병

……

Conclusion

……

Part Three. Corporation (15July, 17Feb)

- Closely held corporation: 비상장회사(주주가 소수인 경우 비상장회사로 presume 한다.)
- Publicly traded corporation: 상장회사
- Promoter = Incorporator: 발기인
- Shareholder = Owner: 주주(주식회사의 소유자)
- Director: 이사(주식회사의 경영자)
- Board of directors (BOD): 이사회

본 파트는 한국법상 주식회사에 해당하는 corporation에 대해 논한다. Corporation은 주주(shareholder)의 출자로 구성되는 자본을 가지고 있는 회사이며, 기본적으로 소유와 경영이 분리되어 있다. 주주(shareholder)가 주식회사의 사원이자 소유자(owner)이고 이사(director) 및 이사회(Board of Directors, BOD)가 경영자이다. 따라서 shareholder는 기본적으로 회사의 경영에 참여할 수 없으나 shareholder이면서 동시에 회사를 경영하는 director가 존재할 수는 있다. 한편, 주식회사 설립의 가장 큰 의의는 유한책임(limited liability)이다. 모든 소유자(주주)와 경영자는 회사채무에 대해 limited liability를 지는 바, 회사의 채무에 대해 직접·무한·연대

책임을 지지 않고 유한책임만을 진다. 다시 말해, 주주는 자신이 출자한 자본(주금액)을 한도로 출자의무만을 부담할 뿐, 주식회사의 채무에 대해 직접·무한·연대 책임을 지지 않는다. 또한 회사 채권자는 회사를 상대로 한 소송만을 제기할 수 있을 뿐, 주주 및 경영자를 상대로 채권을 행사할 수 없다. 이하 주식회사 설립, 회사 구조, 주주 및 이사(또는 officer)의 권리, 의무 및 책임, 그리고 주식회사 관련 연방법 등에 대해 논한다.

Ⅰ. Incorporation

A. Formalities

주식회사 설립은 promoters간에 주식회사 설립을 위한 계약체결을 함으로써 시작되어, Articles of Incorporation(AOI)이 제출됨으로써 완성된다. 즉, 주식회사는 Articles of Incorporation(AOI) 제출 시점에 설립(be incorporated)된다. 따라서 AOI를 제출하기 이전에 존재하는 설립중의 회사는 unincorporated corporation이며, AOI를 제출한 이후 설립된 주식회사는 incorporated corporation 또는 corporation라 일컫는다.

1. General Rule

A corporation is a **distinct legal entity** from its owners.

The main reason to incorporate is to avoid liability for obligation of a business enterprise. All owners and directors are limited liable for the corporation's liability.

2. Articles of Incorporation (AOI)

The Articles of Incorporation with the Secretary of State must contain:

ⅰ. The corporate name;

ⅱ. The number of shares the corporation is authorized to issue;

ⅲ. The address of the corporation's initial registered office and the name of its initial registered agent at that office; and

ⅳ. The name and address of each incorporator.

> **TIP** "ABC Inc."와 같이 회사명에 Inc.로 명시되어 있는 경우 corporation 의 규정을 적용한다.

B. Creation of Corporation

본 챕터에서는 주식회사 설립에 관해 논한다. 주식회사 설립은 주(州) 법에서 요구하는 모든 설립요건을 만족하여 그 설립이 인정된 de jure corporation과 모든 설립요건을 만족하지는 못하였으나 법적으로 설립을 인정하는 경우들이 있다. 후자의 경우에는 de facto corporation과 corporation incorporated by estoppel doctrine이 있다. De facto corporation이란, 설립요건이 미충족되었 더라도 promoter에게 주식회사를 설립하고자 하는 선의(good-faith)가 있었 고 promoter가 설립중의 회사를 주식회사로서 대우하여 행동한 경우 인정되 는 주식회사를 뜻한다. 하지만 promoter가 설립요건 미충족 사실을 인지하고 있었는데도 불구하고 주식회사를 위한 계약을 체결했다면, promoter는 해당 계약의 당사자(active participants)로서 계약에 대한 책임을 진다(personally liable). 설립자가 두 명 이상일 경우 그들은 해당 계약에 대해 jointly and severally liable하므로, 계약 상대방은 promoters 중 아무나 임의로 선택해서 소송하더라도 full recover할 수 있다. Promoter가 악의로 제3자와 계약을 체 결했고 이후 설립된 주식회사가 해당 계약을 adopt 하더라도 promoter의 책 임은 지속된다. 즉, 주식회사와 promoter 모두 책임을 진다. 한편 corporation incorporated by estoppel doctrine은 계약 상대방이 사원의 자산이 아닌 회사 의 존재에 의존하여 계약을 체결한 경우 회사의 설립을 인정해주는 경우이다.

1. De Jure Corporation

De jure corporation is formed when all the statutory requirements are met. The incorporators must sign and file **Articles of Incorporation (AOI)** **with the Secretary of State.**

a. Articles of Incorporation (AOI)

Articles of Incorporation (AOI) should include:

i . Corporation's name and address for corporation's initial registered office;

ii . Name and address of each incorporator;

iii. Initial agent's name for the corporation; and

iv. Authorized number of shares.

[Initial Agent]

The initial agent receives important legal, tax, and corporate compliance documents for the company.

2. De Facto Corporation

De facto corporation의 경우, 회사와 제3자와의 모든 거래에서 회사의 존재가 인정되나 quo warranto 소송에서는 회사의 존재가 인정되지 않는다. Quo warranto 소송은 office에 대한 점유권 및 소유권에 대한 소송을 뜻한다.

a. General Rule

A business is treated as corporation when there were:

i . **Good-faith attempt** to incorporate; and

ii . **Actual use** of the corporate form.

b. In Quo Warranto proceeding

In a quo warranto proceeding, the state may **deny** corporate entity status.

Quo warranto is a legal action used to resolve a dispute over the legal right to hold the public office that a party occupies.

c. When No Good-Faith

If promoters **knew** that there is no incorporation and acted on behalf of the corporation, they are **jointly and severally liable** (personally liable) to the third party.

Even after incorporated corporation adopts the contract, **those** persons are still liable. Thus, **both** corporation and promoters are liable for the contract.

3. Incorporation by Estoppel Doctrine

Under the incorporation by estoppel doctrine, corporate limited liability is recognized **in contract cases,** when:

ⅰ. A third party deals solely with the corporation; and

ⅱ. Has not relied on the personal assets of the promoter.

C. Corporate Purpose

It is presumed that corporations are formed for any lawful business purposes.

If there is a specified corporate purpose but it acts outside of the purpose, such actions are called "ultra vires."

D. Promoters

Promoter는 설립중의 회사를 incorporate하기 위해 일하는 사람으로서, "incorporator"라고도 한다. Promoter는 incorporate 과정에서 발생하는 모든 거래에 대해 personally liable하며, 설립중의 회사(pre-incorporated business)는 책임이 없다. 이는 아직 설립되지 못한 주식회사가 계약에 대해 책임을 질 수 없다고 보기 때문이다. Promoter의 personal liability는 주식회사가 설립(incorporated)된 이후에도 유지되며, 심지어는 설립된 주식회사가 해당 계약을 인정(adopt)하는 경우에도 그 책임이 유지된다. 다만, 해당 거래의 모든 당사자 동의를 요하는 novation이 있는 경우에 한해 promoter의 책임이 면제되고 설립된 주식회사만이 해당 계약에 대해 책임을 진다. 한편, promoter는 주식회사 설립 또는 출자에 관하여 타 promoter, corporation 그리고 계약의 상대방에게 fiduciary duty를 진다.

1. Personal Liability

Generally, a promoter is **personally liable** for the pre-incorporation actions, until:

    ⅰ. There is **novation** that replaces the promoter's liability with that of the corporation; or

    ⅱ. There is a contrary agreement.

2. Corporation's Adoption

Corporation is not liable for pre-incorporation actions, but it has liability when it **adopts** the liability.

Promoter is still liable even after the corporation adopted, unless there is a novation.

3. Fiduciary Duty

Promoters owe fiduciary duties to other promoters, the corporation, and to those persons who invest in it.

E. Corporate Structure

1. Shareholders, Directors, and Officers

a. Shareholders

★Owners are shareholders. Shareholders own stock or equity. Shareholders have **no** right to manage.

b. Directors and Officers

★The **right to manage** is centralized to board of directors (BOD). Officers and committees act on behalf of BOD, by implementing the board decisions and carrying out operations. They have authority based on agency. In other words, directors delegate authority to them.

2. Limited Liability

All of owners and directors are **limited liability** for the corporation's liability. Thus, only the corporation itself can be held liable for corporate obligations, unless such persons are personally liable for their own torts.

3. Documents

Articles of Incorporation (AOI) are filed with the Secretary of State to establish the corporation.

Bylaws contain management provisions which are adopted by the board.

4. Stock

주주가 주식을 매입하는 경우 반드시 consideration이 있어야 하며, 유형 및 무형의 자산 그리고 회사에 이익이 되는 모든 것은 consideration으로 인정된다. 다만, 미래에 제공할 서비스와 담보권이 설정되어 있지 않은 채권을 consideration으로 인정할 것인가에 대해서는 각 주가 보는 시각이 다르다. RMBCA를 채택하는 주에서는 미래에 제공할 서비스와 담보권이 설정되어 있지 않은 채권 또한 consideration으로 인정하나, 캘리포니아 주에서는 consideration으로 인정하지 않는다. 한편, 캘리포니아 주는 주주에게 신주우선인수권(preemptive right)이 없다고 본다.

a. Consideration for Stock Shares

In exchange for stock shares, consideration is requires.

Any tangible or intangible property and anything that can be benefits for the corporation can be consideration.

However, in California, future services and an unsecured debt are not considered as consideration.

b. Preemptive Rights

Preemptive right is a right that the existing shareholders can maintain their percentage of ownership in a corporation when a new stock is issued for cash.

In modern California, shareholders do not have preemptive right, unless the articles of incorporation (AOI) state otherwise.

II. Directors and Officers

본 챕터는 corporation을 manage하는 directors(BOD)와 officers에 대해 논하며, 그 내용은 크게 이들이 회사에 대해 지는 책임과 의무, 이들을 보호하는 rules, 이들이 회사에 대해 가지는 권리, 이렇게 세 부분으로 이루어져 있다. 본 챕터에서 논하는 내용은 director와 officer에게 동일하게 적용가능하나 편의를 위해 이하 내용은 director에 관한 내용으로 서술하였다.

A. Duties and Liability

Director가 회사에 대해 지는 의무에는 이사회를 개최할 의무(duty to hold meetings)와 신의칙의 의무(fiduciary duty)가 있다. Fiduciary duty는 corporation 내부에서 회사의 운영을 책임지는 director에게 주어지며, 본 의무는 director로부터 경영에 대한 업무를 위임받은 officer에게도 동일하게 적용된다. 뿐만 아니라, 특정 corporation의 모회사(parent corporation)가 자회사의 director 선임 등과 같이 자회사 경영에 관여(control)하는 경우에는 모회사가 자회사에 대해 fiduciary duty를 진다. 다시 말해, fiduciary duty는 사람뿐만 아니라 회사에도 주어지는 의무이다. 한편, director는 회사채권에 대해 유한책임(limited liability)을 진다.

1. Duty to Hold Meetings
- Quorum: 정족수
- Plurality: 최다득표(receiving the most votes)
- Count: 유효투표로 인정하다(v.)

a. General Rule
The board of directors must hold meetings. Regular meetings are held following the bylaws without notice. Special meetings are

held, but it requires at least two days notice.

b. Quorum

To be a valid action, **quorum** must be **present at the time of vote** unless bylaws or articles state otherwise.

Quorum means the majority of the board of directors.

c. Participation

Participation is valid only if all directors **simultaneously hear each other** during the meeting.

Breaking quorum **is allowed.**

d. Exception

When there are written consents of all directors, an action may be taken without a meeting.

2. Duty of Care

A director owes corporation fiduciary duties, including duty of care and duty of loyalty.

★The duty of care requires a director acts **in good faith as reasonable person** in a manner he reasonably believes is **in the best interest.**

3. Duty of Loyalty

★Directors have duty of loyalty including:

ⅰ. Duty not to **self-dealing** (conflicting interest transaction);

ⅱ. Duty to **disclose** material information;

ⅲ. Duty to refrain from **unfair competition** (not to compete with the company's business before its dissolution); and

ⅳ. Duty not to **usurp**^{빼앗다} corporate **opportunities.**

4. Liability

Directors have **limited liability,** unless they committed intentional wrongful acts or crimes.

B. Rules protecting Directors (15July, 17Feb)

앞서 언급한 바와 같이, director는 회사의 경영권을 가진 자로서 회사에 fiduciary duty를 진다. 즉, director가 회사 경영에 대해 내리는 모든 결정은 duty of care와 duty of loyalty에 위배되지 않아야 하며, 그렇지 않은 경우에는 breach of fiduciary duty에 대해 책임을 져야 한다. 다만, 본 의무를 너무 엄격히 적용하는 경우 director가 결정을 내리는데 있어 자유롭지 못할 수 있다. 따라서 director의 비교적 자유로운 결정을 위해 "director의 결정은 fiduciary duty를 지킨 선에서 이루어졌다"고 추정함으로써 그들을 보호한다. 본 추정은 BJR과 safe harbor rule 등에 입각한다.

Business judgment rule(BJR)은 duty of care에만 적용되는 rule이다. BJR이란, director가 회사를 위해 내린 결정은 good-faith가 있다(duty of care를 지킨 행위이다)고 추정하여 director들을 보호해주는 rule이다. 따라서 "director의 행위에 BJR이 적용될 수 없다(Director는 duty of care를 위반했다)"고 주장하는 자는 director was not good-faith임을 증명하여, BJR의 추정을 반박해야 한다(rebut presumption). Director's duty of care는 good-faith, reasonable for best interest of corporation, full informed, 이 4개 요소를 포함하므로, BJR의 추정을 rebut하고자 하는 자는 이에 대한 반증을 제시해야 한다.

Director가 duty of loyalty에 관한 행위를 한 경우에는 BJR을 적용할 수 없지만 director 스스로 fairness를 증명하면 보호받을 수 있다. Fairness를 증명할 때에는 substantive fairness와 procedural fairness 모두 증명해야 한다. 일반적으로 director는 자신이 체결한 계약의 fair price와 fair dealing을 증명한다. 한편, duty of loyalty 중 self-dealing에 관한 행위에는 safe harbor rule이 특별히 적용될 수 있다. Safe harbor rule은 director가 회사를 위해 내린 결정이 '합리적'이었다고 추정하여 director의 결정을 보호하는 rule이다. Self-dealing의 합리성 추정 요건은 qualified approval과 full disclosure이다. 다시 말해, director의 duty of loyalty 위반을 주장하는 자는 not approved by qualified directors/shareholders 또는 not fully informed임을 증명해서 safe harbor rule의 추정을 rebut해야 한다.

한편, 상기 rule들은 director 뿐만 아니라 회사 경영에 대해 내리는 자들에 모두 적용되는 바, general partnership(GP)의 partner, limited partnership(LP)의 general partner 등에게도 동일하게 적용된다.

> **TIP**　Conflicting interest transaction에 관한 내용인 경우, ① safe harbor rule을 우선 적용하고, safe harbor rule의 요건을 만족하지 못한 경우에는 ② fairness에 대해 추가적으로 analysis한다.

[도표 2-7]

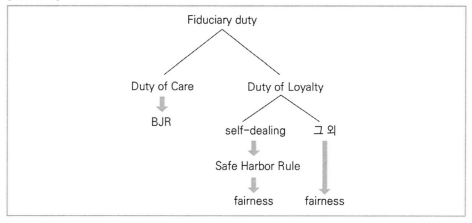

1. Business Judgment Rule (BJR)

a. General Rule

★The business judgment rule (BJR) is a **presumption** that, in making a business decision, the directors of a corporation **acted in good faith** and in the belief that the action taken was **in the best interest of the company.**

b. Rational Business Purpose

BJR을 적용하는 것은 director 또는 parent corporation의 결정을 방해하지 않는 것으로 볼 수 있다. BJR은 그들의 결정을 존중하기 위한 rule이므로, director 또는 parent corporation이 자신들의 결정에 rational business purpose가 있다는 것을 보여주면 BJR이 적용되어 법원은 이들의 결정을 disturb할 수 없다.

According to the business judgment rule, the decisions will not be distributed by a court if they can be attributed to any rational business purpose.

Judicial inquiry is prohibited which is made into actions of corporate directors taken in good faith and in the exercise of honest judgment in the lawful and legitimate furtherance of corporate purposes.

2. Safe Harbor Rule

★Under the safe harbor rule, a director's **self-dealing** is protected when:

ⅰ. There is an approval by **disinterested directors** (or shareholders);

ⅱ. A director **fully disclosed** all relevant information; and

ⅲ. A director **played no part** in the disinterested directors' vote directly or indirectly.

3. Fairness

a. General Rule

Even if the transaction was not properly authorized, the directors can satisfy their fiduciary duty of loyalty by showing that the transaction was fair to the corporation.

Fairness includes not only the market fairness of the terms of the deal but also whether the transaction was one that was reasonably likely to make favorable results for the corporation.

b. Entire Fairness Review

★Generally, the **directors** have the burden to show that the transaction as a whole was fair in terms of **"fair price" and "fair dealing."**

★However, **in intra-group corporate dealings,** the entire fairness review (showing both fair price and fair dealing) is not required.

The absence of fair price is critical.

C. Rights

1. Right to Compensation

A director is entitled to fair compensation.

2. Right to Indemnification

주식회사가 director에게 하는 indemnification 유형에는 두 종류가 있다. Director가 주식회사의 업무를 대리하는 과정에서 지불한 비용과 회사가 director를 상대로 제기한 소송에서 director가 승소한 경우 해당 소송 과정에서 director가 지불한 비용은 강제적 indemnification으로서, 회사가 '반드시' director에게 해당 비용을 indemnify해야 한다. 한편, 제3자가 director를 상대로 제기한 소송에서 director가 패소한 경우 director가 good-faith를 가지고 회사의 이익을 위해 최선을 다한 경우에 한해 해당 소송 과정에서 director가 지불한 비용은 선택적 indemnification으로 인정되는 바, 회사가 director에게 해당 비용을 indemnify '할 수' 있다.

The corporation **must** indemnify a director for expenses incurred on behalf of the corporation and expenses incurred in a proceeding brought by the corporation in which a director prevails.

The corporation **may** indemnify directors for expenses incurred in a proceeding in which directors were unsuccessful. Such indemnification occurs only when directors acted in good faith and in the best interest of the corporation.

3. Right to Inspection

Directors have right to a reasonable inspection of corporate records or facilities.

Ⅲ. Shareholders

본 챕터에서는 주식회사의 주인인 shareholder의 권리와 의무에 대해 논한다. Shareholder는 임시주주총회소집권, 의결권(right to vote), 자료열람권(right to inspect), 이익배당권(right to dividend) 등을 가지고 있다. Shareholder는 경영권을 갖지 않으므로 원칙적으로 회사에 대한 fiduciary duty도 없으나, 최근에는 대주주의 경우 회사 결정에 막대한 영향력을 끼칠 수 있으므로 타 주주에 대한 fiduciary duty가 있다고 본다.

Owners are shareholders. Shareholders own stock or equity. Shareholders have **no** right to manage.

A. Rights

1. Right of Meeting

Shareholders have right to hold meetings as to corporate management issues. There are two types of meetings: general meetings and special meetings.

a. General Meeting

General meetings (annual meetings) are held once a year which requires 10-60 days notice.

b. Special Meeting

Special meetings are held upon reasonable notice as to the date, time, place, and the purpose of the meeting.

[표 2-2]

	Shareholders	Directors
Notice on 'regular' meeting	tm: 10~60 days notice contents: date, tm, place + purpose	×
Notice on 'special' meeting		tm: 2 days notice contents: date, tm, place
Breaking quorum (투표 전에 leave 하면 break quorum 되는가?)	× (quorum요건 만족한 후, 주주가 leave하더라도 해당 안건 확정가능)	○ (Director가 투표 전 leave하는 경우 해당 안건 확정불가
Quorum	majority of the shares entitled to vote	majority of the fixed number of directors
Right to manage/control	×	○
Fiduciary duty	×	○

2. Right to Vote

- Authorized shares: the maximum number of shares a corporation may issue

- Outstanding shares: the total number of shares issued by the corporation and held by the shareholders

  ⇒ Each outstanding share is entitled to one vote.

- Treasury shares: shares required by a corporation, and are considered authorized but not outstanding ⇒ **not** count

a. Quorum

Quorum is a majority of outstanding shares represented. A quorum must attend a meeting before a vote may validly be taken.

An action on a matter is approved if votes are cast in favor of the action.

b. Proxy

의결권 있는 주주가 의결권을 행사하기 위해 주주총회에 반드시 참여해야하는 것은 아니다. 주주가 특정인에게 proxy를 주면, 그 특정인(proxy holder)은 주주를 대리하여 의결권을 행사할 수 있다. Proxy는 주주가 서면으로 작성하고 서명해야 그 효력이 인정된다(valid). 원칙적으로 proxy는 철회 가능(revocable)하지만, 특정인에게 주어진 proxy가 그 특정인의 채권과 관련된 경우라면 철회 불가하다.

ⅰ. General Rule

A shareholder may vote her shares without physically attending the meeting through the use of proxy.

Proxy must be written and signed by shareholder.

ⅱ. Revocable v. Irrevocable

Shareholder proxies generally are **revocable.**

Proxies are irrevocable when they are coupled **with an interest.**

The irrevocable proxy must be so labeled.

c. Vote Calculation

There are two methods on vote calculation: straight voting and cumulative voting for directors.

ⅰ. Straight Voting

In straight voting, each shareholder casts one vote per share held.

ⅱ. Cumulative Voting

Cumulative voting 방식을 취하는 경우, 주주는 자신이 가지고 있는 shares를 선출할 director의 인원수에 곱한 만큼의 투표권을 가진다. 예컨대, 주주가 5개 주(株)를 가지고 있고 2명의 director를 선출하고자 하는 경우 해당 주주는 10개의 투표권을 가지게 된다. 주주는 자신의 모든 투표권을 한 명의 director 후보에게 투표할 수 있다.

In cumulative voting for directors, a shareholder is entitled to cast votes which are calculated by multiplying the number of shares by the number of directors to be elected. Shareholders can cast all votes for one or more directors.

d. Fundamental Changes

ⅰ. General Rule

A majority shareholder vote is required to approve fundamental changes to the corporation.

Fundamental changes to the corporation include merger, share exchange, substantial asset sale, amendment, dissolution, etc.

ⅱ. Procedure

Fundamental changes are made through board's resolution^{결의안} adoption, shareholders' approval, and the updating of the change in the articles.

3. Right to Inspect

적절한 사유가 있는 경우에 한해 주주는 주주총회 회의록, 회계장부 등 회사의 서류를 열람할 수 있다. 주주의 권리와 관련된 사안은 대부분 '적절한 사유'로 인정된다. 서류 열람 신청을 할 경우 주주는 최소 5일 전에 서류열람 목적을 명시한 서면으로 신청해야 한다.

a. General Rule

ⅰ. Right to Inspect

A shareholder has a right to inspect corporate books and records, including minutes of board meetings and accounting records **for a proper purpose.**

ⅱ. Procedural Requirements

Shareholder must make a **five days written notice.** The demand must be made **in good faith** and describes **particular purpose** which is related to a shareholder's interest.

4. Right of Dividends

Shareholders have right to receive dividends, which are distribution of cash, property, or stock from the corporation.

5. Derivative Suit and Direct Suit (17Feb)

본 파트는 주주가 주식회사에 관해 제기할 수 있는 소송인 derivative suit 와 direct suit에 대해 논한다. Derivative suit란, director가 회사경영을 함에 있어 회사에 대한 fiduciary duty를 위반한 경우 주주가 회사를 대신하여 director를 상대로 제기하는 소송이다. Direct suit는 "personal suit"라고도 하며, 주주의 권리가 침해당했을 때 주주가 자신의 권리를 행사하기 위해 제기하는 소송이다. 따라서 주주가 제기하는 소송의 유형은 주주가 소송의 성격을 정하기 나름이다. 한편, derivative suit의 경우 board of directors(BOD)에 대한 주주의 사전(事前) demand가 요구되는 반면, direct suit는 demand 없이 제기할 수 있다. 주주가 derivative suit를 제기했다 하더라도, 과반수 이상의 directors가 이에 대한 적절한 자료와 함께 해당 소송의 진행으로 인해 회사에 불이익이 생길 것으로 예상하여 선의로 소송을 기각시킬 수 있다. 여기서 '적절한 자료'란, 판단에 유용할 정도의 조사가 요구될 뿐 완벽한 조사가 요구되지는 않는다.

a. Derivative Suit

i . General Rule

★If the shareholders bring a suit **on behalf of the corporation,** it may be a derivative suit. In other words, the derivative suit is for **the director's breach of fiduciary duty owed to the corporation.**

ii . Requirements

★To be a valid derivative suit, the shareholder must:

① **Own stock** at the time of the alleged breach;

② Adequately **represent** the corporation's interests; and

③ First make a **demand** to the board of directors, unless it is futile^{소용없는}.

The shareholder represents the corporation's interests when shareholder has **enough shares** to adequately represent the shareholders.

The derivative action may be brought within a reasonable time after the demand. The demand requirement may be waived if the demand is deemed futile.

✔ When there are only two shareholders — 위 ii 요건 충족
✔ When a majority of the board would be defendants in the derivative suit — futile(사전 demand 없이 제소가능)
✔ When there are few directors and all are related (e.g., family member) — futile(사전 demand 없이 제소가능)

TIP Arguable point: Shareholder 갑이 director 을의 행위에 대해 derivative suit를 제기하는 경우, 을은 갑이 사전 demand를 요청하지 않았음을 근거로 해당 소송이 invalid하다고 주장할 것이다. 이에 대해 갑은 주어진 상황에서 demand를 하는 것은 futile하다는 점을 근거로 해당 소송이 valid하다고 주장할 것이다.

iii. Remedy

Recovery is provided to the corporation and the shareholder is entitled to reimbursement for the litigation expenses.

✔ 주식 액면가(par value)보다 낮은 금액으로 주식을 발행한 경우 (**watered stock**을 발행한 경우) → derivative suit 제기 가능 → Directors가 par value와 발행된 금액의 차액에 대해 책임을 진다.
⇒ 문제 본문에 par value가 명시되어 있는 경우, derivative suit 와 연관이 있을 가능성이 높다.

b. Direct Suit

★If the shareholders bring a suit **for their own right,** it may be a **direct suit.**

ⅰ. Oppression Doctrine

- Majority shareholders = Controlling shareholders
- Minority shareholders = Non-controlling shareholders

Oppression doctrine에 따르면, 비상장회사에서 대주주는 타 주주와 주식회사에 대해 신의칙의 의무를 지는 바, 타 주주의 합리적 기대(reasonable expectation)를 저버리는 행위를 한 경우 이에 대한 책임을 져야 한다.

① General Rule

★Under the oppression doctrine, **majority shareholders owe fiduciary duties** of care and loyalty to both minority shareholders and corporation only in **closely-held corporation.**

The oppression doctrine is applicable when actions by controlling shareholders **violate the reasonable expectations** of non-controlling shareholders.

② **Remedies in Oppression**

If a majority shareholder oppressed a minority shareholder, a **minority** shareholder may raise a **direct** claim for oppression remedies.

Remedies in oppression include:

(a) A mandatory **repurchase** by the corporation of the **minority shareholder's stock;** and

(b) **Mandatory dissolution** of the corporation.

B. Duties

1. Fiduciary Duties

Generally, shareholders owe **no** fiduciary duty to the corporation and may act in their own personal interests.

However, in modern, **controlling shareholders owe a fiduciary duty to both corporation and minority shareholders.** A controlling shareholder is one who has substantial impact on the corporation **with a strong voting power.**

2. Liability

a. General Rule

Shareholders are not personally liable for the corporation obligations.

★However, shareholders are jointly and severally liable for:

ⅰ. Unpaid stock;

ⅱ. **A pierced corporate veil;** and

ⅲ. Absence of de jure corporation when the shareholder knew that there was no incorporation.

답안요령 │ Derivative v. Direct suit

Q: <u>Does 갑 have a cause of action against 을, either derivatively or personally?</u> <u>Minority shareholder인 갑이 majority shareholder인 을의 행위에 대해 derivative</u> <u>action과 direct action 중 어떤 유형의 소송을 제기할 수 있는가? (주식회사는</u> <u>closely-held라고 가정한다.)</u>

---

1. Derivative action
   ① 기본 rule(요건×3)
   ② 을's fiduciary duty to corporation 유무판단
   ③ Duty of care
   ④ Duty of loyalty
2. Direct action 기본 rule
   ① 기본 rule

---

② 을's fiduciary duty to 갑 유무판단(oppression doctrine)★
③ Duty of care
④ Duty of loyalty

TIP1 Shareholder가 제기한 소송과 관련한 답안은 피고(을)의 '신분'에 따라 전체적인 내용이 달라진다. 예컨대, 을이 majority shareholder 인 경우 oppression doctrine에 의거하여 을은 갑에 대해 신의칙의 의무를 지는 바, 갑은 을을 상대로 direct action을 제기할 수 있다. 또한 modern law에 따르면 majority shareholder는 회사에 대해 신의칙의 의무를 지는 바, 갑은 을을 상대로 derivative action을 제기할 수 있다. 만일 을이 director인 경우라면 을은 회사에 대해 신의칙의 의무를 지는 바, 그가 duty of care 및 duty of loyalty를 위반한 행위는 BJR, safe harbor rule 그리고 fairness와 연관 지어 답안을 작성한다. 본 답안요령 및 모범답안은 전자의 경우를 바탕으로 작성되었다.

TIP2 Derivative suit와 direct suit를 큰 title로 하여 작성한다.

TIP3 Derivative suit와 관련한 내용에는 갑이 derivative suit의 요건을 만족하였는지 그 여부와 을이 위반한 신의칙의무에 대한 내용이 포함된다.

모범답안 009

1. Derivative suit

Derivative suit

If the shareholders bring a derivative suit on behalf of the corporation when the director breached the fiduciary duty owed to the corporation. To be a valid derivative suit, the shareholder must: (1) own stock at the time of the alleged breach; (2) adequately represent the corporation's interests; and (3) first make a demand to the board of directors, unless it is futile.

(1) Own stock

(ANALYSIS: In this case, 갑 owned stock when 을 breached fiduciary duty to the corporation. Thus, first requirement for derivative suit is satisfied.)

(2) Represent the corporation's interests

Shareholders must have enough shares to adequately represent the shareholders.

(ANALYSIS: In this case, there are only two shareholders, 갑 and 을. 갑 adequately represent the corporation's interests. Thus, second requirement for derivative suit is satisfied.)

(3) First petition/futile

The derivative action may be brought within a reasonable time after the demand. The demand requirement may be waived if the demand is deemed futile.

(ANALYSIS: 을 may argue that 갑 did not make a demand prior to the derivative action. However, 갑 may argue that there are two directors who are family members each other and the demand is futile. 갑's argument may be successful and, therefore, third requirement for derivative suit is satisfied.)

을's fiduciary duty to corporation

A shareholder owes no fiduciary duty to the corporation. However, in modern, majority shareholders have substantial impact on the corporation and owes fiduciary duty to the corporation.

(ANALYSIS: In this case, 을 is a majority shareholder of ABC and he owes fiduciary duty to corporation.)

Duty of care

......

Duty of loyalty

......

2. Direct suit

Direct suit

If the shareholders bring a suit for their own right, it may be a direct suit.

Oppression doctrine

Generally, a shareholder owes no fiduciary duty to the corporation. However, under the oppression doctrine, majority shareholders owe fiduciary duties of care and loyalty to the minority shareholders only in closely-held corporation.

(ANALYSIS: In this case, 을 is a majority shareholder of ABC and ABC is a closely-held corporation. Thus, 을 owes fiduciary duty to 갑.)

Duty of care

......

Duty of loyalty

......

Conclusion

In conclusion, 갑 may raise both derivative and direct suit against 을.

b. Piercing Corporate Veil (17Feb)

Corporation의 shareholder와 director는 회사 채무에 대해 limited liability를 가진다. 즉, 회사 채권자는 shareholder(또는 director)를 상대로 소송할 수 없다. 하지만 예외적으로 shareholder가 회사채권에 대해 personal liability를 지는 경우가 있는데, 그 경우는 다음과 같다. 첫째, pierce the corporate veil한 경우이다. Pierce the corporate veil을 직역하면 "corporation의 베일을 벗기다"이다. Corporation에서는 limited liability를 인정하기 때문에 shareholder가 corporation에 관해한 행동의 모든 책임은 회사로 귀속된다. 즉, shareholder가 자신이 한 행위에 대해 corporation이라는 존재 뒤에 숨어 그 책임을 corporation에 떠넘길 위험이 있다. 따라서 shareholder가 corporation의 존재를

부적절하게 사용하는 경우 corporation이라는 베일 뒤에 숨은 주주의 잘잘못을 따져 그에게 직접 책임을 묻는 데, 이를 "pierce the corporate veil한다."고 표현한다. Pierce the veil 해야 하는 상황은 shareholder 가 자신과 corporation을 별개의 개체로 여겼는지 그 여부를 기준으로 판단한다. 만약 shareholder가 corporation을 별개의 개체가 아닌 자신과 동일한 개체(alter ego)로 여겼다면, pierce the veil한다. 일반적으로 주주가 자신의 자산과 corporation의 자산을 혼용해서 사용(commingle)하는 경우 "alter ego"로 보고 주주에게 직접 책임을 묻는다. Corporation의 해산 또는 청산 과정을 합법적으로 처리하지 않은 경우에도 corporation이 아닌 shareholder 당사자가 책임을 진다.

한편, deep rock doctrine에 따르면 회사가 파산하였고 piercing the corporate veil된 경우 주주가 회사에 가지는 채권은 제3자의 채권보다 변제순위가 낮다. 이는 주주들의 주식배당금 권리는 그들이 자회사에 빌려준 돈에 대한 채권과 동일하게 취급되어야 하기 때문에, 주주들이 자회사에 대해 가지고 있는 채권이 제3자가 자회사에 대해 가지고 있는 채권보다 변제순위가 낮다는 대법원의 판결[Taylor v. Standard Gas & Elec. Co., 306 U.S. 307 (1939)]로부터 도출되었다.

i. General Rule

★When the court **pierces the corporate veil,** shareholders are **personally liable** for the corporation obligations.

★The veil is pierced when there are following reasons:

① **Alter ego** (when the shareholders treat the corporation as an alter ego);

② Undercapitalization (when shareholder invested insufficiently to cover foreseeable liabilities);

③ Fraud (when a corporation is formed to commit fraud); and

④ Estoppel (when shareholder represents that he is personally liable)

ⅱ. Alter Ego

When the shareholders fail to treat the corporation as a separate entity, the corporation's veil can be pierced.

- ✔ 주주의 개인 자산과 회사 자산이 commingle되어 관리 및 사용되는 경우 — alter ego 인정(주주를 상대로 소송가능)
- ✔ Director's meeting을 정기적으로 개최하지 않는 경우 → disregard for corporate formalities → alter ego 인정(주주를 상대로 소송가능)

ⅲ. Undercapitalization

When the shareholder's **initial capital contributions** at the inception of the corporation were **insufficient** to cover the corporation's **foreseeable future liabilities,** the corporation's veil can be pierced.

- ✔ 갑이 주식회사 ABC Inc.를 설립할 당시 10만원을 투자하였고 주식회사에 5억원을 빌려주었다. 이후 회사 사무실을 위한 10년간의 임대차계약을 체결하였다면, 해당 주식회사를 설립할 당시 임대차계약에 따른 비용은 충분히 예상가능(foreseeable)했던 future liability이므로 undercapitalization이 인정된다. 따라서 주식회사의 veil can be pierced.

ⅳ. Fraud

When a corporation is formed to commit fraud using a corporation as a shield the shareholder's existing liability, the corporation's veil can be pierced.

c. Deep Rock Doctrine (17Feb)

★Under the deep rock doctrine, when corporate veil is pierced, any loans made by the **shareholders** to the corporation is **subordinated** to the corporation debts made by **a third party.**

답안요령 | Piercing the corporate veil

Q: <u>What claims, if any, does 갑 have against 을? Discuss.</u>
<u>Corporation ABC의 shareholder인 을이 사업운영을 하는 과정에서 갑과 계약</u>
<u>을 체결하였으나, 해당 계약을 이행하지 않았다. 한편, 을은 자신의 자산과</u>
<u>ABC의 자산을 commingle하며 사업을 운영하였다. 갑이 사원 을을 상대로 채</u>
<u>무불이행에 대한 소송을 제기한 경우, 갑이 승소할 가능성을 논하라.</u>

1. Corporation 회사 특징
2. ABC 회사의 사원 을이 피고인 경우
   ① Limited liability(원칙)
   ② Piercing corporate veil(예외)

TIP1 '회사의 특징'에 관한 문제가 별도로 출제되지 않았다 하더라도 답
안의 첫 문장에 작성하는 것이 고득점 포인트다.

TIP2 생각 route: 본래 shareholder는 회사의 채무에 대해 limited liability
를 진다. → 다만, 소송사유가 shareholder 개인의 행위에 근거한 경
우에는 piercing the corporate veil한다. → Shareholder가 예외적
으로 personal liability를 진다.

TIP3 위 2번: Piercing corporate veil이 인정되는 네 개의 '근거'를 title화
하여 각 근거에 대해 analysis를 한다.

TIP4 Arguable point: 을은 shareholder의 limited liability를 주장하며 자
신의 책임을 부정할 것이나, 이에 대해 갑은 piercing corporate
veil이 인정되어 을에게 책임이 있다고 주장할 것이다.

을 may argue that he has limited liability for the contract, since
he is a shareholder. However, 갑 may argue that the court
pierces the corporate veil.

모범답안 010

Corporation

A corporation is formed by filing Articles of Incorporation with the Secretary of State. All owners and directors are limited liability for the corporation's liability.

1. 갑 against 을

Limited liability

All shareholders are limited liability for the corporation's liability. (ANALYSIS: 을 may argue that he has limited liability for the contract, since he is a shareholder.)

Piercing corporate veil

However, 을's argument would fail and 갑 may argue that the court pierces the corporate veil. The veil is pierced and shareholders are personally liable for the corporation debts when there are alter ego, undercapitalization, fraud, or estoppel.

(1) Alter ego

When the shareholders treat the corporation as an alter ego, shareholders are personally liable.

(ANALYSIS: In this case, 을 commingled corporate funds with his personal funds. His action shows that he treated ABC as an alter ego. Thus, 을 is personally liable for the contract.)

(2) Undercapitalization

When shareholders invested insufficiently to cover foreseeable liabilities, shareholders are personally liable.

(ANALYSIS: In this case, there are no facts indicating undercapitalization.)

(3) Fraud

When a corporation is formed to commit fraud, shareholders are personally liable.

(ANALYSIS: In this case, there are no facts indicating that ABC is formed to commit fraud.)

(4) Estoppel

When shareholders represent that he is personally liable, shareholders are personally liable.

(ANALYSIS: In this case, there are no facts indicating that 갑 reasonably relied on 을's representation that he is personally liable.)

Conclusion

In conclusion, 을 treated ABC as an alter ego and the court would pierce the corporate veil, Thus, 갑 could raise claim against 을 and he is personally liable for the contract.

Ⅳ. Federal Securities Laws

본 챕터에서는 주식회사 및 주식 거래에 관한 연방법에 대해 논한다. Securities Exchange Act(SEA)의 Section 16(b)는 내부자거래 중 단기매매(short-swing trading profits)를 금하는 조항으로서, 주주와 이사가 6개월 이내에 단기매매를 하였고 이로부터 이익이 발생하였다면 이는 회사에 귀속되어야 한다. Section 10b-5는 내부자거래를 금하며, 주식매매에 있어 사기(fraud)행위를 한 자에게 책임을 지운다. 이는 회사의 내부기밀을 이용한 거래를 금하기 위한 법률로서, 내부자와 직접 거래한 자, 내부자, 회사기밀 제공자 등이 본 법률의 적용대상이 될 수 있다. 여기서 "faud"는 torts 과목에서의 misrepresentation과 동일한 개념으로서, 거래인의 intent, material misrepresentation, reliance가 증명되어야 그 책임이 인정된다. 한편, Sarbanes-Oxley Acts는 상장회사의 회계부정 사건에 의한 주가폭락 등을 방지하고자 회계법인을 감독하는 기관을 설립한 법안이다.

A. Section 16(b)

1. General Rule

If a **corporate insider** makes **short-swing trading profits within a six-month period**, those profits must be disgorged to the corporation.

a. Corporate Insider

Corporate insider includes officer, directors, and shareholders who own more than 10% of the corporation's shares.

Directors and officers must be in their positions when they **either** purchase **or** sale their shares.

Shareholders must be in their positions when they purchase **and** sale their shares.

b. Trading

Trading menas a profitable purchase and sale of company equity stock.

2. Requirements

To apply Section 16(b), corporation must:

ⅰ. Be a corporation listed on a national exchange; or

ⅱ. Have $10 million or more in assets and at least 2,000 shareholders.

B. Section 10b-5

- Tipper: A person who **provides** insider information
- Tippee: A person who **receives** insider information
- Misappropriator: 내부자 외에 다른 방법으로 내부정보를 획득한 자(예: 의뢰인으로부터 confidential한 내부정보를 가지게 된 변호사)

Under the section 20-5, insider trading of security is illegal and any person who directly or indirectly uses fraud or deception in transaction of any security has liability. This is to prohibit any security trading based on nonpublic corporate information.

1. Application

Section 10b-5 is applicable to:

ⅰ. A direct trading by an insider;

ⅱ. Tippers when the information was shared for improper purpose;

ⅲ. Misappropriators; and

ⅳ. Tippees only when:

① The tipper breaches fiduciary duty;

② The tippee knew the breach; and

③ The tipper personally benefited.

2. Damages and Remedy

Damages are the difference between actual proceeds based on nonpublic corporate information and the real value of the stock.

Damages should be disgorged to the company.

C. Sarbanes-Oxley Acts

The Acts created a board that oversees accounting industry to set standards for publicly traded companies.

The Acts enhanced reporting requirements and even provide criminal penalties.

Part Four. Limited Liability Companies

Limited liability company(LLC)는 한국법상 유한회사에 해당하며, 합자회사(general partnership)의 특징과 주식회사(corporation)의 특징을 복합적으로 가지고 있다. GP와 같이 세금혜택이 있으며, corporation과 같이 member들이 limited liability 를 가진다. GP와 LLC는 모두 소득세가 감면되는 혜택이 있다. 한편, LLC의 member 는 shareholder처럼 회사의 지분을 가지고 있기 때문에 "shareholder"라고 표현되기도 하나, LLC의 member는 소유권과 경영권을 모두 가지고 있어 명확히는 소유권과 경영권이 분리되는 corporation의 shareholder와 구별되는 개념이다.

A. Basic Rules

1. Definition

★A LLC is a form of business association that combines the features of corporations and partnerships.

Like general partnerships, LLCs have tax advantages and do not pay income taxes.

Like corporations, a LLC generally provides its members (investors) limited liability for firm debts.

2. Formalities

To form a LLC, the members must:

ⅰ. File the Articles of Organization with the state;

ⅱ. Identify the name of the LLC;

ⅲ. Identify the address of the registered office and agent;

3. Types of LLC

LLC 유형에는 member-managed LLC와 manager-managed LLC가 있다. Member-managed LLC는 모든 사원에게 동등한 경영권이 있는 형태의 LLC이며, manager-managed LLC는 일부 사원에게만 경영권이 인정되는 LLC이다. Certificate of Organization(CO)상에 LLC 유형이 명시되어 있지 않은 경우에는 member-managed LLC로 추정한다.

a. Member-Managed LLC

Each member in a member-managed LLC has **equal rights** in the management and conduct of the company's activities.

b. Manager-Managed LLC

A manager-managed LLC is operated by managers who are

appointed to run the company.

c. Presumption

An operating agreement may identify how the LLC is to be managed.

In the absence of an operating agreement, the LLC is presumed to be **member-managed.**

B. Members

Members are owners of a LLC. Members have **limited liability** for the company liability. In other words, members are not personally liable beyond their own capital contributions.

However, **courts may pierce the LLC veil of limited liability.**

답안요령 | LLP와 사원간 책임문제

Q: What claims, if any, does 갑 have against ABC and 병? Discuss. Member-managed LLC인 회사 ABC의 사원 을이 갑과 계약을 체결하였고, 해당 계약에 대한 채무를 이행하지 않았다. 이에 대해 갑이 회사 ABC와 ABC의 또 다른 사원 병을 상대로 소송을 제기한 경우, 갑이 승소할 가능성을 논하라.

---

1. LLC 회사 특징
2. ABC 회사가 피고인 경우
   ① Agency rule
   ② Authority 존부 파악
   ③ Ratification★
3. ABC 회사의 또 다른 사원인 병이 피고인 경우
   ① Limited liability

TIP1 '회사의 특징'에 관한 문제가 별도로 출제되지 않았다 하더라도 답안의 첫 문장에 작성하는 것이 고득점 포인트다.

TIP2 각 '피고'를 title화하여 작성한다.

Limited liability corporation

A limited liability company (LLC) is a hybrid company. A LLC is a form of business association that combines the features of corporations and partnerships. Like general partnerships, LLCs have tax advantages. Like corporations, a LLC generally provides its investors (members) limited liability for firm debts. To form a LLC, the Articles of Organization with the state must be filed.

1. 갑 against ABC

......

2. 갑 against 병

Like corporations, a LLC generally provides its investors (members) limited liability for firm debts.

(ANALYSIS: In this case, 병 is a member of ABC and he has limited liability for the contract. Thus, 갑 could not raise a claim against 병.)

Conclusion

In conclusion, 갑 could raise a claim against ABC, but not against 병.

C. Dissolution

LLC가 해체되는 사유는 다양하다. LLC의 operating agreement상 해체되는 사유를 명시하였고 해당 사유가 발생하는 경우, member 없이 90일 이상 지속되는 경우, 불법적인 행위 등을 근거로 한 법원명령(judicial decree), 그리고 매년 보고서를 제출해야 할 의무 위반 등을 근거로 한 행정명령(administrative decree)이 이에 해당한다.

1. Traditional Rule

The member's dissociation causes dissolution in a LLC.

2. Modern Rule

A LLC is dissolved upon the occurrence of:

ⅰ. The happening of an event specified in the operating agreement;

ⅱ. No members for 90 days;

ⅲ. Upon judicial degree; or

ⅳ. Upon administrative decree.

3장
Community Property

//

Community property(CP)는 부부의 '공동자산'을 의미하는 용어로서, 기본적으로 혼인생활 중 생성된 자산을 뜻한다. Community property law는 부부관계가 종료된 경우, 즉 배우자 일방이 사망했거나 부부가 이혼한 경우 부부의 자산을 어떻게 분배하는지에 대해 규정하고 있는 법으로서, California 주를 포함하여 Louisiana, Nevada, Texas 등 9개의 주에서 채택하고 있다. Community property law에 따르면 부부의 공동자산은 부부간 동등하게 나누어 가지는데, 이는 marital property를 각 상황에 따라 equitably 분배하는 방법과 대비되는 방법이다. 한편, 부부 각자의 '개인자산'은 separate property(SP)라 일컫는데, 이는 부부간 나누어 가지지 않고 그 자산을 단독으로 소유한 배우자 일방이 일체의 권리를 가진다. 다시 말해, 각 자산의 배분 방법은 자산의 유형(community property 또는 separate property)을 기준으로 결정된다.

본 장은 community property law에 관한 기본적인 개념 및 추정, 추정을 깨는 반증(자산 유형 결정에 영향을 미치는 요소), 이혼 및 배우자 일방의 사망 후 자산 분배, 배우자간 fiduciary duty, 이렇게 네 개의 파트로 구분되어 있다.

- Community property (CP)
- Quasi−community property (QCP)
- Separate property (SP)
- Intestate: 유효한 유언장 작성 없이 사망한 자(n.), intestate 방법으로(adv.)
- Deceased = Decedent: 고인(故人)
- Descendant: 자손
- Acquiring spouse: 자산을 단독으로 취득한 배우자 일방
- Surviving spouse: 사망한 자의 배우자

☑ 글쓰기 Tips

1. Community property에 관한 모든 답안은 Community Property Law에 대한 기본적인 설명으로 시작되어야 한다.

2. Community property는 Wills와 Trusts 과목과 연계되어 출제되는 경우가 많다. 배우자 일방이 will 또는 trust에서 자신이 소유한 자산을 언급한 후 사망한 경우 해당 자산을 어떻게 분배할 것인가에 대해 논하는 형태로 출제된다.

3. Community property에 관한 문제를 읽을 시, 가장 먼저 at divorce에 의한 사건인지 또는 at death에 의한 사건인지 확인한다. 역대 기출문제에서는 대부분 divorce 한 경우가 출제되었다.

4. 자산에 대한 각 spouse의 권리 및 책임에 대해 논하는 문제가 출제된다.
   Q: What are 갑's and 을's rights and liabilities, if any, regarding [the van]? Answer according to California Law.
   Q: What are 갑's and 을's respective rights regarding [the house]? Answer according to California Law.
   ⇒ 자산의 유형을 파악한 후, 자산의 분배방법에 대해 논한다.
   ⇒ ① presumption, ② source tracing (commingled source), ③ contribution/improvement, ④ special rules, ⑤ transmutation, ⑥ distribution(at divorce/at death) 순서로 판단한다.

5. 자산에 대한 권리 및 책임 중 구체적인 논점이 출제되기도 한다.
   Q: Should 갑 be required to reimburse the community for the down payment for his house and, if so, in what amount? Answer according to California Law.

[Community Property Law]

California is a community property (CP) state. Under the community property law, all property acquired from the date of the marriage until separation is generally presumed to be CP. On the other hand, property that is acquired before marriage, after the separation, or by gift, bequest, or devise is presumed to be separate property (SP). Quasi-community property (QCP) a property obtained by the spouses during marriage while they lives in a non-community property state, but it would have been considered community property if obtained in California.

Ⅰ. Introduction

A. Community Property Law

Community property law에 따르면 부부관계 종료 시 부부가 소유하고 있는 자산을 CP와 SP로 구분하여 분배한다. 이때 CP는 배우자간 동등하게 분배되고 SP는 해당 자산을 단독으로 소유한 배우자 일방에게 일체로 분배된다. 그렇다면 "부부관계가 종료된다"는 것은 구체적으로 어떤 상황을 의미하는가. 부부 중 일방이 사망한 경우, 부부가 이혼한 경우 그리고 부부가 permanent separation한 경우를 뜻한다. Permanent separation은 부부가 혼인 생활을 재개할 intent 없이 별거(신체적으로 분리됨)하고 있는 상태를 뜻하는 바, 이들이 이혼을 신청(file a dissolution)한 시점은 본 개념과 무관하다.

1. General Rule

California is a community property state. When married couples **domiciled in California**, community property system will apply automatically.

★At death of a spouse, divorce, or permanent separation, all community property are separated equally and separate property remains separate property.

2. Permanent Separation (15July, 16July)

Permanent separation occurs when the marital community ends. The marital community ends when there are both permanent **physical separation** and an **intent** not to resume the marriage.

✔ 2010년에 부부가 permanently separated and 갑 moved away. 2011년에 을 filed for dissolution. ⇒ In 2010, 갑 and 을 permanently separated. 따라서 자산분배는 2010년을 기준으로 한다.

B. Types of Property

1. Community Property (CP)

★A property acquired **during the marriage** is **presumptively** community property.

A property **held in joint form** is presumed to be community property. All **family expenses** are presumed to be paid with community property.

✔ Earnings during the marriage
✔ House bought during the marriage
✔ Car bought by 갑 with his earnings during the marriage
✔ Car bought by 갑's earnings during the marriage which 갑 titled in his name
✔ A condominium held by wife and husband in joint tenancy
✔ 갑's account used for household expenses
✔ CP에서 초과되어 사용된 household expenses
   Any funds spend on household expenses exceeding the amount of community property is deemed to be a gift to the community.

2. Separate Property (SP)

★Separate property is a property acquired:

ⅰ. **Before marriage;**
ⅱ. After a divorce or a permanent separation;
ⅲ. **By gift, bequest, or devise;** or
ⅳ. Using separate property.

3. Quasi-Community Property (QCP)

Quasi-community property란, 부부가 community property rule이 적용되지 않는 주(州)에서 거주하는 동안 자산을 획득하였으나 만일 해당 자산을 캘리포니아 주에서 획득하여 community property law가 적용되었다면 community property(CP)로 구분되었을 자산을 뜻한다. 본 개념은 해당 자산을 단독으로 획득한 배우자 일방(acquiring spouse)이 사망하거나 부부관계가 종료된 시점에 부부가 캘리포니아 주에 거주(domicile)하고 있는 경우에 한해 해당 자산에 부여되는 명칭이다. QCP에는 CP에 적용되는 rules가 동일하게 적용된다. 한편, acquiring spouse가 해당 자산을 획득한 시점부터 QCP로 분류되는 시점 이전에는 acquiring spouse의 SP로 분류된다. 예컨대, equitable division state인 유타 주에서 거주하는 동안 갑이 혼인 중 월급을 저축한 돈으로 해당 주에 있는 콘도를 매입하였고 갑의 이름만을 title에 올렸다. 만일 갑·을 부부가 캘리포니아 주에서 거주하는 동안 해당 콘도를 매입하였다면, 이는 CP(갑의 혼인 중 월급)로 매입한 CP이므로 갑이 사망하거나 갑·을의 혼인 관계가 종료되는 시점에 콘도는 quasi-community property로 구분되고, 그 이전에는 갑의 SP로 인정된다. 한편, acquiring spouse의 배우자(을)가 사망하는 경우에는 갑의 SP로 인정된다.

a. Definition

★Quasi-community property (QCP) is a property obtained by the spouses during marriage while they lives in a non-community property state, but it would have been considered community property if obtained in California.

b. Characterization

Prior to the death of acquiring spouse or dissolution of marriage, the property is treated as **separate property** of the acquiring spouse. ★In other words, such property is considered **quasi-community property upon death of a spouse or divorce.**

When a spouse predeceased the acquiring spouse, such property is considered as SP of the acquiring spouse.

4. Quasi-Marital Property (QMP)

Quasi-martial property (QMP) is a property obtained by **putative**

spouses during their putative marriage.

C. Spouses

본 장은 혼인한 자가 소유하는 자산에 대해 논하는 바, 용어 '부부'의 의미를 파악하는 것이 중요하다. 캘리포니아 주에서 '부부'는 법적 혼인관계가 인정되는 양자(兩者)뿐만 아니라 동거하는 양자(domestic partnership)를 모두 포함하는 개념이다. Domestic partnership은 사실혼을 의미하는 common law marriage와 비교하여 법적 혼인관계가 형성되지 않았음에도 법적으로 법률적 혼인과 동일한 혜택 및 취급을 받는다는 점에서 유사한 개념이나, common law marriage는 domestic partnership보다 더 많은 요건을 필요로 한다는 점 등에서 차이가 있다. 캘리포니아 주에서는 common law marriage를 인정하지 않고 있으나, 타 주에서 인정된 common law marriage는 인정해야 한다 (conflict of laws principles).

1. Common Law Marriage

In California, common law marriage is abolished.

However, under the conflict of laws principles, a valid marriage is valid anywhere, unless it violates public policy of another states.

a. General Rule

To establish a valid common law marriage, it requires that the spouses:

ⅰ. Cohabitated;

ⅱ. Made present agreement to be married; and

ⅲ. Held themselves out to others as a married couple.

Once formed, a common law marriage can only be dissolved through divorce or annulment^{무효선언}.

2. Putative Spouse Doctrine

Under the putative spouse doctrine, a spouse who participated in a marriage ceremony with a **good-faith but mistaken belief** in its validity is treated like a spouse.

3. Domestic Partners

In California, registered domestic partners are treated same as married persons.

Domestic partners are partners who:

ⅰ. Share lives in an intimate^{친밀한} and committed^{헌신적인} relationship of mutual caring; and

ⅱ. Are same-sex or opposite-sex, and one party is 62 years old or older.

Ⅱ. Distributions

본 챕터에서는 부부자산의 분배(distribution)에 대해 논한다. 즉, 부부는 그들의 자산을 부부관계가 종료되는 시점에 나누어 가지는데, 이때 각 배우자가 어떤 자산을 얼마만큼 분배받는지에 대해 논한다. 우선 부부관계가 종료되면 그 근거가 무엇인지 관계없이 community property law의 기본 rule에 따라 각 배우자는 CP와 자신의 SP 전체에 대해 권리를 가진다. 따라서 부부가 이혼(divorce)한 경우에는 각 배우자가 CP의 절반과 자신의 SP 전체를 분배받는다. 그렇다면 배우자 일방이 사망(death)한 경우에는 고인의 권리, 즉 CP의 절반과 고인의 SP 전체를 어떻게 분배해야 하는가. 사망한 자는 권리를 가질 수 없으므로 그 자의 권리를 누군가에게 이전해야 하는데, 이때 어떤 rule에 입각하여 이전해야 하는지가 문제인 것이다.

고인(갑)의 권리분배는 고인의 유효한 유언장이 있는 경우와 없는 경우로 구분된다. 여기서 '갑의 권리'는 CP의 절반과 갑의 SP 전체를 뜻한다. 고인의 유효한 유언장이 있는 경우에는 본래 유언장에 따라 분배하는 것이 원칙이나, community property law에서는 고인의 배우자(surviving spouse, 을)가 갑의 will에 따라 자신(을)에게 분배되는 interest와 intestate law에 입각하여 분배되는 interest를 비교하여 더 큰 interest가 분배되는 방법을 스스로 선택할 수 있도록 하였다. 즉, CP의 절반과 고인(갑)의 SP 전체에 대해 갑이 작성한 will 의 내용과 community property law에서 규정하고 있는 intestate law의 내용 을 비교하여 선택할 수 있다. 그렇다면 intestate law는 고인(갑)의 권리에 대 해 어떻게 규정하고 있는가. Intestate law에 따르면, CP의 절반은 surviving spouse(을)에게 분배되고, 고인(갑)의 SP는 고인(갑)의 생존한 직계가족(child, parent, siblings, or issue)의 수에 따라 surviving spouse와 고인(갑)의 생존 한 직계가족에게 분배된다. 따라서 surviving spouse(을)는 부부관계가 종료 됨에 따라 CP의 절반을 분배받았고 갑이 사망함으로써 intestate law에 따라 CP의 절반을 분배받았으므로, 결과적으로 CP 전체에 대해 권리를 가지게 된 다. 한편, 고인의 유효한 유언장이 없는 경우에는 intestate law에 입각하여 고 인의 권리(CP의 절반과 갑의 SP 전체)를 분배한다. 한편, 부부가 permanent separation을 한 경우에는 대개 별도의 이혼절차를 밟으며, 이러한 경우에는 부부가 이혼(divorce)한 경우 적용되는 rules를 적용하면 된다.

QCP의 경우 원칙적으로 CP와 동일한 rule이 적용되나, 부부관계가 종료되는 시점에 자산의 성격이 SP에서 QCP로 변경되는 특성으로 인해 별도의 rule이 적용되는 경우가 있다. 이에 대한 자세한 내용은 이하 「B. Quasi-Community Property (QCP)」에서 논하도록 한다.

[도표 3-1]

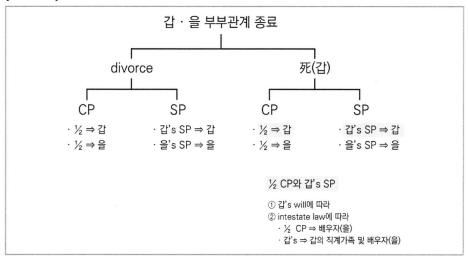

A. General Rule

1. At Divorce

At divorce, all community assets and debts are **divided evenly,** and each spouse retains their separate property debt and assets. QCP is treated as CP.

2. At Death

On the death of a spouse, **a surviving spouse can choose** either to take an **intestate share** under the community property intestacy law or to take **under the terms of the will** written by the deceased spouse.

a. By Will

At death, the decedent can freely devise **half of the community property** and **all of his separate property** through his will.

b. Intestacy Law (Community Property Law)

i. Decedent's CP

If the decedent dies intestate, the surviving spouse is entitled to the decedent's share of the CP (half of the CP). Thus, the surviving spouse is entitled to all of CP.

ii. Decedent's SP

Surviving spouse receives decedent's SP, depending on whether the decedent has surviving issue or parents.

① If there is no child, parent, siblings, or issue of deceased sibling, the surviving spouse receives **all SP.**

② If there ie one child or issue, parent, siblings, or issue of deceased sibling, the surviving spouse receives **half of the SP.**

③ If there are more than one child or issue, parent, siblings, or issue of deceased sibling, the surviving spouse receives **one-third of the SP.**

B. Quasi-Community Property (QCP) (14July−Trusts, 19Feb)

QCP를 분배하는 경우 CP를 분배하는 모든 방법이 적용된다. 즉, 각 배우자가 QCP의 절반씩 나누어 가진다. 한편, 배우자 일방(갑)이 '사망'한 경우에는 surviving spouse(을)는 QCP를 intestate law에 따라 분배할지 또는 갑의 will이 있다면 이에 따라 분배할지 선택하고 그 선택에 따라 분배한다.

한편, acquiring spouse가 해당 자산을 획득한 시점부터 부부가 이혼하거나 배우자 일방이 사망하기 '이전'에는 QCP는 SP로 인정된다. 하지만 SP라 하여 acquiring spouse가 임의로 소유권을 변경할 수 있는 것은 아니다. 따라서 acquiring spouse(갑)가 SP(QCP가 SP인 경우)의 소유권을 임의로 변경하면 배우자(을)는 일정 권리를 행사할 수 있다. 구체적인 내용은 부부가 이혼한 경우와 사망한 경우에 따라 다르다. 우선 갑·을이 '이혼'한 경우 이혼 이전에 발생한 소유권 변경은 상대방 배우자(을)와 상의 없이 이루어진 transfer로서 voidable하다고 본다. 다만, 이혼 시 을의 권리는 CP의 절반에 대해서만 인정되는 바, 을은 QCP의 절반에 대해서만 voidable transfer를 주장할 수 있다. 한편, 갑이 '사망'한 경우에는 갑이 캘리포니아 주에 거주(domicile)하는 동안 이루어진 suspect conveyance(inter vivos transfer)에 한해 을이 transferee에게 transfer된 자산의 절반을 갑의 estate에 되돌려놓으라고 요구할 수 있다. 여기서 'suspect conveyance'란, 고인(갑)이 해당 자산을 점유하고 있거나 사용하고 있을 때 consideration 없이 이루어진 transfer 또는 고인(갑)이 사망할 당시 해당 자산에 대해 power to revoke, power to dispose, right of survivorship 중 하나를 가지고 있는 경우 이루어진 transfer를 의미한다. 자산 가치의 절반에 대해서만 주장할 수 있는 것은 앞서 언급한 바와 같이 을이 해당 자산(CP가 된 QCP)의 절반에 대해서만 권리를 가지고 있기 때문이다.

1. At Divorce

a. General Rule

At divorce, QCP is treated exactly same as CP.

b. Transfer

When a spouse makes a transfer of CP (or QCP) **without consent** of the other spouse, the transfer is **voidable.**

Acquiring spouse is not free to inter-vivos transfer quasi-community property during his life without the other spouse.

2. At Death

a. General Rule

The surviving spouse has right to make an election between her share of the CP (or QCP) following the intestate law and following the decedent's will.

b. Inter Vivos Transfer

When the owner spouse made **inter vivos transfer** (transfer during his life) the surviving spouse is able to compel the reconvey of **half of it to the decedent's estate** if:

ⅰ. The inter vivos transfer is made while the decedent is **domiciled in California;**

ⅱ. Transfer was made **to a third party without consent** of the surviving spouse; **and**

ⅲ. The transfer was a **suspect**^{의심스러운} conveyance.

c. Suspect Conveyance

Suspect conveyance is a transfer that:

ⅰ. There is **no consideration** and decedent spouse **retained possession or enjoyment of property** at time of death; or

ⅱ. Decedent spouse retained **right to revoke, right to dispose, or right of survivorship** at the time of the death.

Ⅲ. Characterization

Community property law를 채택하는 주에서는 기본적으로 '자산의 유형(SP 또는 CP)'을 기준으로 배우자간 자산을 분배하기 때문에, 자산에 대한 배우자의 권리 및 책임을 판단함에 있어 자산의 유형을 판단하는 것, 즉 자산의 characterization을 판단하는 것이 매우 중요하다.

Community property law는 자산의 characterization을 판단할 때 우선 자산에 대한 추정을 하고 해당 자산의 자원(資源, source), 투자(contribution and improvement), transmutation 등을 통해 그 추정을 반박하는 방법을 이용한다. 그중 자원(source)은 자산이 생성되는데 있어 사용된 자원의 흐름을 tracing 하여 자산의 유형을 판단하는 방법이다. 만약 자원이 SP와 CP가 혼합되어 (commingled) 있는 형태, 예컨대 SP와 CP가 섞여져 예금되어 있는 account 라면, 적용하는 rule에 따라 자산의 유형이 다르게 판단될 수 있다. 투자 (contribution and improvement)란, 명의변경, 리모델링, loan에 대한 지불 등과 같이 돈으로 구매하는 방법을 제외한 나머지 방법으로 자산을 생성 및 증자하는데 기여하는 행위를 뜻한다. 이러한 행위들에 관해서는 투자된 자산과 증자된 자산의 유형에 따라 rule을 적용하여 자산의 유형을 판단한다. 한편, transmutation은 '변형'으로 직역되며 자산의 유형을 변형시키고자 취하는 행위를 뜻한다. CP 자원으로 배우자 일방의 gift를 구매하는 것이 transmutation 의 전형적인 예시이다.

A. Presumptions

1. CP Presumption

★A property purchased during marriage is presumptively community property.

> **TIP** ① 혼인기간 중 취득한 자산, ② title이 배우자 일방의 이름만으로 되어 있는 자산, ③ 배우자 일방의 이름으로 되어 있는 account에 대해 논하는 경우, CP presumption을 analysis하는 것이 고득점 포인트다.
> Property titled in one spouse's name alone is not presumptively SP. The property using funds from 갑's account is not presumptively SP.

2. Married Women's Special Presumption

Title이 부인의 이름 단독으로 되어 있는 자산은 해당 여성의 separate property로 추정한다. 본 추정은 1975년 이전에 title이 확정된 자산에 한해 적용되는 바, 1975년 이전에는 남편이 가정의 자산에 대해 독자적인 관리를 해왔던 관습에 따라 만들어진 rule이다. 본 추정에 대해 남편은 부인에게 선물로서 title을 인정한 것이 아니고, 채권자의 소송을 피하기 위한 목적 등 단순히 부인의 이름을 빌리고자 함이었다는 증거 또는 부인이 남편의 동의 없이 title을 가졌다는 증거를 통해 해당 추정을 깰 수 있다.

A property taken in the **married woman's name alone** is presumed to be her **separate property.** This presumption is applicable only to the property acquired prior to 1975.

a. Rebut

The presumption can be rebutted by evidence showing that:

ⅰ. Husband did not intent to make a right to wife but had other reason for taking title in her name; or

ⅱ. Wife took title without husband's knowledge or consent.

3. Joint Title (14Feb, 16July)

Title, 즉 자산의 명의는 기본적으로 자산 유형을 결정하는데 있어 영향을 미치지 않는다. 자산이 배우자 중 일방의 이름으로 되어있다 하더라도 해당 자산이 CP로 인정될 수 있다는 것이다. 예컨대, 혼인기간 중 CP로 배우자 일방의 이름만을 title에 올린 부동산을 매입하였다면 이는 혼인기간 중 획득한 자산으로서 CP로 구분된다. 따라서 자산 유형은 title과 무관하게 source, contribution 등으로 판단되는 것이 원칙이나, SP가 source이면서 부부의 이름 모두가 title(jointly titled)에 올라가 있는 경우에는 Lucas rule 또는 Anti-Lucas rule이 예외적으로 적용된다. Lucas rule은 부부관계가 배우자 중 일방의 '사망'으로 인해 종료된 경우, Anti-Lucas rule은 부부관계가 '이혼'에 인해 종료된 경우에 적용된다. 두 rule 모두 양자의 이름으로 title한 자산은 CP로 추정하고 양자간 별도의 합의가 있는 경우 이 추정은 깨진다고 규정한다는 점에서 동일하나, source를 제공한 배우자, 즉 해당 자산을 구입하기 위해 사용된 SP의 소유자가 reimbursement 를 받을 수 있는지 그 여부에 대해서는 다르게 규정한다. Lucas rule의 경우 투자된 SP는 CP를 위한 gift로 보고 SP의 소유자에 대한 reimbursement를 인정하지 않는 반면, Anti-Lucas rule의 경우 reimbursement를 인정한다. 예컨대, 갑·을 부부가 혼인기간 중 갑의 SP로 부동산을 매입하였고 해당 부동산의 title을 갑과 을의 이름(title)으로 부동산을 매입한 후 이혼하였다면, 해당 부동산은 CP로 추정되고 Anti-Lucas rule의 경우 갑은 해당 부동산에 대해 지불한 선결제금(down payment), 투자금(payments for improvement), 대출금(payments that reduce the principal of a loan)에 해당하는 금액을 reimburse 받을 수 있다.

[표 3-1]

Lucas rule	Anti-Lucas rule
SP로 생성한 jointly titled 자산 ⇒ CP로 추정	
by death인 경우 적용	by divorce인 경우 적용
reimbursement ×	reimbursement ○

Title alone does not establish the character of property for community law purposes.

When jointly titled property is purchased or contributed by separate property, there are two rules applicable: Lucas rule and Anti-Lucas rule.

✔ 갑의 SP로 '매입한' 아파트를 갑을 부부의 이름으로 title 하는 경우
✔ 갑을 부부의 이름으로 title되어 있는 아파트를 갑의 SP로 '리모델링한' 경우

a. Lucas Rule

Lucas rule is applicable when the marriage ends **in death.**

Under the Lucas rule, all jointly titled property **is presumed to be community property** at the death of either spouse, unless there is an express agreement contrary. The agreement must be stated that the parties intend to hold titled differently.

There is **no right to reimbursement** for separate contributions. This is because a contribution of the separate property is presumed to be **a gift to the community property**.

b. Anti-Lucas Rule

Anti-Lucas rule is applicable when the marriage ends **in divorce**. Under the Anti-Lucas rule, all jointly titled property **is presumed to be community property** at divorce, unless there is an express agreement contrary.

There is a **right to reimbursement** for separate contributions.

c. Reimbursement

> "DIP" — Down payment, Improvements, Principal of a loan

★Reimbursement is allowed for expenditures made **for down payment, improvements, and to reduce the principal of a loan.**

B. Source and Tracing

1. Source of Funds

A court will trace source, the assets used to purchase a property, to determine its character.

a. Community Property

A property is characterized as community property, when it was **acquired using community property funds.**

> ✔ 갑이 혼인생활 동안 저축한 근로소득으로 갑의 이름만을 title에 올려 콘도를 매입한 경우
> ⇒ 혼인생활 동안 저축한 근로소득 = CP ⇒ 콘도 is CP.

b. Separate Property

A property is characterized as separate property, when it was acquired using separate property funds.

✔ 혼인 후, 갑이 자신의 부모로부터 10억을 상속받았고, 그 10억으로 매입한 콘도

⇒ 콘도 is presumed as CP, since it is acquired during the marriage. However, 10억 is 갑's SP. Therefore, 콘도 is SP.

2. Commingled Funds (18July)

Commingled funds란, community property와 separate property가 함께 뒤섞여 있는 자산이라는 뜻으로서, 배우자 일방의 혼인 전 근로소득과 부부의 혼인생활 동안의 근로소득이 함께 저축되어 있는 은행 계좌(account)가 그 예이다. 그렇다면 혼인생활 중 commingled funds로 구매한 특정 자산의 유형은 무엇인가. 우선 혼인생활 중 구매한 자산이므로 community property로 추정되나, separate property라고 주장하는 배우자가 commingled funds 중 separate property만이 사용되었음을 증명하여 해당 추정을 반박할 수 있으며, 추정을 반박하는 방법에는 direct-in-direct-out method 와 exhaustion rule, 이렇게 두 가지가 있다. Direct-in-direct-out method (또는 direct tracing method)는 commingled funds에 충분한 separate property가 있었으며 해당 자산을 separate property로서 구매했다는 배우자(separate property라고 주장하는 배우자)의 의도(intent)를 증명하는 방법이다. 한편, exhaustion rule은 commingled funds에 있는 community property는 family expenses로서 모두 소진되었고 separate property만이 남아있었음을 증명하는 방법이다.

a. General Rule

If there is a property funded by commingled funds with both separate property funds and community property funds, there are two methods of accounting: direct in direct out method and the exhaustion rule. The burden of proof is on the **spouse claiming** that the property acquired is **separate property** which is funded by separate property.

b. Direct-In-Direct-Out Method (Direct Tracing Method)

Under the direct-in-direct-out method, the spouse needs to show that there were **separate funds available** at the time the asset was purchased, and the spouse **intended** to use separate funds to purchase the asset as an separate property.

c. Exhaustion Rule

Under the exhaustion rule, the spouse needs to show that community funds in the account **had already been exhausted** by the payment of family expenses at the time the asset was purchased, and separate funds must have been used to purchase the asset.

답안요령 Commingled property

---

1. Community property law 기본 rule
2. CP에 대한 presumption
3. Analysis (commingled funds)
4. Direct-in-direct-out method
   + analysis
5. Exhaustion rule
   + analysis

TIP1 혼인중 취득한 자산의 경우 ① CP로 추정하고(위 2번) ② 다양한 rule을 통해 반박함으로써(위 4, 5번) characterization을 파악한다.

TIP2 Arguable point: Commingled fund의 소유자(bank account의 예금주)는 commingled fund로 구입한 자산이 SP임을 주장할 것이나, 다른 배우자는 해당 자산을 CP와 commingled된 자산으로 구입하였으므로 CP라고 주장할 것이다.

TIP3 Exhaustion rule에서 family expenses에 대해 analysis하는 것이 고득점 포인트다.

Community property law

California is a community property (CP) state. Under the community property law, all property acquired from the date of the marriage until separation is generally presumed to be CP. On the other hand, property that is acquired before marriage, after the separation, or by gift, bequest, or devise is presumed to be separate property (SP). Quasi-community property (QCP) a property obtained by the spouses during marriage while they lives in a non-community property state, but it would have been considered community property if obtained in California.

Automobile

A property purchased during marriage is presumptively community property.

(ANALYSIS: In this case, the automobile is purchased during marriage and it is presumptively community property.)

Commingled funds

Additionally, the automobile is purchased by 갑's bank account. 갑 deposited his earnings both prior to the marriage and during the marriage. Thus, the bank account is commingled funds and the automobile is purchased by commingled funds. 을 may argue that community property is commingled and the automobile is a community property. However, 갑 may argue that the automobile is a separate property. If there is a property funded by a commingled funds with both separate property funds and community property funds, there are two methods of accounting: direct-in-direct-out method and the exhaustion rule.

(1) Direct-in-direct-out method

Under the direct-in-direct-out method, the spouse needs to show that there were separate funds available when the asset was purchased, and the spouse intended to use separate funds to purchase the asset as an separate property.

(ANALYSIS: In this case, it is unclear whether separate funds were available at the time the automobile was purchased.)

(2) Exhaustion rule

Under the exhaustion rule, the spouse needs to show that community funds in the account had already been exhausted by the payment of family expenses at the time the asset was purchased, and separate funds must have been used to purchase the asset.

(ANALYSIS: In this case, family expenses were spent from 갑's bank account. Family expenses are community property and 갑 could argue that his separate funds must have been used to purchase the automobile. Thus, the automobile is 갑's separate property.)

Conclusion

In sum, the automobile is 갑's separate property.

C. Contributions and Improvements

본 챕터에서는 CP 또는 SP가 다른 property에 투자된 경우 해당 property가 어떤 유형에 해당하는지에 대해 논한다. 여기서 '투자'는 자산을 생성하는데 있어 돈(source)으로 직접 구매하는 방법을 제외한 나머지 방법으로 자산의 가치를 증가시키는 행위, 예컨대 명의변경, 리모델링, loan에 대한 지불 등을 포괄한다. Contribution 및 improvement가 이루어지는 경우는 크게 CP를 SP에 투자하는 경우, SP를 CP에 투자하는 경우, 그리고 SP를 SP에 투자하는 경우로 구분된다. 기본적으로 투자된 가치는 reimburse하는 것이 원칙이나, '사업'에 투자되는 경우와 CP를 'SP 부동산'에 투자하는 경우에는 별도의 rule이 적용된다.

1. CP contributions to SP

a. General Rule

Although different rules are applicable in each jurisdiction, **CP is generally reimbursed.**

b. Child Support Payments (15July)

배우자 일방(갑)이 이전 혼인관계로 인한 양육비(child support) 지급 의무가 있는 경우, 해당 양육비는 갑의 separate debt이다. 그럼에도 불구하고 갑의 separate property와 community property 모두 본 채무이행을 위해 사용될 수 있고, 갑의 현재 배우자, 즉 갑이 재혼한 자(을)의 separate property는 사용될 수 없다. 다만, community property는 갑의 separate property가 부족한 경우에 한해 사용되는 보증적 자산으로서, 채무를 이행할 수 있는 갑의 separate property가 존재함에도 불구하고 이를 사용하지 않고 community property를 사용하여 채무를 이행하였다면, 갑·을이 이혼 시 community는 가용성이 있었으나 CP에 우선하여 사용하지 않은 SP만큼을 갑(갑의 SP)으로부터 보상(reimbursement) 받을 수 있다. 예컨대, 갑·을의 혼인 중 갑의 아버지가 사망하여 1,000만원을 유산 받아 투자를 하였고 그 투자로 하여금 매달 10만원의 이익이 발생하였으나 이를 사용하지 않고 갑의 양육비를 community property로 5개월 동안 지급해왔다면, 갑·을 이혼 시 갑은 자신의 separate property로부터 50만원(10만원*5개월)을 community에 reimburse해야 한다. 즉, 매달 10만원(SP)을 가용할 수 있었으나 이를 사용하지 않고 대신 사용한 액수(50만원)는 community property로서, 이혼 시 갑·을이 동등하게 나누어 가진다.

i. General Rule

Child support obligation from previous marriage is **a parent spouse's separate debt.** However, **both** community property and parent spouse's separate property **are liable.**

ii. Reimbursement

The community is entitled to reimbursement for child support payments at dissolution if the payments are made with community funds **when separate property was available and not used.**

답안요령 Child support payment

---

1. Community property law 기본 rule
2. Child support obligation 기본 rule
   + analysis
3. CP에 대한 reimbursement 여부
   + analysis
4. Distribution(결론)

모범답안 013

Community property law

California is a community property (CP) state. Under the community property law, all property acquired from the date of the marriage until separation is generally presumed to be CP. On the other hand, property that is acquired before marriage, after the separation, or by gift, bequest, or devise is presumed to be separate property (SP). Quasi-community property (QCP) a property obtained by the spouses during marriage while they lives in a non-community property state, but it would have been considered community property if obtained in California.

갑's child support obligation

Child support obligation from previous marriage is a parent spouse's separate debt. However, both community property and parent spouse's separate property are liable.

(ANALYSIS: 갑's child support obligation is for a child from a prior relationship. It is his separate debt, but both community property and 갑's separate property are liable.)

Reimbursement

The community is entitled to reimbursement for child support payments at dissolution if the payments are made with community funds when separate property was available and not used.

(ANALYSIS: In this case, 갑 inherited 1천만원 and 갑 put 1천만원 in a bond and the bod had profits of 20만원 per month. Thus, the community is not liable 갑's child support obligation and it is entitled to reimbursement for child support payments at dissolution for 100만원. This is because the community was used for five months(20만원*5 months).

Conclusion

At divorce, all community assets and debts are divided evenly.

(ANALYSIS: In this case, 100만원 will be divided equally between 갑 and 을.)

2. SP contributions to CP and SP contributions to SP (14Feb)

  a. Traditional Law

    Contributed SP is considered a gift and reimbursement is not allowed.

  b. Modern Law

    ★Reimbursement is allowed for expenditures made **for down payment, improvements, and to reduce the principal of a loan.**
    Thus, SP is entitled to a right of reimbursement from the community.

    ✔ 갑이 혼인생활동안 저축한 earnings(CP)로 집을 매입하였고, 이혼 후 자신의 earnings(SP)로 이를 리모델링 한 경우 — SP contributions to CP

3. CP contributions to SP Real Property (18July)

  • Proration rule = Pro rata rule

Under the **proration rule,** the community receives an **interest** in the property when community property is used to pay **installment payments on separate property.**

A prorated interest is calculated by the amount of community property spent for the installment payment over the total purchase price.

> CP prorated interest = SP 할부에 소비된 CP / SP 총가격

✔ 갑이 혼인생활 중 부모로부터 상속받은 1억(SP)으로 집에 대한 down payment를 지불하였고 해당 집의 title에 자신의 이름만 올렸다. 이후 집에 대한 mortgage를 갑·을의 혼인생활 중 earnings (CP)로 지불하였는데, 그 금액이 총 1천만원이다.

⇒ Down payment: SP & mortgage payment by CP ⇒ CP contributions to SP real property installment

⇒ SP의 가치 1억 중 10%(1천만원/1억), 즉 1천만원은 CP로 인정되고, 나머지 9천만원은 SP로 인정된다.

4. CP contributions to SP Business (14Feb)

배우자 일방이 separate property로 소유한 사업이 있었고 혼인기간 동안 해당 사업의 가치가 증가한 경우, 해당 사업의 가치 및 사업으로부터의 수입을 배우자 중 일방이 사망하였거나 또는 이혼 시 어떻게 배분할 것인가. 즉, SP인 사업이 CP에 의해 contribution이 이루어진 경우 배우자간 자산 분배가 어떻게 이루어지는가. 본 논점에 관해 두 가지의 접근하는 방식이 있는데, 하나는 pereira approach, 다른 하나는 van camp approach이다. Pereira formula는 증가된 사업 가치를 community property의 투자 결과로 본다. 즉, 혼인 기간 동안의 사업 운영은 community property으로서, 소유자 배우자의 separate property에 community property가 투자된 것이다. 따라서 초기 투자 금액과 이에 대한 혼인 기간 동안의 이자(interest)는 소유자 배우자의 separate property이고, 나머지는 community property로 본다. 예컨대, 갑이 을과 혼인 전 1억을 투자하여 운영하던 사업 ABC

가 있었고 10년간의 혼인 생활동안 ABC의 가치가 3억으로 증가된 경우, 초기 투자금액인 1억과 그 1억에 대한 10년간의 이자가 갑의 separate property이며, 3억 중 갑의 separate property를 제한 나머지의 금액은 community property로 구분된다. 여기서 '이자율'은 법원이 여러 상황을 종합적으로 고려하여 책정되나, 일반적으로 법정 이자율인 10%가 사용된다.

Van camp formula는 증가된 사업 가치를 소유자 배우자의 사업 운영에 의한 것이 아니라 시장 트렌드, 새로운 기술력 등과 같은 외부적 요인, 즉 CP가 아닌 요소에 의한 것으로 본다. 따라서 소유자 배우자가 그의 사업 운영에 대한 합리적인 대가(월급 등)를 받아왔는지 확인하여 이를 혼인생활 동안의 배우자 소득으로서 community property로 구분하고 나머지 금액은 소유자 배우자의 separate property로 구분한다.

There are two formulas used to determine how to allocate the business and the earnings from the business which is owned by a spouse: pereira approach and van camp approach.

a. Pereira Approach

Pereira approach favors CP estate.

The court considers sum of SP contribution and reasonable rate of return (typically 10%) as SP.

The rest of the value of the business is considered CP.

> SP = 초기투자금액 + (초기투자금액 × 이자율(10%) × 배우자가 사업에 종사한 년수)
>
> CP = 사업value − SP

b. Van Camp Approach

Van camp approach favors SP estate.

The court calculates CP multiplying a reasonable rate of earnings for the working spouse and the number of years the spouse worked during the marriage.

The rest of the value of the business is considered SP.

> CP = 배우자의 소득×혼인기간 중 근속년수
>
> SP = 사업value − CP

5. SP contributions to CP Business

When SP is contributed to a CP business after a divorce or a permanent separation, reverse Pereira and Van Camp approach are used.

a. Pereira Approach

The court considers sum of CP contribution and reasonable rate of return (typically 10%) as CP.

> CP = 이혼 당시의 사업value + (이혼 당시의 사업value×이자율(10%)×투자년수)
>
> SP = 사업value − CP

b. Van Camp Approach

> SP = 배우자의 소득×혼인기간 중 근속년수
>
> CP = 사업value − SP

D. Special Rules

1. Personal Injury Award (15July)

A judgment or settlement obtained by a spouse for a **cause of action** occurred during the marriage is presumptively community property.

a. Characterization

The judgment or settlement will be awarded **to the injured spouse at divorce,** unless it would be inequitable to the other spouse.

The judgment or settlement will be divided evenly **upon death.**

✔ 갑·을은 2010년~2025년의 혼인관계를 유지하다가 이혼하였다. 갑이 2011년에 사고를 당해 injury가 발생했고 이에 대해 2030년에 settlement를 한 경우 → Cause of action이 혼인생활 중 발생하였으므로 해당 settlement는 CP로 구분되나 personal injury award에는 별도의 rule이 적용되어 injured한 갑에게 전액 지급된다.

✔ 상기 예시에서 갑이 사망하여 갑·을간 혼인관계가 종료되었다면, cause of action이 혼인생활 중 발생하였으므로 해당 settlement는 CP로 구분되고 갑의 personal injury award는 갑(갑의 estate)과 을이 동일하게 나누어 가진다.

2. Debt and Loan

a. Debt incurred During Marriage (17July)

원칙적으로 혼인 중 발생한 채무는 부부 공동의 채무, 즉 community debt이다. Community debt와 separate debt의 구분 기준은 채무의 주체가 아닌 '채무가 발생된 시점'이다. 다시 말해, 부부 중 일방(갑)이 상대방(을)의 동의 없이 임의로 지게 된 채무라 하더라도 해당 채무가 혼인 중 발생했다면, 이는 community debt으로 구분된다. 다만, 채권자가 갑의 separate property를 근거로 채권을 형성하였다면 해당 채무는 갑의 separate debt로 구분된다. 한편, 갑의 신용도(community credit)는 부부 공동의 신용도에 포함되는 바, 채권자가 갑의 신용도(credit)를 근거로 채권을 형성하였다 하더라도 해당 채무는 community debt로 구분된다는 점에 유의해야 한다.

A loan taken out **during the marriage is a community debt.**
However, if the lender **relied solely on the borrowing spouse's separate property** for repayment in determining whether to loan one spouse the money, a loan taken out during the marriage is a **separate debt.**

b. Debt After Permanent Separation (16July)

   ⅰ. General Rule

     Generally, debts incurred post-separation are the separate debt of the debtor spouse and only the spouse is liable for that debt.

   ⅱ. Exception

     However, there is a **necessaries of life exception** which is applicable to debts incurred **post-separation but before divorce.** This is because both spouses owe to each other a duty to take care of each other during marriage.

     ✔ Permanently separate한 이후 배우자 일방(갑)이 응급 수술을 받은 경우의 수술비 — community debt

---

답안요령 Debt after separation

> 1. Community property law 기본 rule
> 2. Permanent separation
> 3. Debt after permanent separation 정의 + 기본 rule
>   + analysis
> 4. Necessaries of life exception
>   + analysis
> 5. Distribution(결론)

TIP Arguable point: Debt를 incur한 자(갑)의 배우자(을)는 permanent separation 이후에 발생한 채무임을 근거로 separate debt라 주장할 것이다. 이에 대해 갑은 necessaries of life exception을 근거로 community debt라 반박할 것이다.

모범답안 014

Community property law

California is a community property (CP) state. Under the community property law, all property acquired from the date of the marriage until separation is generally presumed to be CP. On the other hand, property that is acquired before marriage, after the separation, or by gift, bequest, or devise is presumed to be separate property (SP). Quasi-community property (QCP) a property obtained by the spouses during marriage while they lives in a non-community property state, but it would have been considered community property if obtained in California.

Hospital bill

Permanent separation

Permanent separation occurs when there are both permanent physical separation and an intent not to resume the marriage.

(ANALYSIS: In this case, 갑 leaved the house and both 갑 and 을 had no intent to resume the marriage. Thus, permanent separation occurred.)

Debt after permanent separation

Generally, debts incurred post-separation are the separate debt of the debtor spouse and only the spouse is liable for that debt.

(ANALYSIS: In this case, 을 may argue that 갑's hospital bill is the separate debt of 갑. 갑's hospital bill incurred in 2022 and the permanent separation occurred in 2020.)

Necessaries of life exception

However, 갑 may argue that necessaries of life exception is applicable. The exception is applicable to debts incurred post-separation but before divorce. This is because both spouses owe to each other a duty to take care of each other during marriage.

(ANALYSIS: In this case, 갑's hospital bill was for emergency operation and it is necessary of life. Even though 갑's hospital bill incurred after the permanent separation, but it is before divorce in 2025. Thus, 갑's hospital bill is community debt.)

Conclusion

In conclusion, at divorce, either 갑 or 을 may be personally liable for the hospital bill. If community property was available, either spouse is entitled to reimbursement.

c. SP Debt incurred Before Marriage

If separate debt is incurred **before** marriage, all SP of the debtor spouse is used for debt satisfaction **and then** all CP.

✔ 갑이 전(前) 부인 사이에서 낳은 병에 대해 child support를 지고 있는 경우

d. SP Debts incurred During Marriage

If separate debt is incurred **during** marriage, only the debtor spouse's SP is used for debt satisfaction.

3. Pension (18July)

Regarding a pension plan or other form of retirement, time rule is used for apportionment purpose.

If a pension plan was earned during marriage, it is community property.

If a pension plan was earned before or after marriage, it is separate property.

> **case**

① 갑은 teacher로서 10년간 근무했고, 2015년에 퇴직하면서 pension의 절반을 받았고, 나머지 절반은 일정금액을 받기로 하였다. 2020년 갑은 을과 혼인을 하였고, 갑은 혼인 생활 중에도 지속적으로 pension을 받았다. 갑·을이 이혼할 경우, 갑의 pension은 어떤 유형으로 구분되는가?
⇒ 갑의 pension 전체(2015년에 받은 pension의 절반과 매달 받은 나머지

절반)는 모두 갑의 SP이다. 갑의 pension을 혼인 생활 중에 받았다 하더라도 갑의 혼인 전 근로에 대한 소득이므로 SP이다.

② 갑은 2015년부터 teacher로 일했고, 2020년 을과 혼인을 하였다. 혼인생활 동안에도 갑은 꾸준히 근무하였고, 2040년에 퇴직하였다. 퇴직하면서 갑은 pension으로 1억을 받았다. 갑이 퇴직 후 을과 이혼할 경우, 갑의 pension은 어떤 유형으로 구분되는가?

⇒ 2015년에서 2020년(결혼 전)까지에 대한 pension은 갑의 SP, 2020년(결혼 후)부터 2040년까지에 대한 pension은 CP로 분류된다.

4. Stock Options (15July)

a. Vests During Marriage

If the stock options vest during the marriage, it is community property. Vesting is when a person realizes his right.

b. Exercisable After Marriage Ends

When the stock options are granted during the marriage but are exercisable after the marriage ends, special rule is applicable. Exercising is when a person actually purchases the stock.

Whether stock options are community property or separate property depends on whether those were granted **as a reward** for past services or **as an incentive** to continue working.

ⅰ. As a Reward

A community will take proportion of interest in the stock options. The proportion is calculated by **the years of employment** during the marriage divided by the years of employment until exercise. The rest of the interest in the stock options will be taken by a receiving spouse.

$$Community Property = stock option \times \frac{결혼생활 \ 중 \ 근속연수}{stock option을 \ 받기까지의 \ 근속연수}$$

ⅱ. As an Incentive

A community will take proportion of interest in the stock options. The proportion is calculated by **the years of marriage** from the grant of the option divided by the option's grant to its being exercisable

$$CP = stock\, option \times$$
$$\frac{stock\, option 을\, 계약한\, 시점부터\, 이혼\, 시점까지의\, 연수}{stock\, option 을\, 계약한\, 시점부터\, stock\, option 을\, 실제로\, 받은\, 시점까지의\, 연수}$$

Ⅳ. Altering Characterization

A. Premarital Agreement (16July)

- Premarital agreement = Prenuptial agreement

1. General Rule

Community property system could be avoided when there is an effective premarital agreement.

To be effective premarital agreement, it must:

ⅰ. Be in writing and signed by both couples;

ⅱ. Not be involuntary; and

ⅲ. Not be unconscionable at the time of the execution.

a. Voluntariness

To prove voluntariness of the premarital agreement, **a proponent** may prove that:

ⅰ. The other party was represented by a separate attorney when signing the agreement;

ⅱ. The other party was fully disclosed information about the proponent's property and finances before he signs the agreement **(adequate disclosure),** if not represented by an attorney; and

ⅲ. The other party had at least 7 days between receiving the agreement and signing it.

b. Unconscionabiliy

To prove conscionability, a proponent may prove that:

ⅰ. The other party was fully disclosed information about the proponent's property and finances;

ⅱ. The other party waived a right to fully disclosed information; or

ⅲ. The other party actually knew or had reason to know such information.

B. Transmutation (14Feb, 15July, 17July)

Transmutation을 직역하면 '변형'으로, 자산의 유형(SP 또는 CP)을 변형하는 행위를 뜻한다. 대개 한 배우자가 다른 배우자에게 선물로 무언가를 사주는 방식으로 출제된다. Transmutation의 유형에는 ① 배우자 일방(갑)의 SP를 상대방 배우자(을)의 SP로 변형하는 행위, ② 배우자 일방의 SP를 CP로 변형하는 행위 그리고 ③ CP를 배우자 일방의 SP로 변형하는 행위가 있다.

Transmutation은 반드시 서면으로 이루어져야 하는 바, 그 서면에는 transmutation 이 불리하게 작용하는 자의 transmute하고자 하는 intent가 명시되어 있어야 하며 그의 서명이 있어야 한다. 필요한 경우에는 서면 외에 해당 transmutation 이 불리하게 작용하는 자의 intent도 고려하여 transmutation의 유효성을 판단하기도 한다. 본래 writing 요건이 없었으나, 1985년 1월 1일부터 시행된 개정안에서는 writing이 추가로 요구됨으로써 구두상 합의내용 등과 같이 서면이 아닌 증거는 transmutation을 증명할 수 없게 되었다. 즉, transmutation 에 대한 증명은 서면 증거로만 가능하게 되었다. 한편, transmutation에 대한 writing 요건의 예외가 있는데, 변형된 자산, 예컨대 CP로 구입한 배우자 일방의 선물(SP)이 개인적으로 사용(personal use)되고 고가(高價, substantial in value)가 아닌 경우 writing이 없어도 유효한 transmutation으로 인정된다. 여기서 "personal use"는 목걸이와 같이 타인과 공유하지 않고 주로 한 사람에 의해 사용된다는 의미이다. 자산의 가치는 부부의 자산상황을 고려하여 판단하는데, 대부분의 경우 자동차는 고가의 자산으로 취급되어 gift exception 을 적용할 수 없다. 예컨대, 갑이 CP로 배우자 을에게 목걸이를 사준 경우 갑이 해당 목걸이를 선물하고자 하는 intent를 서면으로 작성하지 않았더라도 CP가 을의 SP로 변형된 transmutation이 인정된다.

Transmutation is a change of the character of an asset.

1. General Rule

To be a valid transmutation, it must be:

ⅰ. **In writing** describing the change in ownership; and

ⅱ. Be signed **by the adversely affected spouse.**

2. Exception

When one spouse gives a gift to other spouse, a writing is not required.

★This exception is applicable only when:

ⅰ. The gift was for the receiving spouse's **personal use;** and

ⅱ. Gift is **not substantial in value.**

Whether a property is substantial in value is determined considering spouses' status in life, such as their asset and child support obligation.

✔ 갑이 혼인기간 동안 번 돈(CP)으로 을 이름으로 캠핑카를 사준 경우 → 을이 '캠핑카는 gift임'을 주장할 수도 있으나, 자동차는 오직 한 사람이 사용하는 자산으로 보기 어려우므로 personal use에 해당하지 않고, 상당한 가치를 지니는 자산이므로 두 번째 요건도 만족하지 못한다. 따라서 exception rule은 적용불가하며, CP가 SP(gift)로 transmutation이 되기 위해서는 writing 요건을 만족해야 한다.

✔ 갑이 상속받은 돈(SP)으로 을에게 다이아몬드 목걸이를 사준 경우 → 을이 '다이아몬드 목걸이는 gift임'을 근거로 valid transmutation을 주장할 수도 있으나, 다이아몬드 목걸이는 substantial in value이므로 exception rule이 적용될 수 없다. 따라서, SP가 상대방의 SP(gift)로 transmutation이 되기 위해서는 writing 요건을 만족해야 한다.

Transmutation

---

1. Community property law 기본 rule
2. Transmutation 기본 rule
+ analysis
3. Gift exception
+ analysis
4. Distribution(결론)

TIP   Arguable point: Transmutation이 불리하게 작용하는 자, 예컨대 배우자 갑에게 선물을 해준 을은 writing 요건이 미충족되었음을 근거로 invalid transmutation을 주장할 것이다. 이에 대해 갑은 gift exception 이 적용되어 해당 transmutation은 valid하며, 해당 자산이 자신의 SP임을 주장할 것이다.

모범답안 015

Community property law

California is a community property (CP) state. Under the community property law, all property acquired from the date of the marriage until separation is generally presumed to be CP. On the other hand, property that is acquired before marriage, after the separation, or by gift, bequest, or devise is presumed to be separate property (SP). Quasi-community property (QCP) a property obtained by the spouses during marriage while they lives in a non-community property state, but it would have been considered community property if obtained in California.

Necklace

Transmutation

Transmutation is a change of the character of an asset. Asset can be changed from CP to SP, SP to CP, or from one's SP to other's SP. To be a valid transmutation, it must be: (1) in writing describing the change in ownership; and (2) be signed by the adversely affected spouse.

(ANALYSIS: In this case, 갑 bought the necklace using his inheritance and gave it to 을 as a birthday gift. 갑's inheritance is his SP and it is changed to 을's SP. It is transmutation. However, there is no fact indicating the writing of the transmutation and 갑 may argue that it is invalid.)

Gift exception

을 may argue that gift exception is applicable. A writing is not required only when: (1) the gift was for the receiving spouse's personal use; and (2) gift is not substantial in value.

(ANALYSIS: In this case, a necklace is for 을's personal use and it is not substantial in value. Thus, gift exception is applicable and a writing is not required.)

Conclusion

In conclusion, the transmutation is valid and necklace is 을's SP. Thus, at divorce, 을 is solely entitled to it.

V. Fiduciary Duty and Management

A. Fiduciary Duties (14Feb, 17July)

Spouses **owe one another** the highest fiduciary duties: duty to act fairly and honestly with each other.

If one spouse breaches his fiduciary duty to the other and takes financial interest, the non-breaching spouse may be able to **set aside the conveyance.**

- ✔ 상대방 몰래 community property를 매매한 경우 — violate fiduciary duty
- ✔ 부부의 월급을 관리하는 갑이 을 몰래 자신의 account를 만들어 돈을 저축한 경우, 갑의 violation of fiduciary duty가 인정되는 바, 해당 account는 community property이며 갑·을이 이혼 시 equally 나누어 가진다.

TIP1 | 갑이 '자신의 이익을 위해' 배우자 을에게 transmutation을 요구하였고 을이 갑·을의 CP를 갑의 SP로 transmutate한 경우, 이는 ① 갑의 breach of fiduciary duty이고 ② 해당 transmutation을 통해 갑이 financial interest를 가지게 되었으므로 을이 transmutation을 set aside할 수 있다.

TIP2 | 부부 중 일방이 accountant인 경우, fiduciary duty 논점과 연관이 있을 가능성이 높다.

B. Equal Right of Management (14Feb, 16July, 17July)

Each spouse has an **equal right to manage** community property and keep the other spouse **reasonably informed** as to the financial situation.

One spouse **cannot** dispose or sell any community property **without consent** of the other spouse.

✔ Community property인 자동차를 상대방 배우자(을)의 동의 없이 갑이 자신의 친구에게 준 경우, 해당 자동차는 여전히 community property이며 갑·을이 이혼 시 equally 나누어 가진다.

✔ 매매 계약 시 두 배우자 모두 참여하지 않고 배우자 일방만이 참여한 경우, 계약의 목적물은 community property이며 갑·을이 이혼 시 equally 나누어 가진다.

4장
Wills and Trusts

///

본 장은 유언장(will)과 신탁(trust)에 대해 논한다. 유언장(will)은 작성자 사후(死後)에 법적효력이 발생하고 상속인, 재산 처분 등의 내용을 포함하는 문서이다. 신탁(trust)이란, '믿고 맡긴다'는 의미로 수탁자(trustee)가 위탁자(settlor)의 특정 재산을 관리·처분 그리고 그 밖에 신탁의 목적달성을 위하여 필요한 행위를 하는 법률관계를 뜻한다. 시중에 있는 일부 교재에서는 유언장과 신탁을 별도의 장으로 구성하여 설명하고 있으나, 양 개념의 관련성이 높은 것을 고려하여 필자는 본 장에서 will과 trust를 두 파트로 구분하여 설명하였다. 미국에서는 유언자가 will을 작성할 당시 trust를 생성하거나 사전에 이미 생성한 trust 내용을 will 내용에 포함시키는 경우가 많다. 즉, trust를 통한 유증이 보편화되어 있다. 따라서 에세이 시험에서도 will과 trust가 각각 별도의 문제로 출제되기 보다는, 사안에서 유언자의 will과 trust 내용을 모두 명시하고 유언자 사후에 유산을 어떻게 분배해야 하는지 판단토록 요구하는 문제가 자주 출제된다. 한편, 캘리포니아 주는 community property law를 채택하고 있어 본 장과 「3장, Community Property」가 연계되어 출제되는 경우도 많다. Community property law에 따르면 혼인한 자는 배우자와 community property(CP)에 대해 동등한 권리를 나누어 가지고 본인의 separate property(SP)에 대해서는 일체의 권리를 가진다. 다시 말해, 혼인한 자는 CP의 절반과 자신의 SP 전체를 자유롭게 alienation 할 수 있다. 이때 alienation은 다양한 방법으로 이루어질 수 있는데, 혼인한 자가 생전에 직접 증여하는 경우, trust를 통해 alienation하는 경우, will 또는 사후 trust(testamentary trust)를 통해 상속하는 경우가 있다. 그중 trust와 will을 통한 alienation이 모두 본 장과 밀접한 관련이 있다. 또한 사망한 자가 생전에 별도의 will을 작성하지 않은 경우 그의 CP 절반과 SP 전체를 법정상속해야 하는 문제가 있어, 이러한 경우에도 본 장의 내용과 연계하여 서술해야 한다. 다만, 본 장에 관한 문제는 특정 will 및 trust에 따라 자산분배가 어떻게 이루어져야 하는지에 초점이 맞춰져 있는 한편, community property에 관한 문제는 특정 자산을 CP와 SP로 구분하고 이를 배우자간 어떻게 분배하는지에 초점이 맞춰져 있다는 점에서 차이가 있다.

- Settlor = Testator: (will) 유언자 또는 피상속인 // (trust) 위탁자 또는 신탁자
- Beneficiary = Legatee: (will) 상속인 // (trust) 수익자
- Trustee: 수탁자
- Intestate: 유효한 유언장 작성 없이 사망한 자(n.), intestate 방법으로(adv.)
- Unattested = No witness
- Stepchild: 여자의 혼외자식
- Nonmarital child: 남자의 혼외자식
- Adopted-out child: 입양 '보낸' 자식
- Bequest (n.): 유증
- Bequeath (v.): 유증하다
- Deceased = Decedent: 고인(故人)
- Descendant: 자손

Part One. Wills

Will은 '유언장'을 뜻하는 바, 본 파트는 주로 will에 따른 유언상속을 다루나 법정상속에 관해서도 다룬다. '유언상속'과 관련해서는 유언장의 유효성 요건, 유언장 해석 및 집행 등에 대해 논하고, '법정상속'은 캘리포니아 주에서 채택하고 있는 community property law에 근거한 intestate law에 대해 논한다.

1. 작성자가 여러 개의 will을 작성하는 경우, will간의 관계를 파악하는 것이 중요하며, 다음과 같은 논점이 주로 출제된다.
   ① Will이 작성된 이후 아이가 태어나거나 배우자가 사망한 경우 또는 유언자가 will 작성 후 재혼한 경우, 해당 아이와 두 번째 배우자에게 어떤 권리가 인정되는가.
   ② 이전에 작성된 will과 이후에 작성된 will의 관계(revocation/republish)는 어떠한가. 이전에 작성된 will은 여전히 유효한가.
   ③ 여러 개의 will 내용이 충돌하는 경우 어떤 will의 내용에 근거하여 유산을 분배해야 하는가.
   ④ Will의 validity를 판단하라.
2. '연도'에 대한 정보가 많아, 주어진 사안을 '연도'별로 요약하는 것이 좋다.
3. 사망한 자의 유산에 대해 상속자간 어떤 권리를 가지는지 판단하는 문제가 출제된다.
   Q: <u>What rights, if any, do 갑, 을, and 병 have in the assets in [정's estate]? Answer according to California law.</u>
   Q: <u>What rights, if any, do 갑, 을, and 병 have in the assets in [the house]? Answer according to California law.</u>
   ⇒ 각 '상속자' 또는 '유산(자동차, 집, account 등)'을 title화하여 답안을 작성한다.
   ⇒ 특정 상속자가 will에 명시되어 있는 상속자인지 파악한다. 만일 다수의 will에 명시되어 있다면, will의 validity 및 wills간 관계를 묻는 문제일 가능성이 높다.

Ⅰ. Types of Wills

1. Holographic Will (17Feb)

Holographic will은 유언장의 유효성 요건을 모두 만족하지 못하였으나 일부 중요 문구가 유언자의 수기(手記)로 작성되었고 유언자의 서명이 있어 그 유효성이 인정된 will을 뜻한다.

a. General Rule

★Holographic will is one that is in the testator's **handwriting** and has no attesting witnesses.

A valid holographic codicil revokes any earlier valid will **to the extent it conflicts with the codicil.**

b. Validity Requirement

To be a valid holographic will:

ⅰ. The will must be **signed** by the testator; and

ⅱ. The **material terms** of testator's will must be in handwriting.

2. Codicil (18Feb)

Codicil of will은 이미 존재하는 유언장을 개폐·수정·변경한 유효성을 갖춘 수정유언장이다. Codicil의 유효성 요건은 will의 유효성 요건과 동일하다. 따라서 기존 will을 수정하는 경우 새로운 will을 작성하는 것처럼 유언자의 서명 등 유효성 요건을 모두 충족해야 한다. 반면, codicil of trust는 trust의 유효성 요건을 만족하지 못하더라도 intent, specification of beneficiaries 그리고 designation of trustee만 있으면 유효하다는 점에 유의해야 한다.

★Codicil is an instrument that amends, revokes, modifies an **existing will.**

★Codicil must satisfy **same formalities as a will.**

[Amendment of (revocable) Trust]

Revocable trusts can be amended or terminated by following any procedures or methods for amendment specified in the trust agreement. If there are no specified procedures, revocable trusts can be amended or terminated by the statement signed by the settlor and delivered to the trustee.

II. Validity (15Feb, 17Feb)

A. Jurisdiction of Validity

본 내용은 will의 유효성을 판단할 재판권(jurisdiction)을 어느 주가 가지고 있는지에 대해 논한다. 캘리포니아 주에서는 ① will이 시행된 state 또는 ② 유언자가 will에 서명했을 당시 또는 사망했을 당시의 거주(domicile) state에서 재판권을 가지고 있다고 보고, 해당 state에서 따르는 법을 적용하여 판단한다.

★The validity of a will is determined:

ⅰ. With the law of the state in which **it was executed;** or

ⅱ. With the law of the place where **the testator was domiciled when he signed** his will or **when he died.**

B. Validity Requirements

1. General Rule

To be a valid will, the will:

ⅰ. Must be in **writing;**

ⅱ. Must be **signed** by the testator;

ⅲ. Must be attested by **two witnesses;** and

ⅳ. Testator has **testamentary capacity.**

> **TIP1** ⅱ 요건
>
> ① 유언자의 서명 없이 작성된 유언장은 위 ⅱ요건(서명요건)을 만족하지 못하기 때문에 invalid will이다. 문제 본문에 유언자의 서명여부에 대한 언급이 없고 유언장의 내용에 대해서만 명시하거나, 별도의 서명 없이 testator's name만 있을 경우에는 위 ⅱ요건이 만족되지 못하기 때문에 invalid will이라고 보아야 한다.
>
> ② 유언자가 아니더라도 유언자가 함께 있는 상태에서 그의 지시에 따라 행동한 자(someone in the testator's presence and at his

direction)의 서명도 인정된다.

TIP2 ⅲ 요건: 증인은 반드시 해당 문서가 will이라는 점을 인지해야 하며, ⅱ 요건이 시행되는 것을 직접 목격해야 한다.

① 목격하는 시점에 두 증인이 동시에 서명해야 할 필요는 없으며, 각 증인은 목격한 시점 이후 유언자의 생전에 서명하면 된다.

② 증인이 will의 상세한 내용을 모두 인지하고 있을 필요는 없다. The witness does **not** need to be aware of the **specific details** of a will.

2. Testamentary Capacity

Testamentary capacity exists when a testator is at least 18 years old and understand:

ⅰ. The nature of the testamentary act;

ⅱ. The nature of her property; and

ⅲ. Relations with family members that are affected by the will.

3. Disinterested Witness

Interested witness란, will의 beneficiary, 즉 will로 인해 이권이 생기는 사람이 증인인 경우 그 증인을 뜻한다. 유효한 will을 작성하기 위해서는 최소 두 명 이상의 disinterested witnesses가 증인으로서 will 작성 과정에 참여해야 하는 바, interested witness가 증인으로 참여한 경우에는 해당 will이 그 자의 공갈협박·사기 등에 의해 작성되었다고 추정(rebuttable presumption)한다. 다만, interested witness 외에 다른 두 명 이상의 uninterested witness가 있었거나 해당 유증이 fiduciary capacity에 입각하여 이루어진 경우에는 상기 추정이 적용되지 않는다.

To be a valid will, at least **two disinterested witnesses** are required. If an interested witness involved, a **rebuttable presumption** that the witness procured the devise by duress, menace^{위협}, fraud, or undue influence is created.

However, this presumption is inapplicable if:

ⅰ. There are two other uninterested witnesses; or

ⅱ. The devise is made solely in a fiduciary capacity.

4. Holographic Will (17Feb)

a. General Rule

To be a valid holographic will:

ⅰ. The will must be **signed** by the testator; and

ⅱ. The **material terms** of testator's will must be in handwriting.

b. Material Terms

The material terms of a will that must be in handwriting are ones regarding:

ⅰ. Each gift given under the will; and

ⅱ. A person to whom each gift should go.

c. Date of Execution

작성된 날짜가 적히지 않은 holographic will은 여전히 유효하다. 다만, 유언자의 유언장 작성능력(capacity) 또는 두 개 이상의 will 시행 여부에 대해 다투는 경우에는 날짜가 적힌 will만이 유효하다고 본다.

Even if a holographic will does not contain a statement as to the date of its execution, it is still valid, **unless:**

ⅰ. There is an issue with the testator's capacity; or

ⅱ. There is the possibility that two or more wills should be probated.

TIP1 증인의 참석여부는 holographic will의 유효성과 무관하다.
Attended witness is not required for a valid holographic will.

TIP2 작성된 날짜가 적히지 않은 holographic will은 여전히 유효하다.
The holographic will is still valid even if there is no date of its execution.

III. Defenses against Validity

Will의 유효성은 앞서 will validity 부분에서 언급한 네 요소를 만족하고, 유효성에 대한 defenses가 없는 경우에 비로소 인정된다. 본 챕터에서는 유효성에 대한 defenses에 대해 논하는 바, defenses에는 계약 유효성에 대한 defenses 요컨대 duress, fraud, undue influence 뿐만 아니라 유효성 요건을 충족하지 못했다는 주장도 해당한다. 따라서 유효성 요건 중 하나인 settlor의 testamentary capacity를 만족하지 못했다는 주장도 유효성에 defense로 인정될 수 있다.

To be a valid will, there should be no defenses against validity such as duress, fraud, or undue influence.

A. Testamentary Capacity

To make a valid will, an individual should be **mentally competent** to make a will. The person is competent when he is able to:

ⅰ. Understand the **nature of the testamentary act;**

ⅱ. Understand **his property;** and

ⅲ. Is **not** suffered from **mental disorder** (e.g., delusions).

B. Fraud

Fraud는 fraud in inducement, fraud in execution, 이렇게 두 유형으로 구분된다. Fraud in inducement는 유언자에게 왜곡된 '사실'을 알려줌으로써, 유언자의 의도와는 다른 내용의 유언장을 작성하도록 유도한 경우이다. Fraud in execution는 유언자에게 유언자가 서명한 '서류의 내용과 본질'에 대해 왜곡한 경우이다.

1. General Rule

Fraud occurs when a testator is deceived by a misrepresentation and it led to execute a will that the testator would not otherwise have made.

2. Types of Fraud

a. Fraud in the Inducement

Fraud in the inducement occurs when a person misrepresents **facts**. When fraud in the inducement occurs, **only particular** fraudulent provisions become invalid.

b. Fraud in the Execution

Fraud in the execution occurs when a person misrepresents the **character or contents of the instrument** signed by the testator. When fraud in the execution occurs, **entire will** becomes invalid.

C. Undue Influence (15Feb)

A will is invalid if it was executed as the result of undue influence.

1. Elements

a. Common Law

Under the common law, undue influence is established if:

i . Testator was **susceptible;**

ii . Alleged influencer had the **opportunity** to exert undue influence;

iii. Alleged influencer had a **unnatural disposition** to exert undue influence; and

iv. The will is the **product** of the undue influence.

b. California

In California statute, undue influence is established if:

i . There was **excessive persuasion;**

ii . That **causes another person** to act or refrain from acting;

iii. By **overcoming** that person's **will;** and

iv. It **results in inequity.**

Undue influence may be proven by circumstantial evidence and courts consider several factors, such as vulnerability^{취약성} of the victim, relationship between the influencer and testator, and coercion of influencer.

2. Presumption

a. General Rule

Fraud or undue influence is presumed if:

ⅰ. Testator and wrongdoer has **confidential relationship;**

ⅱ. When a will makes a donative transfer to a care custodian within 90 days of provision of services; or

ⅲ. A donative transfer is made to the person who drafted the will.

✔ The change of will does not bring any benefits to a person. — no confidential relationship between the person and a settlor

b. Exceptions

The presumption is inapplicable when:

ⅰ. Wrongdoer is blood relative or cohabitant;

ⅱ. The transfer is valued at $5,000 or less; or

ⅲ. An independent attorney reviewed.

통상적으로 변호사와 의뢰인 간에 confidential relationship가 있다고 보는 반면 친족(blood relative) 또는 부부간에는 confidential relationship이 없다고 본다. 한편, Civil Procedure 과목 중 issue preclusion과 관련하여 가족간 in privity가 없다고 본다.

Ⅳ. Revocation (17Feb)

Revocation은 유언장을 개폐·수정·변경하는 행위를 뜻하며, revocation 방법에는 크게 법률 및 법규, physical act, 새로운 유언장 작성, 이렇게 세 유형이 있다. 원칙적으로 revoked된 유언장은 효력을 잃는다.

첫 번째 유형, 법률 및 법규에 의한 revocation은 유언자가 유언장을 '작성'한 시점과 유언장을 '집행'하는 시점간 상황이 현저하게 달라, 유언장 내용을 있는 그대로 집행할 경우 그 결과가 유언자의 intent와 현저히 다를 수 있다고 판단되는 경우 법률 및 법규상 허용되는 revocation을 뜻한다. 여기서 "revoke한다"는 것은 본래 유언자가 유언장을 작성한 바와 다르게 유산을 분배한다는 의미이며, 유산을 분배할 때에는 유언자의 intent를 고려한다. 예컨대, 유언자 갑이 "내 유산을 아들 을과 딸 병에게 증여한다."고 작성한 후에 아들 정이 태어났다면 아들 정의 존재 관점에서 유언장을 작성할 시점과 집행할 시점간 상황이 현저하게 다른 바, 법률상 갑의 유산에 대한 아들 정의 권리를 인정한다. 갑이 작성한 유언장에는 아들 정에 대한 유증 내용이 없을 것이나, 갑이 유언장을 작성할 당시 생존해 있던 자녀들에게 증여했다는 점을 미루어보아 아들 정이 그 당시 생존해 있었다면 갑이 정에게도 증여했을 것이라 예상할 수 있기 때문이다. 여기서 아들 정을 "pretermitted child"라 일컫는다. 만일 갑이 유언장에 "내 유산을 부인 무에게 증여하며, 자녀들에게는 일체 증여하지 않는다."고 명시하여 자녀에 대한 증여를 의도적(intentionally)으로 배제하였다면, 갑의 intent를 고려하여 아들 정의 권리는 인정되지 않을 것이다. 상기 rule(pretermitted child)은 유언자의 직계비속뿐만 아니라 배우자에게도 유사한 rule이 적용되며, 그러한 배우자는 "pretermitted spouse"라 일컫는다.

두 번째 유형, physical act에 의한 revocation은 유언장을 손으로 찢는 등 물리적인 방법으로 훼손하거나 변형하는 행위를 통칭한다.

세 번째 유형, 새로운 유언장 작성을 통한 revocation은 기존의 will이 존재하는 상태에서 새로운 will을 작성하여 기존의 will을 revoke한다. 즉, codicil을 작성하여 기존의 will을 revoke하는 방식인데, "기존의 will을 revoke하겠다."라는 문장을 codicil에 직접적으로(expressly) 언급하는 경우와 기존의 will과 충돌하는 내용을 codicil에 작성하여 기존 will의 revocation을 함축하는 경우로 구분된다.

앞서 언급한 바와 같이 revoked된 유언장은 원칙적으로 효력을 잃는다. 다만, 유언자가 사실적 오해 또는 법률적 오해를 바탕으로 invalid revocation을 한 경우에는 유언자가 그 오해를 제대로 인지했다면 revoke하지 않았을 것임이 인정되는 한, 그 revoke된 유언장은 유효하다고 본다(DRR doctrine).

A. By Operation of Law

A bequest may be revoked by operation of law when a change in circumstance occurs that makes it unlikely that the testator would have wanted.

1. Omitted Child (15Feb, 18Feb)

- Omitted child = Pretermitted child

Omitted child란, 유언장이 작성된 이후에 태어난 자녀를 뜻한다. 캘리포니아 주에서는 omitted child에게 will 내용과는 별도로 유언자(omitted child의 부모)의 유산 중 법정상속분(intestate share)만큼의 권리를 인정하고 있다. 이는 omitted child가 유언장이 작성된 시점 이후에 태어났다는 이유만으로 상속에서 제외되는(omitted) 것을 방지하기 위함이다. 다만, 유언자가 omitted child에 대한 상속을 의도적으로(intentionally) 제외하였거나, will을 통해 omitted child의 유언자가 아닌 부모(유언자의 배우자)에게 유산의 상당한 부분(또는 전체)을 상속한 경우 또는 유언자가 해당 will 이외의 방법으로 omitted child에게 상속한 경우에는 omitted child에 대한 법정상속분이 예외적으로 인정되지 않는다. 예컨대, 2020년 갑이 아들 을에게 상속하겠다는 내용의 will을 작성하였고 2030년에 갑의 딸 병이 태어난 후 갑이 사망하였다면, 딸 병은 갑이 will을 작성한 이후에 태어났다는 이유만으로 상속에서 제외되므로, 딸 병에게는 갑 유산에 대한 법정상속분(갑이 will 작성 없이 사망한 경우 딸 병에게 인정되는 권리)이 인정된다. 다만, 갑이 생전에 딸 병에게 집을 상속하였다면, omitted child로서의 법정상속분은 인정되지 않는다.

a. General Rule

A child born to a testator **after the execution** of the will is entitled **intestate share** of decedent's estate.

b. Exceptions

Omitted child is not entitled intestate share of decedent's estate, if:

ⅰ. Omission is **intentional**;

ⅱ. At the time the will is executed, the testator devised **substantially all** of his estate to the **other parent** of the omitted child; or

ⅲ. **The testator provided for the omitted child by a transfer outside of the will.**

2. Omitted Spouse (18Feb)

a. General Rule

A spouse or domestic partner who was married **after the execution** of the will is entitled **intestate share** of decedent's estate.

b. Exceptions

Omitted spouse is not entitled intestate share of decedent's estate, if:

ⅰ. Omission is **intentional**;

ⅱ. The testator provided for the omitted spouse **by a transfer outside of the will**; or

ⅲ. Right to the share is **waived in a valid agreement.**

TIP

① 유언자의 will이 작성된 후 유언자의 아이가 태어난 경우, 해당 아이가 pretermitted child인지 그 여부를 판단해야 한다.

② 유언자가 will 작성 후 혼인을 하거나 이혼 후 재혼한 경우, 유언자가 사망한 시점의 배우자가 pretermitted spouse인지 그 여부를 판단해야 한다.

B. By Physical Acts

The will is revoked when:

ⅰ. Testator has intent to revoke the will; and

ⅱ. The will is burned, torn, destroyed, or cancelled by the testator.

✔ Will을 찢어버리는 행위는 physical act이다.

✔ "Revoke하겠다."라는 문장을 will 모서리 부분에 적는 행위는 physical act이다.

C. By Codicil (15Feb, 18Feb)

1. General Rule

A will is revoked entirely or partially by a codicil (subsequent will) when the codicil:

　ⅰ. Expressly revokes the previous will; or

　ⅱ. Impliedly revokes the previous will through **inconsistencies.**

2. Inconsistent in Terms

★If the codicil is inconsistent in terms, the earlier will is revoked **only to the extent of the inconsistency.** In other words, the will will be revoked **partially** by a codicil.

D. Dependent Relative Revocation Doctrine (DRR Doctrine)

Dependent relative revocation doctrine은 유언자가 사실적 오해 또는 법률적 오해를 바탕으로 invalid revocation을 하였고 유언자가 그 오해를 제대로 인지했다면 revoke하지 않았을 것임이 인정되는 경우, 그 revoke된 유언장은 유효하다고 본다. 다시 말해, 유언자의 오해에 의한 revocation이 인정되는 경우 해당 revocation은 유효하지 않다고 보고 revoke되기 이전의 내용으로 유언장을 집행한다.

★Under the DRR doctrine, if a testator revokes a will or codicil **based on a mistake of fact or law, the revocation is ineffective** if it appears that the testator **would not have revoked but for the mistake.**

갑이 will에 "distribute 2억 to 을"이라고 작성했고, 그 이후 해당 부분에 손으로 두 줄을 긋고 "distribute 5억 to 을"로 수정했다. 갑은 will에 서명하지 않았고, 수정된 내용에 대한 witness도 없었다. 을은 얼마를 유증받을 수 있는가? (DRR에 근거하여 답하라)

⇒ 갑이 "2억 to 을" 부분을 revoke할 당시 갑이 state statute의 서명 요건을 제대로 인지하지 못했고, 이로 인해 invalid revocation이 되었다. 또한 갑이 revoke하려던 내용이 을에게 더 많은 금액을 유증하기 위함이었다는 점을 고려하면, 갑이 그 서명 요건을 제대로 인지했다면 revoke하지 않았을 것으로 예상가능하다. 따라서 revoked된 유언장의 효력이 인정되어 을은 2억을 유증 받을 것이다.

갑's cancellation of the prior will was motivated by a desire to give 을 more money. Under the DRR doctrine, "2억 to 을" is not revoked in consistency with the testator's intention.

TIP1 두 번째 will(상기 예시에서 "5억 to 을" 부분)이 fraud, undue influence 또는 ineffective execution에 의해 그 유효성이 부정되는 경우에는 본 doctrine이 적용되지 않는다.

If a second will is invalid because of fraud, undue influence, or ineffective execution, DRR is inapplicable.

TIP2 여러 번의 revocation이 존재하는 경우, 가장 마지막으로 revoke한 내용이 valid하다고 추정한다. 예컨대, 상기 예시에서 갑이 이후 "distribute 5억 to 을" 부분을 손으로 두 줄을 긋고 "8억 to 을"로 수정하였다면, 을은 8억에 대해 권리가 있다.

Under the DRR, only the most recently revoked instrument is revived.

E. Identical Wills (17Feb)

동일한 will이 두 부 이상 존재했고 유언자가 그중 한 부를 validly revoke한 경우, 다른 will도 revoke되었다고 본다.

There is a presumption that where there are identical originals of one will, the revocation of one constitutes the revocation of the others. In other words, when one of the duplicates is revoked, the will is revoked. When a will is revoked by physical act or codicil but the subsequent will is revoked again, the first will is revived if the testator's intent to revive it is proved.

V. Wills and Other Documents

유언자는 will에 외부 문서를 인용하여 유산을 distribute할 수 있다. 여기서 '외부문서'는 will뿐만 아니라 will이 아닌 기타 문서도 포함한다. 즉, testator 는 will 내용에 will이 아닌 외부의 기타 문서 및 별도의 will(자신이 사전에 작성한 will)을 인용할 수 있다. 'Will이 아닌 외부의 기타 문서'를 인용하는 것을 incorporation by reference라고 한다. 한편, testator가 new will 작성시 '사전에 작성해 놓은 will'을 인용한다면, 그 new will은 codicil이 되고 이러 한 인용을 republication by codicil이라고 한다.

A. Doctrine of Integration

Doctrine of integration은 일정 요건을 만족하면 모든 종이가 한 will을 구성 한다고 보는 이론이다.

Under the doctrine of integration, a document will be integrated into a will if:

 i . Testator **intended;** and
 ii . The document was **physically present at the time of the will's execution.**

Extrinsic evidence is permitted to show testator's intent and the presence of papers.

B. Incorporation by Reference

Incorporation by reference란, will이 아닌 외부의 기타 문서를 인용하는 것을 뜻한다. 예컨대, will에 "반지와 도자기는 서랍 안에 있는 memo에 입각하여 distribute한다."라고 작성한 경우, '반지 서랍 안에 있는 memo'는 외부의 기타문서로서 will에 인용되었으므로, 일정 요건을 만족하는 한 valid한 incorporation by reference가 된다. 한편, 캘리포니아 주에서는 가치가 5,000불 이하(총 합계 25,000불 이하)인 유형(有形)의 동산에 대해 별도의 요건이 적용된다. 상기 예시에서 반지와 도자기는 유형(有形)의 동산이므로 각 가치가 5,000불 이하이고 반지와 도자기의 가치 합계가 25,000불 이하라면, 별도의 요건을 적용한다.

1. General Rule

Incorporated by reference is valid if the writing:

ⅰ. Shows **intent** to incorporate;

ⅱ. Exists **at the time the will was executed;** and

ⅲ. Is **substantially identified** in the will.

2. Tangible Personal Property

In California, there is a special rule for **tangible personal property.**

Disposal of tangible personal property is admitted if the writing:

ⅰ. Was referred in the will;

ⅱ. Is dated and signed by the testator (or handwritten by the testator);

ⅲ. Describes the items and beneficiaries with reasonable certainty; and

ⅳ. Each item may not exceed $5,000 and total value cannot exceed $25,000.

C. Republication by Codicil

Republication이란, 외부문서 전체를 '인용'하는 것을 뜻한다. Republication by codicil은 new will(또는 codicil)을 작성할 때 testator가 이전에 작성한

will(prior will) 전체를 인용하는 것이다. 예컨대, 유증자가 새로운 will(또는 codicil)에 "나머지 부분은 이전 will을 republish한다."는 문구를 작성한다면 이는 사전에 작성한 prior will 전체를 인용한다는 의미이다. 인용된 will은 'new will'이 작성된 시점에 작성되었다고 본다. 만일 codicil이 생성된 이후 이전 will이 revoke된다면, 그 revoked된 내용이 이전 will과 codicil 모두에 반영된다. 반면, codicil이 revoke되는 경우에는 이전 will은 그대로 유지되고 codicil만이 revoke되었다고 본다. 앞서 설명한 DRR doctrine은 will(또는 codicil)을 invalid하게 revoke했을 때 해당 revocation을 valid하다고 인정하는 특별한 경우에 관한 doctrine인 한편, republication by codicil doctrine은 이전 will이 이후 작성된 will(또는 codicil)에 인용된 경우에 관한 doctrine이다.

TIP   ① Republication: 타 문서를 will에 '인용'하는 행위
         ② Revocation: (유언장의) 개폐·수정·변경

1. General Rule

A codicil that refers to an earlier will is said to **republish** that will.
When republication by codicil takes place, the republished will is deemed to be **executed on the same day as the codicil.**

2. Revocation

When a codicil is revoked, an earlier will remains valid.
When the earlier will is revoked, both the earlier will and the codicil are revoked.

[DRR Doctrine]

Under the DRR doctrine, if a testator revokes a will or codicil based on a mistake of fact or law, the revocation is ineffective if it appears that the testator would not have revoked but for the mistake.

2020년 갑's will: 을에게 1억을 유증한다.

2030년 갑's will: 병에게 2억을 유증하고, 2020년 will을 republish한다.

갑 사망 후 을은 갑의 유산 중 얼마를 유증받을 수 있는가?

⇒ 1억. 2030년에 갑의 새로운 will이 작성되었으나, 2020년의 will을 republish한다고 명시한 점을 비추어 2030년의 will은 2020년의 will에 대한 추가적인 유증이라 볼 수 있다. 따라서 을은 2020년의 will 내용에 의거하여 1억을 유증받는다.

"The 2030 will republished the 2020 will and it means adding another gift to the 2020 will. Thus, the gift to 을 is valid and 을 will get 1억."

Ⅵ. Distribution

A. Classification of Gifts

- Specific gift: 특정 물건의 증여("내 목걸이를 준다.")
- General gift: 일정 금액의 증여("300만원을 준다.")
- Residuary gift: Specific과 general 증여 후 남는 유산의 증여("My estate를 준다.")
- Demonstrative gift: 특정된 출처로부터의 일정 금액의 증여("ABC Bank account의 300만원을 준다.")

1. Specific Gift

A specific gift is a gift of **specific and identifiable** property.

2. General Gift

A general gift is a gift from **general assets** of the estate. It is commonly used to give **money**.

3. Residuary Gift

A residuary gift is a gift for the **remainder of an estate** to a specified recipient. Residuary beneficiary receives **residue of an estate**.

4. Demonstrative Gift

A demonstrative gift is a general gift demonstrated **with a specific property or particular fund** from which the gift should be made.

B. Ademption and Abatement

1. Ademption (17Feb)

Ademption을 직역하면 '유증 철회'라는 뜻으로, "ademption을 한다."는 것은 specific gift를 철회한다는 의미이다. Ademption 유형에는 ademption by extinction과 ademption by satisfaction이 있다. Ademption by extinction은 specific gift의 해당 물건이 유언자가 사망한 시점을 기준으로 더 이상 그 유언자의 유산이 아님을 이유로 유증을 철회하는 경우이다. 예컨대, 갑이 유언장에 "내 빨간색 자동차를 을에게 증여한다. Residuary gift to 병."이라고 작성한 후 그 빨간색 자동차를 팔고 파란색 자동차를 샀다면, 빨간색 자동차는 갑이 사망한 시점을 기준으로 더 이상 갑의 유산이 아니므로 파란색 자동차에 대한 유증은 철회(adeem by extinction)된다. 따라서 파란색 자동차는 residuary legatee인 병이 증여받는다. 다만, 갑이 will 작성 당시 ademption by extinction을 원치 않는다는 intent를 가지고 있었거나 ademption 예외에 해당하는 경우에는 을은 specific gift 의 목적물의 가치를 돈으로 환산하거나 specific gift의 목적물이 변경된 형태의 자산을 증여받는다. Ademption 예외에는 유언자가 보유하고 있던 stock을 팔아 다른 stock을 매입하는 경우, executor가 유산을 매매한 경우 그리고 유언자의 자산이 국가에 수용(condemnation)되어 그에 대한 배상(compensation)을 받은 경우가 있다. 한편, ademption by satisfaction이란, 유언자가 생전에 specific gift의 해당 목적물을 이미 증여하였음을 이유로 유증을 철회하는 경우이다. 상기 예시에서 갑이 유언장을 작성한 후 바로 을에게 빨간색 자동차를 증여하였다면, 갑이 사망한 후 을에 대한 유증은 adeem by satisfaction된다.

a. Ademption by Extinction
ⅰ. General Rule
A **specific gift** may be extinguished when the testator no longer owns the specific property at the time of the testator's death. However, when it is proven that the testator had no intent to have the gift adeemed a specific gift may not be extinguished.

ⅱ. Exceptions
There are exceptions to ademption by extinction. A specific gift will not be extinguished when:

① The proceeds of the **sale of one stock** are immediately used to buy another stock;

② The **executor** sells the property; or

③ There was a **condemnation** and the testator receives just compensation.

b. Ademption by Satisfaction
A gift adeems by satisfaction when the subject of the gift which is made during the testator's life is the same as the subject of a provision of the will.

2. Abatement
Abatement는 '감소·경감·완화'라는 뜻을 가진다. "Abatement를 한다."라는 것은 유언자의 유산이 유증액보다 적을 경우, beneficiary에게 유증액을 줄여서 distribute한다는 의미이다. Specific gift, general gift, residuary gift 중에서 가장 먼저 residuary gift를 줄이고, 그 다음으로 general gift를 줄인다. 다시 말해, 세 종류의 gift 중 가장 보호받는 것은 specific gift이다. 만일 유언장 상으로 general gift 또는 specific gift가 다수에게 증여되었다면, 친족이 아닌 자에게 증여된 general gift, 친족에게 증여된 general gift, 친족이 아닌 자에게 증여된 specific gift, 친족에게 증여된 specific

gift 순서로 abate한다.

a. General Rule

When the assets of a testator's estate are insufficient to pay all of the bequest payable under the testator's will, these bequests are reduced or abated.

b. Abatement Order

The order in which a testator's property abates is as follows:

ⅰ. Property passing by intestacy;

ⅱ. Residuary bequests;

ⅲ. General bequests (nonrelatives first, and then relatives); and

ⅳ. Specific bequests (nonrelatives first, and then relatives).

C. Lapse and Anti-Lapse Statute (18Feb)

Lapse를 직역하면 '소멸하다'라는 뜻으로서, beneficiary가 유언자(testator)보다 먼저 사망한 경우 사망한 beneficiary의 몫을 소멸시켜 beneficiary가 아닌 residuary gift를 증여받을 사람(residuary legatee)에게 주는 것을 "lapse한다."고 표현한다. 반면, anti-lapse는 beneficiary가 사망했다 하더라도 일정 요건을 만족하면 beneficiary의 몫을 lapse시키지 않고 beneficiary's issue에게 대신 유증하는 것을 뜻한다. 캘리포니아 주는 anti-lapse statute를 채택하고 있다. 여기서 'issue'는 사망한 beneficiary의 자녀를 포함한 모든 직계비속을 뜻하며, 동일한 촌수의 직계비속 간에는 per capita 방법으로 유산을 분배한다.

1. Lapse Statute

Under the lapse statute, if a beneficiary does not survive the testator, the bequest lapses and a lapsed bequest falls into **residue of the estate.**

Lapse occurred whenever **a beneficiary predeceased the testator** and the testator specified no alternate disposition of the assets in question.

2. Anti-Lapse Statute

California adopts anti-lapse statute.

★When a beneficiary **predeceased** the testator, the bequest to the deceased beneficiary is saved from lapse and the deceased **beneficiary's issue** takes it only when:

ⅰ. Deceased is related **by blood** to the testator;

ⅱ. The deceased beneficiary's issue **survives** the testator; and

ⅲ. There is no contrary intention in the will.

> TIP 유언자의 '배우자'는 anti-lapse statute를 적용할 수 없는 대표적 대상으로서, 유언자의 배우자에 대한 유산배분에 대해 판단하는 경우 'anti-lapse statute를 적용할 수 없음'을 analysis하는 것이 고득점 포인트다.

D. Acts of Independent Significance (18Feb)

- Acts of independent significance = Acts of independent legal significance = Non-testamentary acts

Acts of independent significance^{의미}는 '독립적인(별도의) 의미를 가진 행위'로 직역되며, 유언자가 will 작성 후 자신이 작성한 will의 내용을 변경시키고자 하는 intent 없이 시행하였으나, 결론적으로는 유산분배에 영향을 끼친 행위를 뜻한다.

Acts of independent significance are acts that have some significance beyond avoiding the requirements of the will.

A testator can change the disposition of his property without changing a will through such acts.

갑이 자신의 will에 "my bank account to my employees"라고 작성했다. Will을 작성할 당시 을과 병이 employee였으나 이후 갑이 을을 해고하였고 갑이 사망했을 당시 병과 정이 employee로 근무하고 있었다면, 갑의 bank account는 병과 정에게 분배된다.

⇒ 여기서 '갑이 을을 해고한 행위'는 자신의 will 내용을 변경하고자 한 intent가 있었다기 보다는 을의 근로 태도 등 will 내용 변경과는 무관한 별도의 이유가 있었다고 볼 수 있다. 그렇다 하더라도 갑의 행위는 결론적으로 유산분배에 영향을 끼치게 되었으므로, '갑이 을을 해고한 행위'가 acts of independent significance가 된다.

갑이 자신의 will에 "my car to 을"이라고 작성했다. 본 will을 작성할 당시 갑은 빨간색 자동차를 소유하고 있었으나, 이후 해당 자동차를 팔고 파란색 자동차를 새로 구입했다. 이 경우, 을은 파란색 자동차에 대해 권리를 가진다.

⇒ 여기서 '갑이 빨간색 자동차를 팔고 파란색 자동차를 구입한 행위'는 자신의 will 내용을 변경하고자 한 intent가 있었다기 보다는 새로운 자동차를 구매하고자 하는 intent를 가지고 행동했다고 볼 수 있다. 즉, 갑은 will 내용 변경과는 무관한 별도의 이유가 있었다고 볼 수 있다. 그렇다 하더라도 갑의 행위는 결론적으로 유산분배에 영향을 끼치게 되었으므로, 갑의 행위는 acts of independent significance가 된다.

E. Conservator (15Feb, 19Feb)

- Conservatorship: 법원이 conservator를 지정하는 과정(court proceeding)
- Conservator: Conservatee의 자산에 대해 재정적 결정을 하도록 법원이 지정한 자
- Conservatee: 타인(conservator)으로부터 도움을 받는 자

1. General Rule

A court may appoint a conservator who has the power to make **financial decisions** on the conservatee's estate when the conservatee is **unable to make decisions** on his own.

2. Fiduciary Duty

The conservator **owes the conservatee** fiduciary duties, including duty of care and duty of loyalty.

The conservator should make financial decisions in conservatee's best interests.

✔ Conservator가 conservatee(settlor)의 intent와 정면으로 충돌하는 내용으로 새로운 will을 작성한 경우, 새로운 will은 유효하나 법원은 conservator의 breach of fiduciary duty를 이유로 새로운 will의 beneficiary가 받은 자산에 대해 constructive trust를 생성할 수 있다.

3. Abuse of Authority

When a court concludes that a conservator abused his authority, a conservator's power is subject to judicial control.

The court usually finds an abuse of authority when a conservator **changes the will for his own interest** or in a way **contrary to settlor's intent.**

F. Restrictions on Succession

1. Surviving Spouse's Right

The surviving spouse has **right to elect** to take his share following the deceased **spouse's will or** to take his **intestate share (statutory share).** If the spouse chooses to follow the intestate law, he/she is entitled to half of the CP, and SP of the deceased spouse based on the number of issues. As the result, the surviving spouse is entitled to all of the

CP, all of his own SP, and part of SP of the deceased spouse.

2. No-Contest Clause

If there is a no-contest clause in a will, a beneficiary who contests the instrument without probable cause on the defenses against validity, or revocation will be penalized.

3. Slayer Statute

Slayer statute provides that a person who **intentionally caused the decedent's death** cannot take his share in the estate of a decedent.

Ⅶ. Intestate Distribution (17Feb, 18Feb)

Intestate succession은 '법정상속'을 뜻하는 바, 본 챕터에서는 고인(故人)이 생전에 유효한 will을 작성하지 않고 사망한 경우 그의 유산을 어떻게 분배해야 하는지에 대해 논한다. Community property law를 채택하는 캘리포니아 주에서는 will을 작성하지 않고 사망한 고인의 유산을 community property (CP)와 separate property(SP)로 구분하여 intestate succession을 시행한다. 여기서 '고인의 유산'은 CP의 절반과 고인의 SP 전체를 뜻한다. 배우자 일방이 사망하는 경우 각 배우자는 CP 절반과 각자의 SP 전체에 대해 권리를 가지기 때문이다. Community property law에서 규정하는 intestate succession에 따르면, 고인이 CP의 절반에 대해 가지고 있는 권리는 생존한 배우자 (surviving spouse)에게 모두 상속된다. 즉, intestate succession이 이루어지면 surviving spouse는 자신이 본래 가지고 있는 CP의 절반에 대한 권리와 고인으로부터 상속 받은 CP의 절반에 대해 권리를 가지게 되므로, 결론적으로 CP 전체에 대해 권리를 가지게 되는 것이다. 고인의 SP는 CP와 달리 고인의 배우자(surviving spouse)에게 전적으로 그 권리가 인정되지 않고, 고인의 직계비속(issue), 부모(parent), 형제자매(sibling) 또는 조카(issue of sibling)의 생존여부 및 명수(名數)를 기준으로 surviving spouse와 고인의 혈족간 분배된다. 예컨대, 유언자 사망 당시 유언자의 혈족 1명과 배우자가 생존하고 있었다면 배우자는 SP의 1/2에 대해 권리를 가지고, 유언자의 혈족간 per capita 또는 per stirpes 방법으로 SP의 2/3를 나누어 가진다. 만일 유언자 사망 당시 생존하고 있는 유언자의 혈족이 없고, 오직 배우자만이 생존하고 있었다면 배우자가 SP 전체에 대해 권리를 가진다.

한편, 고인(故人)이 생전에 유효한 will을 작성했다 할지라도 surviving spouse의 선택에 따라 intestate succession이 이루어지는 경우도 있다. 고인이 생전에 유효한 will을 작성한 경우 surviving spouse는 ① 고인의 will에 따라 유언상속을 받을지 또는 ② intestate law에 따라 법정상속을 받을지 선택할 수 있는 권리가 있는데, 후자의 경우를 택하면 상기의 방법으로 유산상속이 이루어진다. Surviving spouse가 상속받는 방법을 선택하는 것을 "surviving spouse's election"이라 표현한다. 예컨대, will에 따른 유언상속분이 법정상속분보다 적은 경우 surviving spouse는 ② 방법을 택하여 법정상속분(CP의 1/2과 고인의 SP 전체 또는 일부)을 받을 수 있다.

A. Surviving Spouse

1. Community Property

The surviving spouse takes half of the community property (CP) and quasi-community property (QCP).

2. Separate Property (17Feb)

The surviving spouse takes all or some of the decedent's separate property (SP), depending on whether there is decedent's surviving issue, parent, siblings^{형제자매}, or issue of siblings.

a. No Surviving People

The surviving spouse takes **all** of the decedent's SP, **only if** there is **no** decedent's surviving issue, parent, siblings, or issue of siblings.

b. With Surviving People

ⅰ. The surviving spouse takes **one-half** of the decedent's SP, when there is decedent's **one** surviving issue, parent, siblings, or issue of siblings.

ⅱ. The surviving spouse takes **one-third** of the decedent's SP, when there is decedent's **more than one** surviving issue, parent, siblings, or issue of siblings.

B. No Surviving Spouse

When there is no surviving spouse or there is a portion of the estate remaining after the surviving spouse receives his share, decedent's estate passes as follows:

ⅰ. Issue (per capita between them);

ⅱ. Decedent's parent (or parents equally);

ⅲ. Issue of the parents;

ⅳ. Grandparent (or grandparents equally);

ⅴ. Issue of grandparents;

ⅵ. Issue of a predeceased spouse;

ⅶ. Next of kin (= decedent's closest surviving blood relative);

ⅷ. Parents of a predeceased spouse;

ⅸ. Issue of parents of a predeceased spouse; and

ⅹ. Escheat to state [상속인 없는 재산이 state에 귀속됨].

a. Per Capita with Representation

본 방법은 다수의 주에서 채택하고 있는 방법으로서, 사망자의 직계비속 중 생존한 자가 있는 첫 번째 generation에서 권리를 동등하게 나누어 가진다(equally divide). 만일 첫 번째 generation에 있는 자 중 predeceased 한 자가 있다면 그의 몫은 그 다음 세대가 '대리'하여 권리를 가지는 바, 'predeceased한 자의 자손'간 equally divide한다.

> **case 1**

갑에게 세 명의 자녀(A, B, C)가 있었고, 그중 A와 B는 predeceased 갑. A에게는 자녀 A1가 있었고 B에게는 B1, B2, C에게는 C1이 있다. 갑이 사망 후

per capita with representation 방법을 사용하는 경우, 갑의 유산은 어떻게 분배되어야 하는가?

⇒ A1은 1/3, B1, B2는 각각 1/6, C는 1/3, C1은 nothing.

① 갑의 유산은 생존한 자가 있는 generation 즉, A, B, C가 동등하게 나누어 가져야 하나, A와 B는 predeceased 갑.

② A, B, C는 각각 갑의 자산에 대해 1/3씩 권리를 가진다. 따라서 갑 사망 시 생존한 C는 갑의 자산 1/3에 대해 권리를 가진다. 즉, C1은 갑의 자산에 대해 권리가 없다.

③ Predeceased한 A와 B의 issue들은 '자신의 부모 몫'을 동등하게 나누어 가진다(A1은 1/3, B1과 B2는 1/3*1/2).

case 2

갑에게 세 명의 자녀(A, B, C)가 있었고, A, B, C 모두 predeceased 갑. A의 자녀 A1, B의 자녀 B1, B2, C의 자녀 C1가 모두 갑 사망 시 생존해 있었다. 갑 사망 후 per capita with representation 방법을 사용하는 경우, 갑의 유산은 어떻게 분배되어야 하는가?

⇒ A1, B1, B2, C1은 각각 갑 유산의 1/4에 대해 권리를 가진다.

① A, B, C 모두 predeceased 갑이므로, 갑 유산에 대한 권리는 생존한 자가 있는 generation, 즉 A1, B1, B2, C1가 존재하는 generation이 가진다.

② A1, B1, B2, C1는 동등한 generation에 있으므로 갑 유산을 동등하게 나누어 가진다. 즉, A1, B1, B2, C1은 각각 갑 유산의 1/4에 대해 권리를 가진다.

b. Per Capita at Each Generational Level

본 방법은 per capita with representation에서 발전된 형태로서, 근래에 다수의 주에서 채택하는 경향이 있다(modern trend). Per capita with representation 방법과 동일하게 사망자의 직계비속 중 생존한 자가 있는 첫 번째 generation에서 권리를 동등하게 나누어 가진다(equally divide). 다만, 첫 번째 generation에 있는 자 중 predeceased한 자의 권리를 분배하는 방법에 있어 양자 방법에 차이가 있다. Predeceased한 자의 권리를 그의 자손에게 이전하는 per capita with representation과 달리, per capita at each generation 방법에서는 predeceased한 자의 몫을 그 다음 '세대'에 이전한다. 만일 predeceased한 자가 한 명 이상인 경우에는 그들의 권리 전체를 그 다음 세대에 이전하여 '동일한 세대에 있는 자'들간 equally divide한다.

case 1

갑에게 세 명의 자녀(A, B, C)가 있었고, 그중 A와 B는 predeceased 갑. A에게는 자녀 A1이 있었고 B에게는 B1, B2, C에게는 C1이 있다. 갑 사망 후 per capita at each generation level 방법을 사용하는 경우, 갑의 유산은 어떻게 분배되어야 하는가?

⇒ A1, B1, B2는 각자 갑 유산의 2/9, C는 1/3, C1은 nothing.

① 갑의 유산을 생존한 자가 있는 첫 번째 generation 즉, A, B, C가 동등하게 나누어 가져야 하나, A와 B가 predeceased 갑 하였다.

② 갑 사망 후 생존한 C는 갑의 자산 1/3에 대해 권리를 가진다.

③ Predeceased한 A와 B의 몫은 그 다음 generation으로 이전되고, 동일한 generation간, 즉 A1, B1, B2간 동등하게 권리를 나누어 가진다 (2/3*1/3). 즉, A1, B1, B2가 각각 갑의 자산 2/9에 대해 권리를 가진다.

case 2

갑에게 세 명의 자녀(A, B, C)가 있었고, A, B, C 모두 predeceased 갑. A의 자녀 A1, B의 자녀 B1, B2, C의 자녀 C1가 모두 갑 사망 시 생존해 있었다. 갑 사망 후 per capita at each generation level 방법을 사용하는 경우, 갑의 유산은 어떻게 분배되어야 하는가?

⇒ A1, B1, B2, C1은 각각 갑 유산의 1/4에 대해 권리를 가진다.

① A, B, C 모두 predeceased 갑이므로, 갑 유산에 대한 권리는 생존한 자가 있는 첫 번째 generation, 즉 A1, B1, B2, C1가 가진다.

② A1, B1, B2, C1는 동등한 generation에 있으므로 갑 유산을 동등하게 나누어 가진다. 즉, A1, B1, B2, C1은 각각 갑 유산의 1/4에 대해 권리를

가진다.

c. Per Stirpes

• Per stirpes = Strict per stirpes

본 방법은 소수의 주에서 채택하는 방법으로서, 사망자 자손의 predeceased 여부와 무관하게 사망자의 유산은 그의 child(ren)에게 권리가 이전된다. 만일 children 중 predeceased한 자가 있다면, 그의 몫은 그대로 그의 자손에게 이전된다.

---

case 1

갑에게 세 명의 자녀(A, B, C)가 있었고, 그중 A와 B는 predeceased 갑. A에게는 자녀 A1이 있었고 B에게는 B1, B2, C에게는 C1이 있다. 갑이 사망 후 per stirpes 방법을 사용하는 경우, 갑의 유산은 어떻게 분배되어야 하는가?
⇒ A1은 1/3, B1, B2는 각각 1/6, C는 1/3, C1은 nothing.

① 갑 자녀의 생존여부와 무관하게 갑의 유산은 A, B, C가 동등하게 나누어 가진다.

② 갑 사망 후 생존한 C는 갑의 자산 1/3에 대해 권리를 가진다.

③ Predeceased한 A와 B의 issue들은 '자신의 부모 몫'을 동등하게 나누어 가진다. (A1은 1/3, B1과 B2는 1/3*1/2)

---

case 2

갑에게 세 명의 자녀(A, B, C)가 있었고, 그중 A, B, C 모두 predeceased 갑. A의 자녀 A1, B의 자녀 B1, B2, C의 자녀 C1이 모두 갑 사망 시 생존해 있었다. 갑 사망 후 per stirpes 방법을 사용하는 경우, 갑의 유산은 어떻게 분배되어야 하는가?
⇒ A1은 갑 유산의 1/3, B1, B2은 1/6, C1은 1/3에 대해 권리를 가진다.

① 갑 자녀의 생존여부와 무관하게 갑의 유산은 A, B, C가 동등하게 나누어 가진다.

② A, B, C 모두 predeceased하였으므로, 그들의 권리는 그들의 직계비속에게 각각 이전된다.

③ A1은 A의 몫인 1/3에 대해 권리를 가진다. B1, B2는 B의 몫인 1/3을 동등하게 나누어 가진다(1/3*1/2). C1은 C의 몫인 1/3에 대해 권리를 가진다.

C. 120-Hour Rule

For intestate succession purpose, a person who **fails to survive** the decedent **by 120 hours** is deemed to have **predeceased** the decedent.

The 120-hour survival requirement would not apply if it would result in the escheat of property to the state^{상속인 없는 재산이 state에 귀속됨}.

D. Advancement

If a person dies intestate, property that the decedent gave **during lifetime** to an heir is treated as an **advancement** against that heir's share of the intestate estate only if:

ⅰ. The decedent declares; and

ⅱ. The heir acknowledges in writing.

Part Two. Trusts

본 파트는 신탁(trust)에 대해 논하는 바, 그 내용은 크게 신탁 유효성(validity) 요건, 수탁자(trustee)가 수익자(beneficiary)에 대해 지는 신의칙의 의무(fiduciary duty) 그리고 신탁 해석 및 집행으로 구분되어 있다.

1. 주어진 사안을 전체적으로 파악하여 상속자의 권리를 판단하는 will 문제와는 달리, trust 문제는 fiduciary duty, 채권자의 권리 등과 같이 세부적인 논점을 다루는 문제가 많다.
2. Trust에 관한 답안은 'trust validity'에 대한 내용으로 시작되어야 한다. Trust 문제가 타 과목과 혼합되어 출제된 경우, 'trust validity'에 대한 별도의 문제가 없다 하더라도 이에 대한 analysis를 가장 먼저 작성한다.
3. Trust에 따라 위탁자(settlor)의 자산을 어떻게 분배해야 하는지 판단하는 문제가 주로 출제된다.
   Q: What rights, if any, does 갑 have in the trust assets? Discuss.
4. Trustee의 fiduciary duty에 관한 문제도 자주 출제된다.
   Q: What duties, if any, has 갑 violated as trustee, and what remedies, if any, does 갑 have against him?
   Q: What is the likely result of 갑's suit against 을? Discuss.
5. 세부적인 논점에 관해 출제되는 경우도 많다.
   Q: Is 갑's petition likely to be granted?
   ⇒ 지문에서 갑의 petition 내용을 우선 파악한 후, 관련된 rule을 적용한다.
     15Feb 기출문제에서는 갑이 trust를 modify하겠다는 내용의 petition을 구하였고, 이는 trust의 유형(revocable/irrevocable)과 modify하는 방법에 대해 논하는 문제였다.
   Q: Will 갑's creditors be able to reach the trust assets?
   ⇒ Spendthrift clause 또는 trust의 유형(revocable/irrevocable)에 관한 문제이다.

Ⅰ. General Concepts

본 챕터는 신탁에 대한 기본적인 정의, 신탁의 유효성 요건, 그리고 신탁의 유형에 대해 논한다. 앞서 언급한 바와 같이 신탁은 수탁자(trustee)가 위탁자(settlor)의 특정 재산을 관리·처분 그리고 그 밖에 신탁의 목적달성을 위하여 필요한 행위를 하는 법률관계를 뜻한다. 즉, trust는 trustee와 settlor간의 fiduciary relationship으로서, trustee는 수익자(beneficiary)에게 신의칙의 의무(fiduciary duty)를 진다. 한편, trust의 유효성 요건에는 settlor의 trust를 생성할만한 능력(capacity), settlor의 trust를 생성하겠다는 의도(intent), 합법적인 trust의 목적(purpose), 신탁자산(trust property) 그리고 명확한 beneficiary가 있다. Trust가 반드시 서면으로 작성되어야 하는 것은 아니나, trust의 목적물이 부동산과 같이 Statute of Frauds(SOF)의 적용대상인 경우에는 서면으로 작성되어야만 유효한 trust로 인정된다. 또한 trust는 일반적으로 기한이 별도로 정해져 있지 않아 beneficiary의 이익이 무기한 연기될 수 있는 위험이 있어, 자선 외의 목적을 가진 trust의 trustee는 그 역할 기간이 21년에 한한다(21-year rule).

A. Trusts

★A trust is a fiduciary relationship where the settlor gives legal title the trustee as to certain property.

The trustee is subject to fiduciary duties for the benefits of certain **beneficiaries**, who have equitable rights in the property.

B. Trust Creation

1. Trust Validity (16Feb)

A valid express trust requires:

ⅰ. A definitive **beneficiary**;

ⅱ. Trust **property**;

ⅲ. A valid trust **purpose**;

ⅳ. An **intent** to create a trust; and

ⅴ. A settlor with **capacity**.

TIP1 Trust가 반드시 서면으로 작성되어야 하는 것은 아니나, trust의 목적물이 부동산과 같이 statute of frauds(SOF)의 적용대상인 경우에는 서면으로 작성되어야만 유효한 trust로 인정된다.

The trust is not required to be in writing, unless it is required by the Statute of Frauds.

TIP2 Trustee가 명시되어 있지 않거나 trustee로 지목된 자가 거절하는 경우에도 여전히 유효한 trust이다. Trustee가 명시되어 있지 않은 경우에는 법원에서 지명(appoint)한다.

When a trustee is not named in the trust, the court will appoint one.

Trust에 관한 답안은 "trust validity"에 대한 내용으로 시작되어야 한다.

★A trust is fiduciary relationship where the settlor gives legal title the trustee as to certain property. The trustee is subject to fiduciary duties for the benefits of certain beneficiaries, who have equitable rights in the property. A valid express trust requires: (1) a definitive beneficiary; (2) trust property; (3) a valid trust purpose; (4) an intent to create a trust; and (5) a settlor with capacity.

(ANALYSIS: In this case, 을 is a beneficiary and 갑's house and 10억 are trust property. There is no fact indicating invalid trust purpose and 갑 had an intent to create his trust with capacity. Thus, the trust is valid.)

2. Other Limitations

a. Real Property

A trust for real property must be **in writing and signed** either by the trustee or the trustee's agent.

b. Personal Property

An oral trust for personal property may be established only by clear and convincing evidence.

c. 21-Year Rule

A trustee may perform **only for 21 years as a trustee** for a non-charitable purpose or unincorporated society. This rule applies regardless of the terms of the trust.

C. Types of Trusts

Trust의 유형은 '생성시점'을 기준으로 inter-vivos trust와 testamentary trust, '수정 및 종료 가능 여부'를 기준으로 revocable trust와 irrevocable trust로 구분된다. 이 중 revocable trust와 irrevocable trust로 구분하는 것이 중요한데, 이는 유형에 따라 trust의 성격이 달라 trust 수정 등 trust의 시행에 있어

많은 영향을 미치기 때문이다. 일반적으로 settlor가 trust의 유형을 명시하나, 그렇지 않은 경우 캘리포니아 주에서는 revocable하다고 본다. 위 네 유형의 trust 외에도 trust의 성격에 따라 다양한 trust가 존재하는데, settlor의 사후 (死後)에 효력이 발생하는 pour-over trust, trustee에게 재량권이 인정되는 discretionary trust, beneficiary의 기본적 생활수준을 돕기 위해 설계된 support trust, will상 특정인에게 증여하였으나 실제로는 그 특정인이 상속인 이 아닌 trustee인 secret trust 등이 있다.

1. Inter-Vivos Trust and Testamentary Trust (16Feb)

Inter-vivos trust는 "living trust"라고도 일컬으며, 작성자가 생전에 작성 하는 trust로서 작성 당시 trust가 실행될 시점이 정해진다. 즉, inter-vivos trust는 trust가 작성된 후 바로 실행될 수도 있고, 작성자가 사망한 이후에 실행될 수도 있다. 보통은 작성된 후 바로 실행되는 trust를 뜻한다. 한편, testamentary trust는 testator가 will을 작성함과 동시에 생성되는 trust로 서, testator가 '사망한 후'에 실행되는 trust를 뜻한다.

a. Inter-Vivos Trust

An inter-vivos trust is a fiduciary relationship used in estate planning created **during the lifetime of the settlor.** This trust has a duration that is determined **at the time of the trust's creation** and can entail^{수반하다} the distribution of assets to the beneficiary during or after the trustor's lifetime.

b. Testamentary Trust

Testamentary trust is created **through the provisions of a settlor's will,** and does not take effect **until the settlor's death.**

2. Revocable Trust and Irrevocable Trust (16Feb)

Trust는 수정 및 종료 가능 여부를 기준으로 revocable trust와 irrevocable trust로 구분된다. Revocable trust는 수정 및 종료가 가능한 trust를 의미 하는 반면, irrevocable trust는 수정 및 종료가 불가한 trust를 뜻한다. 캘 리포니아 주는 settlor가 별도의 언급을 명시하지 않는 한 revocable trust

로 보는 소수설을 취하고 있으며, 만일 settlor가 revocation의 요건을 명시하였다면 해당 요건을 만족해야만 revocation이 인정된다. Revocation 요건을 만족하지 못한 경우에는 최초로 작성한 trust에 의거한다. 한편, irrevocable trust일지라도 모든 income beneficiaries가 competent한 상태에서 trust를 종료하는 것에 동의하고 trust의 종료가 trust의 목적을 좌절시키지 않는 경우에는 trust가 종료될 수 있다.

a. General Rule

★Under the minority, including California, a trust is **revocable** unless stated otherwise.

★**A power to revoke includes the power to amend.**

If there is specific instructions for revoking in a trust, a revocation is valid only when the instructions are followed.

✔ "It is revocable in writing by a document signed by co-trustees and delivered to co-trustees."

b. Amendment of Revocable Trust

Revocable trusts can be amendment or terminated by any procedures or methods for amendment specified in the trust agreement.

If there are no specified procedures, revocable trusts can be amended or terminated by the statement signed by the settlor and delivered to the trustee.

c. Amendment of Irrevocable Trust

ⅰ. By Beneficiary

Irrevocable trusts can be amended or terminated **by beneficiary** when:

① All beneficiaries are **competent;**

② They **unanimously consent;** and

③ The termination does **not frustrate trust purpose.**

[표 4-1] Irrevocable trust

By Whom	How
Trustee	**no** power to terminate
Beneficiary	요건×3
Court	when purpose becomes impossible/illegal/frustrated

3. Pour-Over Trusts

Pour-over trust는 위탁자(settlor)가 사망 시 자산을 분배하도록 설계된 trust를 뜻한다. 일반적으로 위탁자의 will에 pour-over trust를 인용하는 형태의 case가 출제된다. 즉, settlor가 '이미 생성되어 있는' trust를 자신의 will에 인용하는 방법으로 생성되는데, 이는 settlor가 will 작성 시 생성되는 trust인 testamentary trust와는 trust 생성 시점에서 차이가 있다. Pour-over provision의 전형적인 case는 다음과 같다. Settlor가 생전에 inter-vivos trust이면서 amendable trust를 작성한 후, will을 작성한다. Will에 "내 probate estate를 trust principal로 넣겠다"는 내용을 삽입한다. 그 이후 will에 삽입된 trust를 amend한다. 이 경우, settlor가 사망하면 어떤 trust의 내용에 따라 유산을 분배해야 하는가. Settlor가 자신의 자산을 trust에 투자할 때, 모든 자산을 trust에 투자해야 하는 것은 아니지만, 보통은 모든 자산을 trust에 pour하는 case로 출제된다. Will에 trust를 인용하는 것은 will이 아닌 문서를 인용하는 것이므로, incorporation by reference doctrine이 적용된다.

A pour-over trust is a trust that is structured to receive and dispose of assets at the settlor's death.

4. Discretionary Trusts

Discretionary trusts란, 수탁자(trustee)에게 재량권이 주어지는 trust를 의미한다. 따라서 discretionary trust의 trustee는 trust의 모든 운영 및 분배에 관해 재량권을 가지고 있다.

In discretionary trusts, **a trustee** has discretion to distribute or withhold payments, principal, or income to the beneficiary.

5. Support Trusts

Support trusts란, settlor가 beneficiary의 기본적인 생활수준 유지를 돕기 (support) 위해 설계한 trust로서 beneficiary의 생활비뿐만 아니라 건강, 교육 등에 관한 비용도 지급가능하다. Beneficiary의 채권자는 beneficiary 가 본 trust로부터 영위하는 혜택에 대해 채권을 주장할 수는 있으나, 그 채권 주장의 정도가 beneficiary의 생활수준 유지를 방해하지 않는 선으로 제한되어 있다.

A support trust is a trust to pay for the beneficiary's support, health, maintenance, or education.
A creditor of beneficiary cannot access to the distributions to the extent it would interfere with the support.

6. Secret Trust

Secret trust란, settlor(갑)가 will을 통해 특정인(을)에게 자산을 증여하였 으나 실제로는 그 특정인(을)이 상속인이 아닌 trustee인 경우의 trust를 뜻한다. 갑이 will상 을에게 자산을 증여하고, 해당 will을 작성하기 전 갑 과 을간 을이 trustee의 역할을 하도록 협의한 경우 secret trust가 인정된 다. 따라서 을은 갑 생전에 trustee로서 해당 자산을 관리하다가 갑이 사 망하면 해당 자산을 수익자에게 배분한다. 즉, secret trust란 settlor가 will 상 trust의 존재 및 trust 자산에 대해 언급하지 않고 secret하게 유지하는 trust를 뜻한다. 한편, half secret trust는 settlor가 will상 trust의 존재는 언 급하였으나 trust beneficiary는 명시하지 않은 형태의 trust를 뜻한다. 예 컨대, settlor 갑이 자신의 will에 "I leave 15억 to 을 to act as a trustee." 라고 작성하였다면, 을이 trustee임을 명시하였으나 trust상의 beneficiary 를 secret하게 유지하였으므로 half secret trust라 할 수 있다.

a. Secret Trust

- Secret trust = Full secret trust

A secret trust is created when there is a settlor's gift to the beneficiary on the face of settlor's will **without indicating an intent to create a trust** in the will, but trust is created relied on a **promise** that the trust beneficiary will hold the property for another.

b. Half Secret Trust

- Half secret trust = Semi-secret trust

A half secret trust is created when the settlor's gift on trust is on the face of settlor's will, but **the identity of the trust beneficiary is kept in secret** and is communicated to the secret trustee.

II. Fiduciary Duties (14July, 16Feb)

Trust는 trustee와 settlor간 형성된 fiduciary relationship으로서, trustee는 beneficiary에게 신의칙의 의무(fiduciary duty)를 진다. 만일 trustee가 한 명 이상인 경우에는 trustee간에도 신의칙의 의무가 인정된다. 따라서 trustee의 신의칙의무 위반에 대해 beneficiary 또는 타 co-trustee는 의무를 위반한 trustee를 상대로 소송을 제기하거나 그의 지위를 박탈할 수 있다. Fiduciary duty는 크게 duty of care와 duty of loyalty 이렇게 구분되며, 각 duty는 세부적인 의무들을 포함하고 있다. Duty of care는 trustee가 trust를 운영하는 데 있어 합리적으로 행동할 것을 요구하며, duty of loyalty는 beneficiary의 최대 이익을 위해 행동할 것을 요구한다.

★A trustee owes fiduciary duties to the beneficiaries of a trust.
A beneficiary or a trustee (co-trustee) may bring a suit against a trustee who breaches the fiduciary duties, and may remove the trustee from his

position.

A. Duty of Care

1. General Rule

★Under the duty of care, a trustee must act as a **reasonable prudent person** when he deals with trust affairs.

2. Duty to Investigate and Duty to Diversify

★Under the prudent investor rule, a trustee owes duty to **investigate** any investment and duty to **diversify** investments.

Under the common law, the trustee's performance is measured based on the statutory lists of good investments. Under the Uniform Prudent Investor Act (UPIA), **trust portfolio** is used to measure the performance.

✔ Investing all assets in ABC stock — violate the duty to diversify
✔ Sell all assets and invest the proceeds in one building — violate the duty to diversify

3. Duty to Account and Inform

A trustee owes duty to account and inform the beneficiaries regarding income and expenses of the trust.

4. Duty to Segregate

★A trustee must **segregate**^{분리하다} trust funds with his own funds and should **not commingle** them.

5. Duty to Defend

A trustee must defend actions resulting in a loss to the trust and raise claims.

B. Duty of Loyalty

A trustee owes duty of loyalty to act **in the best interest of beneficiaries.**

1. Duty to avoid Self-Dealing

A trustee cannot engage in self-dealing. ★A trustee should not use the trust asset **for his own benefits.**

Under the "no further inquiry" rule, there is no need to inquire into the motivation for the self-dealing transaction or even its fairness.

Any trust beneficiary can cause a self-dealing purchase by a trustee to be **set aside** (**rescind** the contract) or obtain a **damages award.**

✔ Trust asset으로 trustee 자신이 소유한 빌딩을 매입한 경우 — self-dealing (violate the duty of loyalty)

✔ Trustee가 rent fee 없이 거주하고 있는 집을 trust asset으로 매입한 경우 — self-dealing (violate the duty of loyalty)

✔ Trustee가 trust asset인 부동산을 개인적으로 매입하는 경우 — self-dealing (violate the duty of loyalty)

a. Set Aside

If a beneficiary elects to set aside (rescind) the transaction, the trust property purchased by the trustee is returned to the trust and the amount the trustee paid for the property is refunded by the trust.

b. Damages Award

$$(fair\ mkt\ value) - (trustee's\ purchase\ \$)$$

If a beneficiary seeks damages, those damages are based on the difference in the fair market value of the trust assets at the time of the self-dealing transaction and the amount paid by the trustee.

2. Duty to Avoid Conflicts of Interest

A conflict of interest occurs when the trustee acts on behalf of others to whom the trustee also owes obligations.

A trustee owes beneficiaries duty to avoid conflicts of interest.

3. Duty to Act Fairly

A trustee should act **fairly and impartially** towards **all beneficiaries.** The trustee should **not favor one** beneficiary in investment or distribution. If a duty to act fairly is breached, a **constructive trust** is allowed for the interest of favored beneficiary.

> **case**

갑's testamentary trust: "나의 집에 대한 rent income to 을 for life, then to 병." 갑이 지정한 trustee인 정이 갑 사망 후 3년 후 을과 병이 모두 생존한 시점에 집을 적정한 금액에 판매했다. What duties, if nay, has 정 violated as trustee of the trust?

⇒ 갑의 trust에서 을은 present beneficiary, 병은 remainderman이다. 정은 을과 병을 공평히 대우할 의무가 있다. 즉, 을과 병의 interest를 적절히 균형을 이루도록(balance) 하여야 하는데, 정이 trust asset인 집을 판매함으로써 병의 interest가 완전히 소멸하게 되었다. 따라서 정은 breached the duty to be impartial이다.

C. Remedies (14July, 16Feb)

Trustee가 신의칙 의무를 위반한 경우, beneficiary의 구제로는 손해배상 (damages) 청구, constructive trust, equitable lien 등 다양한 방법이 있다. 본 내용은 「5장 Remedies」에서의 내용과 동일하나, trustee의 breach of fiduciary duty에 대한 remedy만을 설명한다. 손해배상액(damages)은 상황에 따라 beneficiary의 손실 등을 고려하여 산정되는데, trustee가 self-dealing을 한 경우에는 시세(fair market value)와 trustee가 trust property를 매입한 금

액의 차액으로 산정한다. 한편, trustee는 자신의 breach of fiduciary duty를 주장하는 beneficiary를 상대로 laches, unclean hands 등의 equitable defenses를 주장할 수 있다.

1. General Rule

There are several remedy options for breach of trust:

ⅰ. Damages;

ⅱ. **A constructive trust;**

ⅲ. Equitable lien on the property;

ⅳ. Ratification and waiver of the breach;

ⅴ. **Set aside (rescind);**

ⅵ. Suit for resulting loss(추가적인 손해);

ⅶ. **Removal of the trustee;** and

ⅷ. **Tracing and retrieve assets.**

a. Constructive Trusts

Constructive trust는 법원이 가상으로 생성한 trust이다. Trustee의 breach of fiduciary duty를 통해 누군가 부당이득으로(unjustly enrichment) trust property를 취득하게 된 경우 해당 자산을 constructive trust의 asset로, 부당이득으로 취득한 자를 해당 자산을 관리하는 trustee로 봄으로써, 해당 자산의 본래 소유자, 즉 beneficiary를 보호하는 equitable remedy의 일종이다.

★A constructive trust is one of **equitable restitutions** by requiring the defendant to transfer title/interest back to the plaintiff. It is a remedy to **prevent unjust enrichment** when:

ⅰ. Self-dealing or breach of fiduciary duty occurs;

ⅱ. Fraud in the inducement or undue influence occurs;

ⅲ. Secret trusts are involved; or

ⅳ. Oral real estate trusts are created.

✔ When a wrongful transfer of property is made to a third party **who knows** he receives trust property, the third party holds the property **as a constructive trustee** and is **liable for any losses** to the trust.

✔ Conservator가 자신이 settlor의 유산을 상속받는다는 내용으로 새로운 will을 작성하였고 본 내용이 settlor의 intent와 충돌하는 경우, 새로운 will은 유효하나 법원은 conservator의 breach of fiduciary duty를 이유로 새로운 will의 beneficiary가 받은 자산에 대해 constructive trust를 생성할 수 있다.

b. Equitable Lien

Equitable lien은 법원이 가상으로 생성한 security interest로서, 기본적인 법리는 constructive trust와 유사하다. 이는 trustee가 부당이득으로(unjustly enrichment) 취득한 자산을 beneficiary에 대한 채무의 '담보'로 봄으로써, 해당 자산의 본래 소유자, 즉 beneficiary를 보호하는 equitable remedy의 일종이다.

Equitable lien makes property act as collateral for the money owed to the plaintiff. In other words, equitable lien creates a security interest in property held by the defendant.

c. Ratification

본래 ratification이란, agent가 authority 없는 상태에서 계약을 체결했고 그 이후에도 authority가 생기지 않았지만 principal이 그 계약의 존재를 인지한 후 agent의 권한과 관계없이 계약을 승인 및 재가(裁可)하는 것을 뜻한다. Trust 과목에서 본 개념은 trustee가 신의칙 의무를 위반하였다 하더라도 settlor 및 beneficiary가 trustee의 행위를 승인 및 재가하여 그의 breach에 대한 책임을 면제(waive)하는 것을 뜻한다.

Ratification occurs when an agent took action without authority, and the principal **subsequently approves** the action **with capacity and full knowledge of material terms.**

Agent is no longer liable once ratification occurs.

d. Set Aside (Rescind)

When a wrongful transfer of property is made **not** to a bona fide purchaser, the beneficiary can **set aside (rescind)** the transaction.

When a wrongful transfer of property is made to a **bona fide purchaser,** it **cuts off** the beneficiary's interest.

e. Tracing and Retrieve

When self-dealing occurred and assets are invested, the beneficiary can trace the trust property and retrieve them for the benefit of the trust.

2. Trustee's Defense

When beneficiaries bring a suit against the trustee for the breach of fiduciary duty, the trustee may argue **equitable defenses,** such as laches and unclean hands.

a. Laches

Laches^{태만} defense arises when a party (beneficiaries) **delays** in bringing an equitable action and the delay causes **prejudice** on the defendant.

If the delay did **not** cause any **harm to the defendant (trustee),** laches defense is **unavailable.**

b. Unclean Hands

The unclean hands arises when a beneficiary is engaged in **wrongdoing related to the contract.**

Breach of fiduciary duty

---

1. Trust validity★
2. Fiduciary duty 기본 rule
   + analysis
3. Breach된 fiduciary duty
   + analysis
4. Remedies
   + analysis
5. Defenses★
   + analysis

TIP1   Trust에 관한 답안은 "trust validity"에 대한 내용으로 시작되어야 한다.

TIP2   2번 analysis: Trustee의 breach of fiduciary duty를 주장하는 자에게 그러한 주장을 할 수 있는 권리가 있는지 그 여부를 판단한다.

TIP3   3번: 주어진 사안에서 trustee가 '위반한 fiduciary duty'를 title화하여 작성한다.

TIP4   별도의 문제가 출제되지 않았다 하더라도 trustee가 주장할 수 있는 defenses에 대해 판단하는 것이 고득점 포인트다.

모범답안 016

Trust validity

A trust is fiduciary relationship where the settlor gives legal title the trustee as to certain property. The trustee is subject to fiduciary duties for the benefits of certain beneficiaries, who have equitable rights in the property. A valid express trust requires: (1) a definitive beneficiary; (2) trust property; (3) a valid trust purpose; (4) an intent to create a trust; and (5) a settlor with capacity.

(ANALYSIS: In this case, 을 is a beneficiary and 갑's house and 10억 are trust property. There is no fact indicating invalid trust purpose and 갑 had an intent to create his trust with capacity. Thus, the trust is valid.)

Fiduciary duty

A trustee owes fiduciary duties to the beneficiaries of a trust. A beneficiary or a trustee (co-trustee) may bring a suit against a trustee who breaches the fiduciary duties, and may remove the trustee from his position. (ANALYSIS: In this case, 을 may bring a suit against the trustee 병.)

Breach of fiduciary duties

(1) Duty to investigate and duty to diversify

Under the duty of care, a trustee must act as a reasonable prudent person when he deals with trust affairs. Under the prudent investor rule, a trustee owes duty to investigate any investment and duty to diversify investments.

(ANALYSIS: In this case, 병 sold all trust property and bought ABC stock using the proceeds. His action was not an act that a reasonable prudent person would do. He did not diversify investments. Thus, 병 breached the duty to investigate and duty to diversify.)

(2) Duty to avoid self-dealing

A trustee cannot engage in self-dealing. A trustee should not use the trust asset for his own benefits. Under the no further inquiry rule, there is no need to inquire into the motivation for the self-dealing transaction or even its fairness.

(ANALYSIS: In this case, ······.)

Remedies

For the breach of fiduciary duties mentioned above, 을 can bring a suit against 병. Any trust beneficiary can cause a self-dealing purchase by a trustee to be set aside (rescind the contract) or obtain a damages award.

(1) Set aside

If a beneficiary elects to set aside (rescind) the transaction, the trust property purchased by the trustee is returned to the trust and the amount the trustee paid for the property is refunded by the trust.

(ANALYSIS: In this case, 을 may rescind the contract 병 made and 병 would return the building to the trust and the trust would pay 8억 to 병.)

(2) Damages

If a beneficiary seeks damages, those damages are based on the difference in the fair market value of the trust assets at the time of the self-dealing transaction and the amount paid by the trustee.

(ANALYSIS: In this case, 을 may seek 2억 (10억-8억) as damages.)

Defenses

When beneficiaries bring a suit against the trustee for the breach of fiduciary duty, the trustee may argue equitable defenses, such as laches and unclean hands.

(ANALYSIS: In this case, there are no facts indicating that equitable defenses are applicable.)

Conclusion

In conclusion, the trustee 병 breached the duty to investigate and duty to diversify, and the duty to avoid self-dealing. There are no applicable defenses and the beneficiary을 may bring a suit against 병.

Ⅲ. Rules Regarding Execution

A. Cy Pres Doctrine (15Feb)

Cy Pres는 "as near as possible"이라는 뜻을 가진 용어이며, cy pres doctrine 은 trust에 '기부의 목적'으로 사용될 trust asset, 즉 charitable trust의 asset을 settlor가 trust에 명시한 방법으로 운영 및 분배하기 어려운 상황일 경우 해당 trust를 어떻게 처리해야 하는지에 대한 이론이다. 법원이 cy pres power를 행사할 경우, 기부의 목적으로 사용될 trust 자산을 trust에 명시된 방법 이외 의 방법으로 운영 및 분배할 수 있다. Cy pres power 행사 여부는 법원에서

settlor가 trust 작성 시 가지고 있었던 의도(intent)를 기준으로 판단하는 바, general charitable intent를 가지고 있었던 경우에는 trust의 내용을 변경하고 그렇지 않은 경우에는 해당 trust를 settlor의 유산으로 본다. 다시 말해, 본 doctrine은 charitable trust에만 적용되는 doctrine으로서 법원이 settlor가 생성한 trust의 내용을 변경하는 경우에 해당한다.

When the trust property to be used for a **charitable purpose** could not be distributed as directed in the trust, the court determines whether to exercise its cy pres power.

If settlor has a **specific** charitable intention, the property **reverts**^{되돌리다} to the settlor.

If settler has a **general** charitable intention, another substitute can be chosen in consistency with the **settlor's intention**.

B. Conditions of Trust (14July)

1. General Rule

A settlor may make express conditions for distribution of trust interest. When a beneficiary violates the condition of the trust, the trustee **can sue for return** of the income used in violation of the trust terms.

2. Wish v. Condition

In determining whether the terms of a trust is merely showing settlor's wish or is an express condition of distribution, the court considers **totality of the circumstances**.

| 답안요령 | Conditions of trust |

Q: <u>What is the result of 병's suit against 을?</u>
<u>갑이 을을 beneficiary, 병을 trustee로 하는 trust를 생성했다. 이후 trust interest가 을에게 지급되었고, 병은 을이 해당 interest를 사용하는데 있어</u>

조건을 만족하지 못했음을 근거로 을을 상대로 소송을 제기하였다. 병의 승소가능성에 대해 논하라.

---

1. Trust validity★
2. Express conditions에 대한 기본 rule
3. Wish v. Condition
   + analysis★
4. 결론(remedy)

TIP1 Trust에 관한 답안은 "trust validity"에 대한 내용으로 시작되어야 한다.

TIP2 Arguable point: Beneficiary는 trust상 문구가 단순히 settlor's wish에 불과하다고 주장할 것이나, 이에 대해 trustee는 express condition임을 주장하여 beneficiary에게 수익반환을 요구할 것이다.

TIP3 Settlor 사망 후 trust에 의거하여 모든 trust property가 beneficiary에게 지급되는 경우, beneficiary는 express condition이 아닌 settlor's wish임을 주장할 것이다.

모범답안 017

1. What is the result of 병's suit against 을?

Trust validity

A trust is fiduciary relationship where the settlor gives legal title the trustee as to certain property. The trustee is subject to fiduciary duties for the benefits of certain beneficiaries, who have equitable rights in the property. A valid express trust requires: (1) a definitive beneficiary; (2) trust property; (3) a valid trust purpose; (4) an intent to create a trust; and (5) a settlor with capacity.

(ANALYSIS: In this case, 을 is a beneficiary and 갑's house and 10억 are trust property. There is no fact indicating an invalid trust purpose and 갑 had an intent to create his trust with capacity. Thus, the trust is valid.)

Express conditions

A settlor may make express conditions for distribution of trust interest.

(ANALYSIS: In this case, the settlor, 갑 directed that the trust income to be paid to 을 to be spend only for her education.)

Wish v. Condition

In determining whether the terms of a trust is merely showing settlor's wish or is an express condition of distribution, the court considers totality of the circumstances.

(ANALYSIS: In this case, 을 may argue that the terms of the trust is merely a general wish of 갑. At 갑's death, 을 may receive all trust principal and income and she is entitled to use the funds as she wants. However, trustee 병 may argue that the terms of the trust expressly limit the use of funds. In sum, the court likely determines that the terms of the trust is an express condition of distribution and 을 violated the condition.)

Conclusion

In conclusion, 을 violated the condition and the trustee 병 can sue for return of the income used in violation of the trust terms.

C. Creditor's Rights (19Feb)

Settlor 및 beneficiary의 채권자는 trust property에 대해 채권을 행사할 수 있는가. 이는 trust상 '채무자의 권리'를 기준으로 판단되는 바, 채권자는 채무자가 trust에 대해 가지고 있는 권리에 한해 채권을 행사할 수 있다. Settlor의 경우, 자신이 작성한 trust의 성격에 따라 trust에 대한 settlor의 권리 범위가 다르다. Revocable trust의 경우, settlor는 자신이 작성한 trust에 대해 제한 없는 권리를 가지는 바, settlor의 채권자는 trust property 전체에 대해 채권을 행사할 수 있다. 다만, settlor가 사망하면 사망 시점을 기준으로 trust는 irrevocable한 성격을 띠게 되어 settlor의 채권자는 더 이상 trust property에 대해 채권을 행사할 수 없게 된다. 한편, beneficiary의 채권자는 settlor의 채권자와 마찬가지로 beneficiary가 trust상 가지고 있는 권리, 즉 수익권에 한해 채권을 행사할 수 있다. 예컨대, settlor 갑이 10억을 신탁하였고 이를 운영하는 과정에서의 수익(interest)을 을(beneficiary)에게 for life로 지급하는 경우, 을의 채권자는 10억이 아닌 을에게 지급될 또는 지급된 interest에 한해 채권을 행사할 수 있다. 다만, beneficiary의 권리를 보장하기 위해 trust상 "beneficiary의 채권자는 beneficiary의 이익에 대해 채권을 행사할 수 없다"는 내용의 조항이 명시되어 있는 경우에는 채권자는 beneficiary에게 '지급되어야 하는' 수익에 대해 채권을 행사할 수 없다. 이 같은 조항을 "spendthrift clause"라 일컫는다. 여기서 유의해야 할 점은 spendthrift clause는 '미지급된' beneficiary의 이익에 한해 적용될 뿐, 이미 beneficiary에게 지급된 이익에 대해서는 적용되지 않는다는 것이다. 상기 예시에서 trust상 spendthrift clause가 명시되어 있고 을이 신탁재산의 수익 1천만원을 지급받아야 하는 경우, 을의 채권자는 1천만원에 대해 채권을 행사할 수 없으나, 을이 이미 1천만원을 지급받은 후에는 채권을 행사할 수 있다. 다만, spendthrift clause가 존재한다 하더라도 public policy상 채권자의 채권행사를 제한하기에 무리가 있는 경우에는 채권자의 권리가 보장된다. 채권자가 furnished necessities, 채권자가 양육비를 받아야 하는 아이, alimony를 받을 권리가 있는 전 부인과 같이 법원의 판결 및 명령에 의거한 채권을 가진 자인 경우 등이 이에 해당한다.

1. General Rule

a. Settlor's Creditor

When a settlor has **right to revoke,** creditors of the settlor **can** generally reach the trust assets.

However, upon the settlor's death, creditors cannot reach the trust assets. A revocable inter vivos trust becomes irrevocable, when a settlor died.

b. Beneficiary's Creditor

The beneficiary's creditor can reach **the interest of the beneficiary,** not the trust assets itself.

2. Spendthrift Clause

a. General Rule

★A spendthrift clause restricts the trust beneficiary from transferring his rights to a third party, including creditors of him.

b. Exceptions

However, a creditor **can** reach the beneficiary's income interest when:

  i . A judgment creditor has provided services for the protection of a beneficiary's interest in the trust;

  ii . A creditor **furnished necessaries;**

  iii. There is an order for **child support or alimony;**

  iv. There is a claim by the state or federal government; or

  v . There is a **self-settled trust** where the settlor has an interest.

| 답안요령 | Creditor's right |

```
1. Trust validity★
2. Creditor's right
   + analysis
3. Spendthrift clause
   + analysis
4. Spendthrift clause 예외
   + analysis
```

| TIP1 | Trust에 관한 답안은 "trust validity"에 대한 내용으로 시작되어야 한다.

| TIP2 | Trust 자산에 대해 채권을 주장하는 creditor가 settlor와 beneficiary 중 누구의 creditor인지 확인한다.

① Settlor의 채권자가 채권을 행사하고자 하는 사안인 경우, trust 의 유형(revocable/ irrevocable trust)을 파악한다.

② Beneficiary의 채권자가 채권을 행사하고자 하는 사안인 경우, spendthrift clause를 중점으로 출제된 문제일 가능성이 높다.

| 모범답안 018 |

1. Will 갑's creditor 을 be able to reach the trust assets?

Trust validity

A trust is fiduciary relationship where the settlor gives legal title the trustee as to certain property. The trustee is subject to fiduciary duties for the benefits of certain beneficiaries, who have equitable rights in the property. A valid express trust requires: (1) a definitive beneficiary; (2) trust property; (3) a valid trust purpose; (4) an intent to create a trust; and (5) a settlor with capacity.

(ANALYSIS: In this case, 을 is a beneficiary and 갑's house and 10억 are trust property. There is no fact indicating invalid trust purpose and 갑 had an intent to create his trust with capacity. Thus, the trust is valid.)

Creditor's right

The beneficiary's creditor can reach the interest of the beneficiary, not the trust assets itself.

(ANALYSIS: In this case, the creditor 을 is a creditor of 갑, who is a beneficiary of the trust. Thus, 을 can reach the interest of 갑.)

Spendthrift clause

A spendthrift clause restricts the trust beneficiary from transferring his rights to a third party, including creditors of them.

(ANALYSIS: In this case, there is a spendthrift clause in the trust and 갑 cannot transfer his rights, 1천만원, to his creditor 을. Thus, 을 cannot reach 1천만원.)

Exceptions

However, a creditor can reach the beneficiary's income interest under the public policy. A creditor can reach when: (1) a judgment creditor has provided services for the protection of a beneficiary's interest in the trust; (2) a creditor furnished necessaries; (3) there is an order for child support or alimony; (4) there is a claim by the state or federal government; or (5) there is a self-settled trust where the settlor has an interest.

(ANALYSIS: In this case, 을 is 갑's child and 갑 has child support obligation. Thus, the creditor 을 can reach the 갑's income interest under the public policy.)

Conclusion

In conclusion, 을 can reach 1천만원 although there is a spendthrift clause in the trust. This is because 갑 has child support obligation to 을.

5장
Remedies

//

Remedies는 권리 침해에 대한 법적 '구제방법'을 뜻하는 바, 민사소송에서 원고가 소송을 제기함으로써 구제받을 수 있는 법적 방법에 대해 논한다. 원고가 피고의 채무불이행(breach of contract)에 대해 소송을 제기하는 경우, 위법행위(torts)에 대해 소송을 제기하는 경우, 정부가 제정한 ordinance의 위헌성에 대해 소송을 제기하는 경우, 이 모든 경우에 remedies가 고려된다. 즉, 본 장은 Torts, Contract, Real property 또는 Constitutional law 과목과 연계되어 출제되며, 지난 7년간 두 번째로 자주 출제된 만큼 중요도가 높은 과목 중 하나이다.

Remedies의 유형은 remedy at law, restitution 그리고 remedy in equity로 구분된다. Remedy at law는 금전적인 배상을 뜻하는 바, 손해배상이 이에 해당한다. 다만, 계약당사자간 의도가 계약서에 제대로 반영되지 못한 경우 또는 피고가 위법하게 취득한 자산이 희귀하여 원고가 반드시 돌려받아야 하는 경우 등과 같이 상황상 손해에 대한 금전적 배상이 적합하지 않은 경우가 있다. 이러한 경우 법원은 형평성을 고려한 구제방법을 취하게 되는데, 이를 remedy in equity라고 한다. 계약서를 재작성하도록 명하는 것(reformation), 동산 및 부동산을 원고에게 돌려줄 것을 명하는 것(replevin/ejectment), 작위 또는 부작위를 명하는 것(specific performance/TRO and PI) 등이 해당된다. 한편, restitution은 부당이득(unjust enrichment)에 의해 발생한 손해에 대한 구제방법으로서, legal restitution과 equitable restitution으로 구분된다. 기본적으로 상기 세 유형의 remedies는 모든 소송에서 적용가능하나, 각 소송의 유형별로 적용되는 세부적인 방법에는 다소 차이가 있다.

1. 본 장에 관한 문제는 소송당사자에게 적합한 remedy를 찾거나 주어진 사안에서 소송당사자가 주장하는 remedy의 적합성을 판단토록 요구한다.

   Q: <u>How should the court rule on 갑's claim for relief?</u>

   Q: <u>What is the likelihood of success of 갑's claim, and what defenses can 을 reasonably raise?</u>

   Q: <u>What remedies can 갑 reasonably seek?</u>

   Q: <u>What is the likelihood of 갑's success in obtaining a TRO/PI?</u>

   ① 소송당사자가 remedy를 특정하는 경우

   ⇒ 갑 filed a complaint against 을 for rescission of the contract. What is the likelihood of 갑's success in obtaining rescission?

   ② 소송 당사자의 적합한 remedy를 찾는 문제

   ⇒ 갑 filed a complaint against 을 for fraud. What remedies can 갑 reasonably seek?

   ⇒ Remedy at law, restitution, remedy in equity 중 갑에게 적합한 remedy를 찾는다.

2. Constitutional law와 remedies가 혼합되어 출제되는 경우, ① justiciability, ② remedy 순서로 작성한다.

3. Equitable remedies의 적합성을 판단토록 요구하는 문제가 출제된 경우, ① 해당 equitable remedy와 ② 이에 대한 equitable defenses를 모두 서술한다.

I. Basic Concepts

There are three types of remedy: remedy at law, restitution, and remedy in equity. The plaintiff may choose one of available remedies.

1. Remedy at Law

Remedy at law, which is called as legal remedy, is **money damages** to compensate the plaintiff.

2. Restitution

★Restitution is **to prevent the unjust enrichment.** There are two types of restitution: legal restitution and equitable restitution.

3. Remedy in Equity

a. General Rule

★Remedy in equity is judicial remedy by courts of equity. It is allowed **only when remedy at law is inadequate.**

The court has broad discretion in deciding the award of an equitable remedy. The court will consider the equities of the situation, considering the **fairness** of the remedy to both parties.

b. Equitable Defenses

There are several equitable defenses, such as laches and unclean hands.

[표 5-1]

| | Remedy at Law | Restitution | | Remedy in Equity |
		Legal Restitution	Equitable Restitution	
Contracts	• compensatory damages • expectation damages • consequential damages • incidental damages • reliance damages • liquidated damages • nominal damages	• quasi -contract • replevin • ejectment	• rescission • reformation	• TRO • preliminary injunction • specific performance
Torts	• compensatory damages • pure economic loss • nominal damages • punitive damages	• money restitution • replevin • ejectment	• construc-tive trust • equitable lien	• TRO • preliminary injunction • permanent injunction
Real Property	Torts와 Contracts의 모든 remedies를 동일하게 적용			

Ⅱ. Remedies

A. Remedy at Law

Remedy at law, 즉 monetary damages는 보호되어야 할 법익이 침해된 것에 대한 '금전적 배상'을 뜻하는 바, 구체적으로는 계약법상 채무불이행으로 인한 손해와 Torts상 피고의 위법행위로 인한 손해에 대한 금전적 배상을 의미한다. 계약법상 monetary damages 유형은 원고 및 피고의 상황을 기준으로 compensatory damages, nominal damages, punitive damages 그리고 liquidated damages로 구분된다. Compensatory damages는 채무불이행에 대한 구제 중 가장 보편적인 손해배상이며, nominal damages는 상대방이 계약을 위반하였으나 실질적 손해가 없는 경우의 손해배상, 즉 명목상 손해배상을 의미한다. Punitive damages는 징벌적 손해배상을 뜻하는 바, 계약법상에서는 인정되지 않고 위법행위로 인한 피해에 한해 인정된다. Liquidated damages는 계약을 체결할 당시 계약당사자간 계약위반에 대한 배상액수를 사전에 합의한 바를 그대로 따르는 구제방법으로서, 징벌적 배상의 성격을 띠지 않는 경우에 한해 그 유효성이 인정된다. 한편, compensatory damages는 일반적으로 expectation damages, incidental damages 그리고 consequential damages의 합계에 원고가 계약상 부담해야 할 비용을 뺀 액수로 산정된다. Torts상 monetary damages 유형에는 compensatory damages, pure economic loss, nominal damages 그리고 punitive damages가 있다. Torts상 compensatory damages는 피고의 위법행위로 인해 발생된 원고의 신체적 및 자산적 불이익을 금액으로 산정하여 배상한다. Pure economic loss는 신체 및 자산에 대한 물리적인 피해 없이 발생한 금전적 손해를 뜻한다. Nominal damages와 punitive damages는 앞서 언급된 계약법상 개념과 동일하며, punitive damages는 torts상에서만 인정된다.

1. Compensatory Damages

a. In Contracts

★The compensatory damages is to put the non-breaching party in as good a position as if the other party had fully performed.

Compensatory damages is generally measured by adding expectation damages, incidental, and consequential damages.

  ⅰ. Expectation Damages

★Expectation damages is measured as **the value of the breaching party's performance that was lost.**

  ⅱ. Incidental Damages (UCC2)

★It is recognized **only in UCC2.** Incidental damages means any expenses reasonably incurred by the parties (either seller or buyer) during the performance process.

  ⅲ. Consequential Damages

★Consequential damages are caused by the **non-breaching party's special circumstances.**

★It is recoverable only when:

① **Foreseeable** (proximate causation);

② **Reasonably certain** (damages are not speculative); and

③ **Unavoidable** (plaintiff's duty to mitigate).

  ⅳ. Reliance Damages

★When expectation damages are **too speculative,** non-breaching party may recover reliance damages as the **loss incurred reasonably relying on the contract.**

It is to put the plaintiff in the position **as if the contract had never been made.**

b. In Torts

The compensatory damages is awarded to compensate the plaintiff **for injury or loss.**

2. Nominal Damages

Nominal damages is awarded when there is a breach but **no actual loss.**

3. Punitive Damages (Torts)

Punitive damages is the damages awarded to punish defendant's **wrongful conduct.** It could **not** be awarded in contract cases.

4. Liquidated Damages (Contracts)

Liquidated damages is damages enforced upon the clause of the contract.

★It is admissible only when:

ⅰ. Damages are **difficult to calculate;** and

ⅱ. Damages are **unreasonable** (characterized as **penalty**).

5. Pure Economic Loss (Torts)

Pure economic loss는 신체 및 자산에 대한 물리적인 피해 없이 발생한 금전적 손해를 뜻하며, 본 손해에 대한 배상액은 주로 원고의 지출 (expenditure), 이익의 손실(loss of profit) 등을 포함한다. 이는 torts case 중에서도 negligent misstatement 또는 intentional interference with business relations에 한해 드물게 인정된다. 한편, 본 개념은 물리적인 피해 없이 발생한 금전적 피해라는 점에서 consequential damages와 구별된다. 예컨대, 피고의 negligence로 인해 원고가 다리를 다쳤고 회복하는 동안 수입이 없었다면, loss of earnings는 신체적 피해로 인한 consequential damages로 인정된다.

Pure economic loss is awarded when it is occurred **without** any physical injury or property loss.

Generally, pure economic loss is not recoverable in torts, but in negligent misstatement or intentional interference with business relations cases.

B. Restitution

앞서 언급한 바와 같이, restitution은 부당이득(unjust enrichment)에 의해 발

생한 손해에 대한 구제방법으로서, legal restitution과 equitable restitution으로 구분된다.

Restitution is a remedy **to prevent unjust enrichment.**
There are two types of restitution: legal restitution and equitable restitution.

1. Legal Restitution

Restitution 유형 중 legal restitution은 quasi-contract, money restitution, replevin 그리고 ejectment를 포함한다. Quasi-contract란, 계약법상에서만 인정되는 구제방법으로서 계약 성립요건(offer, acceptance, consideration)을 만족하지 못하였으나 부당이득을 얻은 자가 있으므로 법원이 인정하는 가상의 계약이다. 즉, 양자의 합의는 없었으나 공정성(fairness)을 위해 계약이 체결되었다고 보고, 법원이 부당이득을 본 자에게 상대방에 대한 배상을 하도록 명한다. 그 배상액은 부당이득의 가치 또는 해당 이득을 제공하는데 있어 든 비용으로 산정된다. Money restitution은 quasi-contract와 동일한 법리에 따른 개념으로서 Torts에서 인정하는 구제방법이다. Replevin과 ejectment는 부당이득으로 취한 동산 및 부동산을 원고에게 돌려주는 구제방법을 뜻하는 바, replevin은 원고에게 동산을 돌려주는 방법이고 ejectment는 부동산을 돌려주는 구제방법이다.

a. Quasi-Contract (Contracts)
• Action in quasi-contract = Action for an implied in law contract
= Action for quantum meruit

Quasi-contract is recognized when a party has **derived a benefit from no legally binding contract.**
Generally, it is measured by the **value of the benefit conferred or the cost in conferring the benefit.**

✔ 계약당사자간 체결한 실제 금액(서비스비)은 무관하다.

⇒ Arguable point: 피고는 계약당사자간 체결한 계약상 서비스비인 $5,000로 배상액을 산정해야 한다고 주장할 것이나, 계약당사자간 체결한 실제 금액은 무관하며, 배상액은 원고가 제공한 benefit의 가치 또는 benefit을 제공하는데 있어 든 비용으로 산정된다. The defendant may argue that the damages should be measured as $5,000 under the contract between the parties. However, the damages is measured by the value of the benefit conferred or the cost in conferring the benefit. Thus, the plaintiff would recover $8,000.

b. Money Restitution (Torts)

It is measured by the **value of the benefit conferred.**

c. Replevin

Replevin allows the plaintiff to recover a specific **personal property** which was wrongfully taken from the plaintiff.

d. Ejectment

Ejectment allows the plaintiff to recover specific **real property** which was wrongfully taken from the plaintiff.

2. Equitable Restitution

Equitable restitution은 피고의 부당이득(unjust enrichment)에 대해 형평법상 인정되는 구제수단이다. 이는 다른 equitable remedies와 마찬가지로 remedies at law를 적용하기 부적합한 경우에 한해 채택된다.

계약법상 equitable restitution 유형에는 당사자의 본래 의도를 반영하여 새롭게 계약을 체결하는 reformation과 당사자간 체결한 기존의 계약을 무효화하는 rescission이 있다. 일반적으로 reformation은 계약을 지속적으로 유지시키고자 하는 측이 주장하는 remedy인 반면, rescission은 계약을 더 이상 유지시키고 싶지 않은 측이 주장하는 remedy이다. 예컨대, 갑이 을에게 부동산을 매매하는 과정에서 주차장을 사용할 수 있다고 언급하였으나 계약을 체결한 후 알고 보니 주차장을 사용할 수 없고 해당 부동산이 을에게 더 이상 가치가 없다면 을은 rescission을 주장할 것이다. 보험회사와 피보험자간 계약서상 보장액이 실제 금액보다 낮게 반영되어 있는 경우, 보험회사는 rescission을 주장하는 반면 피보험자는 reformation을 주장할 것이다.

한편, torts case에서는 피고가 부당이득으로 취득한 자산을 trust asset로 보는 constructive trust와 담보로 보는 equitable lien을 생성하는 remedy를 취한다. Constructive trust는 법원이 가상으로 생성한 trust이다. 피고가 부당이득으로(unjustly enrichment) 취득한 자산은 constructive trust의 asset로, 피고를 해당 자산을 관리하는 trustee로 봄으로써, 해당 자산의 본래 소유자를 보호하고자 하는 equitable remedy의 일종이다. 예컨대, 갑이 을에게 3억을 맡겼으나 을이 이를 자동차를 구입하는데 사용한 경우(embezzlement), 법원은 constructive trust가 생성되었다고 보고 을을 자동차를 관리하는 trustee로 본다. 을이 갑에게 3억을 변제하거나 해당 자동차의 title을 갑에게 이전하면 constructive trust는 종료되며, 종료되기 이전까지 발생한 interest는 모두 갑에게 귀속된다. Equitable lien은 법원이 가상으로 생성한 security interest로서, 기본적인 법리는 constructive trust와 유사하다. 이는 피고가 부당이득으로(unjustly enrichment) 취득한 자산을 원고에 대한 피고의 채무의 담보로 봄으로써, 해당 자산의 본래 소유자를 보호하고자 하는 equitable remedy의 일종이다. 상기 예시에서 갑이 을에게 3억을 맡겼으나 을이 이를 자동차를 구입하는데 사용한 경우, 법원은 equitable lien이 생성되었다고 보고 해당 자동차를 을이 갑에게 가진 채무 3억에 대한 담보로 본다. 을이 갑에게 3억을 변제하거나 해당 자동차의 title을 갑에게 이전하면 equitable lien은 종료된다.

Equitable restitution은 equitable remedy로서 equitable defenses가 적용되는 바, non-moving party는 moving party(equitable restitution을 주장하는 측)의 laches, unclean hands 등을 주장할 수 있다. Parol evidence rule은 equitable defense가 아니나, 상대방의 equitable restitution 주장에 대해 사용될 가능성이 높은 항변사유로서 본 파트에 그 내용을 실었다. 다만, 사안에 적용하다보면 rule의 예외에 해당되는 경우가 많아 본 defense가 받아들여지는 경우는 극히 드물다.

a. Reformation (Contracts)

Reformation is the court's order **to rewrite a contract** reflecting the true agreement of the parties.

b. Rescission (Contracts)

Rescission is the court's order to **make a contract invalid** and make the parties left as a contract **had never been made (is discharged).** When the original contract is voidable and rescinded, rescission remedy can be recovered.

Generally, it is available when a party has a valid **defense to the formation,** such as fraud, mistake, illegality, and unconscionability.

c. Constructive Trust (Torts)

Constructive trust is a trust made by a court where **the defendant acts as trustee** for the unjustly obtained property.

It is to order the defendant to convey title of unjustly obtained property to the plaintiff.

d. Equitable Lien (Torts)

Equitable lien is a security interest made by a court where **the property acts as collateral** for the money owned to the plaintiff.

It is to order the defendant to convey title of unjustly obtained property to the plaintiff.

e. Equitable Defenses

   i . Laches

      • Laches^{태만} = Aacquiescence^{묵인}

Laches defense arises when a party **delays** in bringing an equitable action and the delay causes prejudice on the defendant.

If the delay did **not** cause any **harm to the defendant,** laches defense is **unavailable.**

Arguable point: 을(피고)은 갑(원고)이 당사자간 mutual mistake를 쉽게 발견할 수 있는 위치에 있었음에도 reformation 신청에 태만 했다고 주장할 것이다. 이에 갑은 mutual mistake에 대해 인지하지 못했음을 주장할 것이다. 법원은 을도 계약당사자 중 한 명으로서 해당 mutual mistake를 쉽게 발견할 수 있었으며, 갑의 태만으로 인한 을의 불이익이 발생하지 않았음을 근거로 을의 laches 주장을 받아들이지 않을 것이다.

을 may raise laches defense, arguing that 갑 easily could have become aware of the mutual mistake, but he delayed in bringing a reformation action. 갑 may argue that he was unaware of the mutual mistake. 을's argument will fail. 을 was a party of the contract who reduced the contract and he was able to discover the mistake. Moreover, the delay did not cause any harm to 을 and therefore laches defense is unavailable.

ii. Unclean Hands

The unclean hands arises when the party seeking equitable remedies is engaged in **wrongdoing related to the contract.**

iii. Parol Evidence Rule

★Under the parol evidence rule, the parties **cannot** provide **extrinsic evidence** of prior agreements that is **inconsistent** with the contract terms when there is a **written** contract which is **finally expressed and is a complete integration.**

However, such evidence **is** allowed when it is to prove **mistake, clerical errors, or fraud.**

TIP 당사자간 의도한 바가 계약서에 온전히 반영되지 못하여 당사자 중 일방이 equitable restitution을 주장하는 경우, parol evidence rule 에 대한 arguable point를 언급하는 것이 고득점 포인트다.

✔ 갑이 을에게 부동산을 매매하는 과정에서 주차장을 사용할 수 있다고 언급하였으나, 계약을 체결한 후 알고 보니 주차장을 사용할 수 없는 상황이었고 해당 부동산이 을에게 더 이상 가치가 없다면 을은 rescission을 주장할 것이다. 이때 을은 갑이 계약체결 전 언급한 "주차장을 사용할 수 있다"는 진술을 증거로 제출하여 갑의 fraud에 근거한 rescission을 주장할 것이다. 이에 대해 갑은 해당 증거는 parol evidence rule에 위배된다고 주장할 수도 있으나, 계약체결 전 합의 내용을 fraud 입증을 위해 제출하는 parol evidence rule의 예외에 해당되는 바, 갑의 defense(parol evidence rule)는 받아들여질 수 없다. 즉, 을의 증거는 admissible하다.

갑 may argue that 을 cannot use his statement under the parol evidence rule. Under the rule, the parties cannot provide extrinsic evidence of prior agreements that is inconsistent with the contract terms when there is a written contract which is finally expressed and is a complete integration. However, the statement is used **to prove fraud** and it falls within the exception. Thus, 갑's argument will fail and the evidence is admissible.

✔ 갑은 1,000개의 창고를 소유하고 있으며, 그중 25번째 창고를 을에게 매매하기로 하였다. 하지만 갑 비서의 실수로 양자간 계약서에는 35번째 창고로 기입되었고, 이에 대해 을은 reformation을 주장하며 계약 체결 전 갑이 을에게 언급한 "25번째 창고를 판매하겠다."는 진술을 증거로 제출하였다. 이에 갑은 해당 증거는 parol evidence rule에 위배된다고 주장할 가능성이 있으나, 계약체결 전 합의 내용을 mistake 입증을 위해 제출하는 parol evidence rule의 예외에 해당되는 바, 갑의 defense(parol evidence rule)는 받아들여질 수 없다. 즉, 을의 증거는 admissible하다.

갑 may argue that 을 cannot use his statement under the parol evidence rule. Under the rule, the parties cannot provide extrinsic evidence of prior agreements that is inconsistent with the contract terms when there is a written contract which is finally expressed and is a complete integration. However, the statement is used **to prove mistake** and it falls within the exception. Thus, 갑's argument will fail and the evidence is admissible.

✔ 피보험자 갑과 보험회사 ABC간 $20,000을 한도로 보장하는 보험계약을 체결하였다. 이후 갑의 요청으로 해당 계약의 보장액을 $70,000로 변경하고자 하였으나, ABC 직원의 실수로 보험계약서상 보장액이 $50,000로 기입되었다. 이후 갑에게 교통사고가 발생하자 ABC는 계약서상 내용에 따라 $50,000를 지급하겠다고 밝혔다. 이에 대해 갑은 계약 수정 전 양자간 합의된 내용("$70,000 보장액")에 대한 증거를 근거로 reformation을 주장하였다. ABC는 해당 증거는 parol evidence rule에 위배된다고 주장할 가능성이 있으나, 계약체결 전 합의 내용을 mistake 입증을 위해 제출하는 parol evidence rule의 예외에 해당되는 바, ABC의 defense(parol evidence rule)는 받아들여질 수 없다. 즉, 갑의 증거는 admissible하다.

ABC may argue that 갑 cannot use his statement under the parol evidence rule. Under the rule, the parties cannot provide extrinsic evidence of prior agreements that is inconsistent with the contract terms when there is a written contract which is finally expressed and is a complete integration. However, the statement is used **to prove mistake** and it falls within the exception. Thus, ABC's argument will fail and the evidence is admissible.

Equitable restitution

Q: <u>What is the likelihood of success of 갑's complaint for [rescission]?</u>

---

1. Rescission에 관한 기본 rule
2. Rescission 주장의 근거
   + analysis
3. Defenses★
   (+ analysis — parol evidence rule)★
   + analysis — laches, unclean hands

TIP1 위 2번: 소송당사자가 주장하는 remedy에 대한 근거(들)을 title화
한다.

TIP2 Equitable remedy에 대한 근거 중 fraud(misrepresentation) 또는
mistake가 자주 출제되는데, 이들은 소송당사자간 arguable points
가 많은 close call이다.

"갑 may argue that ……. 을 may argue that ……."

"It is a close call, but it is likely for the court to decide that
……."

⇒ Arguable point ①

갑(원고)은 을(피고)의 진술이 계약에 있어 material fact에 대한 내
용이라고 주장할 것이나, 이에 대해 을은 단순히 부수적인 fact에
대한 진술일 뿐이라고 반박할 것이다.

갑 may argue that the statement is **material,** [since the parking
lot was the key factor in determining the price]. **을 may argue**
that the location is **collateral** to the purchase, and therefore
there is no misrepresentation of material fact. **The court is likely
to view** the parking lot material.

⇒ Arguable point ②

갑(원고)는 을이 해당 사안을 알면서도 알리지 않은 것은 misrepre-
sentation에 해당한다고 주장할 것이다. 이에 을(피고)은 자신은 해당
사안에 대해 갑에게 어떠한 언급도 하지 <u>않았으므로</u> misrepresentation
은 발생하지 않았다고 주장할 것이다. 부작위에 의한 misrepresentation

이 인정되는 바, 법원은 을의 misrepresentation을 인정할 것이다.

갑 **may argue** that 을 made a misrepresentation because he knew that parking lot was unavailable but he did not notice to 갑. 을 **may argue** that he did not mention any statement regarding the parking lot and therefore there is no mis-representation. Failure to disclose could be a misrepresentation based on omission, and the court **is likely to recognize** the misrepresentation.

TIP3   별도의 질문이 없다 하더라도 equitable remedy에 관한 문제에서는 equitable defenses에 대해 서술하는 것이 고득점 포인트다.

모범답안 019

1. Likelihood of success of 갑's complaint for [rescission]

Rescission

Rescission is an equitable remedy. It is the court's order to make a contract invalid and make the parties left as a contract had never been made. Generally, it is available when a party has a valid defense to the formation, such as fraud, mistake, illegality, and unconscionability. The court has broad discretion in deciding the award of an equitable remedy. The court will consider the equities of the situation, considering the fairness of the remedy to both parties. Rescission is subject to equitable defenses, such as laches, acquiescence, unclean hands, and estoppel.

Grounds for rescission

Fraud

Rescission may be allowed based on fraud, which occurs when a party: (1) made a misrepresentation of material fact; (2) with the intent that the other party rely on the misrepresentation; (3) the other party in fact relied on the misrepresentation; and (4) the other party suffered damages.

(1) Misrepresentation of material fact

(ANALYSIS: In this case, 을's statement is false because ……. 갑 may argue that the statement is material, since the location was the key factor in determining the price. 을 may argue that the location is collateral to the purchase, and therefore there is no misrepresentation of material fact. The court is likely to view the location material.)

(2) With the intent

(ANALYSIS: 갑 may argue that 을 knew the fact and had an intent to defraud him. 갑 may argue that ……. 갑 will very likely prevail.)

(3) Reliance

(ANALYSIS: 갑 spent $100,000 in relying on 을's statement. ……)

(4) Damages

(ANALYSIS: 갑 was damaged and he spent cost for repairs.)

Conclusion

In conclusion, it is a close call, but it is likely for the court to decide that 을 made misrepresentation. Rescission may be allowed based on fraud.

Mistake

Rescission may be allowed based on either mutual mistake or unilateral mistake.
Mutual mistake occurs when: (1) ……, (2) …….
Unilateral mistake occurs when: (1) ……, (2) …….

Conclusion

In conclusion, it is a close call, but it is likely for the court to decide that there was mutual mistake between 갑 and 을. Rescission may be allowed based on mutual mistake.

Defenses

Rescission is an equitable remedy and equitable defenses are applicable.

Laches

......

Unclean hands

......

Conclusion

In conclusion, there are no defenses applicable in this case.

Conclusion

In conclusion, 갑's complaint for rescission based on fraud would be successful, since there are no defenses applicable in this case.

C. Remedies in Equity

1. Temporary Restraining Order and Preliminary Injunction (17July, 19July)

a. Temporary Restraining Order

★A temporary restraining order (TRO) is **to preserve the status quo for limited time.**

ⅰ. Notice of Hearing

Generally, **notice of the hearing** for the issuance of the TRO must be given before a TRO is issued.

★However, TRO can be granted **without notice** of hearing (called as **"ex parte TRO"**) when the moving party:

① Shows that there is **immediate and irreparable injury;**

② Shows that he made a **good-faith effort to make a notice** to the opposing party and the reason his failure; and

③ Provides some **security.**

ⅱ. Considering Factors

법원은 원고가 소송에서 승소할 가능성이 높고, TRO가 허가되지 않을 시 원고의 회복할 수 없는 피해가 예상되며, TRO가 허가되지 않을 경우 예상되는 원고의 피해와 TRO가 허가되었을 경우 예상되는 피고의 피해를 비교형량하여 원고의 피해가 큰 경우, TRO를 허가한다. 여기서 '원고가 소송에서 승소할 가능성'이라는 것은 원고가 피고를 상대로 제기한 주된 소송이 승소할 가능성을 뜻하는 바, TRO가 받아들여질 가능성이 아니라는 점에 유의해야 한다. 예컨대, 원고가 breach of contract를 주장하면서 피고에 대한 TRO를 신청한 경우, 법원은 breach of contract에 대한 원고의 승소가능성을 판단한다. 원고가 정부의 ordinance에 대해 violation of the First Amendment를 주장하면서 정부에 대한 TRO를 신청한 경우라면, 법원은 원고의 violation of the First Amendment 주장이 받아들여질 가능성을 판단한다. 한편, 'TRO가 허가되지 않을 경우'라는 것은 PI를 위한 심의(PI hearing)를 개최하기 전까지의 기간 동안 TRO가 허가되지 않을 경우를 뜻한다. 법원이 원고와 피고의 피해를 비교형량할 때에는 공공의 이익(public interest)과 의도성(misconduct willfulness)이 고려되어 원고의 피해를 더 크게 보아 TRO를 허가한다.

★In determining whether to grant a TRO, the court usually consider:

① The **probability** that the plaintiff will succeed on the merits;

② The threat of **irreparable harm** to the plaintiff if the injunction is not granted; and

③ The balance between this **harm to the movant** without the injunction and the **injury to the defendant** with the injunction.

✔ 정부(피고)가 ordinance를 몇 주 후에 시행하겠다고 발표함. — **not** an irreparable harm(위 ②번 미충족) & injunction을 허가한다 하더라도 이로 인한 정부의 피해가 비교적 적을 것이다(위 ③번 미충족).

✔ 계약의 목적물이 매우 희귀하여 원고가 피고 외에 구입할 수 있

는 방법이 없는 경우 — irreparable harm(위 ②번 충족)

✔ 위헌적인 ordinance를 금함. → Injunction을 허가함으로써 보호되는 public interest가 크다. → harm to π > injury to Δ (위 ③번 충족)

✔ 피고가 의도적으로 계약을 파기함. → 피고측의 misconduct willfulness가 인정됨. → harm to π > injury to Δ(위 ③번 충족)

iii. Period

The temporary restraining order would last **no longer than 14 days.**

The order can be extended only when there is a good cause or the opposing party consents to it.

b. Preliminary Injunction

★A preliminary injunction is **to preserve the status quo until a full hearing on the merits.**

In determining whether to grant a preliminary injunction, the court consider same factors using in determining whether to grant a TRO.

[표 5-2] TRO v. Preliminary Injunction

	TRO	PI
Purpose	to preserve the status quo for limited time	to preserve the status quo until a full hearing on the merits
Period	no longer than 14 days	through the pendency of the litigation
Notice	○ (예외요건×3 ⇒ ex parte TRO)	○
Security	need	
Considering factors	① The probability that the plaintiff will succeed on the merits; ② Irreparable harm to the plaintiff if the injunction is not granted; and ③ The balance between this harm to the movant without the injunction and the injury to the defendant with the injunction.	

답안요령 TRO

Q: <u>What is the likelihood that 갑 will obtain a TRO?</u>

---

1. (Justiciability) ★
   + analysis
2. TRO 기본 rule
3. Ex parte TRO
   + analysis (ex parte 요건 3개)
4. 고려요소
   + analysis ★

TIP1 원고가 피고 행위의 위헌성을 주장함과 동시에 TRO 및 PI를 주장하는 경우, ① 해당 사건의 justiciability 유무여부와 ② TRO 및 PI의 요건에 대해 서술한다.

TIP2 위 4번: 법원이 TRO/PI 승인여부에 판단할 때의 '고려요소'에 대해 상세히 analysis하는 것이 고득점 포인트다.

모범답안 020

1. Likelihood that 갑 will obtain a TRO

Justiciability

Standing

A plaintiff 갑 must have standing in order to bring a lawsuit against the State in the federal court. To establish standing, 갑 must show an injury in fact, causation, and redressability.

(1) Injury in fact

......

(2) Causation

......

(3) Redressability

......

Ripeness

......

Mootness

......

In conclusion, the federal court will hear the case, because the case involves case or controversy.

TRO

A temporary restraining order (TRO) is to preserve the status quo for limited time. Generally, notice of the hearing for the issuance of the TRO must be given before a TRO is issued.

Ex parte TRO

TRO without notice of hearing is called ex parte TRO. It can be granted when the moving party: (1) shows that there is immediate and irreparable injury; (2) shows that he made a good-faith effort to make a notice to the opposing party and the reason his failure; and (3) provides some security.

(1) Immediate and irreparable injury

(ANALYSIS: ·······.)

(2) Good-faith effort

(ANALYSIS: In this case, ·······.)

(3) Security

(ANALYSIS: In this case, ·······.)

Conclusion

In conclusion, all requirements for ex parte TRO are satisfied and notice of hearing is not required in this case.

Considering factors

In determining whether to grant a TRO, the court usually consider: (1)

the probability that the plaintiff will succeed on the merits; (2) the threat of irreparable harm to the plaintiff if the injunction is not granted; and (3) the balance between this harm to the movant without the injunction and the injury to the defendant with the injunction.

(1) Probability that the plaintiff will succeed on the merits

(ANALYSIS: In this case, 갑 raised his claim for declaratory relief that the ordinance violates the First Amendment. The ordinance facially discriminates against churches. Thus, there is high probability that 갑 will succeed on the merits.)

(2) Irreparable harm to the plaintiff

(ANALYSIS: In this case, In this case, the State indicated that the ordinance would not resume for three weeks. Thus, there is no irreparable injury.)

(3) Balancing test

(ANALYSIS: In this case, the ordinance violates the First Amendment and it causes a big harm to the movant if the injunction is not granted. This is because the harm caused by a violation of the constitutional right is profound. On the other hand, the State postponed the execution of the ordinance. It shows that the State would suffer small injury with the injunction. Moreover, prohibiting the violation of the constitutional right protects public interest. Thus, the balancing test favors 갑.)

Conclusion

In conclusion, there is no irreparable harm to 갑 and therefore 갑 will not obtain TRO.

Conclusion

In conclusion, 갑 has standing for his claim but TRO would not be granted because there is no irreparable harm to 갑. Thus, 갑 will not obtain TRO.

2. Specific Performance (Contracts) (17July, 20F−Contracts)

Specific performance is an **equitable remedy** in which the court orders a party **to perform his duties under the contract.**

a. Requirements

★It is available when:

i . There is a **valid contract;**

ii . **Legal remedy is inadequate;**

iii. The enforcement is **feasible;**

iv. **Both** parties are **eligible** to have their performance; and

v . There are **no equitable defenses.**

b. Valid Contract

There must be offer, acceptance, and consideration. Moreover, there should be no applicable **defenses to formation,** such as mutual mistake and misrepresentation.

c. Inadequate Legal Remedy

Legal remedy is inadequate when:

i . The contract is for **unique** property;

ii . Money damages are **speculative**^{추측에 근거한};

iii. There is **potential loss** and money damages are inadequate; or

iv. **Replevin or ejectment is unavailable.**

✔ A contract for **real property** = unique property → 위 ⅰ요건 충족

✔ A contract for personal property that is **very rare or customized** = unique property → 위 ⅰ요건 충족

d. Feasibility of Enforcement

Specific performance is inadequate when it is difficult for the court to enforce it. To be a feasible enforcement,

i . The court should have **jurisdiction** over either the defendant or the property;

ⅱ. Negative injunctions are easier to enforce in compared to affirmative injunctions; and

ⅲ. Contractual duty requiring **series of acts** over the period, duty requiring **taste**^{감각} or **skill,** and **personal services** are difficult to enforce.

e. Mutuality

Both parties should be allowed to perform their duties by law. For instances, there are no issues of sale of illegal goods or the minority of contracting party.

Both parties should be willing and able to perform their obligations.

f. No Equitable Defenses

Specific performance is inapplicable when there is applicable equitable defense, such as laches and unclean hands.

답안요령 | Specific performance

1. CL/UCC2★
2. Specific performance 기본 rule
3. Specific performance 요건(×5)
+ analysis (valid contract 요건★)

TIP1 Specific performance 적용여부는 해당 계약의 유효성을 통해 판단되는 바, 해당 계약에 적용되는 법률(CL 또는 UCC2)을 먼저 파악해야 한다.

TIP2 위 3번 analysis: 각 '요건'을 title화하여 작성한다. 그중 첫 번째 요건 valid contract는 ① 성립요건 3개(offer, acceptance, consideration) 뿐만 아니라 ② defenses to formation도 고려해야 한다.

모범답안 021

1. Specific performance

Governing rule

A contract for the sale of goods is governed by UCC2. The term "goods" means things that is tangible, movable, and identifiable at the time of making a contract. All other contracts are governed by the common law. (ANALYSIS: In this case, 갑 and 을 made contract for painting service. Thus, the contract between them is governed by CL.)

Specific performance

Specific performance is an equitable remedy in which the court orders a party to perform his duties under the contract. It is available when: (1) there is a valid contract; (2) legal remedy is inadequate; (3) the enforcement is feasible; (4) both parties are eligible to have their performance; and (5) there are no equitable defenses.

(1) Valid contract

To be a valid contract, there must be offer, acceptance, and consideration. (ANALYSIS: In this case, 갑 made an offer to 을 for the painting service. 을 accepted it and $100,000 is consideration.)

Defenses

However, the contract is invalid when there are applicable defenses of formation, such as misrepresentation and mistake.

Misrepresentation
……

Mistake
……

(2) Inadequate legal remedy

Legal remedy is inadequate when the contract is for unique property or money damages are speculative.
(ANALYSIS: In this case, 갑 breached the contract and he can compensate him with expectation damages. Thus, legal remedy is adequate and specific performance is inadequate remedy.)

(3) Enforcement is feasible

Specific performance is inadequate when it is difficult for the court to enforce it. Contractual duty requiring series of acts over the period, requiring taste or skill, and personal services are difficult to enforce.
(ANALYSIS: In this case, the contract is for painting service, personal service. It is difficult for the court to enforce 을 to do painting. Thus, feasibility requirement is not satisfied.)

(4) Eligibility

Both parties should be willing and able to perform their obligations.
(ANALYSIS: In this case, 을 already completed his performance but 갑 breached the contract. Thus, eligibility requirement is satisfied.)

(5) No equitable defenses
Laches

......

Unclean hands

......

Conclusion

In conclusion, the first requirement for specific performance is not satisfied. Thus, 갑 will not obtain specific performance.

답안요령	Contracts & Remedies

Q: What remedy or remedies may 갑 reasonably seek and what is the likely outcome? Discuss.

1. CL/UCC2★
2. Contract 성립
   + analysis
3. Breach 주장에 대한 근거
4. Remedies

① Legal remedies
② Restitution
③ Equitable remedies

TIP1 소송당사자의 적합한 구제방법(remedies)은 우선 '소송당사자(갑) 의 승소가능성'에 대해 논해야 하는 바, ① 당사자간 계약에 대한 analysis를 통해 상대방(을)의 breach of contract에 대해 논한 후 ② 이에 대한 갑의 remedies에 대해 판단해야 한다.

TIP2 위 2번: 계약성립여부는 계약성립요건 3개뿐만 아니라 defenses against validity도 고려해서 판단한다.

TIP3 위 4번: '세 유형의 remedies'를 title화하여 작성하고, 각 remedy에 대한 analysis에서 갑의 duty to mitigate를 논하는 것이 고득점 포인 트다.

모범답안 022

CL v. UCC2

A contract for the sale of goods is governed by UCC2. The term "goods" means things that is tangible, movable, and identifiable at the time of making a contract. All other contracts are governed by the common law. (ANALYSIS: In this case, the contract was made for painting service and CL is applicable.)

Contract validity

......

Anticipatory repudiation

......

Remedies
Legal remedies
Compensatory damages

The compensatory damages is to put the non-breaching party in as good a position as if the other party had fully performed. Compensatory damages is generally measured by adding expectation damages, incidental, and consequential damages.

Expectation damages

Expectation Damages is measured as the value of the breaching party's performance that was lost.

(ANALYSIS: In this case, 갑 was going to be paid for 1천만원. 갑 expected to receive it after the completion of the project. Thus, 갑 would receive 1천만원 as expectation damages.)

Incidental damages

It is recognized only in UCC2.

(ANALYSIS: In this case, the contract is made for service and CL is applicable. Thus, 갑 cannot recover incidental damages.)

Consequential damages

Consequential damages are caused by the non-breaching party's special circumstances.

(ANALYSIS: In this case, 갑 may argue that he could recover consequential damages since he lost his repudiation because of 을's breach.)

(1) Foreseeable

(ANALYSIS: In this case, 갑 may argue that 을 has known that ……. Thus, foreseeability requirement is satisfied.)

(2) Reasonably certain

To recover consequential damages, damages should not be speculative.

(ANALYSIS: In this case, 갑 is seeking for consequential damages, arguing his reputation is reduced. However, the damages for reputation is too speculative. Thus, reasonable certainty requirement is not satisfied.)

(3) Unavoidable

Unavoidability requirement is satisfied when the plaintiff satisfied his duty to mitigate.

(ANALYSIS: In this case, there are no ways for 갑 to reduce the damages. Thus, 갑 did not violate his duty to mitigate and unavoidability requirement is satisfied.)

Conclusion

In conclusion, 갑 would not recover consequential damages.

Reliance damages

When expectation damages are too speculative, non-breaching party may recover reliance damages as the loss incurred reasonably relying on the contract. It is to put the plaintiff in the position as if the contract had never been made.

(ANALYSIS: As mentioned above, 갑 is arguing that his reputation is reduced, but the damages for reputation is too speculative. Thus, 갑 would recover reliance damages and the damages would include money spent by 갑.)

Restitution

Restitution is a remedy to prevent unjust enrichment. There are two types of restitution: legal restitution and equitable restitution.

Legal restitution (Quasi-contract)

Quasi-contract is recognized when a party has derived a benefit from no legally binding contract. Generally, it is measured by the value of the benefit conferred or the cost in conferring the benefit.

(ANALYSIS: In this case, ……. 을 may argue that the damages should be measured as $5,000 under the contract between the parties. However, damages is measured by the value of the benefit conferred or the cost in conferring the benefit. Thus, 갑 would recover $8,000.)

Equitable restitution

Reformation is the court's order to rewrite a contract reflecting the true agreement of the parties. Rescission is the court's order to make a contract invalid and make the parties left as a contract had never been made (is discharged).

(ANALYSIS: In this case, …….)

Equitable remedies
Specific performance

Specific performance is an equitable remedy in which the court orders a party to perform his duties under the contract. It is available when: (1) there is a valid contract; (2) legal remedy is inadequate; (3) the enforcement is feasible; (4) both parties are eligible to have their performance; and (5) there are no equitable defenses.

(1) Valid contract
……

(2) Legal remedy is inadequate
……

(3) Enforcement is feasible
……

(4) Eligibility
……

(5) No equitable defenses
……

Conclusion
……

Conclusion

In conclusion, 갑 would recover reliance damages or legal restitution.

3. Permanent Inunction

a. General Rule

Permanent injunction is a court order to take or to refrain from certain actions. It is issued after a full lawsuit.

b. Requirements

It is recoverable only when:

ⅰ. Legal remedy is **inadequate**;

ⅱ. There is a protectable **property interest**;

ⅲ. The enforcement is **feasible**;

ⅳ. The hardship to plaintiff outweighs the hardship to defendant; and

ⅴ. There are **no equitable defenses**.

c. Property Interest

Traditionally, an injunction is allowed only for the **property interest**. However, in modern California, an injunction is also allowed when there are **protectable personal rights**.

d. Balancing Test

The court balances the hardship to plaintiff if the injunction is not granted against the hardship to defendant if the injunction is granted.

The injunction is granted when the balancing test **favors the plaintiff**.

CEE/MBE

6장
Real Property

//

본 장은 부동산에 관한 권리 및 권리변동에 대해 논하며, 한국법상 '부동산사법'에 가깝다. 지난 7년간 에세이 기출문제에서 자주 다루었던 논점을 중심으로, 토지에 관한 권리(estate in land), 임대차 관계(tenancy), 비점유권 권리(non-possessory interests), 소유권 이전(conveyance), 부동산을 담보로 하는 채권(security interest), 용도지역 조례(zoning ordinance) 등에 대해 논한다. 그중 zoning ordinance는 수정헌법 5조 및 14조에 따른 Taking Clause와 밀접한 관련이 있는 바, 이는 다양한 판례들과 헌법상의 권리를 함께 이해하는 것이 중요하다.

☑ 글쓰기 Tips

1. Real property는 지난 7년간 에세이 기출문제 중 타 과목과 비교하여 가장 적은 출제 빈도수를 가지고 있는 과목이다.
2. Real property에 관한 문제는 torts, remedies, constitutional law 등 다양한 과목들과 연계되어 출제된다.
3. Real property에 관한 전형적인 문제가 있는 것은 아니고, 각 논점에 따라 법원의 판결에 대해 논하거나 주어진 부동산에 대한 등장인물의 권리에 대해 논하는 문제들이 출제된다.
   Q: What right, title, or interest in ABC land, if any, held by 갑, 을, and 병? Discuss.
   ⇒ 각 '등장인물'을 title화하여 작성한다.
   Q: What is the likely outcome of 갑's action?
   Q: How is the court likely to rule on 갑's claim?
   ⇒ 주어진 사안을 읽으면서 논점을 찾아야 한다.
4. 문제에 구체적인 논점이 드러나 있는 경우도 있다.
   Q: How is the court likely to rule on 갑's claim for the share of the proceeds from any foreclosure sale? Discuss.

Ⅰ. Estates in Land (15July#2)

A. Present and Future Interests

1. Fee Simple Determinable

When 갑 conveyed a **fee simple determinable** interest to 을, 갑 retains **possibility of a reverter.** 갑(grantor) does **not** need to take any action to regain access to the property.

2. Possibility of Reverter

When 갑 conveyed a **fee simple on condition subsequent** to 을 and the court implies the forfeiture provision, 갑 has the **power of termination.** 갑(grantor) needs to take action to regain access to the property.

B. Restraint on Alienation

When an interest in property is subject to condition that completely bars alienation, the condition is **void** and the interest is fee simple absolute.

> **case**

갑이 을에게 "so long as 을 does not make any transfer of ABC토지"라는 조건으로 자신의 ABC토지에 대한 interest를 증여하였다. 이후 갑이 사망하였고, 을은 병에게 ABC토지를 매도하였다. What property interest in ABC, if any, is the court likely to find possessed by 갑's issues, 을, and 병?

⇒ 병 ownes fee simple absolute interest. 상기 문구에 따르면 을은 fee simple determinable, 갑(및 갑의 issues)은 possibility of reverter이다. 다만, 해당 조건은 을의 소유권 이전(移轉)을 제한하는 조건(restraint on alienation)으로서 그 유효성이 부정되는 바, 을은 fee simple absolute interest를 가지고 갑은 어떠한 권리도 갖지 않는다. 즉, 을은 병에게 ABC토지를 매도할 수 있는 권리가 있으며, 을·병간 매매계약은 유효하다. 따라서 해당 토지에 대해 병 ownes fee simple absolute interest.

C. Co-Tenancy (15Feb, 15July)

1. Joint Tenancy v. Tenancy in Common

   a. Joint Tenancy

      ⅰ. General Rule

         ★A joint tenancy exists when two or more individuals own property with the right of survivorship.

         ★Under the common law four-unities test, four unities are required to create a joint tenancy: unity of time, unity of title, unity of interest, and unity of possession.

      ⅱ. Severance

         A lifetime conveyance of one of the joint tenants to third party severs the joint tenancy, and may create a tenancy in common.

   b. Tenancy in Common

      A tenancy in common is a concurrent estate with no right of survivorship and each tenant has the interest is freely alienable.

2. Contribution

   A contribution should be made to another co-tenant when the co-tenant fully paid for necessary improvements, principle on the mortgage, or taxes on the property.

II. Landlord and Tenant

A. General Concepts

1. Types of Tenancy (15July)

A **tenancy for years** is one that is to continue **for a fixed period of time.**

A **periodic tenancy** is one that continues **for successive periods** until the tenant gives the landlord termination notice. If a tenant goes into possession **after the termination date,** the tenancy is treated as a **periodic tenancy.**

A **tenancies at will** is one that is terminable by either landlord or tenant.

✔ "갑 leases ABC상가 to 을 from 2030-09-29 to 2031-09-28." — tenancy for years

✔ "갑 leases ABC상가 to 을 from month to month." — periodic tenancy

2. Statute of Frauds

★The **statute of frauds** requires that a lease creating a tenancy **for more than one year be in writing.**

If the writing requirement is not satisfies, a tenancy will be treated as a **periodic tenancy.**

B. Assignment v. Sublease (15Feb)

1. Assignment

Assignment is a tenant's transfer of the **entire** remaining leasehold interest.

★When a tenant assigns his interest in a lease, the **privity of estate** arises between landlord and new tenant, and the **privity of contract** remains between landlord and assignor.

2. Sublease

Sublease is a tenant's transfer of **any part** of the remaining leasehold interest.

Both privity of estate and privity of contract remain between landlord and assignor.

A covenant does not run with the land, and the subleasee is **not personally liable to the landlord.** He is only liable to the original tenant.

C. Duties of Landlord and Tenant (19Feb)

1. Landlord's Duties

a. Duty to Deliver Possession

In the majority of jurisdictions, a landlord must deliver **actual possession** to a tenant.

In the minority of jurisdictions, the duty is satisfied when a landlord gives the tenant the **legal right to possession.**

b. Duty to Disclose Defects

A landlord has duty to disclose the dangerous condition when:

ⅰ. The landlord **knew or should have known** the condition at the time of making the lease ("latent defects"); and

ⅱ. The tenant could **not discover** the condition upon **reasonable** inspection.

c. Duty for Quiet Enjoyment

A landlord should not interfere the tenant's quiet enjoyment and possession of the premises.

The duty for quiet enjoyment is breached when a landlord:

ⅰ. **Evicts** a justifiable tenant prior to its termination;

ⅱ. **Fails to deliver possession** of the premises to the tenant at the beginning of the term; or

iii. **Fails to make premises** suitable for human residence.

d. Implied Warranty of Habitability

- Implied warranty of habitability = Implied warranty against latent defects = Implied warranty of quality = Implied warranty of merchantability = Implied warranty of fitness

i . General Rule

A landlord owes an implied warranty of habitability to make the premises suitable **for human residence.**

★Under the implied warranty of habitability, a **landlord** has **duty to repair** in **residential** leases.

✔ No hot water — warranty 적용대상 ○

✔ Stove problem — warranty 적용대상 ×

The implied warranty of habitability does not typically extend to include household appliances(가전제품에는 적용되지 않는다).

ii . Tenant's Remedies

When a landlord breaches the implied warranty, a tenant must **give notice** before he adopts any options in the following:

① Tenant **terminates the lease** (no duty to pay rent);

② Tenant may **make repairs and offset the cost** against future rent obligations;

③ Tenant may reduce or abate rent to an amount equal to the **fair rental value;** or

④ Tenant may **seek damages** against the landlord.

TIP   Arguable point

목적물이 거주의 목적을 지니는 경우, 임대인은 임차인에게 implied

warranty of habitability에 따라 duty to repair가 있다. 임대인이 본 의무를 이행하지 않는 경우, 임차인이 해당 목적물을 향유하는데 있어 제약을 받으므로 constructive eviction이 인정되는 바, 임대인 은 duty to quiet enjoyment 또한 breach하게 된다. 다시 말해, 목적 물이 거주의 목적을 지니는 경우, 임대인이 duty to repair를 breach 한다면 이는 implied warranty of habitability와 duty to quiet enjoyment 모두를 breach하는 것이다.

In every **residential lease**, there is an **implied warranty of habitability** and the landlord owes duty to repair to the tenant. If the **duty to repair** is breached, the tenant's ability to use and to enjoy the property is impaired and **constructive eviction** is recognized. Thus, when the landlord breaches duty to repair, implied warranty of habitability, and **duty to quiet enjoyment** are breached.

2. Tenant's Duties

a. Duty to Pay Rent

i. Common Law

Under the common law, lease covenants are independent, and a tenant has duty to pay rent even after a landlord breaches his duty.

ii. Modern Law

Under the modern law, covenants are dependent, and landlord's breach of his duty relieves tenant's duty to pay rent.

When the tenant has no appropriate reason, the landlord is entitled to damages **for the unpaid rent** with **duty to mitigate** the losses by re-letting the premises.

b. Duty to Repair

A **tenant** has duty to repair only in **nonresidential** leases.

A **landlord** has duty to repair only in **residential** leases under the implied warranty of habitability (in nonresidential, no duty).

c. Duty Not to Waste

A tenant has duty not to waste on the leased premises.

D. Surrender (Abandonment) (19Feb)

Surrender는 임차인이 목적물을 포기했음을 의미하는 바, 임차인이 임대차 종료일 이전에 해당 임대차 계약을 해지(intent not to return) 할 의도로 목적물을 비우고(vacate) 차임을 지급하지 않는 경우를 의미한다. Surrender가 발생하면, 임차인에게 세 가지의 옵션이 주어진다. 임대인의 surrender를 받아들여(accept) 임대인의 duty to rent가 종료되고 임차인은 그 피해를 최대한 줄이도록 노력(duty to mitigate)하거나, 임대인을 대신하여 해당 목적물을 제3자에 임대하거나, 임차인의 surrender를 받아들이지 않고 해당 목적물을 그대로 두어(leave) 임차인의 duty to rent가 지속되는 경우가 그것이다.

1. General Rule

★When there is surrender, landlord has three options to:

ⅰ. **Accept** the surrender;

ⅱ. **Re-let or attempt to re-let** the premises on the tenant's behalf; or

ⅲ. **Leave** the premises vacant.

a. Accept the Surrender

If the landlord accepts the surrender, the tenant's duty to pay rent ends and the landlord has **duty to mitigate** losses.

b. Re-Let or Attempt to Re-Let

ⅰ. **Re-Let or Attempt to Re-Let**

If the landlord re-lets (or attempts to re-let) the premises, he would be entitled to the difference between the rent owed under the lease and the rent under the new lease.

ⅱ. **Fail to Re-Let or Attempt to Re-Let**

If the landlord failed to re-let the premises, he would be entitled to the difference between the rent owed under the lease and fair market value.

The landlord has **duty to mitigate** losses.

c. Leave the Premises Vacant

If the landlord leaves the premises vacant, the tenant's duty to pay rent continues and the landlord can recover for unpaid rent as it accrues.

[표 6-1]

Options	Landlord's Recovery	Duty to Mitigate
Accept	−	○
Re-let (Attempt to re-let)	(original tenant rent fee) − (re-letting rent fee)	
Fail to re-let	(original rent fee) − (fair market value)	○
Leave vacant	unpaid original rent fee	

III. Non-Possessory Interests

A. Easement (16July, 18Feb)

An easement is a right in land granted to a third party.

1. Types of Easement

a. Affirmative and Negative Easement

An **affirmative** easement allows the holder to do something, while a **negative** easement prevents the holder from doing something.

b. Appurtenant Easement and Easement in Gross

When there is a **dominant estate**, the easement is **appurtenant easement** which **runs with the land** to subsequent takers who has notice of the easement. When there is no dominant estate, the easement is **easement in gross.**

2. Creation of Easement

There are three ways to create an easement: creation by express grant, by implication, and by prescription.

a. By Express Grant

Easement is expressed in writing, since statute of frauds applies to an interest in land.

b. By Implication

Easement is implied and created by operation of law without writing. There are three types of such easement: an easement implied from an existed use, an easement implied from a recorded subdivision, and an easement by necessity.

c. By Prescription

An easement is implied by prescription, using the similar principal as adverse possession.

Easement by prescription requires: actual, open and notorious, hostile, and continuous use. Acquiring easement by prescription is similar with acquiring property by adverse possession, but exclusive use is not required.

i. Actual

The use must be same with how a **reasonable landowner would have used** it if in possession.

ii. Open and Notorious

The use must put an landowner **on notice** of adverse possession if the owner inspected the land.

iii. Hostile

The use must have been **without landowner's permission.**

iv. Continuous

The use must have lasted the **statutory period** and the period can be aggregated when the adverse possessors are in privity.

B. Real Covenant (15Feb)

Covenant는 '약속'을 의미하며, real covenant는 특정 토지상에서의 작위 또는 부작위를 내용으로 하는 약속을 뜻한다. 예컨대, 특정 토지에 펜스를 치겠다는 약속, 특정 토지를 상업적으로 사용하지 않겠다는 약속, 임대차 계약에서 임차인이 화재보험을 들어야 한다는 약속 등이 이에 해당한다. Real covenant와 관련된 가장 중요한 논점은 해당 covenant의 run with the land 여부이다. 즉, covenant로 인해 의무를 지는 토지(servient estate) 및 해당 covenant로 인해 이익을 얻는 토지(dominant estate)의 점유권 및 소유권이 변경된 경우 새로운 소유권자 및 점유권자(successor) 간에도 해당 covenant 가 유효한지 그 여부가 가장 중요한 논점이다. 본 개념은 토지의 title이 변경된 경우뿐만 아니라 임대차 계약 후 임차인이 자신의 임차권을 제3자에게 assign한 경우에도 적용된다는 점에 유의해야 한다.

Servient estate에 대한 권리가 타인(successor)에게 이전된 경우 다섯 요건 (intent, notice, horizontal privity, vertical privity, touch and concern)이 만족되어야만 해당 의무가 runs with the land하여 successor에게도 해당 covenant에 대한 의무가 인정된다. 예컨대, ABC토지 주인 갑이 DEF토지 주인 을에게 높은 빌딩을 세우지 않겠다는 covenant를 하였고 이후 ABC토지를 병에게 판매하였다. 이 경우 ABC토지는 servient estate에 해당하며, 상기 다섯 요건이 만족되는 경우에 한해 병에게도 높은 빌딩을 세우지 않겠다는 covenant를 이행할 의무가 인정된다. 즉, 다섯 요건이 모두 만족되었으나 병이 높은 빌딩을 세운 경우 을은 병을 상대로 손배청구를 할 수 있다. 한편, dominant estate에 대한 권리가 타인(successor)에게 이전된 경우에는 세 요건(intent, vertical privity, touch and concern)이 만족되는 경우에 한해 covenant에 근거한 권리가 runs with the land하여 successor에게도 권리가 인정된다. 예컨대, 상기 예시에서 주인 을이 해당 토지에 대한 권리를 정에게 이전하였고, 정이 병을 상대로 권리를 주장하는 경우에는 세 요건이 만족되어야 한다.

1. General Rule

★A real covenant is a **written promise** to do something on the land or a promise not to do something on the land.

2. Requirements to Run

a. Requirements for Burden

★The **burden** of covenant runs with the land if:

ⅰ. The covenanting parties **intended** that the covenant runs with the land;

ⅱ. The covenant **touches and concerns** the land;

ⅲ. A subsequent purchaser of the servient estate has **notice** on it;

ⅳ. There is **horizontal privity**; and

ⅴ. There is **vertical privity.**

b. Requirements for Benefit

★The **benefit** of covenant runs with the land if:

ⅰ. The covenanting parties **intended** that the covenant runs with the land;

ⅱ. The covenant **touches and concerns** the land;

ⅲ. A subsequent purchaser of the servient estate has **notice** on it; and

ⅳ. There is **vertical privity.**

Ⅳ. Conveyance

A. Marketable Title

1. General Rule

★In every land contract, the seller makes an **implied covenant** (implied warranty) that he will provide the buyer **with a marketable title at the time of closing.**

Once the deed is delivered, the land sale contract merges with the deed and any rights to sue under the contract is extinguished.

2. Marketability

Title is unmarketable when there is a **defect in the chain of title**, there is an **encumbrance**, or the estate violates **zoning ordinance**.

Encumbrance is any right in a third party that reduces the value or interferes with the use and enjoyment of the land, such as mortgages, easements, and covenants.

B. Deeds

미국 등기에는 general warranty deed, special warranty deed, quitclaim deed, 이렇게 세 유형이 있으며, 각 유형별로 해당 토지에 대해 보장하는 매수인의 권리 내용 및 범위가 다르다. 토지에 대한 보장을 "covenants for title"이라 일컫는 바, 이는 매도인과 매수인간 계약을 체결하면서 별도로 한 약속이 아니라 등기(deed)의 속성상 당연히 함축되는 보장을 의미한다. 매도인과 매수인간 계약을 체결하여 별도로 한 약속은 real covenant이다. Covenants for title에는 매도인이 해당 토지를 이전할 수 있는 권리를 가지고 있다는 보장(covenant of right to convey), 해당 토지에 대해 encumbrance 가 없다는 보장(covenant against encumbrance) 등이 있다. 한편, marketable title은 매매될만한 자격(marketability)을 갖추고 있는 title을 의미하는 바, 해당 목적물이 소유권상 문제가 없고, encumbrances가 없으며, zoning ordinance를 위반하지 않아야 한다. Marketability의 내용과 covenants for title의 내용은 비슷하나, marketable title은 등기가 매수인에게 양도되기 이전까지 보장되는 내용으로서 marketability는 계약상의 문제인 반면, covenant for title은 등기가 매수인에게 양도된 시점 또는 그 이후부터 보장되는 내용으로서 deed상의 문제이다.

1. Covenants for Title

Covenants for title are assurances that a grantor gives to the grantee.

The scope of covenants is determined based on the types of the deeds. There are three types of deeds: the general warranty deed, the special warranty deed, and the quitclaim deeds.

2. General Warranty Deed

Usually, a general warranty deed contains six covenants: covenant of seisin, covenant of right to convey, covenant against encumbrances, covenant for quiet enjoyment, covenant of warranty, covenant for further assurances.

3. Special Warranty Deed

The special warranty deed guarantees that there was no prior conveyance of same estate and there is no encumbrance on the estate.

4. Quitclaim Deeds

A quitclaim deed creates **no covenants** for title.

C. **Records** (15Feb, 16July)

1. Common Law

At common law, **"first-in-time, first-in-right" principle** is used and the grantee first in time takes priority.

2. Modern Law

In modern, recording acts require a grantee to make **a recording for priority purpose.**

a. Notice Statutes

Under a notice recording statute, a **subsequent** purchaser can prevail over prior grantee only if:

　ⅰ. The **prior** conveyances were **unrecorded** at the time of conveyance;

ⅱ. Subsequent purchaser **paid value** for the land; and

ⅲ. The subsequent purchaser took **without either actual, constructive, or inquiry notice** of the prior conveyances.

b. Race—Notice Statutes

Under a race-notice statute, a subsequent **bona fide purchaser** (BFP) is protected only if she **records** before the prior grantee.

[Bona Fide Purchaser (BFP)]

A BFP is a party who **pays value** and takes **without notice** of prior recordings that may affect his title to the property.

c. Race Statutes

Under a race statute, **whoever records first** wins.

3. Shelter Rule

★Under the shelter rule, when a buyer acquires property free of an encumbrance, **any subsequent buyer** acquires title free of a prior encumbrance.

V. Security Interests (14Feb)

A. Types of Security Interests

A security interest in real property secures other obligation. There are several types of security interests, such as mortgage, deed of trust, installment land contract, and absolute deed.

1. Mortgage

When a mortgage is made, a **debtor** usually holds a deed and the property stands as collateral for a debt owed. The debtor and mortgagor can be different people.

When a debtor fails to make payments, a creditor can initiate **foreclosure**.

2. Deed of Trust

When a deed of trust is made, a **third party** holds a deed in a trust to stand as collateral for a debt owed.

When a debtor fails to make payments, a creditor can initiate **foreclosure**.

B. Foreclosure

1. General Rule

★When a creditor forecloses on a property, **the junior interest is extinguished** at the sale of the property **only if** the creditor provides **notice** to the junior interest. A **senior interest remains** intact on the property.

2. Purchase Money Mortgage (PMM)

Purchase money mortgage(PMM)는 특정 물건을 구매하는 과정에서 해당 물건을 담보로 하는 채무를 뜻하며, 채권자가 매매계약의 당사자(매도인)인 경우도 있고 제3자인 경우도 있다. 예컨대, 갑이 을로부터 냉장고를 1,000만원에 구입하는데 돈이 모자라 해당 냉장고를 담보로 하여 을에게 800만원을 빌리는 경우 800만원에 대해 PMM이 생성된다. 기본적으로 PMM은 해당 물건을 담보로 하는 채권들에 우선하는데, 이는 PMM이 채무자가 담보에 대해 소유권을 이전받기 '이전'에 진 채무이고, 일반적인 mortgage는 채무자의 소유권이 이전된 이후에 발생하는 채무이기 때문이다.

A purchase money mortgage has priority over other creditor interests. The record of PMM does not affect the priority.

a. Vendor v. Lender

Usually, the **vender** has priority over the third-party lender, unless **only one party** has notice.

When **only one party** has notice, the recording acts would apply.

b. Lender v. Lender

A lender who made the mortgage **first** has priority over the others. The recording acts do not apply.

---

case

① 갑·을간 토지 매매계약을 체결하였다. 갑은 매매가격 10억 중 3억은 을에게 deed of trust를 담보로 하는 promissory note를 작성하였고, 나머지 7억은 ABC은행에서 해당 토지를 담보로 하는 mortgage를 받았다. ABC은행은 해당 mortgage를 record했고, 갑·을간의 promissory note에 대해 인지하고 있었다. 갑이 을과 은행에 모두 채무불이행(default)하였다. 본 재판권은 adopts race-notice statute. Who has priority?

⇒ 을 has priority over ABC은행. 을의 promissory note와 ABC은행의 mortgage는 모두 갑이 토지를 매입하는 과정 중 생성되었고 해당 토지를 담보로 하는 채권이므로 purchase money mortgage(PMM)이다. 한편, 을은 매매계약의 당사자이므로 vendor, ABC은행은 제3자이므로 third party lender에 해당하며 당사자 중 ABC은행만이 을의 promissory notice에 대해 has notice. 따라서 recording act(race-notice statute)가 적용되는 바, 을 has priority over ABC은행.

② 갑·을간 토지 매매계약을 체결하였다. 갑은 매매가격 10억 중 3억은 을에게 deed of trust를 담보로 하는 promissory note를 작성하였고, 나머지 7억은 ABC은행에서 해당 토지를 담보로 하는 mortgage를 받았다. ABC은행과 을은 서로의 채권에 대해 no notice이다. 갑이 을과 은행에 모두 채무불이행(default)하였다. 본 재판권은 adopts race-notice statues. Who has priority?

⇒ 을 has priority over ABC은행. 을의 promissory note와 ABC은행의 mortgage는 모두 갑이 토지를 매입하는 과정 중 생성되었고 해당 토지를 담보로 하는 채권이므로 purchase money mortgage(PMM)이다. 을은 매

매계약의 당사자이므로 vendor, ABC은행은 제3자이므로 third party lender에 해당한다. 한편, 을과 ABC은행은 서로의 채권에 대해 no notice 이므로 recording act가 적용되지 않고 vendor의 채권이 third party lender의 채권에 우선한다는 rule에 따라 을이 ABC은행에 우선한다.

3. Proceeds of Foreclosure

The **proceeds** of the foreclosure are used in the following order:

ⅰ. Expenses for foreclosure;

ⅱ. Paying off the senior interest;

ⅲ. Paying off the junior interest; and

ⅳ. Mortgagor.

Ⅵ. Taking Clause and Zoning Ordinance (14Feb, 15July−Con.law, 18Feb)

본 파트에서는 헌법상의 Taking Clause와 zoning ordinance에 대해 논한다. Taking Clause는 정부가 taking을 시행하는 경우 개인에게 반드시 보상 (compensation)해야 한다는 내용의 헌법상 조항이다. 여기서 'taking'이란, 정부가 사유재산을 물리적으로 이용하는 경우(complete taking) 또는 규제를 통해 그 재산의 사용을 제한하는 경우(regulatory taking)를 뜻한다. 한편, total taking 또는 complete taking은 사유재산 '전체'를 정부가 물리적으로 또는 규제를 통해 그 사용을 제한하는 것을 뜻한다. Zoning ordinance는 정부가 police power에 입각하여 토지의 이용 및 건축물의 용도 등에 대한 제한을 내용으로 하는 조례를 뜻하는 바, '용도지역 조례'로 이해하면 되겠다. 본래 Taking Clause는 Constitutional law 과목에서 논하는 내용이나, 캘리포니아 에세이 시험(CEE)에서 Real property와 Constitutional law 내용이 연계되어 출제된 바 있고 정부의 목적을 위해 사유재산을 이용한다는 점에서 Real property 과목의 zoning ordinance 논점과 밀접한 관련이 있어, 필자는 본 파트에서 Taking Clause와 zoning ordinance를 함께 논하기로 한다.

A. Taking Clause

1. General Rule

★Under the Fifth Amendment Taking Clause, the governmental taking of private property for public use is prohibited without just compensation.

2. Taking

a. Total Taking (Complete Taking)

Total takings are recognized when the government:

ⅰ. **Physically occupy** a landowner's land or real property (physical taking); or

ⅱ. Denies **all economic value** of the private property, the regulation is a taking (regulatory taking).

b. Regulatory Taking

ⅰ. **General Rule**

The governmental regulation (e.g., zoning ordinance) that decreases economic value is not a taking, **as long as the regulation leaves an economically viable use for the property.**

ⅱ. **Balancing Test**

★In determining whether the regulation is a **taking**, courts do multi-factor balancing test considering:

① The **social goal** and the value to the community;

② The **economic impact** on the claimant; and

③ The extent of **interference with the investment-backed expectation** of the owner.

✔ Regulatory taking이 실행될 경우, claimant의 본래 사용목적을 위해 추가적인 비용이 반드시 발생한다는 사실은 위 ③ 요건(interference)에 해당되지 않는다. 추가적인 비용이 발생될 뿐, 그 목적을 위한 토지사용이 전면적으로 불가능해지는 것은 아

니기 때문이다.

The regulation leaves an economically viable use for the property, and therefore it is not regulatory taking.

✔ When a business has been for a long period — 위 ③요건 미충족(오랜 기간 동안 사업을 하였으므로 사용자는 투자한 자본에 대해 return을 받았다고 볼 수 있다.)

✔ When a business has newly open — 위 ③요건 충족(개업을 하였으므로 사용자는 투자한 자본에 대해 return을 받았다고 볼 수 없다.)

3. Public Use

A public use is recognized when it is **rationally related** to a public purpose.

✔ Protecting children pedestrians

4. Compensation (18Feb)

Compensation is measured as the **full market value at the time of the taking** based on comparable properties.

The government may be liable for losses resulting from reliance on the assumption that there would be no taking.

✔ 해당 property의 작년 시세가 — compensation 책정 시 고려 ✕
✔ Cost for purchasing the taken property — compensation에 포함 ✕
✔ Cost of recent improvements — compensation에 포함 ○ (다만, claimant 가 no taking이라는 정부의 정책에 의존하여 improve한 경우에 한한다.)
✔ Cost for relocation (cost of finding a replacement property) — compensation에 포함 ✕

B. Zoning Ordinance

Zoning ordinance는 정부가 police power에 입각하여 토지의 이용 및 건축물의 용도 등에 대한 제한을 내용으로 하는 조례를 뜻하는 바, '용도지역 조례'로 이해하면 되겠다. Zoning ordinance는 정부의 목적을 위해 사유재산을 이용한다는 점에서 taking clause와 밀접한 관련이 있다. 앞서 언급한 바와 같이 Taking clause는 정부가 taking을 시행하는 경우 개인에게 반드시 보상(compensation)해야 한다는 내용의 헌법상 조항이다. 여기서 'taking'은 정부가 사유재산을 물리적으로 이용하는 경우(physical taking)와 규제를 통해 그 재산의 사용을 제한하는 경우(regulatory taking)를 통칭한다. Zoning ordinance도 규제의 일종이기 때문에 regulatory taking에 해당할 수 있으나, 모든 zoning ordinance가 regulatory taking인 것은 아니고, 사유재산의 '모든' 경제적 가치가 하락한 경우와 소유자의 투자에 대한 기대를 꺾은(interfere) 경우에 한해 regulatory taking으로 인정된다.

Zoning ordinance가 제정되면 본래 일정 지역에 일괄적으로 적용하는 것이 원칙이나, 그것이 여의치 않은 경우 정부가 zoning ordinance 내용에 위배되는 토지 및 건축물 사용을 일부 허용하기 위해 nonconforming use 또는 variance를 인정하기도 한다. Nonconforming use와 variance는 zoning ordinance의 내용에 위배되는 토지 및 건축물 사용을 허용한다는 점에서 동일하나, 약간의 차이가 있다. Zoning ordinance가 제정된 시점 '이전'부터 존재했던 토지 및 건축 이용을 그대로 허용해주는 것은 nonconforming use라 하고, zoning ordinance가 제정된 시점 '이후'에 그 내용에 위배되는 토지 및 건축 이용을 허용해주는 것은 variance라 한다. Nonconforming use는 zoning ordinance를 제정하였다 하더라도 이를 단기간 안에 일괄적으로 적용하기에 현실적으로 어려움이 존재하므로 인정하는 것으로서, 대개 토지 이용자가 새로운 토지를 찾을 수 있도록 일정 기간(amortization)을 제공하고 해당 기간 동안의 nonconforming use를 허용한다. 한편, variance는 zoning ordinance가 제정된 시점 이후에 그 내용에 위배되는 토지 및 건축 이용을 예외적으로 허용해주는 것을 의미하는 바, 그 유형에는 area variance와 use variance가 있다. Area variance는 건축물의 크기 및 치수(dimension)가 zoning ordinance를 미미하게 위배한 경우 허용하는 예외를 뜻하고, use variance는 건축물의 용도가 zoning ordinance를 위배한 경우 허용하는 예외를 뜻한다. Use variance를 신청하는 건축물 사용자는 zoning ordinance에 따른 어려움(hardship)과 해당 variance가 허용되었을 경우 주변 사용자들에게 피해가 없다는 점을 증명해야 한다.

1. General Rule

Zoning ordinances are regulations on the land use by states and localities. It is allowed pursuant to the police power. However, a person who violates the zoning ordinance can seek for nonconforming use or variance.

a. Zoning ordinance and Taking

★Zoning ordinance is a taking only when:

ⅰ. It denies **all economic use** of the property; or

ⅱ. It **unreasonably interferes with investment-backed expectations.**

2. Nonconforming Use

a. General Rule

★Nonconforming use is allowed to continue if:

ⅰ. The use **existed prior to the change** of the ordinance; and

ⅱ. The use does **not cause harm** to neighborhood.

b. Amortization

Amortization is to allow the owner to find a new location for the activity.

3. Variance

A variance is an individual exception for the zoning ordinance.

There are two types of variance: area and use variance.

a. Area Variance

An area variance allows a building to exist in dimensions that slightly violate the zoning ordinance.

b. Use Variance

★A use variance allows a person to operate a structure for a purpose that is not permitted by the zoning ordinance.

For a use variance, an individual must show that:

ⅰ. His **hardship** with the ordinance; and

ⅱ. No **damage or harm to the neighborhood** caused by the variance.

---

case

① 갑이 manufacturing facility를 운영하고 있었는데, ABC City에서 해당 지역을 only for residential purpose로 지정하는 zoning ordinance를 제정하였다. 갑은 해당 facility를 운영하기 위해 10억을 투자한 상태였다. ABC City는 use variance를 허용할 수 있는가?

⇒ No. 갑은 해당 facility의 운영을 위해 막대한 금액을 투자하였으므로 해당 사업을 지속하지 못하는 경우 economic hardship이 예상된다. 하지만 거주지역에서 manufacturing facility 운영은 지속적인 소음을 발생시키고 특히 제조과정에서 유해물질이 다루어지는 경우 상당한 피해가 예상되는 바, use variance는 허용될 수 없다.

갑 paid substantial amount of money for the business and it would be a substantial economic hardship if the use variance is not permitted. However, manufacturing facility would harm the neighborhood with subsequent noise in residential area and substantial harm would be caused if the manufacturing involves toxic materials or chemicals.

② 상기 예시에서 해당 지역을 only for retail stores로 지정한다는 내용의 zoning ordinance를 제정하였다면, ABC City는 use variance를 허용할 수 있는가?

⇒ May be yes. Retail stores가 있는 공간에서 manufacturing의 소음은 그다지 큰 피해로 예상되지 않는 바, use variance는 허용될 수 있다.

In the area surrounding with the retail stores, it is unlikely that the manufacturing would likely cause significant harm to the neighborhood with noise.

⇒ May be no. 해당 ordinance의 목적은 retail store로 구성된 커뮤니티를 형성하고자 하는데 있으므로 manufacturing facility는 그러한 커뮤니티에 방해의 요소가 될 수 있다.

The ordinance is to make a community comprised of retail stores. The manufacturing facility may make distraction and interference to the community.

답안요령 Taking Clause & Zoning ordinance

Q: <u>Was the ruling by the court correct? Discuss.</u>

<u>ABC City는 해당 지역을 only for commercial purpose로 지정한다는 내용의 zoning ordinance를 only for residential purpose로 변경하였다. 이에 따라 법원은 레스토랑을 갓 오픈한 갑에게 3개월 이내로 상업을 중단해야 한다고 판결하였다. 본 판결에 대해 논하라.</u>

1. Zoning ordinance 기본 rule
2. Taking Clause 기본 rule
3. Physical taking
   + analysis
4. Regulatory taking
   + analysis
5. (Nonconforming use and variance)

TIP1 문제가 Constitutional law의 Taking Clause와 nonconforming use 및 variance 중 어느 논점에 초점이 맞춰져 있는지 파악하는 것이 중요하다. Taking Clause에 초점이 맞춰져 있는 경우, 주어진 zoning ordinance의 합헌여부를 논한다. 한편, nonconforming use 및 variance에 초점이 맞춰져 있는 경우, 갑의 상황이 각 요건에 부합하는지 그 여부를 판단한다. 본 답안요령은 전자(前者)의 경우를 기준으로 작성되었다.

TIP2 Zoning ordinance에 대해 논하는 문제이므로 이에 대한 기본적인 rule과 Taking Clause에 대한 기본적인 rule 모두 작성해야 한다.

TIP3 위 3번: Regulatory taking도 taking에 해당한다는 점을 Lucas case 와 관련지어 언급하는 것이 고득점 포인트다.

모범답안 023

Zoning ordinance

Zoning ordinances are regulations on the land use by states and localities. It is allowed pursuant to the police power, according to Euclid case. However, a person who violates the zoning ordinance can seek for nonconforming use or variance.

(ANALYSIS: In this case, City ABC amended the zoning ordinance and it is allowed under the police power.)

Taking Clause

Under the Fifth Amendment Taking Clause, the governmental taking of private property for public use is prohibited without just compensation. Takings are recognized when the government: (1) physically occupy a landowner's land or real property (physical taking); or (2) denies economic value of the private property, the regulation is a taking (regulatory taking).

Physical taking

When the government physically occupy an individual property, it must be with just compensation.

(ANALYSIS: In this case, the zoning ordinance merely prohibit the commercial use and there is no physical occupation of 갑's property. Thus, there is no physical taking issue here.)

Regulatory taking

According to Lucas case, when a regulation denies all economical values of the property, a taking occurs. When a regulation unreasonably interferes with investment-backed expectations, it is also a taking. In determining whether the regulation is a taking, courts do multi-factor balancing test considering: (1) the social goal and the value to the community; (2) the economic impact on the claimant; and (3) the extent of interference with the investment-backed expectation of the owner [Penn case].

(ANALYSIS: In this case, City ABC amended the regulation (zoning ordinance).)

(1) Social goal and value to the community

(ANALYSIS: In this case, City ABC regulated the zoning ordinance for …….)

(2) Economic impact on the claimant

(ANALYSIS: In this case, the restaurant was very popular and 갑 would suffer big economic impact. Moreover, there are lots of equipment needed in the restaurant business and the cost for remodeling or rebuilding would be very high.)

(3) Extent of interference with the investment-backed expectation of the owner

(ANALYSIS: In this case, 갑 newly opened the restaurant and he may argue that his investment-backed expectation is interfered. The restaurants are capital intensive and it takes time to recover the capital costs.)

Conclusion

In conclusion, the zoning ordinance is not a taking.

Nonconforming use

Nonconforming use is allowed to continue if: (1) the use existed prior to the change of the ordinance; and (2) the use does not cause harm to neighborhood. Amortization is to allow the owner to find a new location for the activity.

(ANALYSIS: In this case, 갑 already opened the restaurant before the City ABC regulated the ordinance and running the restaurant causes no harm to residence. Thus, nonconforming use would be allowed. However, the ordinance was dramatically changed and three months amortization seems unreasonable.)

Conclusion

In conclusion, the zoning ordinance is not a taking and amortization is too short.

답안요령 | Nonconforming use & Variance

Q: How is the court likely to rule on 갑's request that ABC City issue a building permit?

갑이 manufacturing facility를 운영하고 있었는데, ABC City에서 해당 지역을 only for residential purpose로 지정한다는 내용의 zoning ordinance를 제정하였다. 갑은 해당 ordinance가 제정되기 이전에 이미 공장을 매입하기 위해 10억을 투자한 상태였고, ABC City에 공장설립 허용을 신청하였다. 법원은 어떤 판결을 내리겠는가?

> 1. Zoning ordinance 기본 rule
> 2. Nonconforming use 기본 rule
>   + analysis
> 3. Variance 기본 rule
>   + analysis

TIP1 문제가 Constitutional law의 Taking Clause와 nonconforming use 및 variance 중 어느 논점에 초점이 맞춰져 있는지 파악하는 것이 중요하다. Taking Clause에 초점이 맞춰져 있는 경우, 주어진 zoning ordinance의 합헌여부를 논한다. 한편, nonconforming use 및 variance에 초점이 맞춰져 있는 경우, 갑의 상황이 각 요건에 부합하는지 그 여부를 판단한다. 본 답안요령은 후자(後者)의 경우를 기준으로 작성되었다.

TIP2 위 1번: "정부는 police power에 입각하여 zoning ordinance를 제정할 수 있다"고 판시한 Euclid case와 연계하여 작성하는 것이 고득점 포인트다.

TIP3   위 2번: Nonconforming use의 '허용요건'을 title화하여 작성한다.

TIP4   위 3번: Variance의 '허용요건'을 title화하여 작성한다.

모범답안 024

Zoning ordinance

Zoning ordinances are regulations on the land use by states and localities. It is allowed pursuant to the police power according to Euclid case. However, a person who violates the zoning ordinance can seek for nonconforming use or variance.

Nonconforming use

Nonconforming use is allowed to continue if: (1) the use existed prior to the change of the ordinance; and (2) the use does not cause harm to neighborhood.

(ANALYSIS: In this case, the facility existed prior to the zoning ordinance. However, manufacturing facility would harm the neighborhood with subsequent noise in residential area and substantial harm would be caused if the manufacturing involves toxic materials or chemicals. Thus, nonconforming use would not be permitted.)

Variance

A variance is an individual exception for the zoning ordinance. There are two types of variance: area and use variance. An area variance allows a building to exist in dimensions that slightly violate the zoning ordinance. A use variance allows a person to operate a structure for a purpose that is not permitted by the zoning ordinance. For a use variance, an individual must show that: (1) his hardship with the ordinance; and (2) no damage or harm to the neighborhood caused by the variance.

(ANALYSIS: In this case, 갑 wanted to use the building for manufacturing purpose and he is seeking for a use variance.)

(1) Hardship with the ordinance

(ANALYSIS: In this case, 갑 paid 10억, substantial amount of money, for the business and it would be a substantial economic hardship if the use variance is not permitted. Thus, 갑 has hardship with the ordinance.)

(2) No damage or harm to the neighborhood

(ANALYSIS: In this case, 갑 wants to use the building for manufacturing purpose. However, as mentioned above, manufacturing facility would harm the neighborhood with subsequent noise in residential area and substantial harm would be caused if the manufacturing involves toxic materials or chemicals. Thus, the second requirement for use variance is not satisfied.)

Conclusion

In conclusion, the use variance would not be granted, since the second requirement for use variance is not satisfied.

Conclusion

In conclusion, the court would not permit both nonconforming use and use variance.

C. Relating Cases

1. Penn Case

Penn case는 regulation이 taking에 해당하는지 그 여부를 판단하는 기준을 제공하였다. 즉, multi-factor balancing test를 제시하였다.

Several factors must be weighed in determining whether a taking occurred are: (1) the **economic impact** on the claimant, (2) the extent to which the regulation has interfered with distinct **investment backed expectations**, and (3) the character of the government action [Penn Central Transportation Co. v. New York City, 438 U.S. 104 (1978)].

2. Euclid Case

Euclid case에 따르면 정부는 police power에 입각해 zoning ordinance를 제정할 수 있으며, 이는 합헌이다.

To be constitutional zoning ordinance, it must have its justification in aspect of the **police power,** such as the public health, safety, morals, or general welfare [Euclid v. Ambler Realty Co. - 272 U.S. 365, 47 S. Ct. 114 (1926)].

3. Lucas Case

Lucas case에서 법원은 정부가 물리적으로 사유자산을 이용하는 것뿐만 아니라 자산의 경제적 혜택을 모두 없애는 규제 또한 taking에 해당한다고 판시하였다.

When a regulation denies **all economical values** of the property, a taking occurs [Lucas v. South Carolina Coastal Council, 505 U.S. 1003 (1992)].

7장
Contracts

///

본 장은 계약 및 이에 따른 법률관계를 다루며, 크게 계약 성립, 계약서상 내용 및 채무내용, 채무불이행에 대한 remedy, 이렇게 세 부분으로 나뉜다. Contracts에서는 주어진 사안을 전체적으로 파악하여 계약당사자의 승소가능성 및 구제방법을 판단하는 문제가 대부분이다. 또한 계약 당사자 행위들이 계약 성립 과정의 일부인 경우가 많아, 각 당사자의 행위를 자세히 analysis하는 것이 중요하다. 본 장에 관한 답안은 크게 네 파트로 구성되는 바, ① 해당 사안에 적용되는 법률(CL 또는 UCC2), ② 유효한 계약의 생성여부, ③ 계약서상 내용 및 채무내용 파악 그리고 ④ 채무불이행에 대한 구제방안(remedy)이 그것이다.

- Aggrieved party = Non-breaching party = Injured party
- Breaching party: 계약을 불이행한 측
    = The party to be charged
    = The party sought to be bound
    = The party against whom the contract is being enforced

☑ 글쓰기 Tips

1. 모든 문제의 답안은 아래의 큰 틀에서 벗어나지 않는다.
   ① CL/UCC2
   ② Contract validity + Defenses to formation
   ③ Breach 여부 + Defenses
   ④ Remedy (damages)
2. 모든 문제는 가장 먼저 목적물의 유형을 통해 CL/UCC2 중 어느 법률이 적용되는

지 파악하고, UCC2가 적용되는 경우 당사자가 merchant인지 그 여부도 확인하여 작성해야 한다.

3. '당사자 일방이 제기한 소송의 승소 가능성'에 대한 문제는 주어진 사안을 종합적으로 판단할 것을 요구하는 문제이다.

    Q: <u>Is 갑 likely to prevail in his suit? Discuss.</u>

    Q: <u>Is 갑 likely to prevail in his breach of contract lawsuit and if so, what damages will he likely recover? Discuss.</u>

    Q: <u>Have 갑 and/or 을 breached the contract? If so, what damages might be recovered, if any, by each of them? Discuss.</u>

    ⇒ 상대방 을의 breach of contract뿐만 아니라 을의 defense에 대해서도 서술해야 한다.

    ⇒ ① CL/UCC2 판단, ② Contract validity, ③ 을의 breach of contract여부 판단, ④ 을의 defenses(~한 이유로 나에게는 채무가 없다), ⑤ Breach에 대한 remedies(duty to mitigate, monetary, non-monetary, restitution)

4. 당사자 중 일방의 breach를 가정한 질문도 있다.

    Q: <u>What remedy or remedies may 갑 reasonably seek and what is the likely outcome? Discuss.</u>

    ⇒ 상대방 을의 breach of contract가 명시되어 있는 경우로서, remedies에 초점을 두고 서술해야 한다.

    ⇒ ① Monetary remedy, ② Non-monetary remedy, ③ Restitution, ④ 갑의 duty to mitigate

[CL v. UCC2]

A contract for the sale of goods is governed by UCC2. The term "goods" means things that is tangible, movable, and identifiable at the time of making a contract. All other contracts are governed by the common law.

(ANALYSIS: In this case, the contract was made for tomatoes and UCC2 is applicable.)

Merchants are who deals in goods of the kind or having knowledge or skills peculiar to the goods involved in the transaction.

(ANALYSIS: In this case, 갑 is a tomato farmer and 을 is a supermarket owner. Both parties are merchants.)

I. Governing Rule

A. CL and UCC2

★A contract for the sale of goods is governed by UCC2. The term "goods" means things that is tangible, movable, and identifiable at the time of making a contract. All other contracts are governed by the common law.

B. Merchants

Under UCC2, there are special rules for merchants.

★"Merchants" are who deals in goods of the kind or having knowledge or skills peculiar to the goods involved in the transaction.

II. Formation of Contract

A. Mutual Assent and Consideration

1. Mutual Assent

Mutual assent between the parties is shown through offer and acceptance.

a. Offer

ⅰ. General Rule

★An offer is made when a person **communicates** to another his intent to enter into a bargain.

✔ Advertisement — solicitation of offer ○, offer ✕
✔ "I am offering you to sell the car for $500,000." → "the car" 라는 표현이 충분히 definite한지 그 여부에 대한 analysis가 필요하다. → 다른 자동차를 판매하지 않고 오직 한 자동차를 판매하는 경우라면 probably suffice(offer로 인정)일 것이나, 다수의 자동차 중 한 대를 판매하는 경우라면 offer로 인정될 수 없다.

ii. Termination by Death

Generally, an offer is terminated when either parties dies or becomes insane.

[Termination of Contract]

A contract does **not** terminate even if either parties dies or becomes insane.

계약당사자 중 한 명이 죽거나 insane의 상태가 된다면 offer는 종료된다. 반면, 계약이 성립된 이후에는 계약당사자 중 한 명이 죽거나 insane의 상태가 된다하더라도 계약이 종료되지 않는다.

b. Acceptance

i. General Rule

★An acceptance is a manifestation of consent to the offer. It may be made by any reasonable means before the offer is terminated.

ii. Mailbox Rule (19July)

Under the mailbox rule, an **acceptance** is effective **upon dispatch.** In other words, a valid contract is formed when the acceptance is dispatched, even before the offeror has not yet received it.

c. Rejection (16Feb)

Rejection is a manifestation of intent not to accept an offer.

i. Additional Terms

① Counteroffer (16Feb)

Under UCC2, when the offeree expressly made **condition on assent,** his response is recognized as **rejection or counteroffer,** rather than acceptance.

✔ "I'll think about it." — deferral^{유예} of response ○, rejection ×

✔ "The acceptance is expressly made conditional on your assent to the terms of this acceptance." — rejection ○

✔ "I accept your offer, provided that you agree to 10% discount." — rejection ○

② Contracts Between Merchants

Under UCC2, offeree's additional or different terms become part of the contract only when:

(a) **Both** parties are **merchants**;

(b) Those terms do **not materially change** the original terms of the offer; and

(c) Offeror does **not reject** them **within a reasonable time.**

ⅱ. Buyer's Right to Inspect (in UCC2)

Under the UCC2, buyers have right to inspect the goods **before** he accepts.

A buyer may **reject** the goods by notifying the seller the intent to reject **within a reasonable time** of defect.

2. Consideration

★There is consideration if it is bargained for exchange for a return promise or performance. Usually, consideration is proven by the facts that the parties have received **legal benefit or detriment**^{손상} **for the contract.**

B. Promissory Estoppel (16Feb)

• Promissory estoppel = Implied-in-law contract

★Promissory estoppel occurs when a party makes a promise with the **intent to induce the reliance** of the other party, and the other party relies on that promise **to its detriment**^{손상}.

C. Implied-In-Fact Contract

An implied−in−fact contract is formed **by actions, conducts, or circumstances** other than oral or written language.

✔ Shipment of the goods and payment for the goods

D. Statute of Frauds (SOF) (19July)

1. General Rule

> "MY LEGS" – Marriage, performance〉one Year, Land, Executor promises, Goods≥$500, Suretyship

Statute of frauds (SOF) requires agreements be evidenced by a writing **signed by the party sought to be bound** (a party against whom it is being enforced). The statutes apply to:

ⅰ. Promises regarding marriage;

ⅱ. Performance beyond one year;

ⅲ. Interest in land;

ⅳ. Executor Promises;

ⅴ. Goods priced at $500 or more; and

ⅵ. Suretyship promises.

2. Exceptions

> "SMAP" – Special goods, Merchant's confirmatory memo, Admission, Payment

Under UCC2, the writing is not required for the sale of goods totaling $500 or more when:

ⅰ. The goods are **specially manufactured;**

ⅱ. There is a **merchant's confirmatory memo;**

ⅲ. The party sought to be bound **admitted** the contract; or

iv. One party has **partially performed** (partially accepted and paid for the goods).

a. Merchant's Confirmatory Memo

A writing is a merchant's confirmatory memo for the statute of frauds purpose if:

ⅰ. The contract is made **between merchants;**

ⅱ. The sender makes the writing **in confirmation** of the contract **within a reasonable time;**

ⅲ. The writing is received and the receiving party has **reason to know its contents;** and

ⅳ. The receiving party does **not** make **objection** to its contents **within 10 days after it is received.**

E. Defenses to Formation (16July, 17July−civil pro., 18Feb, 20Feb)

1. Mistake

   a. Mutual Mistake

   Mutual mistake occurs when:

   ⅰ. **Both parties** have a **mistaken belief** about **material fact;** and

   ⅱ. Both parties **did not assume** the risk of the mistake.

   b. Unilateral Mistake

   Unilateral mistake occurs when:

   ⅰ. **One party** has a **mistaken belief** about **material fact;**

   ⅱ. The mistaken party **did not bear the risk** of that mistake; and

   ⅲ. The other party **knew/had reason to know** of that mistake.

   ✔ Having superior knowledge = Bearing the risk

2. Non-Disclosure

Non-disclosure occurs when the party who has a **duty to disclose** makes **no comment or disclosure** information.

3. Misrepresentation

a. General Rule

Misrepresentation occurs when a party:

  i . Made a misrepresentation of **material fact;**

  ii . **With the intent** that the other party rely on the misrepresentation;

  iii. The other party **in fact relied** on the misrepresentation; and

  iv. The other party suffered **damages.**

Ⅲ. Performance

A. Modification (18July, 20Feb)

1. Common Law

Under the common law, there must be **consideration** to be a valid modification.

✔ The modification placed an **additional** **$5,000** on 갑, and an **additional burden** should be placed on 을 to be a valid modification.

2. UCC2

Under UCC2, an agreement modifying a contract needs **no consideration** to be binding, but needs **good-faith.**

TIP Modification과 anticipatory repudiation의 관계
계약당사자가 계약 체결 후 자신의 채무에 대해 어려움을 호소하거나 이행하지 못할 가능성을 시사하는 경우, 해당 언급이 modification과 anticipatory repudiation 중 어느 것에 해당하는지 analysis해야 한다. 예컨대, 갑·을간 매매계약을 체결한 후 갑이 을에게 "공장 직원의 파업으로 delay될 가능성이 있다"고 얘기한 경우, 갑은 해당 언급이 modification임을 주장할 것이나 을은 해당 언급이 anticipatory

repudiation이므로 갑이 breach the contract했다고 주장할 것이다.

B. Terms in Contract

1. Mirror Image Rule (16Feb)

a. Common Law

Under the mirror image rule, an acceptance should mirror an offer without modification. In other words, the acceptance must be **exactly same** with the offer.

b. UCC2 (Battle of the Forms)

UCC2 abandoned the mirror image rule, and adopts "battle of the forms" provision. Additional or different terms **is effective** as an acceptance, unless the party expressly stated that the acceptance is made conditional on assent to the additional or different terms.

2. Parol Evidence Rule (20Feb)

a. General Rule

★Under the parol evidence rule, the parties cannot provide **extrinsic evidence** of prior agreements **to vary the terms of writing** when there is a **written** contract which is **finally expressed and is a complete integration.**

b. Integration

In determining whether the writing is completely or partially integrated, the court considers various factors, such as a **merger clause.**

If the writing is completely integrated, the writing discharges prior agreements.

If the writing is partially integrated, it discharges prior agreements **only to the extent that the written agreement is inconsistent** with the prior agreement.

✔ Merger clause is not a sole factor in determining whether the writing is completely or partially integrated, but it is a substantial one.

⇒ 서면으로 작성된 계약의 integration 정도를 판단하는데 있어 merger clause가 없다면 complete integration으로 보지 않는다. 다만, merger clause가 존재한다하여 반드시 complete integration 으로 인정하는 것은 아니다.

3. Dead Man Act (19July)

In some jurisdictions adopting the Dead Man Act, **oral statements** of a deceased **against the descendant's estate** cannot be provided to prove the existence of an agreement.

> TIP 주어진 사안에 Dead Man Act의 적용여부가 명시되어 있지 않은 경우, 본 Act가 적용되는 경우로 '가정'하여 증거의 제출여부를 판단한다. There are no facts indicating whether the jurisdiction adopts Dead Man Act. If Dead Man Act applies, ~.

C. **Warranties** (16Feb)

1. Implied Warranty of Merchantability

When a contract is for **sale by a merchant, every** contract implies a warranty of merchantability.

2. Implied Warranty of Fitness for a Particular Purpose

A contract implies a warranty of fitness for a particular purpose when:

ⅰ. The seller **knows or has reason to know** the **particular purpose** for which the goods are required; and

ⅱ. That the buyer **relies on** the seller's skill or judgment to select or furnish suitable goods.

3. Express Warranty

Express warranty는 판매자 및 공급자가 구매자에게 거래의 기초(basis of the bargain), 즉 거래의 목적물인 제품에 대해 언급한 확언(affirmation) 또는 약속을 뜻한다.

An express warranty arises when a seller or supplier **makes any affirmation** of fact to the buyer relating to the goods that becomes part of the **basis of the bargain.**

4. Disclaimer

Disclaimer는 보증에 대한 '포기'를 뜻하는 바, 계약서 상 "현 상태 그대로를 보증하며 그 외의 보증은 인정하지 않는다(as is, with no warranties as to the condition of the house)."는 조항으로 표현될 수 있다. 이러한 조항을 "as is" provision이라 일컬으며, 본 조항이 있는 경우 모든 유형의 warranty가 모두 waive되는 것이 원칙이다. 그렇다면 "as is" provision이 존재하는 경우 판매자가 구매자를 기만한 사실에 대해서도 판매자는 이에 대해 책임을 지지 않아도 되는가. 예컨대, 매도인 갑이 매수인 을에게 아파트 천장의 누수 사실에 대해 속였고 아파트 매매계약서에 "as is" provision이 존재한다면 을은 rescind the contract를 주장할 수 없는가. 본 사안에서는 당사자의 misrepresentation 및 unilateral mistake가 인정되는 바, 법원은 in the interests of justice에 입각하여 rescission을 인정할 것이다.

Even though there is an "as is" provision in the contract, a court may find that the misrepresentation was significant enough to **rescind** the contract **in the interests of justice.**

D. Discharge (16July, 18July)

1. Impossibility

When impossibility occurs, the contractual duties are discharged.

★Impossibility occurs when an **unforeseeable** event makes the contractual performance impossible.

✔ 갑·을간 construction contract를 체결하였고 이후 친환경 목재만을 사용하라는 법규가 unforeseeably 제정된 경우, 친환경 목재가 더 많은 cost를 야기한다 할지라도 채무를 전혀 이행할 수 없는 것은 아니므로 impossibility가 인정되지 않는다.

Even though the new regulation evaluates the cost, the regulation deos not make the party's performance illegal or impossible. Thus, impossibility would not be an effective defense.

2. Impracticability

★When permanent impracticability occurs, the contractual duties are discharged. Impracticability occurs when:

ⅰ. Unforeseeable event makes the contractual performance **extremely and unreasonably difficult;**

ⅱ. The event is as to a **basic assumption** of the contract; and

ⅲ. **Neither party assumed the risk.**

3. Frustration of Purpose

★When frustration of purpose occurs, the contractual duties are discharged.

Frustration of purpose occurs when:

ⅰ. An **unforeseeable** event **frustrates the purpose** of the contract; and

ⅱ. **Neither party assumed the risk.**

✔ 갑이 lifetime care를 위해 보험을 들었고 그 이후 사망한 경우, 계약의 목적이 상실되었으므로 frustration of purpose로 인정된다.

✔ 갑·을간 construction contract를 체결하였고 이후 친환경 목재만을 사용하라는 정부의 unforseeable한 지침이 있었던 경우, 친환경 목재가

더 많은 cost를 야기한다 할지라도 계약의 목적 및 가치가 완전히 상실되었다고 보기 어려우므로 frustration of purpose가 인정될 수 없다. Increased cost does not frustrate the purpose of the contract.

4. Rescission (18Feb)

When rescission occurs, the contractual duties are discharged. Rescission makes the parties left as a contract **had never been made.** When the original contract is voidable, rescission remedy can be recovered.

Ⅳ. Breach

When a party fails to perform as contemplated by^{고려되다} the contract, there has been a breach.

A. Material Breach (CL) (14July, 16July)

1. General Rule

★Under the **common law** doctrine of substantial performance, non-breaching party can recover when there is a **material breach.** A material breach occurs when a party does not provide **substantial performance.**

2. Considering Factors

When courts determine whether there is a material breach, they consider:

ⅰ. Whether the breach was willful or in good faith;

ⅱ. The extent of part performance; and

ⅲ. Cost of fixing the breach.

3. Time of the Essence Clause

When there is an explicit time of the essence clause, failure of timely performance is a **material breach.**

When performance is slightly delayed, it is **not** considered a material breach.

✔ "갑 agrees to start the performance on Sep. 29."

① 계약서에 "time is essence"라는 문구가 명시되어 있지 않은 경우, 적시(適時)에 대한 언급만으로는 time of the essence clause를 인정하기 어렵다.

There was no explicit statement that time is essence and there was mere reference of the timeliness. Thus, time is not of essence.

② Time of the essence clause로 인정된다 할지라도 time of the essence clause는 대개 완료일(completion date)에 적용되는 바, 갑이 9월 29일 이후에 채무를 이행한다 할지라도 material breach로 인정되기는 어렵다.

Although there is the time of essence clause, it is usually as to the completion date rather than the starting date. Thus, delay in starting is not a material breach.

B. Perfect Tender Rule (UCC2)

★Under UCC2, goods should be **perfectly tendered** and a party is required to act in **good faith.**

If the goods does not completely conform to the buyer's specification, the buyer may **reject** them.

✔ "갑 agrees to start the performance on Sep. 29."

① UCC2의 perfect tender rule에 따라 채무자는 합의한 내용(quantity, time of delivery)을 충실히 이행해야 하며, 그렇지 않을 경우 breach of the contract로 인정된다.

Under UCC2 perfect tender rule, delivery on the contracted date is required.

② Arguable point

계약서상 delivery due date는 명시되어 있으나 time is essence라는 점은 명시되어 있지 않은 상태에서 판매자가 due date를 지키지 않은 경우, 판매자는 essence of time을 명시하지 않았음을 근거로 본인 채무를 substantially perform했다(breach하지 않았음)고 주장할 것이다. 이에 구매자는 UCC2상의 perfect tender rule에 근거하여 delivery due date를 지키지 않은 판매자의 breach of the contract를 주장할 수 있다.

Seller may argue that he performed substantially and there is no breach of the contract. However, the buyer could argue that delivery on the contracted date is required under UCC2 perfect tender rule.

C. Anticipatory Repudiation (14July, 15Feb, 16July, 18July)

Anticipatory repudiation이란, 계약당사자들의 모든 채무가 이행되지 않은 경우 행해지는 repudiation을 뜻하는 바, 계약당사자 중 일방이 채무를 이행하지 않겠다는 의지를 표명(unambiguously)함으로서 이루어진다. 일단 계약당사자 중 일방(갑)이 의지를 표명하면, 그 상대방(을)은 repudiating party(갑)를 상대로 소송을 제기하거나, 자신(을)의 채무 기한까지 기다렸다가 갑을 상대로 소송하거나, 갑의 행위를 계약 파기를 위한 offer로 보고 모든 채무가 discharged되었다 여기거나 또는 갑에게 채무이행을 촉구할 수 있다.

1. General Rule

★Anticipatory repudiation is considered a **total breach** of the contract and it occurs if:

i. Both parties have **executory**[불이행의] **unperformed** duties for a **bilateral** contract; and

ii. The party **unambiguously** indicates his intent to repudiate.

2. Remedies

★When anticipatory repudiation occurs, non-repudiating party has following four options:

   ⅰ. **Sue immediately,** treating the anticipatory repudiation like a **repudiation;**

   ⅱ. **Wait** to sue and postpone his own performance **until the due date;**

   ⅲ. Treat the contract **as discharged,** treating the anticipatory repudiation like an **offer to rescind;** or

   ⅳ. **Urge** the promisor to perform, ignoring the anticipatory repudiation.

When one party has **fully performed** his duty **prior to the due date** and the other party repudiates by refusing to party, the non-breaching party must wait **until the original due date** to seek remedies.

3. Anticipatory Repudiation and Perspective Inability and Modification

Anticipatory repudiation은 당사자 중 일방이 더 이상 계약 내용을 이행하지 않겠다(repudiate)는 의사를 표명한 경우 인정되는 바, 당사자 중 일방이 단순히 자신의 채무이행에 있어 '어려움'이 있다는 점을 명시한 경우에는 인정되지 않는다. 후자의 경우 당사자 중 일방이 자신의 "perspective inability를 알렸다"고 표현하는데, 이는 채무를 이행하지 않겠다는 의사표명은 없었다는 점에서 anticipatory repudiation과 차이가 있다. 예컨대, 을에게 토마토를 판매하기로 한 농부 갑이 을에게 "갑작스러운 폭우로 토마토 배달이 지연될 것 같다."고 말했다면 이는 갑의 anticipatory repudiation인가. 이 경우 갑은 토마토 배달이 지연될 것 같다고 밝혔을 뿐, 자신의 채무를 이행하지 않겠다는 의사를 표명한 것은 아니므로 perspective inability로 인정된다.

한편, anticipatory repudiation은 modification과도 구분되어야 한다. Modification은 계약수정을 뜻하는 바, 새로운 계약을 생성하는 것과 같이 offer와 acceptance 요건이 만족되어야 한다. CL의 경우에는 consideration도 요구되나, UCC2에서는 good-faith 요건이 만족되면 consideration이 없더라도 modification이 인정된다. 즉, modification은 당사자간 합의(offer and acceptance)가 있어야만 인정되는 반면, anticipatory repudiation은 당사자 일방의 의사표명이 있으면 인정된다는 점에서 두 개념에 차이가 있다.

★A statement as to **perspective inability to perform** is made when one party **expresses doubts** or reservations about a duty or obligation under the contract.

- ✔ "Heavy rains slowed tomato ripening. Delivery will be two weeks late." — perspective inability
- ✔ "I'll see it is possible to deliver no later than September 29." — perspective inability
- ✔ "Using other equipment would add costs." — perspective inability
  There was no representation that he could not perform because of the increased cost. It merely requested a greater sum of money due to the increased cost of performance.

4. Retraction of Repudiation

- • Retraction = Revocation

★A repudiating party may withdraw his repudiation before his performance is due, unless the other party **considers the repudiation final** or **materially changed her position in reliance on the reputation.**

TIP Arguable point: Breaching party(갑)는 'retract했음'을 주장할 것이나, 이에 대해 non-breaching party(을)는 '상대방(갑)의 repudiation을 final로 여겼음' 또는 '상대방(갑)의 repudiation을 믿고 자신의 상태를 현저히 변화시켰음'을 근거로 갑의 repudiation이 유효하다고 주장할 것이다.

5. Request for Assurances (UCC2) and Anticipatory Repudiation (15Feb, 18July)

한편, UCC2에는 anticipatory repudiation과 관련된 "assurance"라는 개념을 인정하고 있다. 이는 CL에서 인정되지 않는 개념으로서, 목적물이 "goods"인 계약에 한해 적용된다. Assurance란, 계약 당사자가 상대방이 계약 이행을 하지 못할 것 같다고 합리적으로 판단한 경우 그 상대방에게 계약 이행에 대해 요구하는 보장을 뜻한다. 예컨대, 갑이 을로부터 토마토 1톤을 구입하는 계약을 체결하였는데 계약체결 이후 심한 폭우가 내려 토마토를 정상적으로 재배할 수 없다고 합리적으로 판단한 경우, 갑은 을에게 해당 계약을 제대로 이행할 수 있는지에 대한 assurance를 요구할 수 있다(demand for assurance). 갑으로부터 demand for assurance를 받은 을은 일정기간 내로 갑에게 assurance를 주어야하며, 만약 assurance를 하지 않는다면 을이 anticipatory repudiate한 것으로 본다. 갑의 채무는 demand for assurance가 이루어진 이후부터 assurance가 이루어지기까지의 기간 동안 유예된다.

★Under UCC2, a party may demand **assurances in writing** to the other party, if there are **reasonable doubt** that the other party may not perform. The performance of the demanding party **is suspended** until the requesting party receives adequate assurances.

★If the other party did not provide a proper assurance **within 30 days after a justified demand for assurances,** the contract may be treated as **anticipatorily repudiated.**

TIP1   당사자 중 일방이 상대방에게 request for assurance를 한 경우, anticipatory repudiation과 assurance 관계에 대해 언급해야 한다. If a party fails to make a response to the assurance, this failure may be treated as an anticipatory repudiation.

TIP2   Proper demand for assurance가 아닌 경우의 arguable point
갑·을간 소송에서 갑이 '을에게 request for assurance를 하였으나 을의 response가 없었음'을 주장하며 을의 anticipatory repudiation을 주장하는 경우, 을은 이에 대해 proper assurance가 아니었다고 반박할 것이다.

갑 may argue that there was 을's anticipatory repudiation because he failed to make a response to the assurance. However, 을 may argue that 갑 did not made a proper assurance and there is no anticipatory repudiation.

답안요령 | Anticipatory repudiation v. Perspective inability

---

1. CL/UCC2 (+ Merchant)
   + analysis
2. Contract validity + Defenses against validity
   + analysis
3. Anticipatory repudiation 기본 rule
4. Perspective inability
   + analysis

TIP1 Contracts 과목의 모든 답안에는 ① 적용법률(CL/UCC2)과 ② 계약 성립여부를 작성해야 한다.

TIP2 계약성립여부는 계약성립요건 3개뿐만 아니라 defenses against validity도 항상 고려해서 판단해야 한다. 계약성립여부가 주된 논점이 아닌 경우, 계약성립요건에 대한 rule을 자세히 서술할 필요는 없다.

TIP3 Perspective inability에 관한 사안에서는 대개 당사자가 자신의 채무를 delay하거나 이행하지 못할 가능성이 있음을 시사한다. 이 경우, 해당 당사자는 단순히 의문을 가졌을 뿐이며 해당 진술은 anticipatory repudiation이 아닌 perspective inability에 해당한다고 볼 수 있다. 대부분의 경우 perspective inability로 인정된다.

The party did not make an unambiguous repudiation, but he **only expressed doubt** regarding his ability [to do performance].

TIP4 계약당사자가 계약 체결 후 자신의 채무에 대해 어려움을 호소하거나 이행하지 못할 가능성을 시사하는 경우, modification에 관련된 arguable point가 존재할 수 있다. 예컨대, 갑·을간 매매계약을 체결하였고 이후 갑이 을에게 "공장 직원의 파업으로 delay될 가능성이 있다"고 얘기한 경우, 갑은 해당 언급이 modification임을 주장할 것이나 을은 해당 언급이 anticipatory repudiation이므로 갑이 breach the contract했다고 주장할 것이다.

모범답안 025

CL v. UCC2

A contract for the sale of goods is governed by UCC2. The term "goods" means things that is tangible, movable, and identifiable at the time of making a contract. All other contracts are governed by the common law. (ANALYSIS: In this case, the contract was made for tomatoes and UCC2 is applicable.)

Merchants are who deals in goods of the kind or having knowledge or skills peculiar to the goods involved in the transaction.

(ANALYSIS: In this case, 갑 is a tomato farmer and 을 is a supermarket owner. Both parties are merchants.)

Contract validity

To form a valid contract, there should be offer, acceptance (mutual assent), consideration, and no defenses to contract.

(ANALYSIS: In this case, there were offer and acceptance between them and 1천만원 and tomatoes are valuable consideration. In addition, there are no defenses against validity applicable. Thus, 갑 and 을 formed a valid contract for tomatoes.)

Anticipatory repudiation v. Perspective inability
Anticipatory repudiation

Anticipatory repudiation is considered a total breach of the contract and it occurs if: (1) both sides have executory unperformed duties for a bilateral contract; and (2) the party unambiguously indicates his intent to repudiate. When anticipatory repudiation occurs, non-repudiating party has four options: (1) sue immediately, treating the anticipatory repudiation like a repudiation; (2) wait to sue and postpone his own performance until the due date; (3) treat the contract as discharged, treating the anticipatory repudiation like an offer to rescind; or (4) urge the promisor to perform, ignoring the anticipatory repudiation.

Perspective inability

A statement as to perspective inability to perform is made when one party expresses doubts or reservations about a duty or obligation under the contract.

(ANALYSIS: In this case, 갑 indicated that heavy rains slowed tomato ripening and delivery will be two weeks late. 을 could argue that his statement is anticipatory repudiation, but there is no indication that 갑 would not perform his obligation. 갑 merely indicated the delay of delivery. Thus, 갑's statement is perspective inability to perform rather than anticipatory repudiation.)

Conclusion

In conclusion, 갑's statement is perspective inability to perform rather than anticipatory repudiation. Therefore, 을 could not treat the contract as discharged and he should pay for tomatoes.

| 답안요령 | Anticipatory repudiation & UCC2 assurance |

1. CL/UCC2 (+ Merchant)
   + analysis
2. Contract validity + Defenses against validity
   + analysis
3. UCC2 assurance 기본 rule
   + analysis
4. 결론

TIP1   Contracts 과목의 모든 답안에는 ① 적용법률(CL/UCC2)과 ② 계약 성립여부를 작성해야 한다.

TIP2 위 3번: UCC2 assurance와 perspective inability to perform에 대해 모두 analysis해야 하는 경우도 있다. 예컨대, 갑이 토마토 배달이 폭우로 인해 약간 늦어질 수 있다고 언급한 것에 대해 을이 reasonably doubt를 느끼고 request for assurance를 한 경우, 갑의 statement가 perspective inability to perform이라는 점을 우선 analysis하고, 을의 request for assurance를 analysis한다.

TIP3 위 3번에 대한 analysis: ① demand for assurance를 하는데 있어 적합성(reasonability) 여부와 ② demand for assurance의 요청방법 (서면), ③ 상대방이 제공한 assurance의 의의(적합한 assurance/ anticipatory repudiation)

모범답안 026

CL v. UCC2

A contract for the sale of goods is governed by UCC2. The term "goods" means things that is tangible, movable, and identifiable at the time of making a contract. All other contracts are governed by the common law. (ANALYSIS: In this case, the contract was made for tomatoes and UCC2 is applicable.)

Merchants are who deals in goods of the kind or having knowledge or skills peculiar to the goods involved in the transaction.

(ANALYSIS: In this case, 갑 is a tomato farmer and 을 is a supermarket owner. Both parties are merchants.)

Contract validity

To form a valid contract, there should be offer, acceptance (mutual assent), consideration, and no defenses to contract.

(ANALYSIS: In this case, there were offer and acceptance between them and 1천만원 and tomatoes are valuable consideration. In addition, there are no defenses against validity applicable. Thus, 갑 and 을 formed a valid contract for tomatoes.)

<u>Assurance under UCC2</u>

Under UCC2, a party may demand assurances in writing to the other party, if there are reasonable doubt that the other party may not perform. The performance of the demanding party is suspended until the requesting party receives adequate assurances. If the other party did not provide a proper assurance within 30 days after a justified demand for assurances, the contract may be treated as anticipatorily repudiated.

(ANALYSIS: In this case, 을's doubt that 갑 may not perform is reasonable because there was uncommon heavy rain. Moreover, the demand for assurance was made in writing. Thus, the demand for assurance to 갑 is a justified demand and it was within 을's right. 갑 did not provide an adequate assurance since he provided assurance after 2 months after 을 provided the demand for assurance. Thus, the contract may be treated anticipatorily repudiated and 을 may raise suit against 갑.)

<u>Conclusion</u>

In conclusion, although 을 provided a proper demand for assurance, 갑 did not provide a proper assurance. Thus, the contract may be treated anticipatorily repudiated and 을 may raise suit against 갑.

V. Damages

A. Duty to Mitigate (14July, 16July)

Duty to mitigate란, 피해를 최소화하기 위해 노력할 의무를 뜻한다. 계약법에서 duty to mitigate는 non-breaching에게 있기 때문에 non-breaching party는 상대방의 breach를 인지한 후 '합리적인' 대안(replacement, substitute)을 찾아야 한다.

★Duty to mitigate requires the injured party to take all reasonable steps to reduce the damages.

TIP1 상대방의 채무불이행 후 replacement를 찾는 것은 duty to mitigate 에 의한 행위인 바, damages 책정 시 recover 금액을 제하여 계산 한다.

TIP2 계약기간 동안 제3자와의 계약을 금하는 조항이 있는 경우, non-breaching party의 duty to mitigate에 대해 analysis한다.

예문: 해당 조항이 있었기 때문에 타인과의 계약을 통해 mitigate할 수 없었다. 따라서 그는 duty to mitigate를 위배하지 않았다.

Because the provision made 갑 retrain from entering into other contracts, 갑 was unable to mitigate.

B. Non-Monetary Damages

1. Specific Performance (14July, 20Feb)

a. General Rule

When the **legal remedies are inadequate,** nonbreaching party may seek specific performance as an equitable remedy.

Specific performance is a court order which mandates a party to perform their contractual obligations.

Specific performance is only available on contracts **for land** or for **rare and unique goods.** It is unavailable for service contracts.

b. Requirements

★Specific performance is available when a claimant can show that:

i. There is a **valid contract** between the parties;

ii. There are **no disputes as to performance** of non-breaching party (certainty of terms, conditions);

iii. The non-breaching party has **fully performed;** and

iv. **Legal remedy is inadequate.**

c. Equitable Defenses

"LUB" - Laches, Unclean hands, sale to Bona fide purchaser (BFP)

Specific performance is available only when there are no equitable defenses applicable, such as laches, unclean hands, and sale to bona fide purchaser.

 ⅰ. Laches

Laches^{태만} defense arises when a party delays in bringing an equitable action and the delay **causes** prejudice on the defendant.

 ⅱ. Unclean Hands

The unclean hands defense arises when the party seeking specific performance is engaged in wrongdoing related to the contract.

 ⅲ. Sale to Bona Fide Purchaser

If the subject matter of a contract is sold to bona fide purchaser, the original party cannot assert the specific performance.

답안요령	Specific performance

Q: Is 갑 likely to prevail in its lawsuit seeking specific performance against 을? Discuss.

---

1. Specific performance 기본 rule
   + analysis
2. Defenses★
3. 결론

TIP1 특정 remedy 적용 가능성을 판단하는 문제는 대개 동일한 사안에 대한 여러 문제 중 하나로 출제되는 경우가 많은 바, contracts 과목에 공통적으로 작성하는 ① 적용법률(CL/UCC2)과 ② 계약성립여부를 별도로 작성할 필요는 없다.

TIP2 위 1번 analysis: Specific performance의 '요건'들을 title화 하여 각각 analysis한다.

TIP3 Defenses에 대한 별도의 문제가 출제되지 않았다 하더라도 이에 대해 analysis하는 것이 고득점 포인트다.

2. Specific performance

Specific performance

Specific performance is a court order which mandates a party to perform their contractual obligations. Specific performance is available when a claimant can show that: (1) there is a valid contract between the parties; (2) there are no disputes as to the duty of the seeking party; (3) the non-breaching party has fully performed; and (4) legal remedy is inadequate.

(1) Valid contract

As mentioned above, there is a valid contract between 갑 and 을.

(2) No disputes as to the duty of the seeking party

갑 is seeking specific performance against 을. Terms in the contract between 갑 and 을 are certain and definite. There are no any disputes as to his duty.

(3) Fully performed

갑 already paid 을. His performance is already fully performed.

(4) Legal remedy is inadequate

Specific performance is allowed only when the legal remedies are inadequate. Specific performance is only available on contracts for land or for rare and unique goods.

(ANALYSIS: In this case, 을 did not performed his duty, conveying the deed. However, there is no adequate legal remedy, since the land is viewed as unique.)

Conclusion

In conclusion, specific performance is adequate.

Defenses

Specific performance is available only when there are no equitable defenses applicable, such as laches, unclean hands, and sale to bona fide purchaser.

Laches

Laches defense arises when a party delays in bringing an equitable action and the delay causes prejudice on the defendant.

(ANALYSIS: In this case, there are no facts indicating that 갑 delayed in bringing the lawsuit. Thus, laches defense is inapplicable.)

Unclean hands

The unclean hands defense arises when the party seeking specific performance is engaged in wrongdoing related to the contract.

(ANALYSIS: In this case, there are no facts indicating that 갑 engaged in wrongdoing. Thus, unclean hands defense is inapplicable.)

Sale to bona fide purchaser

If the subject matter of a contract is sold to bona fide purchaser, the original party cannot assert the specific performance.

(ANALYSIS: In this case, there are no facts indicating that 을 sold the land to a bona fide purchaser. Thus, the defense is inapplicable.)

Conclusion

In conclusion, there are no applicable defenses.

Conclusion

In conclusion, 갑 is likely to prevail in its lawsuit seeking specific performance against 을.

C. Monetary Damages

미국 계약법상 monetary damages 유형에는 원고 및 피고의 상황을 기준으로 compensatory damages, nominal damages, punitive damages 그리고

liquidated damages, 이렇게 네 가지가 있다. 그중 compensatory damages는 채권자를 채무가 이행되었을 경우와 동일하게 만들고자 하는 목적을 가지는 배상액으로서, 주로 expectation damages, consequential damages 그리고 incidental damages의 합계로 책정된다. 만일 상기 요소들의 구체적인 금액을 산정하기 어려운(speculative) 경우에는 reliance damages로 책정된다. 한편, nominal damages는 채무불이행이 발생하였으나 손해는 발생하지 않은 경우의 손해배상, 즉 명목상 손해배상을 뜻하고, liquidated damages는 계약 당사자간 정해놓은 채무불이행 시의 배상액으로서 reasonable한 경우에 한해 인정된다. Punitive damages는 징벌적 손해배상을 뜻하는 바, 계약법상에서는 인정되지 않고 위법행위로 인한 피해에 한해 인정된다.

매매계약의 목적물이 goods인 경우, 즉 UCC2가 적용되는 계약의 경우에도 상기 손해배상 범위 책정 기준과 유사한 기준을 사용하나 채무불이행을 한 당사자가 누구인지에 따라 expectation damages(compensatory damages의 요소 중 하나)를 책정하는 방법이 다르다. '판매자'가 채무불이행하였고 구매자가 목적물을 인도받지 못한 경우에는 market damages 및 cover damages로 계산하며, 판매자가 채무불이행하였으나 구매자가 목적물을 인도받은 경우에는 lost-value damages로 계산한다. 한편, '구매자'가 채무불이행한 경우에는 market damages 및 cover damages로 계산하나 판매자가 lost volume seller, 즉 계약 당시 채무불이행한 구매자가 아니더라도 해당 제품을 판매할 수 있는 제3자가 충분히 존재하는 상태의 판매자였다면 lost profits로 계산한다.

건축계약(construction contract)의 경우에도 UCC2가 적용되는 매매계약과 마찬가지로 채무불이행한 당사자가 '건축주(owner)'인 경우와 '시공자(builder)'인 경우로 구분하여 손배액을 책정한다. 기본적으로 건축주가 breach한 경우에는 해당 계약에 의한 이익(profit)으로 계산하고, 시공자가 breach(시공자가 시공을 도중에 종료)한 경우에는 완공하기 위해 추가적으로 드는 비용과 완공이 delay되었음에 대한 보상액으로 계산한다.

1. Compensatory Damages

a. Expectation Damages

i. General Rule

★The expectation damages is to put the non-breaching party in as good a position as if the other party had fully performed.

ii. Market Damages (in UCC2)

fair mkt value − K price

Under UCC2, a party is entitled to recover the difference between the fair market price and the contract price.

Buyer's damages are measured as of the time the **buyer learns of the breach**.

Seller's damages are measured as of the time **for delivery**.

iii. Cover Damages (in UCC2) (15Feb, 16Feb, 18July)

cover price − K price

Under UCC2, a party is entitled to recover the difference between the cover price and the contract price when the made a **reasonable contract** for substitute goods **in good faith**.

TIP Arguable point: 갑이 상대방 을의 performance due date 이전에 타 회사 및 타인과 계약(replacement)을 체결한 경우, 을은 갑에게 기한 이전에 다른 계약을 체결하는 행위는 breach of contract임을 주장할 수 있다. 다만, 갑은 이에 대해 을의 breach/anticipatory repudiation을 주장할 것이다.

을 may argue that 갑 breached the contract because he purchased replacement before the due date. However, 갑 may argue that 을 anticipatorily repudiated before he made the replacement contract and, therefore, 갑 did not breach the contract.

iv. Lost Profits (in UCC2) (14July, 16Feb)

$$net\ profit = K\ price - cost$$

Lost profits are used when market damages and cover damages are inadequate compensation in which the seller is a **lost volume seller.** A lost volume seller is the seller who can obtain or manufacture as many goods as he can sell.

Lost profit is measured by the seller's **net profit (contract price with the breaching buyer minus cost to the seller).**

v. Construction Contract (16July)

① Owner's Breach

Generally, builder's damages are measured as **lost profits** if the owner's breach occurred before the construction started. Builder's damages are measured as **lost profits and any costs** incurred to date if the owner's breach occurred during the construction.

② Builder's Breach

Owner's damages are measured as **the cost of completion** if the builder's breach occurred **before** the construction started. Owner's damages are measured as **the cost of completion and reasonable compensation for delay** if the builder's breach occurred **during** the construction.

b. Consequential Damages

Consequential damages are caused by **the nonbreaching party's special circumstances.**

It is recoverable only when:

i. **Foreseeable** (proximate causation);

ii. **Reasonably certain** (damages are not speculative); and

iii. **Unavoidable** (plaintiff's duty to mitigate).

c. Reliance Damages (14July)

When expectation damages are **too speculative,** non-breaching party may recover reliance damages.

Usually, reliance damages is measured as the **cost of the performance** by non-breaching party. The expenses that non-breaching party has **incurred in preparing and partially performing the contract** are included.

> ✔ 차주와 차 딜러간 차 판매금액의 10%의 커미션 계약을 체결한 경우, 신문광고비 등과 같이 차 딜러가 소비한 마케팅 비용

d. Incidental Damages (in UCC2)

It is recognized **only in UCC2**. Incidental damages means any expenses reasonably **incurred** by the parties (either seller or buyer) **during the performance process.**

> ✔ Cost for packaging, shipping
> ✔ Cost for inspection
> ✔ Cost for paperwork
> ✔ Cost for warehouse
> ✔ 구매자가 채무불이행 한 후 판매자가 resell하기까지의 비용

2. Punitive Damages

Punitive damages could **not** be recoverable in contract cases.

D. Restitution (14July)

There are two types of restitution: legal restitution and equitable restitution.

1. Legal Restitution

a. Quasi-Contract

• Action in quasi-contract = Action for an implied in law contract = Action for quantum meruit

Quasi-contract is recognized based on a **unjust enrichment** theory. A party is recoverable when he conferred benefit to other party and it allows the other party to keep that benefit **without compensation**. Generally, it is measured by the **value of the benefit conferred or the cost in conferring the benefit.**

---

case

갑·을간 employment contract를 체결하였고, 어느 날 갑자기 고용주 갑이 을을 해고한 경우, 을은 갑으로부터 어떤 legal restitution을 받을 수 있는가?
⇒ Employment contract의 내용에 대한 별도의 언급이 없는 경우, 해당 근로관계는 at-will employment relationship으로 보는 바, 당사자에 의해 언제든 종료될 수 있다. 따라서 본 사안에서 갑의 행위는 breach로 인정되지 않는다. 다만, 을이 계약 체결일로부터 종료일까지 근무한 것에 대한 임금은 restitution으로서 보상받을 수 있다.

b. Replevin and Ejectment

Replevin applies when the plaintiff wants her **personal property** returned.

Ejectment applies when the plaintiff wants her **real property** returned.

2. Equitable Restitution

Reformation and rescission are included in equitable restitution.

a. Rescission (18Feb)

Rescission makes the parties left as a contract **had never been made (is discharged).** When the original contract is voidable and rescinded, rescission remedy can be recovered.

TIP

Rescission을 구하는 전형적인 근거에는 ① mistakes (mutual/unilateral)와 ② non-disclosure가 있다.

Q: <u>What remedy or remedies may 갑 reasonably seek and what is the likely outcome? Discuss.</u>

---

1. CL/UCC2★ (+ Merchant)
2. Contract validity + Defenses against validity
   + analysis
3. Breach 주장에 대한 근거
4. Remedies
   ① Legal remedies
   ② Restitution
   ③ Equitable remedies

TIP1   소송당사자의 적합한 구제방법(remedies)은 우선 '소송당사자의 승소가능성'에 대해 논해야 하는 바, ① 당사자간 계약에 대한 analysis를 통해 상대방의 breach of contract에 대해 논한 후 ② 이에 대한 remedies에 대해 판단해야 한다.

TIP2   위 2번: 계약성립여부는 계약성립요건 3개뿐만 아니라 defenses against validity도 항상 고려해서 판단해야 한다.

TIP3   위 4번: 세 유형의 remedies를 title화하여 작성하고, 각 remedy의 analysis에서 갑의 duty to mitigate를 논하는 것이 고득점 포인트다.

모범답안 028

CL v. UCC2

A contract for the sale of goods is governed by UCC2. The term "goods" means things that is tangible, movable, and identifiable at the time of making a contract. All other contracts are governed by the common law. (ANALYSIS: In this case, the contract was made for painting service and CL is applicable.)

Contract validity

......

Anticipatory repudiation

......

Remedies

Legal remedies

Compensatory damages

The compensatory damages is to put the non-breaching party in as good a position as if the other party had fully performed. Compensatory damages is generally measured by adding expectation damages, incidental, and consequential damages. Consequential damages are recoverable only when: (1) foreseeable; (2) reasonably certain; and (3) unavoidable.

Expectation damages

Expectation Damages is measured as the value of the breaching party's performance that was lost.

(ANALYSIS: In this case, 갑 was going to be paid for 1천만원. 갑 expected to receive it after the completion of the project. Thus, 갑 would receive 1천만원 as expectation damages.)

Incidental damages

It is recognized only in UCC2.

(ANALYSIS: In this case, the contract is made for service and CL is applicable. Thus, 갑 cannot recover incidental damages.)

Consequential damages

Consequential damages are caused by the non-breaching party's special circumstances.

(ANALYSIS: In this case, 갑 may argue that he could recover consequential damages since he lost his repudiation because of 을's breach.)

(1) Foreseeable

(ANALYSIS: In this case, 갑 may argue that 을 has known that ·······.

Thus, foreseeability requirement is satisfied.)

(2) Reasonably certain

To recover consequential damages, damages should not be speculative. (ANALYSIS: In this case, 갑 is seeking for consequential damages, arguing his reputation is reduced. However, the damages for reputation is too speculative. Thus, reasonable certainty requirement is not satisfied.)

(3) Unavoidable

Unavoidability requirement is satisfied when the plaintiff satisfied his duty to mitigate.
(ANALYSIS: In this case, there are no ways for 갑 to reduce the damages. Thus, 갑 did not violate his duty to mitigate and unavoidability requirement is satisfied.)

Conclusion

In conclusion, 갑 would not recover consequential damages.

Reliance damages

When expectation damages are too speculative, non-breaching party may recover reliance damages as the loss incurred reasonably relying on the contract. It is to put the plaintiff in the position as if the contract had never been made.
(ANALYSIS: As mentioned above, 갑 is arguing that his reputation is reduced, but the damages for reputation is too speculative. Thus, 갑 would recover reliance damages and the damages would include money spent by 갑.)

Restitution

Restitution is a remedy to prevent unjust enrichment. There are two types of restitution: legal restitution and equitable restitution.

Legal restitution (Quasi-contract)

Quasi-contract is recognized when a party has derived a benefit from no legally binding contract. Generally, it is measured by the value of the benefit conferred or the cost in conferring the benefit.

(ANALYSIS: In this case, ……. 을 may argue that the damages should be measured as $5,000 under the contract between the parties. However, damages is measured by the value of the benefit conferred or the cost in conferring the benefit. Thus, 갑 would recover $8,000.)

Equitable restitution

Reformation is the court's order to rewrite a contract reflecting the true agreement of the parties. Rescission is the court's order to make a contract invalid and make the parties left as a contract had never been made (is discharged).

(ANALYSIS: In this case, …….)

Equitable remedies
Specific performance

Specific performance is an equitable remedy in which the court orders a party to perform his duties under the contract. It is available when: (1) there is a valid contract; (2) legal remedy is inadequate; (3) the enforcement is feasible; (4) both parties are eligible to have their performance; and (5) there are no equitable defenses.

(1) Valid contract
……

(2) Legal remedy is inadequate
……

(3) Enforcement is feasible
……

(4) Eligibility

……

(5) No equitable defenses

……

Conclusion

……

Conclusion

In conclusion, 갑 would recover expectation damages or legal restitution.

8장
Civil Procedure

///

본 장은 미국에서 제기되는 민사소송에 대해 논하는 바, 관할권(jurisdiction)과 소송 진행과정(civil procedure), 이렇게 두 파트로 나누어져 있다. 캘리포니아 에세이 시험(CEE) 범위는 연방법원(federal courts)에서 청취하는 민사소송과 캘리포니아 주 법원에서 청취하는 민사소송을 모두 포함하는 바, 각 rule을 Federal rules과 California rules로 구분하여 설명하였다. 첫 번째 파트에서는 관할권(jurisdiction)에 대해 논한다. 다수의 법원 중 어느 법원에서 소송을 청취해야 하는지에 대한 내용으로서, 소송의 내용을 기준으로 한 subject matter jurisdiction(SMJ), 피고 및 소송 목적물을 기준으로 한 personal jurisdiction(PJ), 구역(district)을 기준으로 한 적합한 venue, 이 세 유형의 요건을 모두 만족해야만 연방법원의 관할권이 인정된다. 캘리포니아 주 법원은 PJ와 venue, 이 두 요건을 만족하면 재판권을 가진다. 두 번째 파트에서는 지난 7년간 출제되었던 CEE에서 다루었던 논점을 중심으로 원고가 filing하는 소장(complaint)부터 시작되어 최종판결(final judgment) 후 appeal하는 내용을 포함한 민사소송의 전체적인 진행과정에 대해 논한다.

☑ 글쓰기 Tips

1. 지난 7년간 CEE에서는 California rules보다는 Federal rules에 관해 더 자주 출제되었으며, Evidence와 Constitutional law이 연계되어 출제되기도 하였다.
2. Civil procedure에 관한 모든 문제는 가장 먼저 해당 case가 state court와 federal court 중 어디에 제소되었는지 확인한다.
3. Civil procedure에 관한 전형적인 문제는 없고, 특정 논점에 대해 출제된다.
   Q: <u>Does the federal court have [subject matter jurisdiction] over the suit? Discuss.</u>
   Q: <u>Did the federal court properly deny 갑's motion for [remand]? Discuss.</u>
4. 소송당사자가 신청한 motion에 대해 논하는 문제도 자주 출제된다.

Q: Did the state court properly grant 갑's motion to dismiss?
Q: Did the federal court properly grant 갑's motion for summary adjudication?
⇒ 주어진 사안에서 motion의 근거를 찾는다.

Part One. Jurisdictions (15July, 16July, 17July, 19Feb)

Ⅰ. Subject Matter Jurisdiction (SMJ)

A federal court has subject matter jurisdiction, when it has either federal question jurisdiction or diversity jurisdiction.

A. Federal Question Jurisdiction (FQJ)

★A federal court has federal question jurisdiction when the claim arises out of the federal laws, such as the Constitution, laws, or treaties of the United States.

B. Diversity of Citizenship Jurisdiction (DCJ)

★A federal court has diversity of citizenship jurisdiction when if the amount in controversy exceeds $75,000 and there is complete diversity between the parties.

1. Diversity

Each plaintiff must be diverse from each defendant.

State citizenship for individual U.S. citizen is determined by their domicile when the complaint was filed.

A corporation is a citizen of any state where it has been incorporated and of state where it has its principal place of business.

2. Amount in Controversy (AIC)

When a court determines the amount in controversy, it relies on the plaintiff's **good-faith allegations.**

The recovery which is less than $75,000 does not affect the amount in controversy requirement.

C. Supplemental Jurisdiction (SPJ)

A district court may exercise supplemental jurisdiction over claims that shares **common nucleus of operative fact.** In other words, the court may exercise SPJ over the claims that are part of the **same transactions or occurrences** of the primary claims.

II. Personal Jurisdiction (PJ)

There are three types of personal jurisdiction: in personam jurisdiction, in rem jurisdiction, and quasi in rem jurisdiction.

A. Traditional Basis

A court has in personam jurisdiction over a defendant when:

ⅰ. The defendant is **present** in the forum state;

ⅱ. The defendant is **domiciled** in the forum state; or

ⅲ. The defendant **consents** to jurisdiction.

B. Long-Arm Statute and Constitutional Limitation

1. California's Long-Arm Statute

A state long-arm statute may provide a personam jurisdiction over non-resident defendants.

California adopts long-arm statute which permits the exercise of jurisdiction broadly as is allowed by the **U.S. Constitution.**

2. Specific Long-Arm Statute

Some states adopt specific long-arm statue, which gives the court jurisdiction **over a non-resident defendant** who conducted in specific situations described in the statute.

3. Constitutional Limitation

★Under the **Due Process Clause** of the Fourteenth Amendment, a court has jurisdiction over a defendant if he have established **"minimum contacts"** with the state and the exercise of jurisdiction would be **related** to the defendant's contacts, and it would be **fair play and substantial justice.**

a. Minimum Contacts

A defendant has **minimum contacts** with the state when he **purposefully availed** himself of California and it was **foreseeable** that the defendant will be **haled into court.**

In **stream commerce** cases, purposeful availment is recognized only when the defendant **deliberately targeted** the forum.

[Purposeful Availment]
- ✔ 의사 갑(domiciled in A 주)은 회사 을이 B 주에서 생산된 장비를 이용하여 환자 병을 C 주에서 수술하였고, 그 과정에서 장비의 결함으로 인해 병이 신체적 상해를 입었다. 환자 병이 '의사 갑'을 상대로 B 주에서 negligence case를 제기한 경우, B 주는 의사 갑에 대해 personal jurisdiction이 있는가? → No. 갑 has no purposeful availment of State B.
- ✔ 의사 갑(domiciled in A 주)은 회사 을이 B 주에서 생산된 장비를 이용하여 환자 병을 C 주에서 수술하였고, 그 과정에서 장비의 결함으로 인해 병이 신체적 상해를 입었다. 환자 병이 '회사 을'을 상대로 B 주에서 negligence case를 제기한 경우, B 주는 의사 을에 대해 personal jurisdiction이 있는가? → Yes. 을 has purposeful

availment of State B.

[Stream Commerce Cases]

✔ 독일에서 공장을 운영하고 있는 피고(domiciled in Germany)가 독일 공장에서 생산한 자동차를 LA에 유통한 경우(specifically distribute its cars in LA) → deliberately targeted ○ → purposeful availment 인정 ○ → 피고에 대한 캘리포니아 주의 재판권(personal jurisdiction)이 인정된다.

✔ 독일에서 공장을 운영하고 있는 피고(domiciled in Germany)가 한국 공장에서 생산한 자동차를 유통하였고, 그 결과 LA에서 판매된 경우 → deliberately targeted × → purposeful availment 인정 × → 피고에 대한 캘리포니아 주의 재판권(personal jurisdiction)이 인정되지 않는다.

b. Relatedness

Relatedness between claim and contact is recognized either specifically or generally.

Specific jurisdiction is recognized when the defendant's contacts in the forum is not systematic or continuous, but a **cause of action arises out of his contacts with a jurisdiction.**

General jurisdiction is recognized when the defendant's contacts in the forum is **systematic or continuous** and he is **essentially at home** in the forum.

c. Fairness

Even when a nonresident has the necessary minimum contacts with the forum state, the exercise of the personal jurisdiction may offend **due process,** if it is unfair.

In determining whether the exercise of personal jurisdiction is fair, the court considers several factors, such as **the plaintiff's interest in relief, the defendant's severe disadvantage, and the interest of** forum state.

답안요령 Personal jurisdiction

Q: <u>Does the Superior Court of California in San Diego have personal jurisdiction over 갑?</u>

---

1. Traditional bases
   + analysis
2. Long-arm statute and Constitutional law
3. Analysis
   ① Minimum contacts ("stream of commerce" theory★)
   ② Relatedness
   ③ Fairness

모범답안 029

Traditional bases

A court has in personam jurisdiction over a defendant when: (1) the defendant is present in the forum state; (2) the defendant is domiciled in the forum state; or (3) the defendant consents to jurisdiction.

(ANALYSIS: In this case, ……. Thus, 갑 does not satisfy any of traditional bases of personam jurisdiction.)

Long-arm statute and Constitutional law

A state long-arm statute may provide a personam jurisdiction over non-resident defendants. California adopts long-arm statute which permits the exercise of jurisdiction broadly as is allowed by the U.S. Constitution. Under the Due Process Clause of the Fourteenth Amendment, a court has jurisdiction over a defendant if he have established minimum contacts with the state and the exercise of jurisdiction would be related to the defendant's contacts, and it would be fair play and substantial justice.

(ANALYSIS: In this case, 갑 is domiciled in South Korea and the

California's long-arm statute would be applied.)

Minimum contacts

A defendant has minimum contacts with the state when he purposefully availed himself of California and it was foreseeable that the defendant will be haled into court. In stream commerce cases, purposeful availment is recognized only when the defendant deliberately targeted the forum.

(ANALYSIS: In this case, 갑 deliberately targed California. 갑 manufactures his machines in Germany and he purposefully shipped those machines to San Diego for distribution with the intent to sell them in California. Thus, 갑 has minimum contacts with California.)

Relatedness

Relatedness between claim and contact is recognized either specifically or generally. Specific jurisdiction is recognized when the defendant's contacts in the forum is not systematic or continuous, but a cause of action arises out of his contacts with a jurisdiction. General jurisdiction is recognized when the defendant's contacts in the forum is systematic or continuous and he is essentially at home in the forum.

(ANALYSIS: In this case, 갑 is domiciled in South Korea and he is not at home in California. Thus, he does not satisfy general jurisdiction. However, he sold the machine in California and a cause of action arises out of it. Thus, specific jurisdiction is recognized.)

Fairness

The exercise of the personal jurisdiction should be fair under the due process. In determining whether the exercise of personal jurisdiction is fair, the court considers several factors, such as the plaintiff's interest in relief, the interest of forum state and the defendant's severe disadvantage.

(ANALYSIS: In this case, the exercise of the personal jurisdiction is fair. 갑 suffered physical injury and 갑 has strong interest in the case. California state also has a big interest in protecting the residents and malfunctioned machine. 갑 may argue that he lives in South Korea and it is unfair. However, the modern transportation would not be helpful for alleging unfairness. Thus, the exercise of the personal jurisdiction is fair.)

<u>Conclusion</u>

In this case, the Superior Court of California in San Diego has personal jurisdiction over 갑.

Ⅲ. **Venue** (16July)

본 파트는 재판권 요건 중 하나인 venue에 대해 논한다. 원고가 소송을 연방법원에 제기하였다면 Federal rules에 따라 venue를 판단하고, 캘리포니아 주 법원에 제기하였다면 캘리포니아 주 법원이 따르는 procedural law의 근간인 California Code of Civil Procedure에 따라 venue를 판단한다. California rules는 피고가 거주(reside)하고 있는 곳 또는 소송의 dispute가 발생한 곳을 proper venue라고 규정한다. 따라서 torts case에서는 상해(injury)가 발생한 곳을, contract case에서는 계약내용이 이행될 곳을 proper venue라고 규정한다.

여기서 '피고의 거주지(the place where defendant resides)'는 Federal rules와 California rules에서 다르게 해석된다. Federal rules의 경우, 해당 소송에서의 모든 피고들이 동일한 주에 거주하고 있는 경우에 한해 피고들의 거주지 모두가 proper venue로 인정된다. 예컨대, 피고 두 명이 각각 A district, B district에 reside하고 있고 두 지역 모두 동일한 주에 존재하는 지역인 경우 A district와 B district 모두 proper venue이다. 한편, California rules에 따르면, 소송이 제기될 당시 피고들이 거주하고 있었던 모든 곳이 proper venue로 인정되고, 만일 캘리포니아 주에 거주하고 있는 피고가 없는 경우라면 캘리포니아 주 내의 모든 county가 proper venue로 인정된다. 예컨대, 피고 두 명이 각각 A county, B county에 reside하고 있고 A county가 캘리포니아 주 내의 지역인 경우라면 A county와 B county 모두 proper venue이다. 만일 A county와 B county 모두 캘리포니아 주 내의 지역이 아니라면, 캘리포니아 주 내의 모든 지역이 proper venue이다.

'회사'의 거주지도 다르게 해석된다. Federal rules에서는 PJ가 인정되는 모든 곳이 proper venue로 인정되는 반면, California rules에서는 PPB, 계약이 생성된 곳, 계약이 이행되는 곳, 채무불이행이 된 곳, 채무가 발생된 곳 모두 proper venue로 인정된다.

A. Federal Rules

For civil actions brought in federal court, venue is proper in any district where:

ⅰ. Any defendant **resides** if **all** defendants are residents of the forum state;

ⅱ. A **substantial portion** of the claim occurred;

ⅲ. A **substantial part** of property is located; or

ⅳ. If none of the above apply, then venue is proper in any judicial district in which any defendant is subject to the court's personal jurisdiction.

B. California Rules

1. General Rule

In California, the venue is proper in any county where:

ⅰ. The **defendant resides**; or

ⅱ. The **dispute arose**.

In torts actions, the county where the **injury took place** is another proper venue.

In contract actions, the county where the **contract will be performed** is another proper venue.

In local actions, the county in which the **real property lies** is a proper venue. A local action is a dispute as to land.

2. Reside

a. Person

Where any defendant resides at the time the case is filed is a proper venue.

If there is no defendant who resides in California, any county in California is a proper venue.

b. Corporation

Where the principal place of business (PPB) of the corporation, where the contract was made or performed, where the contract breach occurs, or where liability arises is a proper venue.

IV. Removal (14Feb, 15July, 16July)

1. Requirements

A defendant may remove a civil action from state court to federal court if the action is a type over which the **federal courts have original jurisdiction.**

2. Procedure (30-Days Rule)

Under the 30-days rule, the removal must be sought within 30 days after the defendant discovers (through service of the summons or receiving the initial pleading, whichever period is shorter).

3. In DCJ Cases

To be a valid removal **in diversity of citizenship cases,** there are two additional requirements:

ⅰ. Defendant should not be a citizen of the forum state (in which the state action is brought); and

ⅱ. The removal must be sought within one year **after commencement** in a diversity action (one year rule).

4. Remand

If removal is improper, the **plaintiff** can file a motion to remand the case back to state court.

A motion to remand must be filed **within 30 days of the notice of removal.**

Q: Is 갑's motion to remand proper?

Q: Is 갑's action properly removable to federal court?

> 1. Removal 기본 rule & 30-days rule
> 2. Analysis
>   ① FQJ 해당여부
>   ② DCJ 해당여부
> 3. (DCJ인 경우) 추가요건
>   + analysis

TIP1   생각 route: Removal 신청 가능여부 확인 → 가능한 경우 remand 불가, 불가능한 경우 remand 신청 가능여부 확인

⇒ Remand에 관한 문제는 removal과 remand 모두 analysis해야 한다.

TIP2   위 3번: 주어진 사건이 DCJ인 경우, 추가요건에 대해 반드시 analysis 해야 한다.

모범답안 030

1. Is 갑's motion to remand proper?

Removal

A defendant may remove a civil action from state court to federal court if the action is a type over which the federal courts have original jurisdiction. Under the 30-days rule, the removal must be sought within

30 days of either service of the summons or receiving the initial pleading, whichever period is shorter.

FQJ

A federal court has federal question jurisdiction when the claim arises out of the federal laws, such as the Constitution, laws, or treaties of the United States.

(ANALYSIS: In this case, 갑 raised a claim based on 을's negligence. Thus, the federal court does not have federal question jurisdiction.)

DCJ

A federal court has diversity of citizenship jurisdiction when if the amount in controversy exceeds $75,000 and there is complete diversity between the parties.

(1) Amount in controversy

(ANALYSIS: In this case, 갑 is seeking damages for $80,000. Thus, the amount in controversy requirement is satisfied.)

(2) Complete diversity

Each plaintiff must be diverse from each defendant. State citizenship for individual U.S. citizen is determined by their domicile when the complaint was filed.

(ANALYSIS: In this case, 갑 is domiciled in State A and 을 is domiciled in State B. Complete diversity between 갑 and 을 is satisfied.)

Conclusion

The federal court has diversity of citizenship jurisdiction.

Additional requirements

To be a valid removal in diversity of citizenship cases, there are two additional requirements: (1) defendant should not be a citizen of the forum state (in which the state action is brought); and (2) the removal must be sought within one year after commencement in a diversity action (one year rule).

(1) Defendant
(ANALYSIS: In this case, 을 is a citizen of State B and 을 filed a motion to remove the case to the federal court in State C. Thus, the first requirement is satisfied.)

(2) One year rule
(ANALYSIS: In this case, 을 filed a motion to remove the case to the federal court after four months from the date of commencement of the case. Thus, the second requirement is satisfied.)

Conclusion
In conclusion, 을's motion to remove is proper

Conclusion
In conclusion, 을's motion to remove is proper and, therefore, 갑's motion to remand is improper.

V. Choice of Law (14Feb, 15Feb, 17July)

A. Erie Doctrine

1. General Rule
When the federal court has jurisdiction based on the **diversity,** the **federal court** must apply **forum state law** for the **substantive** rules.

2. Substantive v. Procedural Rules
When it is unclear whether the law is substantive or procedural, several tests are used.

Under the outcome determinative test, an issue is substantive if it is substantially affects the outcome of the case.

Under the balancing test, the law is substantive if it has the **grater interest** to be applied.

Under the forum shopping test, the court should follow the state law when the application of the federal rule **results in forum shopping.**

✔ Statutes of limitations (SOL) — substantive

✔ Rules for tolling statutes of limitations(소멸시효 중단) — substantive

✔ Choice of law rules — substantive

✔ Elements of a claim or defense — substantive

✔ Standards of burden of proof — substantive

✔ Whether or not a testimonial privilege applies — substantive

✔ Measure of damages — substantive

✔ Rule of discovery — procedural

B. California Choice of Law

1. Real Property

The law of the state where **the real property is located** governs the disposition of real property.

2. Torts

The court **balances the interest** of the governments in having their law apply. In other words, the court compares impairment to each state's interest.

3. Contracts

When there is no choice of law provision in the contract, the court **balances the interest** of the governments in having their law apply. When there is choice of law provision and there is no conflict with provision California rule, the provision is applicable.

When there is choice of law provision and there is conflict with provision California rule, the California rule is applicable only when there is **materially greater interest** to apply the rule.

case

California에 위치한 federal court에서 DCJ를 근거로 갑·을간 부동산 소유권에 대한 소송이 제기되었다. 해당 부동산은 ABC 주에 위치해 있다. California rules와 federal rules에 따르면 갑의 소유권이 인정되나, ABC 주에 따르면 을의 소유권이 인정된다. California court는 본 사안에 대해 어떻게 판단해야 하는가?

⇒ ABC 주의 rule에 따라 을의 소유권이 인정된다. Erie doctrine에 따라, federal court에서 제기된 소송이지만 choice of law, 즉 substantive law 에 따라 California rules를 적용해야 한다. California는 논란이 되는 부동 산이 위치한 주의 법에 따르도록 규정하고 있는 바, 본 사안에서는 ABC 주의 rules에 따라 을의 소유권이 인정된다.

Part Two. Civil Procedure

소송개시(filing) → pleadings (rule 12(b)) → 증거수집 및 제출(discovery) → summary judgment → 판결 → new trial or appeal

I. Pleadings

본 챕터에서는 pleadings에 대해 논한다. Federal rules와 California rules는 서로 다른 complaint의 작성 기준을 규정하는 바, Federal rules는 notice pleading, California rules는 fact pleading을 채택하고 있다. 연방법원의 notice pleading은 complaint의 내용이 피고가 해당 사건에 대해 이해할 수

있는 정도를 요하는 바, 그렇지 못한 경우에는 해당 사건은 dismiss된다. 다만, 최근에는 보다 높은 기준인 plausibility 기준을 채택하고 있는데, 이에 대한 자세한 내용은 「Ⅳ. Motions and Trial」 부분에서 논하도록 한다. 한편, 캘리포니아 법원은 소송의 근거, 예컨대 과실(negligence)의 모든 요건에 대한 사안을 설명할 것을 요하는 바, complaint에는 소송의 근거를 지지할 수 있는 결정적인(ultimate) 사안이 설명되어 있어야 한다.

A. General Rules

There are three types of pleadings: complaint, response, and answer.

1. Federal Rules

Federal courts use **notice pleading,** and it is enough to provide reasonable notice of nature and scope of the claims.

Complaint must include: identification of parties, proper subject matter jurisdiction, state of claim, demand for judgment, and the plaintiff's signature.

Generally, the defendant must serve an answer within 21 days after being served with the summons and complaint.

2. California Rules

California courts use **fact pleading,** and it should include **ultimate facts** to support each element of the cause of action.

In complaint, fictitious^{허구의} "Doe" defendant is allowed when the defendant is unknown. A demand for judgment includes the amount of damages.

Generally, the defendant must serve an answer within 30 days after being served with the summons and complaint.

a. Cross Complaint

In California, the term "cross complaint" is used for all third-party actions, such as counterclaim, cross-claim, and impleader.

b. Demurrers

In California, demurrer is typically used to respond to the complaint.

There are two types of demurrer: general and special demurrer. Each type of demurrer has different grounds.

ⅰ. **General Demurrer**

General demurrer is may be filed when:

① Pleadings failed to state facts sufficient to constitute a cause of action; or

② The court lacks subject matter jurisdiction.

ⅱ. **Special Demurrer**

Special demurrer is may be filed based on several grounds, such as:

① Failure to make a definite statement;

② Lack of legal capacity; and

③ Inadequate joinder of parties.

B. Service of Process (16July)

1. Federal Rules

Under the Federal Rules of Civil Procedure (FRCP), service is made:

ⅰ. To the individual personally by a non-party 18 years or older;

ⅱ. To someone of suitable age and discretion at the individual's dwelling or usual place of abode;

ⅲ. To an authorized agent; or

ⅳ. In accordance with the **state law of the forum state or where service is made.**

2. California Rules

A defendant may personally be served by a non-party 18 years or older and handed a summons and one copy of the complaint.

When personal service does not work, service may be made by leaving the process with the defendant's registered agent or a person who resides at the defendant's domicile.

The service may be made by **certified mail** to the defendant's recorded address.

✔ Ordinary mail → is not a certified mail → improper service
✔ First-class mail, airmail → is a certified mail → proper service

II. Joinder

A. Joinder of Claims (17July)

1. General Rule

A plaintiff may join all claims that he has against the defendant regardless of whether they **arise out of the same transaction or occurrence**.

2. Abstention

When a state claim is joined in federal court, there is an abstention issue.

The federal court may **abstain** from hearing the state law claim, **sever** it, and **remand** it to a state court if there is an **important state interest** in the proceeding.

> TIP1   Q: <u>May 갑 join claims for A and B in the same suit against 을?</u>
> ⇒ 특정 claim의 join 가능여부는 ① common nucleus of operative fact와 ② abstention 여부에 대한 analysis를 통해 판단해야 한다.
>
> TIP2   Joinder된 claim의 SMJ 유무여부를 서술하는 경우, ① 해당 claim 이 독립적인 SMJ를 가지고 있는지 그 여부와 ② supplemental

jurisdiction(SPJ)을 가지고 있는지 그 여부(pendent jurisdiction와 ancillary jurisdiction)를 모두 analysis해야 한다.

B. Class Actions

1. Federal Rules

Class action is allowed when four requirements of representative members and the action meets any of the three types of class actions.

a. Representative Requirements

Class action is allowed if:

① The class is so **numerous**;

② There are questions of law or fact **common** to the class;

③ The claims or defenses of the representative parties are **typical of** that of the class; and

④ The representative parties will **fairly and adequately** represent the class.

b. Types of Class Action

Class action is allowed if:

ⅰ. There is a **risk of inconsistent adjudications** or harm the interests of other class members when actions are held separately;

ⅱ. **Injunctive or declaratory relief** is appropriate; or

ⅲ. **Common questions of law or fact** predominate.

2. California Rules

ⅰ. Representative Requirements

Class action is allowed if there is:

① An **ascertainable**^{확인할 수 있는} **class**; and

② A **well-defined community of interest** among class members.

Community of interest is recognized when:

① **Common questions of law or fact** predominate;

② The representative parties will **fairly and adequately** represent the class; and

③ The class action will be **substantially beneficial** to the parties and the court.

ii. Type of Class Action

In California, there is only one type of class action.

III. Discovery (15Feb, 19July)

Discovery is the process in which parties **obtain information from the other party.** A litigant has right to discover **all non-privileged information** which is **relevant** to the subject matter of the case and is **not unduly burdensome** to produce. The information should be **relevant** to the cause of action. However, the information does not need to be admissible evidence.

A. Mandatory Discovery

1. Federal Rules

There are three types of mandatory discovery: initial discovery, expert testimony, and pretrial disclosure.

2. California Rules

There are **no** mandatory discovery, but the party can require such information.

3. Disclosure of Expert

A party **is required** to disclose the names and identities of all **testifying experts** who will testify at trial. Disclosure of consulting experts who are hired in anticipation of litigation but will not testify at trial is not required.

B. Types of Discovery

1. Interrogatories

a. General Rule

i. Federal Rules

Under the Federal rules, a litigant can direct **written interrogatories** to another party. The interrogatories are **limited to 25** unless there is court order or stipulation.

ii. California Rules

In California, **unlimited** interrogatories are generally allowed. However, in some cases, interrogatories are **limited to 35.**

b. Objection

When a responding party objects discovery requests, he must state his objections **specifically.** The party must specify the objection to the relevance, scope, burden, or objectionable basis of the discovery.

✔ "These interrogatories are flawed^{결함있는}." — proper objection ×

✔ "Objection. Privileged." — proper objection ×

c. Request to Produce

i. Federal Rules

Under the Federal rules, requests to produce can be made to any person, including another party and a nonparty. However, subpoena is required for the request to a nonparty.

ii. California Rules

In California, requests cannot be made to a nonparty.

d. Motion to Compel

Before a party files a motion to compel, he must attempt to **meet and confer**^{상의하다} with the responding party in good faith in an effort to resolve any discovery disputes.

2. Deposition

Generally, a party cannot take more than 10 depositions and cannot depose the same person more than once.

When the deposition is sued by party **against another party,** the **notice** of deposition is required.

When the deposition involves **non-party,** the requesting party must issue a **subpoena.**

3. Physical and Mental Examinations

a. Federal Rules

Under the Federal rules, **a court** may order a physical or mental examination only when a party's physical or mental condition **is in issue** based on **good cause.**

Good cause is recognized when the examination is **not overly intrusive.**

✔ Negligence case에서 medical expenses, pain and suffering을 주장하는 원고에게 physical examination을 요청하는 경우 — in issue ○

A physical examination is relevant in determining the extent of plaintiff's injuries and the proper amount of damages.

✔ Negligence case에서 medical expenses, pain and suffering을 주장하는 원고에게 medical examination을 요청하는 경우 — in issue ✕

The plaintiff did not assert emotional distress.

✔ Negligence case에서 lost wage를 주장하는 원고에게 20년 전부터 현재까지의 tax return 자료를 요청하는 경우 ― in issue ×

Producing tax returns for 20 years is unduly burdensome and is not relevant in determining the present lost wage.

> **TIP** 당사자가 상대방에게 physical 'and' mental examination을 요청한 경우, physical과 mental examination 신청을 구분하여 각 신청의 유효성 요건(in issue, good cause) 만족여부를 analysis해야 한다.

b. California Rules

In California, the **defendant** have a right to request **one physical exam** of the plaintiff **without leave of the court**. Other physical or mental examinations require leave of the court.

> **답안요령** Physical/Mental examination

---

1. Discovery 기본 rule
   + analysis (relevance)
2. Physical/Mental examination 기본 rule
3. 요건 × 2
   + analysis

> **TIP1** 위 1번: Evidence law상의 relevance와 discovery에서 요구하는 relevance는 차이가 있다는 점을 서술한다.

> **TIP2** 위 3번: In issue 요건과 good cause 요건을 title화하여 작성한다.

> **모범답안 031**

1. Motion to order the physical and mental examination

(a) Physical examination

Discovery

Discovery is the process in which parties obtain information from the other party. A litigant has right to discover all non-privileged information which is relevant to the subject matter of the case and is not unduly burdensome to produce. The information should be relevant to the cause of action, but the information does not need to be admissible evidence. (ANALYSIS: In this case, 갑 brought an action against 을 for his physical injury. 갑 would obtain information as to 을's physical condition from the physical examination. Thus, the physical examination would be related to the accident.)

Physical examination

Under the Federal rule, a court may order a physical examination only when a party's physical condition is in issue based on good cause. Good cause is recognized when the examination is not overly intrusive and it is relevant.

In issue

To grant a motion to order a physical examination, the physical condition should be at issue.
(ANALYSIS: In this case, as mentioned above, 을's physical condition is in issue since 갑 is asserting 을's negligence.)

Good cause

Good cause is recognized when the examination is not overly intrusive.
(ANALYSIS: In this case, there is no fact indicating that 갑 has no good cause in filing a motion for the physical examination.)

Conclusion

In conclusion, the court should grant the motion to order a physical examination.

(b) Mental examination
Discovery
……

<u>Mental examination</u>

......

In issue

......

Good cause

......

Conclusion

......

C. Privilege

1. Physician-Patient Privilege

a. Federal Rules

Under the Federal Rules of Evidence, there is no physician-patient privilege.

b. California Rules

Generally, most of the state statutes, including California, regulate the doctor-patient privilege which protects **confidential** communications between a doctor and a patient **for medical treatment.**

When the patient puts a physical condition **in issue,** the privilege is inapplicable.

2. Attorney-Client Privilege

Confidential communications between an attorney and a client which are made **for legal advice** are privileged from disclosure.

The privilege extends to agents of the attorney and employees or agents of the corporation client.

3. Privilege Log

A party may assert privilege in response to a discovery request with **privilege log** (document).

The privilege log must include **specific basis** for privilege.

✔ "Objection. Privileged." — proper asserting ✕

TIP1   Privilege와 관련된 discovery 및 evidence(expert의 증언)의 적합성을 판단하는 경우, 반드시 privilege log에 대해 analysis해야 한다.

TIP2   Attorney-client privilege는 work-product doctrine, duty of confidentiality 논점과 항상 연계하여 생각해야 한다.

Ⅳ. Motions and Trial

A. Rule12(b) (17July)

피고는 원고의 complaint 내용이 구체적이지 않을 경우 Rule 12(b)(6)에 따른 motion to dismiss를 취할 수 있다. 앞서 언급한 바와 같이 Federal rules는 complaint의 작성 기준을 "notice pleading"으로 규정하는 바, complaint의 내용이 피고가 해당 사건에 대해 이해할 수 있는 정도에 미치지 못하는 경우 해당 사건은 dismiss된다. Notice pleading의 기준에 따르면 피고에게 구체적인 사안이 명시될 필요는 없다. 다만, Twombly와 Iqbal 판례를 통해 법원은 원고에게 보다 구체적인 pleading을 요구하고 있으며, 그 기준은 "plausibility standard"라 일컫는다. "Plausibility 기준"은 원고가 구체적인 사안을 명시하고 그 사안들을 통해 합리적인 jury가 원고의 주장에 대해 납득할 수 있는(plausible) 수준을 요구한다[Bell Atlantic Corp. v. Twombly, 550 U.S. 544 (2007), Ashcroft v. Iqbal, 129 S. Ct. 1937 (2009)]. 즉, California rules에서 규정한 "fact pleading"에 가깝다.

1. Federal Rules

Based on Twombly and Iqbal cases, **plausibility standard** is required. The plaintiff must allege **specific facts** which is enough for a **reasonable jury could conclude that the allegations were plausible.**

If the plaintiff fails to provide a well-pleaded complaint, which includes insufficient facts, the defendant may file a motion to dismiss for failure to state a claim upon which relief can be granted.

> **case**

원고 갑이 상대방 을의 fraud in the contract를 주장하고자 complaint를 다음과 같이 작성하였다: "fraud in the supposed value." Is 갑's allegation sufficient to state a claim for fraud?

⇒ No. 갑은 을의 fraud를 주장하고 있는 바, 을이 갑과 계약할 당시 해당 내용이 계약에 있어 중요한(material) 부분을 거짓임을 인지(knowing)하면서도 갑을 속이고자 하는 의도(intent)로 갑에게 허위로 진술(misrepresentation)하였음을 complaint에 서술해야 한다. Complaint 내용의 서술은 plausibility standard에 부합해야 하는 바, fraud 요건에 부합하는 사안에 대한 명시 없이 을의 fraud만을 주장하고 있는 갑의 complaint는 well-pleaded complaint로 인정될 수 없다. 따라서 을은 Rule 12(b)(6)에 의거하여 motion to dismiss를 취할 수 있다.

B. Summary Judgment (15July)

- Summary judgment = Summary adjudication

1. General Rule

★A summary judgment motion is granted only if:

i . When there is **no genuine issue of material fact;** and

ii . The movant is entitled to **judgment as a matter of law (JMOL).**

2. Total or Partial Summary Judgment

When some of elements are recognized and some are not in a case, total summary judgment is not appropriate.

A partial summary judgment is permitted.

3. Summary Judgment and Preclusion

Summary judgment는 factual적인 부분에 대해서는 논란이 없고 오직 legal적인 부분에 대한 판단만이 필요한 사건에서 재판에서 더 이상 factual적인 부분에 대해 다투지 않고 주어진 그대로를 바탕으로 법원의 법률적 판단만을 더하여 사건을 판결한 것을 뜻한다. 여기서 'factual적인 부분에 관해 논란이 없다'는 것은 claim preclusion 또는 issue preclusion 을 통해 증명될 수 있다. 이 두 제도는 전소(前訴)의 판결 및 논점을 그대로 가져와 후소(後訴)에서 더 이상 다투지 않는 제도로서, 이들이 인정되면 후소(後訴)에서는 factual적인 부분에 대해 더 이상 다투지 않고 법률적 판단만을 더하여 사건을 종결시킬 수 있다. 즉, 당사자는 motion for summary judgment를 취할 수 있다.

Summary judgment is often related to claim preclusion or issue preclusion.

Both claim and issue preclusion can establish that no genuine material issues of fact exist, and establish that summary judgment is proper.

a. Claim Preclusion

Under the doctrine of claim preclusion, the parties and their privies are **barred** from asserting the **cause of action** in a later lawsuit when:

ⅰ. Earlier judgment is a **final judgment on the merits;**
ⅱ. **Same claimant against same defendant;** and
ⅲ. **Same claim.**

b. Issue Preclusion

Issue preclusion을 주장하고자 하는 경우 전소와 후소의 소송당사자가 다른 경우에도 인정되는가 하는 논점이 있다. 과거에는 issue preclusion을 주장하는 측과 그 상대방측 모두 전소에서의 소송당사자일 것이 요구되었다(mutuality rule). 다만, 최근에는 보다 완화된 rule을 적용하여 이전 소송에서 논한 논점에 대한 판결을 제3자가 자신을 보호하고자 issue preclusion을 주장하고(use defensively) 그것이 fair하다고 판단되는 경우에 한해 허용된다. 반면, 제3자가 자신의 주장을 위해 issue preclusion을 주장하는 경우(use offensively)에도 use defensively의 경우와 마찬가지로 fair하다고 판단되는 경우 허용되나, 법원은 이를 잘 인정하지 않는 경향이 있다. Use offensively인 경우와 관련하여 wait-and-see plaintiff라는 개념이 있는데, 이는 후소의 원고가 전소에 소송당사자로서 충분히 참여할 수 있었음에도 불구하고 참여하지 않은 자를 뜻한다.

ⅰ. General Rule

Issue preclusion arises when:

① Earlier judgment is a **final judgment on the merits;**

② Issue was **actually litigated and determined;** and

③ Issue was **essential** to the earlier judgment.

ⅱ. Non-Mutual Preclusion

Defensive issue preclusion occurs when a nonparty raise it **to avoid liability** in a subsequent case. It is allowed if the party that will be estopped had a **fair and equitable opportunity** to litigate the issue at the prior proceeding.

Offensive issue preclusion occurs when a nonparty raise it to support claim in a subsequent case. It is allowed only when it is **fair and equitable** in a balancing test.

case 1

갑이 식당에서 넘어져 다쳤고, 이에 대해 식당 직원 을을 상대로 negligence case를 제기하였다. 해당 소송에서 jury는 "을 has no negligence"임을 인정하였고 그 결과 갑은 패소하였다. 이후 갑은 식당주인 병을 상대로 negligence case를 제기하였고, 병은 "을 has no negligence"임을 주장하였다. Does the jury's conclusion in 갑·을 case that 을 has no negligence preclude 갑 from litigating that issue in the 갑·병 case?

⇒ Yes. 병(non-party)은 자신의 책임이 없다는 점을 주장하기 위해 해당 issue를 그대로 후소(後訴)에서 주장하고 있으므로, 이는 defensive issue preclusion에 관한 문제이다. 갑은 이전 소송, 즉 갑이 을을 상대로 제기한 소송에서 증인을 부르거나 cross-examination을 하는 등 을의 과실에 대해 논의할 수 있는 기회가 충분히 있었으므로, 후소(갑이 병을 상대로 제기한 소송)에서 해당 issue에 대해 preclusion을 인정하더라도 fair하다. 따라서 갑은 갑·병 소송에서 을의 과실여부를 다시 논할 수 없다.

case 2

ABC회사에서 제조한 자동차를 구매한 갑이 자동차의 결함으로 인한 personal injury를 주장하며 ABC회사를 상대로 소송을 제기하였다. 본 소송에서 jury는 '자동차의 결함'을 인정하였고 그 결과 갑이 승소하였다. 이후 동일한 자동차를 구매한 을이 이전 갑과 ABC회사간 소송에서 논의되었던 '자동차의 결함'을 주장하면서 ABC회사를 상대로 personal injury 소송을 제기하였다. Does the jury's conclusion in 갑·ABC case that defects on the car preclude ABC from litigating that issue in the 을·ABC case?

⇒ Maybe Yes. 을(non-party)은 소송상대방인 ABC회사에 적대적으로(against ABC) 자동차 결함을 주장하므로, 이는 offensive issue preclusion이다. ABC회사는 이전 소송, 즉 갑이 제기한 소송에서 증인을 부르거나 cross-examination을 하는 등 자동차 결함에 대해 논의할 수 있는 기회가 충분히 있었으므로, 후소(을이 제기한 소송)에서 해당 issue에 대해 preclusion을 인정하더라도 fair하다. 따라서 ABC회사는 을과의 소송에서 자동차 결

함여부를 다시 논할 수 없다.

case 3

소비자 갑이 ABC회사의 하자있는 제품을 사용하는 과정에서 injury가 발생했다. 갑은 ABC회사를 상대로 negligence product liability를 주장하였고, 이전에 다른 소비자 을이 ABC회사를 상대로 소송한 내용을 바탕으로 ABC회사 제품의 defects에 대해 유효한 issue preclusion을 주장하였다. 갑이 motion for summary judgment를 취했다면, 받아들여질 수 있는가?

⇒ May be a partial summary judgment. 갑은 negligence case를 제소하였으므로, 그에게 negligence 요건인 duty, breach, causation, damage에 대한 입증책임이 있다. 따라서 갑이 유효한 issue preclusion을 주장하였다 할지라도, 이는 negligence product liability 중 defective product 요건 하나만을 입증했을뿐 그 외의 요소는 입증할 수 없다.

c. Federal Rules v. California Rules

i . Final Judgment

Under the Federal rules, a judgment is final when the **judgment is rendered.**

Under the California rules, a judgment is final when the **appeals have concluded.**

ii . Same Claim

Under the Federal rules, all legal theories arising from the **same transaction or occurrence** are same.

Under the California rules, each **cause of action** may raise different claim even though those arises from the same transaction or occurrence (primary rights theory).

case

갑·을간 자동차 사고에 대해 갑이 을에게 personal injury를 주장하는 소를 제기하였고, 갑이 승소하였다. 이후 갑은 동일한 자동차 사고에 대해 을을 상대로 property damages를 청구하였으나, 이에 대해 을은 claim preclusion을 주장하였다. 갑은 을을 상대로 property damages를 청구할 수 있는가?

⇒ Federal rules에 따르면 갑은 property damages를 청구할 수 없는 반면, 캘리포니아 주에서는 청구할 수 있다. Federal rules에서는 두 청구는 동일한 사건, 즉 동일한 자동차 사고(same transaction or occurrence)에 의해 발생된 것이므로 하나의 claim으로 보나, 캘리포니아 주에서는 두 청구를 별개의 claim으로 본다. 즉, Federal rules에서는 claim preclusion이 인정되고, California에서는 인정되지 않는다.

C. Renewed Judgment as a Matter of Law

- Renewed judgment as a matter of law = Judgment notwithstanding the verdict

1. Federal Rules

A party may renew motion for judgment as a matter of law when:

i. Judgment was entered **against whom the party;** and

ii. The party **raised the motion during the trial** but the court did not grant it.

The motion should be filed <u>within 28 days</u> after entry of the judgment.

2. California Rules

The raising party is not required to raise **the motion during the trial.** The motion should be filed <u>within 15 days after service of notice of entry of judgment, or 180 days after the entry of the judgment.</u>

D. Jury Trial (15Feb, 7July)

1. Federal Rules

a. General Rule

Under the **Sixth Amendment,** a party has the right of **jury trial** in the **legal claim.**

A demand for a jury trial should be made **within 14 days of the filing of the answer to the complaint,** and the **notice** to other party must be made.

b. Legal v. Equitable Claim

When legal claims and equitable claims are joined in one action, **the legal claim** should be tried first to the jury and then the equitable claim to the court.

✔ Damages → remedy at law → legal claim

✔ Injunction (e.g., specific performance) → remedy at equity → equitable claim

c. Jury Composition

6-12 jurors compose a jury and unanimous vote is required.

2. California Rules

a. General Rule

Under the California Constitution, a party has the right of **jury trial** in the **legal claim.**

b. Legal v. Equitable Claim

ⅰ. When legal claims and equitable claims are joined in one action, **the equitable claim** should be tried first and then the legal claim to the jury.

ⅱ. When a claim is mainly equitable, the judge may hear the whole case without jury (equitable clean-up doctrine).

c. Jury Composition

    <u>6 jurors</u> compose a jury and <u>three-quarters vote</u> is required.

E. Appeal (14Feb)

1. General Rule

Litigants may appeal only from final judgments of the district courts. A final judgment is one that ends the litigation on the merits and leaves nothing for the court to do.

2. Exception (Collateral Order Doctrine)

The court may hear an appeal when:

   ⅰ. That issue is **independent (collateral to)** the merits of the action; and

   ⅱ. The losing party would **be precluded from an opportunity to review** its rights on appeal.

✔ Motion to remand에 대한 법원 판결 — not a final judgment(재판 중 당사자가 본 판결에 대해 appeal을 신청한다 하더라도 받아들여질 수 없다.)

✔ Forum-selection clause에 대한 법원 판결 — not a final judgment

✔ Injunctions → not a final judgment, but is a exception → appealable

[표 8-1]

	Federal Rules	California Rules
Pleading	notice pleading (plausibility standard)	fact pleading
Complaint		"Doe" defendant 가능
Response	w/i 21 days	w/i 30 days
Interrogatories	up to 25	unlimited, or up to 35 in limited cases
Request to produce	to another party + nonparty	to another party
Physical and mental examinations	−with leave of the court −in issue −good cause	−△ can request one physical exam −나머지는 leave of the court
Claim/ Issue Preclusion — "final judgment"	when the judgment is rendered	when the appeals have concluded
Claim/ Issue Preclusion — "same claim"	same transaction or occurrence	same cause of action
Jury trial	legal → equitable	equitable → legal
Jury trial	6−12 jurors, unanimous vote	6 jurors, three−quarters vote
Renewed judgment as a matter of law	The party must raise the motion during the trial	is **not** required
Renewed judgment as a matter of law	w/i 28d after entry of the judgment.	① w/i 15d after service of notice of entry of judgment; or ② w/i 180d after the entry of the judgment.
New trial	w/i 28d after entry of the judgment	① w/i 15d after service of notice of entry of judgment; or ② w/i 180d after the entry of the judgment.
Additur	**not** permitted	permitted

- w/i = within
- △ = defendant
- d = days

9장
Torts

//

미국법상 torts는 '위법행위'를 뜻하는 바, 이는 고의 또는 과실로 인해 타인에게 손해를 가하는 위법행위를 뜻하는 한국법상 불법행위보다 넓은 개념이다. 한국법에서는 고의 또는 과실로 인한 위법행위를 일반 불법행위로 정의하고 행위자의 고의 또는 과실이 없더라도 책임을 묻는 무과실책임이 불법행위의 예외로 인정된다. 다시 말해, 한국법상 불법행위는 위법성의 원인인 '고의 또는 과실'에 초점이 맞춰져 있는 개념인 것이다. 반면, 미국법상 torts는 '위법성'에 초점이 맞춰져 있는 개념으로서 고의 또는 과실과 같은 원인을 기준으로 하지 않고 위법성의 성격에 따라 torts의 유형을 구분한다. 본 장은 지난 7년간 캘리포니아 에세이 시험 (CEE)에 출제되었던 논점을 중심으로 intentional torts, other torts, negligence, strict liability 그리고 general considerations에 대해 논한다.

☑ 글쓰기 Tips

1. CEE상 Torts는 지난 7년간 출제된 빈도수가 낮은 과목에 속하나, 타 과목에 비해 주어진 사안을 법률에 적용하는 analysis가 중요한 과목으로서 답안을 꼼꼼히 작성해야 한다는 점에서 난도가 높다. Jury는 동일한 사실관계에 대해 다양하게 해석할 수 있는 바, arguable points를 작성하는 것이 고득점 포인트다.
   ⇒ "갑 may argue that ~. However, 을 may argue that ~."
2. 본 장에 관한 에세이 문제는 주로 피고의 특정 행위에 대해 원고가 제기할 가능성이 있는 claim들을 논하는 문제가 출제된다. 아래에는 연관성이 높아 대개 함께 analyze해야 하는 claim들을 묶어 놓았다.
   Q: <u>What tort causes of action, if any, may 갑 bring against 을?</u>
   ⇒ 소송 승패여부와 상관없이 피고의 행위와 연관된 '모든' claim을 서술한다.
   ⇒ 각 'claim'을 title화하고, 각 claim의 '요소'를 subtitle화하여 작성한다.
   ① 피고가 원고에게 협박한 경우 — IIED, assault
   ② 피고가 원고에 관한 defamatory statement를 언급한 경우 — defamation, IIED,

NIED, invasion of privacy

③ 피고가 원고의 물건(자동차)을 손상시킨 경우 — trespass to chattel, conversion, trespass to land, battery

3. 여러 논점이 구체적으로 나열된 문제도 있다.

Q: <u>What claim(s) may 갑 reasonably raise against 을; what defenses may 을 reasonably assert; what damages, if any, may 갑 recover; what is the likely outcome? Discuss</u>

Q: <u>What tort causes of action, if any, may 갑 bring against 을, and how is each likely to fare?</u>

⇒ 한 문제에 ① 원고가 피고를 상대로 제기할 수 있는 claim, ② 피고의 반박 (defense), ③ 판결내용(누가 승소할 확률이 높은지, 손배액)을 모두 analyze 하도록 출제되었으므로, 세 '논점'을 큰 title로 서술하는 것이 좋다.

4. 등장인물이 여러 명이고 여러 개의 소송이 제기된 경우, 원고와 제기된 claims를 중심으로 사안을 정리하면서 읽어야 실수를 줄일 수 있다.

Part One. Intentional Torts

I. Intentional Torts to Person

A. Battery

★Battery is an intentional infliction of bodily harm caused by harmful or offensive contact to another's person.

Such contact includes harmful or offensive contact to objects that is connected to a plaintiff's body.

✔ 원고가 쓰고 있는 모자를 세게 내려친 경우 — ○ (contact 인정)

✔ 원고가 책상에 벗어놓은 모자를 세게 내려친 경우 — ×

✔ 원고가 타고 있던 차를 세게 내려친 경우 — ○

✔ 원고가 주차장에 세워 둔 차를 세게 내려친 경우 — ×

| TIP | Arguable point: 피고는 자신이 원고의 신체가 아닌 모자를 세게 내

려쳤으므로 battery에 해당하지 않는다고 주장할 수 있으나, 원고의 신체와 연결되어 있는 것에 대한 offensive contact는 battery로 인정된다.

Although 갑 would argue that he made offensive contact on 을's hat, not his body and battery did not occur, harmful or offensive contact to objects that is connected to a plaintiff's body is actionable as a battery.

B. Assault

Assault is the intentional creation of apprehension of immediate bodily harm of another.

★To establish a prima facie case of assault, the plaintiff must show:

ⅰ. Defendant's act that puts the plaintiff in a **reasonable apprehension** of an **imminent harmful or offensive contact;**

ⅱ. Defendant's intent to cause such apprehension; and

ⅲ. Causation.

✔ 갑이 을에게 전화상으로 죽이겠다고 협박한 경우, 을이 멀리 떨어져 있는 갑이 자신에게 immediate bodily harm을 할 것이라고 믿는 것은 unreasonable하다. 따라서 갑의 협박은 assault에 해당하지 않는다.

✔ 갑이 을에게 "만나면 죽이겠다."고 협박한 경우, 을을 미래에 죽일 것이라고 협박하였으므로 을이 자신에게 immediate bodily harm이 발생할 것이라고 믿는 것은 unreasonable하다. 따라서 갑의 협박은 assault에 해당하지 않는다.

갑's statement has a future time condition to the threat, and it does not satisfy immediacy requirement.

C. Intentional Infliction of Emotional Distress (IIED) (16Feb, 20Feb)

Intentional infliction of emotional distress(IIED)는 피고가 충격적인 행위를 통해 원고에게 심각한 정신적 충격을 주고자(intent) 한 경우 또는 원고에게 그러한 충격을 줄 수 있을 것이라 충분히 예상할 수 있었음에도 불구하고 이를 간과(reckless)하고 행위한 경우에 성립되며, 원고가 자신의 심각한 정신적 피해에 대해 입증책임을 진다. IIED는 피고가 원고에 대한 defamatory statement를 언급한 경우 원고의 주장가능한 claim으로서 이 외에도 defamation, NIED, invasion of privacy 등이 있다.

1. Prima Facie Case

★In an intentional infliction of emotional distress action, the plaintiff must show:

ⅰ. Defendant's **extreme and outrageous conduct;**

ⅱ. Defendant's **intent** to cause plaintiff to suffer **severe** emotional distress **or recklessness** about the effect of his conduct;

ⅲ. **Causation;** and

ⅳ. **Damages (severe emotional distress).**

2. Extreme and Outrageous

Conduct is extreme and outrageous if it would cause severe emotional distress in a **reasonable** person or in a particular person when the defendant **has known** about the person's **particular sensitivities.**

Ⅱ. Intentional Torts to Property

A. Trespass to Land (18Feb−Real Prop.)

Trespass to land is an unlawful entry in the other's land.

★For a claim for trespass to land action, the plaintiff must prove:

ⅰ. Defendant's act of **physical invasion** of **plaintiff's real property;**

ⅱ. Defendant's **intent** to bring physical invasion of plaintiff's real property; and

ⅲ. **Causation.**

B. Trespass to Chattel and Conversion

1. Trespass to Chattel

★Trespass to chattel is an interference with plaintiff's right of possession in the chattel.

If an **normal person** in the community feels offensive, inconvenient, or annoying, the interference is substantial.

2. Conversion

★Conversion is an interference with plaintiff's right of possession in the chattel.

3. Differences

a. Degree

Trespass to chattel occurs when the property is **harmed** but not completely destroyed, while conversion occurs only when the property is **completely** destroyed or stolen.

b. Damages

When trespass to chattel occurs, the plaintiff may recover the **cost of repair.**

When conversion occurs, the plaintiff may recover **the market value of the chattel at the time the conversion occurred.**

> **TIP** 피고가 원고의 chattel에 대해 위법행위를 한 경우 ① trespass to chattel과 conversion 소송의 각 요소에 대해 analyze하고 ② 두 claim간 차이점을 명시하는 것이 고득점 포인트다.

III. Defenses

1. Consent

Consent is a defense to intentional torts, and may be express or implied through words or conduct.

The defendant's actions cannot exceed the **scope of the consent** given.

2. Necessity

Defendant's action would be privileged, if his action was necessary to protect some actor's or public interest. Necessity is recognized when the interest is so important to **justify** the harm caused by defendant's action.

3. Self-Defense and Defense of Others (16Feb)

a. General Rule

A defendant is not liable for harm to the plaintiff if he:

 i . **Reasonably believed** that the plaintiff is in danger of immediate bodily harm; and

 ii . Used **reasonable force** that was **necessary** to protect himself or another.

b. Mistaken Self-Defense

피고가 원고가 제3자에게 intentional torts를 행하고 있다고 오인하고 원고에게 torts를 행한 경우, 해당 피고의 mistake가 reasonable한 경우에 한해 defense로 인정된다.

Mistaken self-defense/defense of others is still a valid defense to an intentional tort if the mistake was **reasonable**.

4. Insanity

Insanity is not a valid defense to the intentional torts.

Part Two. Other Torts

I. Defamation (15Feb−Biz Asso., 20Feb)

Defamation은 '명예훼손'을 뜻하며, 명예훼손이 인정되는 경우 위법행위자는 타인의 명예에 부정적인 영향을 끼쳐 야기한 정신적 및 재산적 손해에 대해 배상할 책임을 진다. 다만, 명예훼손은 수정헌법 1조상 보장되는 freedom of speech(표현의 자유)와 개인의 명예 보호라는 두 가치가 충돌하는 문제로서, 그 성립요건은 개인의 신분 및 적시된 내용에 따라 달리 규정된다. 다시 말해, 개인(private person)의 개인적인 내용(private matter)에 대해 적시한 경우 완화된 성립요건을 기준으로 하여 defamation에 대한 책임은 비교적 쉽게 인정되는 반면, 공인(public figure) 또는 공적인 내용(public matter)에 대한 적시는 앞선 경우보다 falsity와 fault, 이 두 요건이 추가적으로 요구되어 비교적 엄격한 기준으로 defamation의 성립이 인정된다. 이는 적시된 내용에 대해 반박할 기회가 적은 개인들의 defamation에 의한 피해가 공인에 비해 더 크다고 여기기 때문이다. 따라서 private person의 private matter에 관한 경우 freedom of speech보다 개인의 명예 보호에 더 가치를 두고, public figure 또는 public matter에 관한 경우에는 freedom of speech를 개인의 명예 보호보다 더 가치를 둔다고 할 수 있다.

A. Prima Facie Case

★For claims of defamation, the plaintiff must show:

ⅰ. **Defamatory statement** by the defendant;

ⅱ. The defamatory language is **of or concerning the plaintiff;**

ⅲ. **Publication;** and

ⅳ. **Damages to the reputation** of the plaintiff.

★**Falsity** of the defamatory statement and defendant's **fault** are required to be proved when the defamatory statement is as to a **public figure or public concern.**

1. Defamatory Language

Defamatory statement is a statement that harms another's reputation. All statements of **fact** are defamatory, but statements of **opinion** are not.

✔ "갑에게 회계를 맡기기에는 믿음직스럽지 못하다."고 얘기한 을

① 을이 갑과 함께 일하는 동안 갑이 dishonest하다고 생각해서 언급했다면, defamatory language.

② 을이 아무 근거 없이 자신의 생각/의견을 언급한 것이라면, mere opinion.

> **TIP** Arguable point: Defamation을 주장하는 원고측은 해당 언급이 '사실'에 관한 언급이라고 주장할 것이나, 이에 대해 피고측은 해당 언급이 언급자의 '의견'이었을 뿐이었다고 반박할 것이다.
>
> Plaintiff will argue that defendant's statement was factual statement. In response, defendant will argue that his statement is his opinion, and therefore, cannot be a defamatory statement.

2. Publication

"Publication" means a communication **to a third person who understands it**. The communication may be made **either intentionally or negligently**.

3. Damages

For defamation, both general and special damages should be proved. Different rules are applicable depending on whether the claim is for libel or slander.

a. Libel

Libel is a **written or recorded** defamatory statement.

For all libels, **general damages are presumed by law** and special damages are not required to be proved.

✔ Radio/TV broadcasts

✔ Written letter

b. Slander

Slander means **spoken** defamation.

   ⅰ. **General Rule**

      Generally, general damages are presumed by law but **special damages are not presumed** (special damages are required to be proved).

   ⅱ. **Slander Per Se**

      However, for **slander per se,** both general and special damages are presumed.

      Business or profession, loathsome^{전염병} disease, crime involving moral turpitude^{부도덕 범죄}, and unchastity^{행실이 나쁨} of a woman are categorized as slander per se.

4. Falsity and Fault

Falsity of the defamatory statement and defendant's **fault** are required to be proved when the defamatory statement is as to a **public figure or public concern.**

a. Falsity

If the plaintiff is a **public figure,** the plaintiff is **required to prove** that the statement was false.

b. Fault

If the plaintiff is a **public figure,** the statement must have been made **with actual malice.** Malice means knowledge that the statement was false or reckless disregard as to its truth or falsity. If the plaintiff is a **private figure,** the standard is **negligence.**

B. Defenses

1. Consent

Consent by a plaintiff is a complete defense to a defamation case.

2. Truth

Truth is a complete defense to a defamation case.

II. Nuisance (18Feb-Real Prop.)

1. Private Nuisance

Private nuisance is a conduct that causes a **substantial and unreasonable interference** with another private individual's **use or enjoyment** of possession.

2. Public Nuisance

Public nuisance is a conduct that causes **unreasonable** interference with the health, safety, or property **rights of the community at large**.

III. Intentional Interference with Business Relations
(14July-Prof. resp.)

A. Prima Facie Case

In a prima facie case of intentional interference with business relations, a plaintiff must prove that:

i . There is a **valid contractual relationship** between the plaintiff and a third party or a **valid business expectancy**;

ii . Defendant had **knowledge** of the relationship or expectancy;

iii. Defendant **intentionally interfered** the relationship or expectancy; and

iv. Plaintiff suffered **damage**.

Part Three. Negligence (14July, 17July, 19Feb)

Negligence란 가해자의 과실, 즉 부주의로 인해 타인에게 위법한 침해가 발생한 행위를 뜻한다. 원고는 피고의 주의의무(duty of care), 의무 위반(breach of duty), 부주의와 손해간 인과관계(causation) 그리고 손해(damage)를 입증해야 한다. '부주의'는 주의의무의 위반을 뜻하는 바, 그 주의의무는 사회의 보통사람(ordinary, prudent, reasonable person)으로서의 주의의무를 기준으로 한다. 다만, 어린아이, 토지 소유자 및 점유자 등 행위자의 신분에 따라 별도로 주의의무 기준을 정한 경우도 있다. 한편, 주의의무의 범위는 가해자가 행위 당시 예견가능(foreseeable)한 자에 한한다. 다시 말해, 가해자는 그의 부주의로 인해 발생할 수 있는 위법한 침해 범위(zone of danger) 내에 있는 자에 한해 책임을 진다. 원고에게 피고의 과실에 대한 입증책임이 있다면, 피고는 assumption of risk 등 항변사유에 대한 입증책임을 진다. Assumption of risk란, 원고가 피해를 예상했음에도 불구하고 이를 감수하고 행위했음을 의미하는 바, 피고의 과실이 인정된다하더라도 원고는 피해에 대해 배상받을 수 없다. 한편, comparative negligence를 인정하는 재판권에서는 원고의 과실만큼을 손해배상액에서 제하는 방법을 취하는 바, 피고가 원고의 과실을 입증하면 손해배상액이 적게 책정된다(pure comparative negligence).

A. Prima Facie Case

★In a prima facie case of negligence, a plaintiff must prove duty, breach, actual and proximate causation, and damages.

B. Duty

1. General Rule

A person owes duty to act all foreseeable plaintiffs.

a. Foreseeability

Under the majority rule (Cardozo view), a person owes duty of care only to **reasonably foreseeable plaintiffs.** Defendant is liable only to the person **in the zone of danger.** This view considers **proximate** causation.

Under the minority rule (Andrews view), a person is liable for all damages caused by the breach of duty regardless of its foreseeability. This views considers actual causation.

b. Standard of Care

　ⅰ. Licensee

Licensee is one who enters on the land with the landowner's express or implied permission **for her own purpose or business.**

A landowner owes licensees a duty to warn dangerous condition that the landowner **knows or has reason to know** and which the licensee **was not likely to discover.**

　ⅱ. Invitee (19Feb)

An invitee is one who enters on the land with the landowner's express or implied **invitation.**

A landowner owes invitees a duty **to warn of or to make safe** dangerous condition that the landowner **knows or has reason to know** and a duty to make reasonable **inspections** of the premises.

c. Negligent Infliction of Emotional Distress (NIED) (20Feb)

모든 사람은 타인에게 정신적 충격을 가하지 않도록 주의할 의무(duty)가 있으며, 이를 이행하지 않는 경우 NIED에 대한 책임을 진다. NIED가 인정되기 위해서는 원칙적으로 두 요건, 즉 ① within the zone of danger인 피해자 그리고 ② 정신적 피해로 인한 신체적 피해를 만족해야 한다. 다만, 아래 내용은 피고가 원고에 대한 defamatory statement를 언급하였고 이에 대해 원고가 NIED를 주장할 수 있는지 그 여부를 판단하는 기출문제를 바탕으로 서술하였다.

To have a negligent infliction of emotional distress claim, plaintiff must show:

    ⅰ. He negligently made a statement; and

    ⅱ. Which caused **physical symptoms** from the distress.

    ✔ 원고가 정신적 충격을 받았으나 병원에서 치료를 받지 않은 경우 (no medical treatment) → 요건 ⅱ 미충족

C. Breach

1. General Rule

A defendant breaches a duty of care when he fails to conform to the requisite standard of care.

2. Negligence Per Se (17July)

a. Elements

    ★For a negligence per se claim, plaintiff must show:

    ⅰ. That the **statute's purpose** is to prevent the type of **harm** that the plaintiff has suffered; and

    ⅱ. That the plaintiff is in the **class of persons** the statute is designed to protect.

b. Presumption

If negligence per se applies, the **duty and breach** elements are **conclusively presumed** when the defendant breaches the statute.

D. Causation

1. Actual Causation

A defendant is actual cause of injury (damage) if **but for** the defendant's conduct the plaintiff would not have suffered the harm.

2. Proximate Causation

The proximate causation test is based on **foreseeability.**

A defendant's conduct is proximate cause of the injury only when the **intervening force is foreseeable.** An independent intervening event is an unforeseeable force which **cuts off** the chain of causation.

> ┌─────┐
> │ TIP │ Arguable point: 피고는 intervening force is unforeseeable임을 주
> └─────┘ 장하고, 이에 원고는 foreseeable임을 주장하며 반박할 것이다.
>
> Defendant will argue that [the intervening force] was unforeseeable. In response, plaintiff will argue that it was foreseeable, and therefore, it proximately causes the [result].

E. Damage

Any personal injury or property damages are sufficient to support a claim of negligence.

F. Defenses

1. Contributory Negligence

In a jurisdiction in which applies contributory negligence, the plaintiff **cannot recover anything** when he is negligent.

2. Comparative Negligence

In a jurisdiction in which applies **pure** comparative negligence, the plaintiff **can** recover amount which is **reduced by the plaintiff's own negligence.**

In **most** jurisdictions in which apply **partial** comparative negligence, the plaintiff **can** recover only when his negligence is **not serious** than that of the defendant.

3. Assumption of Risk

When the plaintiff **knew the risk but voluntarily assumed** it, assumption of risk is created and the plaintiff is barred from recovering.

| Negligence

Q: Under what theory or theories, if any, might 갑 bring an action for negligence against 을, 병, and/or 정(owner), and what is the likely outcome? Discuss

---

1. Negligence 기본 rule
2. 을/병
   ① Duty
   ② Breach
   ③ Causation
   ④ Defenses★
3. 정(owner)
   ① Vicarious liability
   ② Direct negligence★

TIP1   갑이 을, 병, 정을 상대로 negligence를 근거로 소송을 제기하였으므로, 공통적인 내용에 해당하는 negligence 기본 rule을 먼저 작성 후, 각 '피고'를 title화하여 작성한다.

TIP2   피고 행위의 negligence 여부를 판단하는 경우, 피고가 주장할 수 있는 defenses에 대해 논하는 것이 고득점 포인트다.

TIP3   피고가 owner인 경우, ① 그의 직원의 negligence에 대해 책임 (vicarious liability)을 지는 경우와 ② 그의 직접적인 과실(direct negligence)에 대해 책임을 지는 경우를 구분하여 작성하는 것이 고득점 포인트다.

TIP4   위 3①: 만일 직원이 employee가 아닌 independent contractor인 경우라면, independent contractor의 과실이 사용자에게 귀속되는 exception rule에 대해 논해야 한다.

모범답안 032

Negligence

In a prima facie case of negligence, a plaintiff must prove duty, breach, actual and proximate causation, and damages. First, under the majority rule, a person owes duty to care only to reasonably foreseeable plaintiffs.

Defendant is liable only to the person in the zone of danger. Under the minority rule, a person is liable for all damages caused by the breach of duty regardless of its foreseeability. Second, a defendant breaches a duty of care when he fails to conform to the requisite standard of care. Third, a plaintiff must show both actual and proximate causation. A defendant is actual cause of injury (damage) if but for the defendant's conduct the plaintiff would not have suffered the harm. The proximate causation test is based on foreseeability. Fourth, the plaintiff must prove they suffered damages.

을

In this case, 갑 brought a claim against 을 based on negligence.

(1) Duty

Licensee

......

(2) Breach

......

(3) Causation

(a) Actual causation

......

(b) Proximate causation

......

(4) Damages

......

Defenses

Assumption of risk

......

병

......

정

정 is an owner and he can be liable either for vicarious liability or for his direct liability.

Vicarious liability

A principal will be vicariously liable for the agent's tortious conduct only if it occurred within the scope of his employment. Additionally, principal is liable for vicarious liability when principal employed the agent as an employee, rather than an independent contractor. A court will consider several factors in determining the degree of the principal's control over the agent, such as level of skills required, whether work is part or whole of principal's business, payment for regular work, and the length of the relationship.

(ANALYSIS: In this case, 병 is employed by 정. 병 was serving in the restaurant in the working hour. Thus, his negligence occurred within the scope of his employment. Moreover, a servant is a job that requires no special skills and 병's payment was for regular work. A court is likely to consider 병 as an employee, rather than an independent contractor. Thus, 정, the owner, is vicarious liable for 병's negligence.)

Direct negligence

(1) Duty

......

(2) Breach

......

(3) Causation

(a) Actual causation

......

(b) Proximate causation

……

(4) Damages

……

Defenses

……

Conclusion

In conclusion, 갑 might be successful to bring an action for negligence against 을, 병, and 정(owner).

Part Four. Strict Liability

Strict liability는 한국법상의 '무과실책임'과 유사한 개념이다. 행위자의 행위 성격상 행위자에게 안전하게 행동할 의무를 부과할 정도로 충분히 위험한 경우, 행위자가 그 행위로 인한 피해에 대해 지는 책임을 뜻한다. Strict liability 유형에는 동물점유자가 지는 책임을 뜻하는 strict liability for animals와 위험한 행위를 하는 자가 지는 책임인 strict liability for abnormally dangerous activities가 있다.

A. Strict Liability for Animals (19Feb)
1. General Rule

The owner has **strict liability** for any injuries caused by the animal's **dangerous propensities** when:

ⅰ. The injury was caused by a **wild animal;** or

ⅱ. The owner of an **animal** has knowledge on the dangerous propensity.

✔ Puppies — domestic animal (위 ⅰ요건 미충족)

2. With Prior Notice

Usually, the owner of domestic animal does not have strict liability. However, the owner of **domestic animal** has strict liability when the owner of an animal **has knowledge** of the dangerous propensities. The owner has strict liability for the injury caused by the known dangerous propensities.

> **TIP**
>
> Arguable point: 원고는 피고가 그의 domestic animal의 위험성에 대해 인지하고 있었음을 주장할 것이나, 피고는 [인지할 수 있는 기회가 적었음을 주장하며] 위험성에 대해 인지하지 못하고 있었다고 주장할 것이다.
>
> The plaintiff may argue that the defendant has knowledge of domestic animal's dangerous propensities. However, the defendant may argue that he has little opportunity to have notice the dangerous propensities.

B. Strict Liability for Abnormally Dangerous Activities (17July)

A defendant has strict liability for engaging in an abnormally dangerous activity, **regardless of his negligence.**

a. Abnormally Dangerous Activity

- Abnormally dangerous activity = Ultra-hazardous activity

★An abnormally dangerous activity is an activity that

ⅰ. Creates a **substantial risk of bodily harm or death** that **cannot be mitigated** by sufficient care; and

ⅱ. Is **not a common usage in the community.**

b. Common Usage

When the value of the activity to society outweighs the risk and probability of harm, it is common usage.

[Restatement (Third) of Torts §20, comment j]

"The transmitting electricity through wires itself is engaged in by only one party. Even so, electric wires are pervasive within the community. Moreover, most people, though not themselves engaging in the activity, are connected to the activity⋯. The concept of common usage can be extended further to activities that, though not pervasive, are nevertheless common and familiar within the community."

"전기를 전송하는 행위는 한 행위자에 의해 일어난다. 그렇다 할지라도 전기선은 사회에서 만연하다. 게다가 대부분의 사람들은 직접 전기를 전송하는 행위에 개입하지 않는다 할지라도 그 행위에 관련되어 있다. "Common usage" 개념은 사회에서 만연하지 않더라도 사람들에게 익숙하고 친숙한 행위에 확장되어 적용할 수 있다."

C. General Considerations

1. Foreseeable Plaintiffs

In majority jurisdictions, the defendant has strict liability only to **foreseeable** plaintiffs.

The defendant has **no** liability to trespasser.

2. Injuries

The defendant has strict liability for injuries which are caused by **normal dangerous propensities**.

3. Defenses

a. Assumption of Risks

When the plaintiff has **knowledge on the danger** and his unreasonable conduct contributed to the harm from the animal or abnormally dangerous activity, he cannot recover from the defendant.

b. Comparative Negligence

Contributory negligence is not a defense, while **comparative negligence** rules are applicable in many states.

As comparative negligence rules apply, the plaintiff can recover damages reduced proportionately to her fault.

Part Five. General Considerations

1. Transfer of Intent

피고가 assault를 의도했는데 battery가 된 경우, 피고의 battery에 대한 intent가 인정되는가. 이 경우 피고의 assault intent가 battery intent로 이전(transfer)되었다고 본다. 즉, 피고가 행위 당시 의도했던 바와 다른 결과가 나오는 경우, 피고는 "transferred intent"가 있다고 본다(doctrine of transfer of intent). 다만, transferred intent가 모든 종류의 intentional torts에서 인정되는 것은 아니며 assault, battery, false imprisonment, trespass to land, trespass to chattel, 이 다섯 개 유형의 위법행위에 대해서만 인정된다.

Under the doctrine of transfer of intent, intent to commit a tort against one person is transferred to the injured person or to the other tort. The doctrine is applicable where:

ⅰ. The defendant commits a **different tort** against the person against whom he intended;

ⅱ. The defendant commits a tort which he intended to commit **against a different person;** or

ⅲ. The defendant commits a **different tort** against a **different person.**

2. Vicarious Liability (14July)

Vicarious liability는 위법행위를 한 자와 특별한 관계를 맺고 있는 자가 해당 위법행위에 대해 배상해야 하는 책임을 뜻하는 바, 한국법상 사용자책임에 해당한다. 여기서 '특별한 관계'란 대리관계(agency)를 뜻하며, 위법행위를 한 자가 agent, vicarious liability를 가지는 자가 principal에 대응된다. 따라서 본 개념은 사용자와 근로자의 관계, partnerships(합명회사, 합자회사 또는 유한책임회사) 및 joint venture와 사원(partners)의 관계 등에 모두 적용가능하다. 그중 사용자와 근로자의 관계에서 vicarious liability가 인정되려면 두 요건이 만족되어야 하는데, ① 근로자가 고용업무 수행 과정(within the scope of employment) 중 발생한 위법행위인 경우 ② 사용자가 근로자를 통제(control)할 수 있는 경우가 그 요건이다. 사용자가 근로자를 통제(control)할 수 있다는 것은 근로자가 independent contractor가 아닌 employee로 고용되어 있다는 것을 의미하는 바, 통제할 수 있는 정도는 업무상 전문적인 skill이 필요한 정도, 급여 지급 방식, 고용기간 등 다양한 사안들을 통해 종합적으로 판단된다.

The principal is **not** vicariously liable for the agent's **intentional torts or criminal acts.**

a. Within the Scope of Employment

A principal will be vicariously liable for the agent's tortious conduct only if it occurred **within the scope of his employment.**

b. Employee v. Independent Contractor

i. General Rule

Principal is liable for torts committed by the agent, when the agent's manner and method is **under the control** of the principal. In other words, principal is liable for **vicarious liability** when principal employed the agent **as an employee,** rather than an independent contractor.

ii. Considering Factors

A court will consider several factors in determining the degree of the principal's control over the agent, such as:

① Level of skills required;

(Skill을 많이 요하지 않는 업무라면, employee로 본다.)

② Whether work is part or whole of principal's business;

(근로자의 업무가 고용자 사업의 일부라면, employee로 본다.)

③ Payment for regular work; and

(시급이라면 employee로, 프로젝트 별로 급여를 지급한다면 independent contractor로 본다.)

④ The length of the relationship.

(지속되는 관계라면 employee로, 특정 프로젝트 동안에만 유지되는 관계라면 independent contractor로 본다.)

iii. Exceptions

A principal **is** liable for the torts of an independent contractor when the conduct:

① Is **ultra-hazardous;**

② Involves **non-delegable** duties;

③ Is **negligent selection** of the independent contractor; or

④ **Estoppel** applies.

[Non-Delegable Duty]

일반적으로 high duty of care가 요구되는 경우 non-delegable duty가 인정된다.

✔ Maintenance of **taxi**: non-delegable duty

운전사 및 수리공(maintenance)은 택시회사의 independent contractor이나 택시의 안전을 유지할 의무는 non-delegable duty로서, 택시의 불안전함(운전사의 부주의한 운전 또는 택시의 부품결함 등)으로 인해 승객이 피해를 입는 다면 택시회사는 이에 대해 책임을 져야 한다.

✔ Maintenance of **store**: non-delegable duty

상점 주인이 independent contractor를 고용하여 상점을 수리했다 하더라도 상점의 안전을 유지할 의무는 non-delegable duty로서, 상점의 위험한 상황으로 인해 고객이 피해를 입는다면 상점 주인은 이에 대해 책임을 져야 한다.

TIP1 Arguable point: 고용주는 근로자가 independent contractor라고 주장할 것이다. 반면, 고용주를 상대로 소송을 제기한 피해자(원고)는 근로자가 employee라는 점과 independent contractor를 인정한다 하더라도 그의 행위가 exception에 해당한다고 주장할 것이다. The principal may argue that the agent is an independent contractor. In response, the agent may argue that he is an employee. If the principal pursues that the agent is hired as an independent contractor, the agent may argue that principal's [conduct involves non-delegable duty].

TIP2 근로자의 행위에 대해 고용주의 책임유무가 출제된 경우, 근로자의 과실(negligence)에 의한 vicarious liability와 고용주 스스로의 과실(negligence) 모두 analyze해야 한다. 여기서 vicarious liability는 근로자의 과실(negligence)이 인정되는 경우에 한해 적용된다는 점에 유의해야 한다.

3. Jointly and Severally Liable (17July)

본 내용은 수인(數人)이 공동으로 위법행위를 한 경우에 대한 내용이다. 수인이 공동의 위법행위로 타인에게 손해를 가한 때에는 그 손해를 연대하여 배상할 책임이 있다.

★If **more than one defendant** conducted tortious acts, those defendants would be **jointly and severally liable** for the damages.
Each of those defendants is liable for the **full amount** of the plaintiff's damages.

10장
Constitutional Law

//

본 장은 미국의 최고법인 헌법(Constitutional law)에 대해 논한다. 미국은 연방정부와 주 정부가 서로 독립적인 정부를 구성하는 federalism 시스템을 가지고 있으며, 각 정부는 삼권분립이 되어 있고, 연방 정부의 권한이 헌법에 명시되어 있다. 연방정부의 권한은 광범위하면서도 헌법에 의해 제한적이고, 주 정부는 연방 정부가 가지고 있는 권한을 제외한 모든 권한을 가진다. 따라서 법의 합헌성을 판단하는 경우 해당 법을 제정한 주체(연방 또는 주 정부)를 기준으로 해야 한다. 캘리포니아 에세이 시험(CEE)에서 본 장에 관한 문제는 광범위한 논점에서 출제되기보다는 commercial clause, free to speech 등 특정 논점을 위주로 출제되는 경향이 있으며, Torts 과목과 같이 주어진 사안을 꼼꼼하게 analysis하는 것이 중요하다. 본 장은 지난 7년간 출제되었던 문제에서 주로 다루었던 논점을 중심으로 justiciability, federal powers, Equal Protection Clause, Due Process Clause, Taking Clause, individual rights에 대해 논한다.

☑ 글쓰기 Tips

1. Constitutional law에 관한 모든 답안은 justiciability 여부를 판단하는 내용으로 시작한다.
2. 차별적인 법률에 대한 위헌성 여부는 ① Commerce Clause, ② P&I of IV, ③ Due Process, ④ Equal Protection 모두에 대해 analysis해야 한다.
3. 표현의 자유에 관한 사안에서는 ① right to freedom of speech, ② vague and overbreath에 대해 analysis해야 한다.
4. 특정 종교에 관한 규정의 위헌성은 ① Equal Protection Clause, ② Free exercise Clause, ③ Establishment Clause, ④ right to freedom of speech, ⑤ vague and overbreath를 통해 판단한다.
5. Amendment의 조항에 대해 analysis하는 경우, 반드시 ① 적용대상(federal/state

government)과 ② 수정헌법14조를 통한 확대적용에 대해 논한다.

6. "First prong of the Lemon test" "Under this prong, ~"

7. 정부가 제정한 법률의 '위헌여부'에 관한 문제는 관련된 모든 헌법적 issues에 대해 서술해야 한다.

    Q: What claims can 갑 make under the U.S. Constitution and show should the court rule?

    Q: What challenges **under the U.S. Constitution,** if any, could 갑 reasonably raise to the [City ABC]? Discuss.

    ⇒ "Justiciability"에 관한 논점부터 서술한다.

8. 특정 issue에 관한 문제도 있다.

    Q: Did federal government's action violate **the procedural due process?**

    Q: 갑 has filed suit claiming violation of **the First Amendment.** What arguments may 갑 reasonably raise in support of his claim? Discuss.

    ⇒ ① 해당 issue 정의 ② state/federal (14조)

9. 직접적으로 위헌여부 및 헌법적 issue가 명시되어 있지 않은 경우, 주어진 '사안'에서 출제의도를 파악해야 한다.

    Q: What is the likelihood of the [plaintiff]'s success in obtaining declaratory relief in its favor?

    ⇒ Declaratory 신청의 근거에 대해 서술

    Q: How should the court rule on the [plaintiff]'s motion?

    ⇒ Motion 신청의 근거에 대해 서술

10. Declaratory relief를 구하는 경우가 있다.

    Q: 갑 sue the State in federal court seeking a declaration that the ordinance violates the First Amendment. What is the likelihood of 갑's success in obtaining declaratory relief in its favor?

    ⇒ 해당 ordinance의 수정헌법 1조 위헌여부에 대해 서술

    (Declaratory relief는 소송당사자의 권리 및 의무에 대해 확정하는 판결을 뜻하며, 손해배상이나 이행명령을 명하지는 않는다.)

[Justiciability]

When a case is to be heard by the federal courts, several requirements for justiciability should be satisfied. In addition to the federal court's jurisdiction over the subject matter of the case, (1) the case does not give an advisory opinion; (2) the plaintiff must have standing; (3) the case must not be moot; (4) the case must be ripe; and (5) the case does not involve political question. Moreover, the case should not violate the Eleventh Amendment.

[Through the Fourteenth Amendment]

The Due Process Clause is also applicable to state and local governments through the Fourteenth Amendment.

Ⅰ. Justiciability in Federal Court (16July, 18July, 19July)

연방법원에서 합헌성에 대해 소송을 진행하는 경우는 다른 유형의 소송에 비해 그 요건이 매우 까다롭다. 이를 doctrine of strict necessity라 일컫는다. 해당 소송에 대해 연방법원의 재판권(jurisdiction)이 인정되어야 하며, 연방법원에서 진행될만한 사건이어야 하며(justiciability), 수정헌법 11조(The Eleventh Amendment)에도 부합해야 한다. Jurisdiction은 해당 소송에 대해 SMJ, PJ, venue를 모두 만족해야 인정되는 바, 본 내용은 civil procedure 과목에서 다룬다.

Justiciability 인정요건은 ① advisory opinion을 제공하는 사건이 아닐 것, ② 원고가 standing을 가질 것, ③ moot하지 않은 사건일 것, ④ ripe한 사건일 것, ⑤ 사건이 political question에 연관되지 않을 것, 이렇게 다섯 가지가 있다. 첫 번째 요건은 사법권에 관한 Article Ⅲ에서 언급된 "case or controversy" 단어를 해석하는데서 만들어졌다. 이는 추상적(abstract)이거나 가상적인(hypothetical) 사건이 아닌, 즉 판결에서 advisory opinion을 제공하는 사건이 아닌 법적으로 영향을 미칠 수 있는 사건일 것을 요구한다. 두 번째 standing 요건은 원고가 해당 사건에 대해 소송을 제기할 수 있는 '자격'을 의미하는 바, 해당 법률에 의해(causation) 발생된 피해(injury)가 있고 판결을 통해 해당 피해가 제거될 수 있는(redressability) 경우에 인정된다. 세 번째 요건은 moot하지 않은 사건이다. Moot는 '고려할 가치가 없는'으로 직역되며, 이미 해결되어 논점이 없다는 것을 의미한다. 즉, 소송이 진행되는 모든 과정에 있어 사건이 해결되지 않고 논점이 있는 상태가 유지되어야 한다. 예컨대, 형기를 모두 마친 자가 소송진행 과정에서 자신의 헌법적 권리가 침해되었다고 주장한다면 이미 형기를 마쳐 더 이상 해결할 논점이 없으므로, 즉 moot case이므로 연방법원에서 진행될 수 없다. 네 번째 ripeness 요건은 원고가 입은 피해가 이미 발생되었거나 그 피해 발생이 immediate할 것을 요구한다. 다섯 번째 요건은 진행되는 사건이 political question과 연관성이 없을 것을 요구한다. Political question이란, 헌법에 의해 입법부 및 행정부에 위임된 사안 또는 사법권으로는 해결할 수 없는 사안을 뜻하는 바, 이러한 사안에 대해서는 연방법원에서 합헌성 여부를 판단할 수 없다.

한편, 수정헌법 11조 또한 연방법원(Article Ⅲ court)에서 진행하는 합헌성 여부에 대한 소송 요건에 대해 규정하고 있다. 수정헌법 11조에 따르면, '타주민(州民)이나 외국인'이 주 정부를 상대로 손배청구 한 소송은 '연방법원'에서 진행할 수 없다. 한편 state sovereignty에 관한 rule은 주 법원에서 제기된 소송에 대해 규정하는 바, '당해 주 주민'이 자신의 주 정부를 상대로 '주 법원'에 손해배상을 청구하는 소는 금지된다.

A. Advisory Opinion

Advisory opinion is an opinion by a court that does not have the effect on legal case. It is an advice on the constitutionality or interpretation of a law.

B. Standing

1. General Rule

A plaintiff must have **standing** in order for the **federal court** to hear the case.

To establish standing, a plaintiff must show **an injury in fact, causation, and redressability**^{시정}.

2. Injury in Fact

The plaintiff must show that his **constitutional or statutory rights** have been violated. Such injury should be **concrete and particularized.**

✔ Economic harm — can be a concrete injury
✔ Emotional distress — can be a concrete injury

3. Redressability

Redressability requirement is satisfied only when a court order can **remedy the plaintiff's injury.**

C. No Mootness

A federal court may hear a case which is **not** moot^{고려할 가치가 없는}. There should be a **real and live controversy at all stages of review.**

✔ 원고가 Equal Protection Clause를 위반한 정부의 정책으로 인한 고객 유실을 주장하는 경우

⇒ Not moot. 정부는 '고객 유실'이라는 harm이 이미 발생하였으므로 not moot하다고 주장할 것이다. 반면, 원고는 이에 대해 자신의 모든 고객이 유실된 것은 아니며 나머지 고객들에게 harm이 발생할 수 있다는 점을 들어 해당 소송이 moot하다고 반박할 것이다.

The government may argue that the case becomes moot because 갑 has already lost his customers and the harm has already done to him. However, 갑 may rebut that the regulation would further harm the rest of his customers.

D. Ripeness

A federal court may hear a case which is ripe. Ripeness requirement is satisfied when there is an **immediate threat of harm.** When cases are raised for ordinances or laws that have not yet been enacted or have not yet been violated, those will not be heard in federal court.

E. No Political Question

Political question cannot be heard by federal court.

Political questions are issues that:

ⅰ. Are related to **another branch of government;** or

ⅱ. Have **no way** to resolve **by the judicial process.**

F. The Eleventh Amendment (16July)

★Under the Eleventh Amendment, a **state** is immune from suit raised by the **private person of another state or of foreign state for damages in federal court.** Lawsuits against the state in federal court are barred.

[Sovereign Immunity]

Under the sovereign immunity, lawsuits raised **by a private person of the state against the state for damages** in the **state's own court** are barred.

[The Tenth Amendment — Dual Sovereignty]

The states retain a significant measure of **sovereign authority,** and Congress cannot require the states **to govern** according to Congress's instructions.

[표 10-1]

		for injunction	가능
for $	타 주민/외국인 → State (in federal ct)		불가 (11th Amend.)
	해당 주민 → State (in state ct)		불가 (sovereign immunity)

답안요령	Justiciability

> 1. Justiciability 기본 rule
> 2. Analysis — 요건(×5)

TIP1 Constitutional law에 관한 모든 답안은 justiciability를 판단하는 내용으로 시작한다.

TIP2 Justiciability의 다섯 요건 중 특정 요건(standing)만을 논하는 문제가 출제된 적도 있다.

Q: State A have moved to dismiss the suit based on standing. How should the court rule on the State A's motion?

Analysis는 justiciability의 다섯 '요건'을 title화하여 작성한다.

모범답안 033

Justiciability

To be heard by the federal courts, several requirements for justiciability should be satisfied. In addition to the federal court's jurisdiction over the subject matter of the case, (1) the case does not give an advisory opinion; (2) the plaintiff must have standing; (3) the case must not be moot; (4) the case must be ripe; and (5) the case does not involve political question. Moreover, the case should not violate the Eleventh Amendment.

(1) Advisory opinion

Advisory opinion is an opinion by a court that does not have the effect on legal case.

(ANALYSIS: In this case, 갑 would raise a suit claiming unconstitutionality of the Act. Thus, the case does not give an advisory opinion.)

(2) Standing

A plaintiff must have standing in order for the federal court to hear the case. To establish standing, a plaintiff must show an injury in fact, causation, and redressability.

(ANALYSIS: In this case, 갑 has standing. He suffered economic loss by the Act and the loss is caused by the Act, since it prevents him from selling his goods in the state. The judicial decision may redress 갑's injuries by striking down the Act. Thus, second requirement is satisfied.)

(3) Not be moot

A federal court may hear a case which is not moot. There should be a real and live controversy at all stages of review.

(ANALYSIS: The government may argue that the case becomes moot because 갑 has already lost his customers and the harm has already done to him. However, 갑 may rebut that the regulation would further harm the rest of his customers. Thus, the case is not moot.)

(4) Ripeness

Ripeness requirement is satisfied when there is an immediate threat of harm. When ordinances or laws have not yet been enacted or have not yet been violated, he ripeness requirement cannot be satisfied.

(ANALYSIS: In this case, the Act is already enacted and the ripeness requirement is satisfied.)

(5) Political question

Political questions are issues that: (1) are related to another branch of government; or (2) have no way to resolve by the judicial process.

(ANALYSIS: In this case, the Act is discriminating state residents and non-state residents and it can be resolved by the judicial process. Thus, there are no political questions here.)

(6) The Eleventh Amendment

Under the Eleventh Amendment, a state is immune from suit raised by the private person of another state or of foreign state for damages in federal court. Lawsuits against the state in federal court are barred.

(ANALYSIS: In this case, the Act is passed by the State A and 갑, an individual, raised the suit against the State A in the federal court. Thus, the case should be dismissed under the Eleventh Amendment.)

Conclusion

In conclusion, the case raised by 갑 has no justiciability, since it violates the Eleventh Amendment.

II. Federal Powers

A. Commerce Clause (18July)

의회는 Commerce Clause에 의거하여 'interstate commerce와 관련된' channels, people, instrument 그리고 activities만을 규제할 수 있다. 따라서 Congress는 모든 영업장 또는 모든 근로자에게 적용되는 commerce 법규는 제정할 수 없다. 예컨대, Congress는 근로 장소에서의 폭력에 관한 법은 제정할 수 있으나, 일반적인 폭력에 관한 법은 제정할 수 없다.

1. General Rule

★Under the Commerce Clause, Congress may regulates:

i. The **channels of interstate commerce**;

ii. The **people and instrumentalities** that work and travel in the channels of **interstate commerce**; and

iii. Activities that **substantially affect interstate commerce.**

2. Dormant Commerce Clause

Under the Dormant Commerce Clause, **a state or local government** may regulate **interstate** commerce when the regulation:

i. Is not **unduly burdensome** (burden does not outweigh the benefits);

ii. May not **discriminate** against in-staters and out-of-staters; and

iii. Is **necessary to achieve an important government interest** (least restrictive means are used).

a. When Unduly Burdensome

When a regulation is nondiscriminatory but impose burdens on interstate commerce, it is permitted if:

i. The **burden** imposed on interstate commerce **is outweighed by** the **benefits** to the state; and

ii. It is **rationally related** to a legitimate government interest.

3. Exceptions

There are exceptions to the Dormant Commerce Clause:

ⅰ. When a state is acting as a **market participant;** and

ⅱ. When a **traditional public function** is given to the states.

TIP1 Arguable point

위헌을 주장하는 측(원고 측)은 해당 정책이 in-stater와 out-of -stater간 차별을 한다고 주장하여 IR test를 적용하려 할 것이나, 이에 대해 정부(피고 측) 측은 차별은 없었다고 주장하며 RR test를 적용하려 할 것이다.

A plaintiff may argue that there was a discrimination between in-staters and out-of-staters, and therefore IR test should be applied. In response, a defendant may argue that there was no discrimination and RR test should be applied.

TIP2 만일 원고 측의 주장대로 IR test를 적용하였고 요건 ⅲ(least restrictive means)이 미충족 된 경우에는 해당 정책보다 제한적이지 않은 대안을 제시하는 것이 좋다.

TIP3 Commerce Clause에 관한 사안이 제시되는 경우, Privileges and Immunities Clause of Article Ⅳ에도 부합하는지 analysis하는 것이 고득점 포인트다.

---

case

주(州) 정부가 철도회사 ABC를 매수하였고, 해당 철도회사 창고를 주(州) 내에 공장을 가지고 있는 회사에게 우선배분하도록 규정하였다. 이에 타 주 회사 경영자 갑은 창고를 이용하지 못하게 되었고, 이로 인해 제때 상품을 배송하지 못해 많은 고객들을 잃어 경제적 손해를 입었다. Is the regulation constitutional under the Dormant Commerce Clause?

⇒ Unconstitutional. 주 정부는 해당 규정이 주 내의 회사와 타 주의 회사를 차별하는 것이 아니라 in-state에 있는 '공장'에 혜택을 준 것일 뿐이라고 주장할 수 있다. 반면, 갑은 해당 규정이 주 내의 공장에게 우선권을 주어

주 내에 공장을 지닌 회사와 타 주에 공장을 지닌 회사를 다르게 대우하고 있다고 반박할 것이다. 또한, 모든 회사에게 적은 비율의 창고를 배분하는 등과 같은 규정을 통해 보다 비차별적이고 부담이지 않은 방법을 사용할 수 있다는 점에서 요건 iii을 충족하지 못한다.

State may argue that it is not discriminating against out-of-staters, but is favoring factories in the state. 갑 will rebut that the regulation gives in-staters priority space, treating companies differently based on their state of citizenship. Moreover, the regulation is not least restrictive means and it can be more narrowly tailored. **For example, the State can guarantee a small percentage to all companies.**

B. Privileges and Immunities Clause of Article IV (18July)

본 조항은 주(州)가 헌법적 기본권리 및 상업 행위에 대해 주민과 타 주민을 차별하는 것을 금한다. 이는 회사(corporation)와 외국인(alien)에는 적용되지 않는다. 주 규정의 본 조항 위반 여부는 ① 조항의 적용대상(행위)이 기본권리 및 상업 행위에 해당하는지 그 여부와 ② 해당 규정이 주(州)의 목표(interest)를 달성하는데 있어 necessary한지 그 여부를 기준으로 판단한다. 여기서 "necessary하다"는 것은 특정 목표를 달성하는 데 있어 규정의 차별성과 부담성이 최소한에 그친다는 의미이다.

1. General Rule

Privileges and Immunities Clause of Article IV prevents a **state** from **discrimination** against out-of-staters when it affects a **fundamental right or important commercial activities.**

Corporations and aliens are **not** protected under the Privileges and Immunities Clause of Article Ⅳ.

[Article Ⅳ, Section 2, Clause 1]
The citizens of each state shall be entitled to all privileges and immunities of citizens in the several states.

2. Exception

Even if a state law discriminates against out-of-staters, it is permitted when there are **no less restrictive means** to solve the problem. In other words, the discrimination is permitted when the state has a **justification** for it.

TIP　Privileges and Immunities Clause of Article IV에 관한 사안이 제시되는 경우, Commerce clause 위배여부도 함께 analysis하는 것이 고득점 포인트다.

III. Equal Protection Clause (EP) (18Feb, 18July)

1. General Rule

★Under the Fourteenth Amendment Equal Protection Clause, the state shall not treat similarly situated persons differently.

The level of scrutiny depends on what classification is sued by government.

2. Level of Scrutiny

a. Strict Scrutiny Test (SS Test)

When a state uses a suspect classification, the strict scrutiny will be used to determine constitutionality.

★The **government** must show that the challenged classification serves **compelling governmental objectives** when the state discriminates based on race, national origin, and alienage.

b. Intermediate Scrutiny Test (IR Test)

When a state uses a quasi-suspect classification, the intermediate scrutiny will be used to determine constitutionality.

★The **government** must at least show that the challenged

classification serves **important governmental objectives** and the discriminatory means employed are **substantially related to** the achievement of those objectives, when the state discriminates based on gender.

c. Rational Basis Test (RR test)

When a government uses a non-suspect classification, the rational basis test will be used to determine constitutionality.

★The **petitioner** must show that the discrimination is **not rationally related** to legitimate governmental interest when the government discriminates based on other classifications mentioned for SS and IS, such as age.

Ⅳ. Due Process Clause (DP) (16July, 18July)

1. Procedural Due Process

★Under the Due Process Clause of the Fifth Amendment, the **federal** government shall not deprive **a person's life, liberty, or property without due process of law.** The Due Process Clause is applicable to **state and local** governments **through the Fourteenth Amendment.**

a. Person's Life, Liberty, and Property

　ⅰ. Liberty

　　The person has liberty interest when his freedom of movement is restrained or when his constitutional rights are denied.

　ⅱ. Property

　　✔ A tenured^{종신직의} employee, who can only be fired for cause, has a property interest in his employment.

　　✔ A probationary^{가채용의} employee, who may be fired for any cause without notice, has no property interest in his employment.

b. Due Process

The court use **Mathews balancing test** in determining what process was due for the taking.

Generally, **pre-termination notice** is required and additional procedures are required when the Mathews balancing test is satisfied.

Under the test, additional procedures are required when:

ⅰ. The **private interest** is affected by the government actions;

ⅱ. The government has **interest in administration and finance**; and

ⅲ. **The risk** of deprivation^{박탈} **outweighs the value** of additional procedures.

2. Substantive Due Process

a. General Rule

When a law limits a fundamental right, strict scrutiny will be applied. When a law limits a non-fundamental right, rational basis test will be applied.

The Due Process Clause is applicable to **state and local** governments **through the Fourteenth Amendment**.

b. Fundamental Rights

✔ All rights under the First Amendment

✔ Right to travel

✔ Privacy

✔ Voting

답안요령	차별적인 조항

1. Justificiability
   + analysis
2. Dormant Commerce Clause
   + analysis

3. Privileges and Immunities Clause under Article IV
   + analysis
4. Equal Protection Clause
   + analysis
5. Due Process Clause
   + analysis

TIP1 Constitutional law에 관한 모든 답안은 justiciability를 판단하는 내용으로 시작한다.

TIP2 차별적인 법률에 대한 위헌성 여부는 ① Commerce Clause, ② P&I of IV, ③ Due Process Clause, ④ Equal Protection Clause 모두에 대해 analysis하는 것이 고득점 포인트다.

모범답안 034

Justiciability

……

Dormant Commerce Clause

Under the Dormant Commerce Clause ("DCC"), a state or local government may regulate interstate commerce when the regulation: (1) is not unduly burdensome; (2) may not discriminate against in-staters and out-of-staters; and (3) is necessary to achieve an important government interest. The burden imposed on interstate commerce is outweighed by the benefits to the state and it is rationally related to a legitimate government interest.

(ANALYSIS: In this case, …….)

Exceptions

There are exceptions to the DCC: (1) when a state is acting as a market participant; (2) when a traditional public function is given to the states.

(ANALYSIS: In this case, the State A is a contractual party and it is a market participant. Thus, the exception to the DCC is applicable here.)

Conclusion

In conclusion, the Act is constitutional since the exception to the DCC is applicable.

Privileges and Immunities Clause under Article IV

Privileges and Immunities Clause of Article IV prevents a state from discrimination against out-of-staters when it affects a fundamental right or important commercial activities. Even if a state law discriminates against out-of-staters, it is permitted when there are no less restrictive means to solve the problem.

(ANALYSIS: In this case, 갑 is an alien and he is not protected under the Privileges and Immunities Clause of Article Ⅳ.)

Equal Protection Clause

Under the Fourteenth Amendment Equal Protection Clause, the state shall not treat similarly situated persons differently. The level of scrutiny depends on what classification is sued by government.

(ANALYSIS: In this case, the Act discriminates against out-of-staters, and the rational basis test will be used.)

The petitioner must show that the discrimination is not rationally related to legitimate governmental interest.

(ANALYSIS: In this case, the Act is to improve the economy in State A and the Act is rationally related to it. Thus, the Act is consitutional under the Equal Protection Clause.)

Due Process Clause

When a law limits a fundamental right, strict scrutiny will be applied. When a law limits a non-fundamental right, rational basis test will be applied. The Due Process Clause is applicable to state and local governments through the Fourteenth Amendment.

(ANALYSIS: In this case, the Act does not limit a fundamental right and, therefore, RR test should be applied. As mentioned above, the Act is to improve the economy in State A and the Act is rationally related to it. Thus, the Act is consitutional under the Due Process Clause.)

<u>Conclusion</u>

In conclusion, the Act is constitutional.

V. Taking Clause (15July)

1. General Rule

★Under the Taking Clause of the Fifth Amendment, **no property shall be taken for public use without just compensation.** It is applicable to state **and local** governments **through the Fourteenth Amendment.**
"Public use" is interpreted broadly and it includes highway, military base, and even **economic development.**

2. Regulatory Taking

The governmental regulation that decreases economic value is not a taking, **as long as the regulation leaves an economically viable use for the property.**
In determining whether the regulation is a **taking,** courts do multi-factor balancing test considering:
　ⅰ. The **social goal** and the value to the community;
　ⅱ. The **economic impact** on the claimant; and
　ⅲ. The extent of **interference with the investment-backed expectation of the owner.**

✔ Regulatory taking이 실행될 경우 claimant가 본래 사용목적으로 해당 토지를 이용하기 위해서는 추가적인 비용이 반드시 발생한다는 사실은 위 ⅱ요건(interference)에 해당되지 않는다. 추가적인 비용이 발생될 뿐, 그 목적을 위한 토지사용이 전면적으로 불가능해지는 것은 아니기 때문이다.

The regulation leaves an economically viable use for the property, and therefore it is not regulatory taking.

✔ When a business has been for a long period, the economic return expected out of the property — reasonable expectation ○

✔ When a business has newly open, the economic return expected out of the property — reasonable expectation ×

3. Non-Conforming Use

A non-conforming use occurs when the current use of the property becomes in violation of the code because the ordinance subsequently changes.

Nonconforming use is allowed if:

ⅰ. The use **existed prior to the change** of the ordinance; and

ⅱ. The use does **not cause harm** to neighborhood.

4. Reliance on Ordinance

개인이 정부의 ordinance 및 permission을 믿고 자산에 투자를 한 경우 그 투자가 이후 새로운 ordinance에 위배되는 행위가 된다할지라도 적법한 use of property로 인정된다. 즉, 정부가 해당 자산을 public use 목적을 위해 taking하는 경우 자산 소유자에게 just compensation을 해야 한다. 다만, 개인이 '미결정된' ordinance에 근거하여 투자행위를 하였다면 선의로 행해진 투자라 하더라도 부적합한 행위이다.

Once the government makes permission or ordinance is established, the party is entitled to complete the project if the party **substantially relied** on it.

✔ A good-faith belief that the use will be permitted in the future is not enough.

Ⅵ. Individual Rights

A. Establishment Clause (14Feb, 18Feb, 19July)

★Under the First Amendment, Congress shall make no law that has effect of establishing or inhibiting religion.

1. Government's Action

To bring a claim under the U.S. Constitution Establishment Clause, there must be a **government action.**

2. Lemon Test

Under the Establishment Clause, governmental action shall meet **"Lemon" test** to be constitutional. The Lemon test requires governmental action to:

ⅰ. Have **secular**^{세속적인} **purpose** (non-religious purpose);

ⅱ. Have **no** primary effect that **advances** religion; and

ⅲ. **Not** produce **excessive government entanglement** with religion.

✔ 주(州)의 교도소에서 수감자(inmate)들의 교화를 위해 십계명의 일부를 식당 벽에 붙여 놓은 경우, 종교적인 목적이 아닌 수감자들의 교화 목적만이 있었다면 secure purpose로 인정된다.

If the ABC Jail had the purpose only to assist prisoners when they are released from prison, the secular purpose would be recognized.

✔ 화재방지를 위한 교회에서의 촛불 사용 금지 정책(위반할 경우 교회를 close down함) → 촛불 사용은 전형적인 종교 행위로서, 본 정책이 시행될 경우 대부분의 교회가 close down하게 된다. → 요건 ⅱ 만족하지 못함. → unconstitutional

Because the burning candles are common religious practice, the regulation would make many churches close down.

B. Free Exercise Clause (14Feb, 18Feb, 19July)

1. General Rule

The Free Exercise Clause is to prevent government from banning or burdening individuals based on the person's **religious beliefs.**

The government may limit religious conduct only when the regulation:

i. Is **facially neutral;** and

ii. Meets **strict scrutiny test.**

✔ When a law **facially neutral** but **incidentally burdens** the exercise of religion, it is constitutional.

2. Religious Beliefs

The Constitution protects religious belief which is **sincerely asserted** by a person.

The protection extends beyond the traditional religions and religious belief which is false. In other words, the court has very little power to question the validity of a religion.

✔ 본 조항은 정부에게 개인의 종교적 믿음을 인정할 것을 요구하나 그것을 제공할 의무를 부여하지는 않는다. 예컨대, 기독교인 신자인 수감자가 성경책을 읽을 수 있도록 교도소 측에 요청하였으나 거절되었다 하더라도 교도소 측이 해당 수감자의 종교적 믿음을 행할 수 있도록 성경책을 제공해야 할 의무는 없으므로 Free Exercise Clause에 위배되지 않는다.

Although the inmate is allowed to practice his religious belief, the jail is not required to provide him for it.

3. Strict Scrutiny Test (SS Test)

When the government discriminates against religion, the strict scrutiny will be used to determine constitutionality.

★The **government** must show that the challenged regulation is **narrowly tailored** to meet a **compelling governmental interest.** To be narrowly tailored, the government must use the **least restrictive means.**

✔ 화재방지를 위한 교회에서의 촛불 사용 금지 정책(위반할 경우 교회를 close down함) → 화재방지를 위해 스프링클러 설치, 소화기(fire extinguisher) 설치 의무화 등 다른 less restrictive means가 존재한다. → SS test 만족하지 못함. → unconstitutional

There is a variety of less restrictive alternatives, such as the installation of sprinklers, compared to closing down the entire church.

TIP1 Free Exercise Clause v. Establishment Clause
① Free Exercise Clause: 정부의 규정이 일정 행위를 '금지'한 경우
② Establishment Clause: 정부의 규정이 일정 행위를 '장려' 및 '허가'한 경우 또는 정부에서 특정 행위를 '한' 경우

TIP2 특정 종교에 관한 규정이 Equal Protection Clause에 위배되었는지 그 여부는 Free Exercise Clause 및 Establishment Clause와 더불어 판단해야 한다.

C. Free to Speech (14Feb, 16July, 19July)

1. General Rule

★The First Amendment protects the right to **freedom of speech** and it is applicable to the federal government. It is applicable to **state and local** governments **through the Fourteenth Amendment.**

a. Government Employee

Generally, a government employee has a right to free speech only when the matters are **not connected with her employment.** When the government restrict the right, the strict scrutiny will be used to determine constitutionality.

★The **government** must show that the challenged regulation is **narrowly tailored** to meet a **compelling governmental interest.** To be narrowly tailored, the government must use the **least restrictive means.**

2. In Public Forum

a. Content-Based Restriction

All content-based restrictions on speech in a public or designated public forum are subject to strict scrutiny.

★The **government** must show that the challenged classification serves **compelling governmental objectives.**

b. Content-Neutral Restriction

All content-neutral restrictions on speech in a public or designated public forum are subject to intermediate scrutiny.

★Under the intermediate scrutiny, the **state** must show that:

ⅰ. The regulation is not to suppress expression;

ⅱ. The regulation is **narrowly tailored** to achieve a **significant governmental interest;** and

ⅲ. The regulation leaves **open alternative channels** for expressive activity.

TIP1 Free to speech와 관련된 사안이 제시되는 경우, 반드시 prior restraint, vague and overbreadth 여부도 analysis해야 한다.

TIP2 Argument point

위헌을 주장하는 측(원고)은 content-based임을 주장하는 반면, 정부(피고)는 content-neutral임을 주장할 것이다.

A plaintiff may argue that the regulation is content-based restriction, but a defendant may argue that is content-neutral.

3. Time, Place, and Manner Restrictions (T/P/M) (14Feb)

a. In Public Forum

The government may regulate a valid time, place, and manner restriction on speech in public forums if the regulation:

ⅰ. Is **content neutral** and **viewpoint neutral;**

ⅱ. Is **narrowly tailored** to serve an **important** government interest; and

ⅲ. Leaves **open alternative channels of communication.**

b. In Limited and Nonpublic Forums

The government may regulate a valid time, place, and manner restriction on speech in limited or nonpublic forums if the regulation:

ⅰ. Is **viewpoint neutral;** and

ⅱ. Be **reasonably related** to serve a **legitimate government interest.**

4. Symbolic Speech (19July)

Symbolic speech is a communication of an idea using a **symbol or communicative conduct.** Restriction on symbolic speech is unconstitutional. However, the restriction may be consitutional only if the restriction:

ⅰ. Is **content-neutral;**

ⅱ. Further an **important governmental interest;**

ⅲ. Prohibits **no more speech than necessary;** and

ⅳ. Is **within the constitutional power** the government has.

✔ 화재방지를 위한 교회에서의 촛불 사용 금지 정책(위반할 경우 교회를 close down함) → 본 정책은 교회에서의 communication 내용에 근거한 content-based 금지가 아닌 '화재방지'라는 목적을 위한 symbolic speech(촛불사용) 금지이다.

5. Limitations on Freedom of Speech

a. Prior Restraint

Prior restraints put barrier on speech before it even occurs and it is unconstitutional.

To be a valid prior restraint, it must:

   ⅰ. Furthers an **important governmental interest;**

   ⅱ. Involves **no discretion** by the person or group issuing the permit;

   ⅲ. Has **clear criteria** to obtain the permit; and

   ⅳ. There must be a **procedure** in place for **timely resolution** of the permit.

b. Vague and Overbreadth

A overbroad regulation is unconstitutional which regulates more speech than intended.

A vague regulation is unconstitutional which is unclear what speech is prohibited.

답안요령

1. [The First Amendment]
   + analysis
2. Establishment Clause
   + analysis
3. Free Exercise Clause
   + analysis
4. Prior restraint
   + analysis
5. Vague and overbreadth
   + analysis

TIP1 위 1번: Establishment Clause와 Free Exercise Clause에 관한 문제의 경우 the First Amendment에 대해 논한다.

TIP2 위 1번: 수정헌법 14조를 통해 State에도 적용가능하다는 점을 작성하는 것이 고득점 포인트다.

모범답안 035

The First Amendment

The First Amendment applies to Congress and it prohibits Congress from making any law violating an individual's rights. The First Amendment is also applicable to state and local governments through the Fourteenth Amendment.

(ANALYSIS: In his case, the law prohibiting the moon display is regulated by ABC. ABC is a state actor since it functions as a state. Thus, the First Amendment applies to ABC's actions.)

Establishment Clause

Under the First Amendment, the government shall make no law that has effect of establishing or inhibiting religion. Under the Establishment Clause, governmental action shall meet Lemon test to be constitutional. The Lemon test requires governmental action to: (1) have secular purpose; (2) have no primary effect that advances religion; and (3) not produce excessive government entanglement with religion.

(1) Secular purpose

(ANALYSIS: In this case, prohibiting the moon display is to avoid the endorsement of religion. Thus, the first prong of Lemon test is satisfied.)

(2) No primary effect that advances religion

(ANALYSIS: In this case, ABC allowed the christmas tree, but not allowed the moon display. ABC advances a certain religion (Christianity) and the second prong of Lemon test is not satisfied. Thus, ABC violated the

Establishment Clause.)

(3) Not produce excessive government entanglement with religion

(ANALYSIS: In this case, ABC advances Christianity and it results in excessive government entanglement with Christianity. Thus, ABC violated the Establishment Clause.)

Conclusion

In conclusion, ABC violated the Establishment Clause.

Free Exercise Clause

The Free Exercise Clause is to prevent government from banning or burdening individuals based on the person's religious beliefs. The government may limit religious conduct only when the regulation: (1) is facially neutral; and (2) meets strict scrutiny test.

(1) Facially neutral

(ANALYSIS: In this case, ABC regulated a law that is not facially neutral. The law states that all religious symbols cannot be displayed in government buildings, not all symbols. Thus, the first prong is satisfied.)

(2) Strict scrutiny test

The government must show that the challenged regulation is narrowly tailored to meet a compelling governmental interest. To be narrowly tailored, the government must use the least restrictive means.

(ANALYSIS: In this case, ABC may argue that is has a governmental interest, avoiding the governmental endorsement of religion, and it is a compelling governmental interest. However, there are a variety of less restrictive alternatives, such as the moon display without explanation of the religion. Thus, the second prong is not satisfied.)

Conclusion

In conclusion, ABC violated the Free Exercise Clause.

Prior restraints

Prior restraints put barrier on speech before it even occurs and it is unconstitutional. To be a valid prior restraint, it must: (1) furthers an important governmental interest; (2) involves no discretion by the person or group issuing the permit; (3) has clear criteria to obtain the permit; and (4) there must be a procedure in place fore timely resolution of the permit.

(1) Important governmental interest

(ANALYSIS: In this case, ABC has a governmental interest, avoiding the governmental endorsement of religion. Thus, the first prong is satisfied.)

(2) No discretion by the person or group issuing the permit

(ANALYSIS: In this case, there is no clear standard in permitting the display in the building. There is no clear reason to allow only the christmas tree. Thus, the organization with authority to permit has discretion to a person or group issuing the permit. Thus, the second prong is not satisfied.)

(3) Clear criteria to obtain the permit

(ANALYSIS: As mentioned above, there is no clear standard to obtain the displaying permit. ABC allowed the christmas tree, but not the moon display. There is no clear reason to allow only the christmas tree. Thus, the third prong is not satisfied.)

(4) Procedure in place for timely resolution of the permit

(ANALYSIS: In this case, there is no procedure for resolution of the permit. Thus, the fourth prong is not satisfied.)

Conclusion

In conclusion, the law is an invalid prior restrain on speech and, therefore, it is unconstitutional.

Vague and overbreadth

A overbroad regulation is unconstitutional which regulates more speech than intended. A vague regulation is unconstitutional which is unclear what speech is prohibited.

(ANALYSIS: In this case, the law does not specify what a religious display means. The law does not give clear standard to determine whether the moon is a religious display. Thus, it is vague and unconstiutional.)

Conclusion

In conclusion, ABC violated both Establishment Clause and Free Exercise Clause. Moreover, it is an invalid prior restraint on speech and vague.

11장
Evidence

///

Evidence는 증거법으로서, 소송당사자가 수집한 증거들 중 재판에서 사실판단을 담당하는 jury에게 제출할 수 있는 증거들의 유형 및 요건에 대해 규정한다. 즉, 소송당사자가 제출한 증거의 admissibility 판단기준이 되는 법률이다. 본 장은 증거의 관련성(relevance), 서류의 내용 또는 존재 자체가 증거방법이 되는 서증 및 서면(書證, documentary evidence), 사람의 진술이 증거방법이 되는 인증(人證, testimonial evidence), 법정 외부에서 언급된 진술인 hearsay 그리고 사람의 성격에 대한 증거인 character evidence로 구분되어 있다. 한편, CEE 범위는 캘리포니아 주에서 채택하고 있는 법률(California Evidence Code (CEC))과 연방법(Federal Rules of Evidence (FRE)), 이 두 개의 법률이 모두 포함된다. 본 장은 각 법률이 제정한 내용의 차이점에 중점을 두어 작성되었다. 다만, 별도의 언급이 없는 rule은 CEC의 내용이며, FRE에 해당하는 rule은 별도의 표시를 해두었다.

- California Evidence Code (CEC)
- Federal Rules of Evidence (FRE)

1. 캘리포니아 에세이 시험(CEE)의 Evidence 과목은 그 출제범위가 캘리포니아 법률과 연방법이 모두 포함되는 바, 문제에서 요구한 법률의 '용어'를 구분하여 작성하는 것이 중요하다.

2. CEE에서 Evidence는 Professional responsibility, Contracts, Remedies 등 타 과목과 비교하여 자주 출제되는 과목은 아니나, 캘리포니아 법률과 연방법을 모두 암기해야 한다는 점에서 그 범위가 매우 방대하여 어려운 과목에 속한다.

3. Evidence 과목은 주로 재판이 진행되는 과정에서 당사자가 제출하는 증거에 대한 admissibility 판단 문제로 출제되는 바, Civil Procedure 과목과 연계되어 자주 출제된다.

4. 주로 소송당사자가 제출한 증거에 대해 법원이 어떻게 판결해야 하는지 논하는 문제가 출제된다.

   Q: <u>Did the court properly admit the [notes]? Answer according to the California law.</u>

   Q: <u>Should the court have admitted the [notes]? Answer according to the FRE.</u>

   ⇒ 주어진 사안의 facts를 종합적으로 판단하는 문제가 아닌, 특정 증거의 admissibility에 관한 문제이다.

   ⇒ 각 '증거'를 title화하여 답안을 작성한다.

5. 모든 Evidence 문제는 ① 사건유형(civil/criminal case), ② 사안에 적용되는 법률(California law/FRE), ③ 해당 증거의 사용목적(substantive/impeachment)을 파악하는 것이 중요하다.

6. 동일한 문장이 다수의 hearsay exception에 해당하는 경우가 많다. 따라서 주어진 statement의 exception 해당여부와 관계없이 연관성이 있는 hearsay exceptions를 모두 서술해야 고득점 할 수 있다.

   ⇒ Present condition, medical diagnosis/treatment, spontaneous statement, contemporaneous statement는 서로 밀접한 연관성을 가진다.

7. 대부분의 Evidence 문제본문은 사건의 흐름을 보여주고 있기 때문에, ① "At trial, in π's case-in-chief" ② "In Δ's case-in-chief" ③ "In rebuttal" 단계로 구분하여 증거의 admissibility를 파악하는 것이 좋다.

   ⇒ 주어진 증거가 어떤 목적으로 사용되었는지(substantive/impeachment), prior inconsistent statement에 해당하는지 그 여부를 파악하는데 유용하다.

[Logical Relevance]

To be admissible, evidence must be logically relevant. Relevant evidence is any evidence that tends to make the fact more or less probable.

[Legal Relevance]

Under the CEC 352, evidence is legally relevant if its probative value is not substantially outweighed by other factors (misleading the jury, waste of time, injustice prejudice, and confusion of the issues).

[Proposition 8]

Under California's Proposition 8 (Victim's Bill of Rights), in a criminal case, all relevant evidence must be admitted, even if it is inadmissible under CEC. Proposition 8 has some exemptions, such as: secondary evidence rule, hearsay rules, CEC 352, and privileges.

I. Relevance

A. Logical Relevance

To be admissible, evidence must be relevant. ★Relevant evidence is any evidence that tends to make the fact more or less probable.

✔ The credibility of a witness is always at issue.
(Impeach 목적으로 제출하는 증거는 항상 relevant하다.)

✔ The statement is logically relevant that defendant is negligent. This is because it shows that the defendant has notice on it and he knew the problem.

✔ The record is logically relevant because it shows proper maintenance, and it can be used **to rebut** the negligence claim.

✔ The statement is logically relevant because the statement makes it **more likely** that the defendant was negligent.

✔ The record is logically relevant because it **tends to make** the fact of plaintiff's injury **more probable.**

✔ It is logically relevance, because it is the **basis of the claim and is actually in dispute.**

B. Legal Relevance (CEC 352, FRE 403)

★Under the CEC 352 (FRE 403), **evidence is legally relevant if its probative value is not substantially outweighed by other factors** (misleading the jury, waste of time, injustice prejudice, and confusion of the issues).

In other words, a **balancing test** is used to determine legal relevance.

- ✔ The evidence has probative value because it supports whether [증명하고자 하는 내용].
- ✔ The evidence has probative value because it supports a case for [negligence].
- ✔ The evidence has probative value because it supports whether [갑 drove on the red light].
- ✔ The evidence has probative value because it supports whether [갑 suffered damages].

  ⇒ The evidence is legally relevant because its probative value as to whether 갑 suffered damages is not outweighed by other factors.

C. Proposition 8 (California)

Proposition 8은 캘리포니아에서 채택하는 법률로서, Victim's Bill of Rights 라고도 일컫는다. 이는 형소재판에 있어 해당 재판과 연관성이 있는 증거는 캘리포니아 증거법(CEC)에 위배되더라도 모두 채택가능(admissible)하다는 것을 내용으로 한다. 다만, 본 rule에도 예외가 존재하는 바, 일정 rule에 위배되는 경우에는 연관성이 있다 하더라도 증거력이 인정되지 않는다(inadmissible).

1. General Rule

★Under California's Proposition 8, **in a criminal case,** all relevant evidence must be admitted subject to additional **exemptions**^{면제}, **even if objectionable under CEC.**

Proposition is also known as a Victim's Bill of Rights.

2. Exemptions

> "SHE PM ROC" — Secondary evidence rule, Hearsay rules,
> Exclusionary rules (Con.law/Cal.law), Privileges, Member of media, Rape
> shield laws, defendant's Open the door, CEC 352

Proposition 8 is **inapplicable** to the following rules:

ⅰ. Secondary evidence rule;

ⅱ. Hearsay rules;

ⅲ. Exclusionary rules under the Consitutional law (e.g., Confrontation Clause, Miranda) and under the California legislature after 1982;

ⅳ. Privileges;

ⅴ. Member of media (e.g., member of media can refuse to reveal a confidential news source);

ⅵ. Rape shield laws (as to victim's character);

ⅶ. "Open the door" rule for character evidence; and

ⅷ. CEC 352.

D. Public Policy Exclusions (17Feb)

Relevant evidence can be excluded for public policy reasons.

1. Subsequent Remedial Measures (19Feb)

★Subsequent remedial measures are inadmissible **to prove negligence or culpable conduct.**

Those evidence are used to prove ownership or control, unfeasible precaution, and destruction of evidence.

[FRE]

★Subsequent remedial measures are inadmissible to prove negligence, culpable conduct, or a defect in a product or its design.

CEC는 '제품의 하자'를 증명하기 위해 제출된 subsequent remedial measures의 증거력을 인정하나(admissible), FRE는 인정하지 않는다(inadmissible).

2. Offers for Medical Expenses

Offers for medical expenses의 증거력은 substantive evidence로서 제출되는 경우와 impeachment의 목적으로 제출되는 경우를 구분하여 판단해야 한다. Substantive evidence로서 제출되는 경우에는 hearsay exception으로 인정된다 할지라도 public policy exception에 해당하는지 그 여부도 더불어 판단해야 하는 바, 해당 statement가 상대방의 '책임유무'를 증명하기 위해 제출된다면 inadmissible하다. 다만, 상대방의 ownership를 증명하기 위한 경우, 제출하는 측의 책임을 부정하기 위한 경우 또는 그 외의 목적을 위해 증거를 제출하는 경우에는 admissible하다. 한편, impeachment 목적으로 제출되는 경우(상대방의 prior inconsistent statement를 주장하며 impeach하는 경우)에는 hearsay exception 여부와 public policy exception 여부와 무관하게 admissible하다.

CEC에서는 상대방에 대한 의료비 지원 의사(offer)를 언급하는 과정에서 인정한 사실 관계는 offer와 동일하게 취급하여 public policy exception에 해당한다고 본다. 즉, 의료비 지원 의사(offer)와 대화 도중 인정한 사실관계 모두 제출이 허용되지 않는다. 반면, FRE에서는 offer와 사실관계에 대한 언급을 구분하여 offer에 한해서만 public policy exception을 적용하고 사실관계에 대한 언급은 적용되지 않아 admissible하다.

Offers to pay medical expenses are inadmissible to prove **liability for the injury.**

Admissions of **fact** stated with the offers to pay medical expenses **are** also <u>inadmissible</u>.

[FRE]

Admissions of **fact** stated with the offers to pay medical expenses **are** <u>admissible</u>.

3. Disputed Settlement Offers (California)

★A settlement offer is inadmissible if it is used to prove the **validity, liability, or amount** of a disputed claim in civil cases.

Statements **during mediation proceeding** are also inadmissible.

[FRE]

There is no such rule.

✔ 사고 현장에서 갑이 을에게 합의 의사(offer to settle)를 밝힌 경우 → claim is not disputed yet. → exception 적용 × → admissible

✔ 자동차 사고 후 갑이 을을 상대로 negligence case를 제소하자, 을이 합의 의사(offer to settle)을 밝힌 경우 → claim is disputed. → exception 적용 ○ → inadmissible

4. Expressions of Sympathy (California)

Expressions of sympathy regarding to the pain, death, suffering, or death of an accident victim are inadmissible to prove liability.

However, a statement of **fault** shall **not** be inadmissible.

[FRE]

There is no such rule.

5. Plea Negotiations

Under the Proposition 8, offer to plead guilty and statements during plea negotiations are <u>admissible.</u>

[FRE]

Under the FRE, offer to plead guilty and statements during plea negotiations are <u>inadmissible</u> for public policy reason.

1. Logical relevance
2. Legal relevance (CEC352/FRE403)
3. Proposition 8
4. (Authentication—real/doc. evidence)
5. (Public policy exceptions)

TIP1　Evidence에 관한 모든 답안은 첫 단락에 ① logical relevance, ② legal relevance, ③ proposition 8에 관해 서술하고, 각 rule에 대한 analysis는 각 증거에 대한 단락에서 별도로 작성한다.

TIP2　California law를 적용하고 civil suit에 관한 문제인 경우 Proposition 8 rule이 적용되지 않으나, 이에 대한 rule을 작성하고 "본 사안에 적용되지 않는다"는 점을 명시하는 것이 고득점 포인트다.

TIP3　4번: 해당 증거가 real evidence 또는 documental evidence인 경우 authentication에 대해 작성한다.

TIP4　5번: Public policy exceptions는 주어진 증거가 본 논점과 연관된 경우에 한해 작성한다.

모범답안 036-1

Q: Should the court have admitted (a) the [note] and (b) the [recording tape]? Answer according to the California law.

Logical relevance

To be admissible, evidence must be logically relevant. Relevant evidence is any evidence that tends to make the fact more or less probable.

Legal relevance

Under the CEC 352, evidence is legally relevant if its probative value is not substantially outweighed by other factors (misleading the jury, waste of time, injustice prejudice, and confusion of the issues).

Proposition 8

Under California's Proposition 8 (Victim's Bill of Rights), in a criminal case, all relevant evidence must be admitted, even if it is inadmissible under CEC. Proposition 8 has some exemptions, such as: secondary evidence rule, hearsay rules, CEC 352, and privileges.

(ANALYSIS: In this case, it is a civil lawsuit and Proposition 8 does not apply.)

1(a) The note
Logical relevance

See rule above. (ANALYSIS: In this case, the note is logically relevant because it tends to make the fact of plaintiff's injury more probable.)

Legal relevance

See rule above. (ANALYSIS: In this case, the note legally relevant because its probative value as to the case for [negligence] is not outweighed by other factors.)

Authentication

......

Secondary evidence rule

......

Conclusion

In conclusion, the court should have admitted the note.

1(b) The recording tape
Logical relevance

See rule above. (ANALYSIS: In this case, the recording tape is logically relevant because it tends to make the fact of 갑's injury more probable.)

Legal relevance

See rule above. (ANALYSIS: In this case, the recording tape legally relevant because its probative value as to whether 갑 suffered injury is not outweighed by other factors.)

Authentication

......

Secondary evidence rule

......

Public policy exception (offers for medical expenses)

Under the public policy exceptions, offers to pay medical expenses are inadmissible to prove liability for the injury.

(ANALYSIS: In this case, 을 offered 갑 that he will pay medical expenses and 갑 is offering the recording tape to prove 을's liability for his injury. Thus, the recording tape is inadmissible under the public policy exception.)

Conclusion

In conclusion, the recording tape is relevant but public policy exception rule is applicable. Thus, the recording tape is inadmissible.

모범답안 036-2

Q: Should the court have admitted the [note]? Answer according to the Federal Rules of Evidence.

Logical relevance

To be admissible, evidence must be logically relevant. Relevant evidence is any evidence that tends to make the fact more or less probable.

Legal relevance

Under the FRE 403, evidence is legally relevant if its probative value is not substantially outweighed by other factors (misleading the jury, waste of time, injustice prejudice, and confusion of the issues).

1. The note

Logical relevance

See rule above. (ANALYSIS: In this case, ·······.)

Legal relevance

See rule above. (ANALYSIS: In this case, ·······.)

Conclusion

······

Ⅱ. Documentary Evidence (14July, 16Feb, 18July)

본 파트에서는 서류의 존재 자체 또는 그 내용(content)이 증거방법이 되는 서증 및 서면에 대해 논한다. 모든 유형의 서증은 반드시 authentication이 이루어져야 하고, 서류의 '내용'이 증거방법으로 사용되는 경우에는 추가적으로 secondary evidence rule이 적용된다.

A. Authentication

All **non-testimonial evidence** (real evidence and documentary evidence) must be authenticated. There must be enough evidence to support a jury finding that the evidence is **what the proponent ways it is.**

- ✔ 갑이 note의 내용을 증언하는 과정에서 자신이 해당 note를 작성하였음을 명시하였다. → 갑이 해당 note에 대해 personal knowledge를 가지고 있는 바, 해당 note가 갑이 증언한 그 note임을 jury가 인지가능하다. → a proper authentication

  갑 has personal knowledge and the note is properly authenticated.
- ✔ 갑이 을에 대한 defamatory email을 작성하였고 이를 병에게 전송하였다. 을이 갑을 상대로 defamation 소송을 제기하였고, 이에 병이 "갑으로부터 해당 이메일을 받은 적이 있으며, 그 외에도 나는 갑으로부터 많은 이메일을 주고받았다."고 주장했다. → 본 email이 갑으로부터 전송되었다는 것

을 jury가 인지가능하다. → a proper authentication

✔ 갑이 을을 상대로 자동차 사고에 대한 손배청구를 하였다. 갑을 치료한 간호사 병은 갑이 치료받은 당시 "을이 빨간불에 직진해서 나와 충동했다"고 언급하였음을 증언하였고, 이를 작성한 hospital form도 제출되었다. 간호사 병은 "본 form은 내가 작성하였다"고 증언하였다. → 병이 해당 note에 대해 personal knowledge를 가지고 있는 바, 해당 note가 병이 증언한 그 note임을 jury가 인지가능하다. → a proper authentication

✔ 갑이 '자신'의 알리바이를 증명하기 위해 자신의 컴퓨터에서 자동으로 저장되는 날짜와 시간 기록을 제출하면서, "컴퓨터의 날짜와 시간이 정확히 조정되어 있다"고 언급하였다. → 해당 기록이 작성된 날짜와 시간이 정확하다는 것은 알 수 있으나, '갑' 소유의 컴퓨터라는 점은 인지하기 어렵다. → **not** a proper authentication

B. Secondary Evidence Rule

Under the secondary evidence rule (the FRE best evidence rule), **original or duplicate writing** must be provided when the writing is offered to prove its **contents**.

In California, duplicate writing includes photocopy, carbon^{먹지} copy, and <u>handwritten copy.</u>

[FRE—Best Evidence Rule]

Duplicate writing includes photocopy and carbon copy, but <u>handwritten copy is not a duplicate writing.</u>

| 답안요령 | Documentary evidence

Q: <u>Should the court admit the [police record]? Answer according to the California law.</u>

<u>갑·을간 자동차 사고가 발생하였고, 그 현장에 경찰 병이 5분 안에 도착하여 주변에 있던 목격자 정의 진술을 작성한 police record는 admissible한가?</u>

> Logical relevance, Legal relevance, Proposition 8
> 1. Analysis — Logical relevance
> 2. Analysis — Legal relevance (CEC352/FRE403)
> 3. Analysis — Proposition 8
> 4. Authentication
> 5. Secondary evidence rule
> 6. Hearsay + Confrontation Clause

모범답안 037

Logical relevance

To be admissible, evidence must be logically relevant. Relevant evidence is any evidence that tends to make the fact more or less probable.

Legal relevance

Under the CEC 352, evidence is legally relevant if its probative value is not substantially outweighed by other factors (misleading the jury, waste of time, injustice prejudice, and confusion of the issues).

Proposition 8

Under California's Proposition 8 (Victim's Bill of Rights), in a criminal case, all relevant evidence must be admitted, even if it is inadmissible under CEC. Proposition 8 has some exemptions, such as: secondary evidence rule, hearsay rules, CEC 352, and privileges.
(ANALYSIS: Here, it is a civil lawsuit and Proposition 8 does not apply.)

The police record
Logical relevance

See rule above. (ANALYSIS: In this case, the record is logically relevant because it tends to make the fact of plaintiff's injury more probable.)

Legal relevance

See rule above. (ANALYSIS: In this case, the record legally relevant because its probative value as to the case for [negligence] is not outweighed by other factors.)

Authentication

All non-testimonial evidence must be authenticated. There must be enough evidence to support a jury finding that the evidence is what the proponent ways it is.

(ANALYSIS: In this case, the report was properly authenticated the record.)

Secondary evidence rule

Under the secondary evidence rule (the FRE best evidence rule), original or duplicate writing must be provided when the writing is offered to prove its contents. In California, duplicate writing includes photocopy, carbon copy, and handwritten copy.

(ANALYSIS: In this case, 갑 is offering the record to prove the contents of it and the record is an original. Thus, it is admissible under the Secondary Evidence Rule.)

Hearsay

Hearsay is an out-of-court statement offered in evidence to prove the truth of the matter asserted. Proposition 8 does not apply to the hearsay rules.

(ANALYSIS: In this case, the record is a multiple hearsay. The record itself is the outer layer hearsay, and the statements made by 정 which are contained within in are the inner layer of hearsay. The record is admissible only if both layers of hearsay fall within the hearsay exceptions.)

Hearsay exceptions

(1) Business record (outer layer)

......

(2) Present sense impression (inner layer)

......

In conclusion, the police record is admissible because it falls within the hearsay exceptions.

Confrontation Clause

......

<u>Conclusion</u>

In conclusion, the police record falls within the hearsay exceptions and it does not violate the Confrontation Clause. Thus, it is admissible and the court should admit it.

Ⅲ. Testimonial Evidence

A. Competence

A witness must have **personal knowledge** of the matter about which he is to testify, **the ability to communicate,** and the **ability to understand** that she is under a **legal duty** to tell the truth.

B. Opinion Testimony (19Feb)

1. Expert Witness

The witness's opinion can be admitted as an expert opinion if:

ⅰ. The witness is **qualified as an expert;**

ⅱ. The opinion is **helpful to the jury;**

ⅲ. The opinion has **sufficient facts basis;** and

ⅳ. The opinion is based on **reliable** principals and methods that **were reliably applied** by the witness.

2. Lay Witness

Lay witness opinion is admissible **only if:**

ⅰ. The opinion is based on the witness's **firsthand knowledge;** and

ⅱ. The opinion is **helpful to the jury.**

[FRE]

Lay witness opinion is admissible **only if:**

ⅰ. The opinion is rationally based on the witness's **firsthand knowledge;**

ⅱ. The opinion is **helpful to the jury;** and

ⅲ. The opinion is **not based on scientific, technical, or other specialized knowledge.**

답안요령	Testimonial evidence

Logical relevance, Legal relevance, Proposition 8
1. Analysis — Logical relevance
2. Analysis — Legal relevance (CEC352/FRE403)
3. Analysis — Proposition 8
4. Expert witness
5. Lay witness + Competence

TIP1 주어진 증언(testimony)이 '증인의 opinion'에 관한 것이라면, 해당 증언이 expert witness testimony와 lay witness testimony 중 어느 것에 해당하는지 서술한다.

TIP2 Lay witness testimony 요건을 analysis할 때 증인의 competence도 함께 서술하는 것이 좋다.

TIP3 '직업'이 명시되어 있는 witness는 expert witness에 해당할 가능성이 높다. 사안에 witness의 직업이 주어진 경우에는 우선 expert witness testimony 요건을 analysis한 후, 해당 증인이 expert witness가 아닌 경우 lay witness testimony 요건을 analysis한다.

Logical relevance

To be admissible, evidence must be logically relevant. Relevant evidence is any evidence that tends to make the fact more or less probable.

Legal relevance

Under the CEC 352, evidence is legally relevant if its probative value is not substantially outweighed by other factors (misleading the jury, waste of time, injustice prejudice, and confusion of the issues).

Proposition 8

Under California's Proposition 8 (Victim's Bill of Rights), in a criminal case, all relevant evidence must be admitted, even if it is inadmissible under CEC. Proposition 8 has some exemptions, such as: secondary evidence rule, hearsay rules, CEC 352, and privileges.

(ANALYSIS: Here, it is a civil lawsuit and Proposition 8 does not apply.)

1. 갑's statement

Logical relevance

See rule above. (ANALYSIS: In this case, 갑's statement is logically relevant because it tends to make the fact of plaintiff's injury more probable.)

Legal relevance

See rule above. (ANALYSIS: In this case, 갑's statement legally relevant because its probative value as to the case for [negligence] is not outweighed by other factors.)

Expert witness

The witness's opinion can be admitted as an expert opinion if: (1) the witness is qualified as an expert; (2) the opinion is helpful to the jury; (3) the opinion has sufficient facts basis; and (4) the opinion is based on reliable principals and methods that were reliably applied by the witness. (ANALYSIS: In this case, there are no facts indicating that 갑 is qualified as an expert. Even though his statement is helpful to the jury, it cannot be admitted as an expert testimony.)

Lay witness

Lay witness opinion is admissible only if: (1) the opinion is based on the witness's firsthand knowledge; and (2) the opinion is helpful to the jury. (ANALYSIS: In this case, 갑's statement is based on his firsthand knowledge because he saw the accident and it is helpful to the jury to determine whether 을 was negligent. Additionally, there is no evidence indicating that 갑 has no ability to communicate or to understand the nature of his legal duty to tell the truth. Thus, 갑's statement is admissible as a lay witness testimony.)

Conclusion

In conclusion, 갑's statement is admissible as a lay witness testimony.

C. Impeachment (14July, 16Feb, 17Feb, 19Feb, 20Feb)

Impeachment는 증인의 신뢰도를 공격하는 행위를 뜻하는 바, 변호사는 상대방 증인뿐만 아니라 자신의 증인을 상대로 impeach할 수 있다. CEE에서는 증거가 substantive evidence와 impeachment 목적 중 어느 목적으로 사용된 것인지 직접적으로 물어보는 문제는 출제되지 않고, 주어진 증거(testimony)의 admissibility 여부를 묻는 문제를 통해 수험자가 해당 증거의 '사용된 목적'을 판단토록 요구한다. 증거가 사용된 목적이 사안(문제본문)에 명시되어 있는 경우도 있으나 대부분의 경우 이를 명시하지 않고 있어, 수험자 스스로 substantive evidence로 사용된 경우와 impeachment 목적으로 사용된 경우를 구분하여 각 목적에 따른 admissibility를 판단해야 한다. 이때 impeachment 목적으로 사용될 가능성이 매우 낮거나 혹은 가능성이 전혀 없더라도, 이에 대해 analysis하는 것이 고득점 포인트다. 증거가 impeachment 목적으로 사용된 사안의 전형적인 패턴은 다음과 같다.

① 갑의 증인이 증언을 하였고 이에 대해 반대측(을)이 제출한 증거가 갑측 증언 내용에 반대되거나 해당 증언을 반박하는 경우, 반대측(을)이 제출한 증거는 prior inconsistent statement 또는 contradictory facts 방법을 이용한 impeachment 목적을 가질 가능성이 높다.

② 갑이 사건과 '무관한' 타인의 과거 범행(convicted crimes) 또는 도덕적으로 나쁜 행위(bad acts)를 증명하는 경우, 해당 증거는 그 타인에 대한 impeach 목적을 가질 가능성이 높다. 만일 사건과 관련이 '있는' convicted crimes 또는 bad acts를 증명하였다면, 해당 증거는 substantive evidence임과 동시에 impeachment 목적을 가질 가능성이 높다.

Impeachment is to attack the credibility of a witness by cross-examination or by extrinsic evidence.

★The credibility of a witness is always relevant.

There are several types of impeachment: impeachment with prior inconsistent statements, with bias or interest, with criminal convictions, with bad acts, with opinion or reputation evidence, and with sensory deficiencies.

[표 11-1]

Types	Cross-examination	Extrinsic evidence
Prior inconsistent statement	○	(only) when: laying foundation
Contradictory^{모순되는} facts	○	only when: ① material issue (not collateral); ② significant on the issue of credibility; or ③ the subject as to which the opposing party is precluded from offering evidence
Collateral matter	○	×
Deficiencies (capacity)	○	○

Prior convictions of crime	○	○ (record of conviction)
Bac acts	○	×
Bias/Motive	○	○
Reputation/Opinion	○	○ (call other witness)

* 본 표는 CEC와 FRE에 공통적용되나, 각 유형의 세부요건은 CEC와 FRE에서 다르게 규정하고 있다. 예컨대, 주어진 상황에서 prior inconsistent statement가 impeachment 목적으로 사용가능하다면 CEC와 FRE 모두 cross-examination과 extrinsic evidence를 허용한다. 다만, CEC는 under the oath여부와 무관하게 해당 statement의 제출을 허용하는 반면, FRE는 under the oath가 인정되는 경우에 한해 제출을 허용한다.

1. With Prior Inconsistent Statements

A party may use a witness's inconsistent statements **to impeach** the witness only when **foundation is laid** (the witness was given a chance to explain the statement).

Whether the statement was made **under oath is regardless.**

[FRE]

Witness's prior inconsistent statement can be used for impeachment only when **foundation is laid** (the witness was given a chance to explain the statement).

Witness's prior inconsistent statement can be used as **substantive evidence only when the statement was made under oath**. Whether the statement was made under oath is regardless when the statement is used for impeachment.

TIP1   타인의 "prior inconsistent statement의 내용이 사실이다"라는 점을 증명하고자 하는 경우에는 substantive evidence에 해당하고, "이전에는 A라고 언급하였으나 현재 법정에서는 B라고 증언하고 있다"는 점을 증명하고자 하는 경우에는 impeachment 목적을 가지고 있는 것이다.

TIP2 타인의 prior inconsistent statement가 substantive evidence에 해당하는 경우에는 대부분 hearsay exception 중 admission exception 으로서 admissible하다.

2. With Criminal Conviction

CEC에서는 기본적으로 부도덕에 관한 범죄(crime conviction for moral turpitude)와 그 외의 범죄로 구분하여 부도덕에 관한 범죄(crime conviction for moral turpitude)만을 허용한다. Crime conviction for moral turpitude 는 다시 felony와 misdemeanor로 구분되어 felony이면서 CEC 352(balancing test)에 부합하는 경우와 misdemeanor이면서 형소재판인 경우에 한해 허용된다. 반면, FRE에서는 부도덕에 관한 범죄(crime conviction for moral turpitude)와 그 외의 범죄 모두 일정 요건을 만족하는 경우 impeachment 의 목적으로 사용될 수 있다.

A party may use conviction for a crime of **moral turpitude**^{대단히 부도덕한 행위} (a crime involving dishonesty or false statement) to impeach the witness.

Unlike under the Federal Rules of Evidence, CEC does <u>not require a specific time limit</u> for determining remoteness.

✔ Violence에 관한 crime (e.g., battery) — crime for moral turpitude
✔ Forgery — crime for moral turpitude

a. Felony Convictions for Moral Turpitude

Under the CEC, **felony** convictions **for moral turpitude** are admissible if:
  ⅰ. It has not been **expunged**^{지우다}; and
  ⅱ. Subject to legal relevance **balancing test (CEC 352)**.

b. Misdemeanor Convictions for Moral Turpitude

Under the CEC, **misdemeanor** convictions **for moral turpitude** are admissible only in **criminal** cases.

[FRE - Convictions for Moral Turpitude]

Any crime conviction for moral turpitude may be used for impeachment purpose only when the conviction is <u>not too remote.</u> The conviction is too **remote** is more than 10 years passed from the **date of conviction** or the **date of release** from the confinement, whichever is the later date.

The impeachment by such crimes is permitted <u>even when Rule 403 is violated.</u>

[표 11-2, CEC]

Crime conviction for moral turpitude		그 외
Felony	Misdemeanor	
CEC 352 만족해야	only in criminal cases	불가
time limit 없음		

[표 11-3, FRE]

	Crime conviction for moral turpitude	그 외		
① Time	10yr 이내만 가능. BUT P>>D → 10yr 이후도 가능			
② Felony? Misdemeanor?	Both	only Felony		
③ Criminal? Civil?	Both	Criminal case		Civil case (大)
④ W=△? W=W?	―	W=△ (小)	W=W (大)	가능, unless P<<D
결론	가능	가능, only when P>D	가능, unless P<<D	

3. With Bad Acts

A party may use a witness's prior specific bad acts (which have not resulted in a criminal conviction) **to impeach** the witness.

In civil cases, all prior specific bad acts are **not** allowed for impeachment purposes.

In **criminal** cases, Proposition 8 allows both extrinsic evidence and cross-examination as long as the evidence passes legal relevance balancing test.

[FRE]

Under the FRE, a specific bad act is admissible for impeachment purpose only when:

ⅰ. It is inquired into on **cross-examination** (not extrinsic evidence);

ⅱ. The question was made **in good-faith;** and

ⅲ. It passes **legal relevance balancing test (FRE 403).**

TIP　타인의 bad act 또는 crime conviction이 substantive evidence로서 사용된 경우에는 "타인은 A 행동을 했던 사람이다"라는 점을 증명하고자 하는 경우로서, character evidence에 관한 rule을 적용해야 한다. 만일 "타인은 A 행동을 했던 사람으로서 신뢰도가 낮은 사람이다"라는 점을 증명하고자 하는 경우에는 impeachment 목적을 가지고 있는 것이다.

답안요령　impeachment

Q: Should the court admit [병's statement]? Answer according to California law.

갑·을간 자동차 사고가 있었고, 사고발생 후 5분 후 경찰이 해당 현장에 도착하여 주변에 있던 목격자 병의 진술("을이 빨간불에 건넜다")을 police record에 기록하였다. 하지만 을의 case-in-chief에서 병은 "갑이 빨간불에 직진했다"고 증언하였다. 이에 갑은 police record를 증거로 제출하였다. Police record는

admissible한가?

Logical relevance, Legal relevance, Proposition 8
1. Analysis — Logical relevance
2. Analysis — Legal relevance (CEC352/FRE403)
3. Analysis — Proposition 8
4. ★Substantive evidence
   ① Hearsay + Hearsay exception
   ② Analysis
5. ★For impeachment
   ① 기본 rule
   ② The credibility of a witness is always relevant.
   ③ Analysis

TIP1 하나의 증거(police report)가 substantive evidence로서 제출된 경우와 impeachment 목적으로 제출된 경우로 구분하여 각 목적에 따른 admissibility를 판단하는 것이 고득점 포인트다.

TIP2 1번: 주어진 증거(police report)의 relevance에 대한 analysis는 ① substantive evidence(hearsay exception)로서의 relevance와 ② impeachment로서의 relevance 모두 언급해야 한다.

TIP3 4번: Impeachment에 대해 논하는 경우, 해당 증거의 relevance에 관해 언급하는 것이 고득점 포인트다.

The credibility of a witness is always relevant.

TIP4 Crime conviction을 이용한 impeachment에 대해 논하는 경우, CEC와 FRE간 time limit에 있어 차이가 있다는 점을 명시하는 것이 고득점 포인트다.

Unlike under the FRE, CEC does **not** require **a specific time limit for determining remoteness.**

Unlike under the CEC, FRE requires a specific time limit for determining remoteness.

Logical relevance

To be admissible, evidence must be logically relevant. Relevant evidence is any evidence that tends to make the fact more or less probable.

Legal relevance

Under the CEC 352, evidence is legally relevant if its probative value is not substantially outweighed by other factors (misleading the jury, waste of time, injustice prejudice, and confusion of the issues).

Proposition 8

Under California's Proposition 8 (Victim's Bill of Rights), in a criminal case, all relevant evidence must be admitted, even if it is inadmissible under CEC. Proposition 8 has some exemptions, such as: secondary evidence rule, hearsay rules, CEC 352, and privileges.

(ANALYSIS: Here, it is a civil lawsuit and Proposition 8 does not apply.)

1. The police report

Relevance

See rule above. (ANALYSIS: In this case, the police report is relevant for two purposes. First, it tends to make the fact that 을 crossed on the red light more probable. Second, it shows that 병's statement is untruthful. The credibility of a witness is always relevant. Additionally, there is no other factors that substantially outweigh its probative value.)

Substantive evidence

Hearsay

Hearsay is an out-of-court statement offered in evidence to prove the truth of the matter asserted. Proposition 8 does not apply to the hearsay rules.

(ANALYSIS: In this case, the police report is a multiple hearsay. The report itself is the outer layer hearsay, and the statements made by 병

which are contained within in are the inner layer of hearsay. The record is admissible only if both layers of hearsay fall within the hearsay exceptions.)

Hearsay exceptions
(1) Business record (outer layer)

......

(2) Present sense impression (inner layer)

......

Impeachment
Impeachment with prior inconsistent statement
Impeachment is to attack the credibility of a witness by cross-examination or by extrinsic evidence. A party may use a witness's inconsistent statements to impeach the witness only when foundation is laid. Whether the statement was made under oath is regardless.
(ANALYSIS: In this case, during 을's case-in-chief, 병 stated that 갑 crossed on red light. However, the police report shows that 병 has stated that 을 crossed on red light. 병's statement was not made under the oath, but it is admissible since whether the statement was made under oath is regardless. Thus, it is admissible to attack the credibility of 병.)

Conclusion
In conclusion, 병's statement is admissible since it falls within the hearsay exception. Moreover, it is a proper impeachment with the prior inconsistent statement.

D. Privileges

1. Marital Privileges (18July)

a. Spousal Immunity
Only a witness spouse holds the privilege.

The privilege is applicable in <u>both criminal and civil cases.</u>

✔ Live-in boyfriend/girlfriend → cannot invoke marital privileges

[FRE]

Only a witness spouse holds the privilege.

The privilege is applicable <u>only in criminal cases.</u>

2. Attorney-Client Privilege (17July, 19July, 20Feb)

a. General Rule

Confidential communications between an attorney and a client which are made **for legal advice** are privileged from disclosure. The privilege extends to agents of the attorney and employees or agents of the corporation client.

Under the CEC, the privilege allows the privilege holder (client) to prevent **eavesdroppers** from disclosing information.

b. Exceptions

The attorney-client privilege is inapplicable when:

① Legal advice was acquired for **future wrongdoing** that the client knew or reasonably should have known to be a crime or fraud;

② There is a **dispute between attorney and client** (breach of duty by either attorney or client); or

③ <u>A lawyer **reasonably** believe that the disclosure is necessary to prevent a **future** crime which is likely to result **in death or substantial bodily harm.**</u>

[Federal Law]

The attorney-client privilege is inapplicable when:

① Legal advice was acquired for **future wrongdoing** that the client knew/reasonably should have known to be a crime or fraud; or

② There is a **dispute between attorney and client** (breach of duty by either attorney or client).

c. When the Privileged Ends

Under the CEC, the privilege <u>lasts until</u> **the client's estate has been fully distributed.**

[Federal Law]

Under the federal common law, the privilege <u>lasts</u> **even after the client's death.**

3. Work Product Privilege (17July, 19July)

a. Absolute Privilege

An absolute privilege is given to writings that reflect **an attorney's** impressions, conclusions, opinions, or legal research or theories.

Such writings **should not** be discovered **in any circumstances.**

b. Qualified Privilege

A qualified privilege is given to all other documents that are prepared **in anticipation of litigation.**

Such writings are discovered only when a requiring party can show:

ⅰ. A **substantial need** for the documents; and

ⅱ. **Undue hardship** in obtaining substantially equivalent information.

[FRE]

Under the FRE, there is no distinction between documents that are prepared by attorney and others, and qualified privilege rule is used.

TIP1　Work product privilege에 관한 문제의 경우, ① 적용되는 rule 유형(California/FRE)을 파악한 후 California law가 적용되는 경우에

는 ② 해당 자료의 작성인 및 그 내용을 기준으로 privilege 유형을 파악하는 것이 중요하다.

TIP2　Arguable points (qualified privilege):

① Work product privilege를 주장하는 측(해당 자료를 제출하지 않으려는 측) 갑은 ① 상대방 을에게 해당 자료에 대한 필요성이 적다는 점 또는 ② 상대방 을이 다른 방법으로 해당 자료와 유사한 것을 확보하는데 있어 큰 어려움이 없다는 점을 주장할 것이다.

갑 may argue that 을 has no substantial need for the document or 을 could obtain substantially equivalent information without undue hardship.

② 이에 대해 상대방 을측(해당 자료를 요구하는 측)은 해당 자료가 소송을 준비하기(anticipation of litigation) 위해 작성된 것이 아니라, 갑 개인을 위해 작성된 자료임을 주장할 것이다.

을 may argue that the material constitutes an [investigate report] made exclusively for 갑.

Ⅳ. Hearsay

A. General Rule

★Hearsay is an out-of-court statement offered in evidence to prove the truth of the matter asserted.

Proposition 8 does not apply to the hearsay rules.

✔ 컴퓨터에서 자동저장된 기록(날짜, 시간 등) → not assertions by human
　→ Hearsay rule 적용 ×

B. Multiple Hearsay

• Multiple hearsay = Layered hearsay = Double hearsay (FRE)

Each level of hearsay (outer layer and inner layer of hearsay) must fall within hearsay exception to be admissible.

C. Nonhearsay (16Feb, 19Feb)

CEC에서는 statement를 hearsay와 관련하여 크게 non-hearsay, hearsay, hearsay exception으로 구분한다. 그중 non-hearsay는 hearsay의 정의에 맞지 않아 hearsay가 아닌 statement를 의미하며, hearsay exception은 hearsay이나 예외적으로 admissible하다고 보는 statement를 의미한다. 반면, FRE에서는 non-hearsay, officially non-hearsay, hearsay, hearsay exception, 이렇게 네 유형으로 구분하는 바, FRE상 officially hearsay는 CEC상 hearsay exception으로 구분된다. Officially non-hearsay는 "hearsay exemption"으로도 표현되며, 이는 정의상 명확히 따져보면 hearsay에 해당하나 상대방측이 해당 hearsay를 언급한 declarant를 상대로 cross-examination 할 기회가 있는 것과 다름없으므로 FRE상에서만 non-hearsay로 인정하는 statement를 의미한다. Officially non-hearsay 유형에는 prior statement by available witness와 admissions가 있다.

Statements are not hearsay when:

ⅰ. They are used to prove its **legal effect** or whether the statements were made;

ⅱ. They are offered to show **effect on the listener;** or

ⅲ. They are offered to show **declarant's state of mind.**

✔ Defamation case에서 피고가 원고에 대한 defamatory statement를 언급한 장면이 담긴 인터뷰 영상 — legal effect (legal significance)

✔ Contracts case에서 제출된 원고·피고간 체결한 contract 원본 — legal effect (legal significance)

✔ 갑이 을에게 "차 엔진이 망가져 곧 수리해야 한다."고 언급하였고, 이를 들은 병이 갑·을간 negligence case에서 갑의 statement를 증언하는 경우 — show effect on the listener (을이 차 엔진의 결함을 인지하고 있었음)

✔ 갑이 을에게 "차 엔진이 망가져 곧 수리해야 한다."고 언급하였으나 을은 수리하지 않았고, 이후 을을 상대로 제기된 negligence case에서 갑이 '자신의' statement를 언급하는 경우 — show effect on the listener (을이 차 엔진의 결함을 인지하고 있었음)

D. Hearsay Exceptions

1. Prior Inconsistent Statement (PIS) (17Feb, 18July)

A prior inconsistent statement made by an available witness can be used **either as substantive evidence or for impeachment** only when **foundation is laid** (the witness was given a chance to explain the statement).

Whether the statement was made **under oath is regardless.**

[FRE]

Witness's prior inconsistent statement can be used either as substantive evidence or for impeachment only when **foundation is laid** (the witness was given a chance to explain the statement).

Witness's prior inconsistent statement can be used as **substantive evidence only when the statement was made under oath.** Whether the statement was made under oath is regardless when the statement is used for impeachment.

> TIP 특정 증인의 증언을 해당 증인이 앞서 언급한 statement와 비교하여 그 내용이 동일할 경우에는 prior consistent statement(PCS), 동일하지 않을 경우에는 prior inconsistent statement(PIS)로 구분된다. 그중 PIS는 substantive evidence와 impeachment의 목적으로 모두 사용될 수 있는 바, 양 목적을 구분하여 각 admissibility를 판단해야 한다.

갑·을간 자동차 사고에 대한 negligence case에서 갑이 "을이 정지 신호에서 직진을 하였다"고 증언하였고, 이에 대해 을의 witness 병이 "갑이 사고 현장에서 나에게 을은 직진 신호에서 직진을 하였다고 언급하였다"고 증언하였다. Is 병's statement admissible?

① CEC

⇒ 병의 증언이 substantive evidence로서 제출된 경우 이는 hearsay에 해당하나 prior inconsistent statement(hearsay exception)로서 갑에게 해당 사안에 대해 설명할 기회(laying foundation)가 주어지는 한 admissible하다. 한편, impeachment 목적으로 사용되는 경우에는 갑에게 해당 사안에 대해 설명할 기회(laying foundation)가 주어지는 한 admissible하다.

② FRE

⇒ 병의 증언이 substantive evidence로서 제출된 경우, 이는 under oath상태에서 이루어진 발언이 아니므로 prior inconsistent statement(officially non-hearsay)로 인정되지 않아 inadmissible하다. 한편, impeachment 목적으로 사용되는 경우에는 oath 여부와 관계없이 admissible하다.

2. Admissions (14July, 16Feb, 17Feb, 19Feb)

A statement **made by an opponent party** and offered **against that party** is admissible as a hearsay **exception.**

When the declarant and the party have agency or employment relationship, co-conspirators, or partners, the declarant's statement is admissible as a party admission.

[FRE]

A statement **made by an opponent party** and offered **against that party** is admissible **as a non-hearsay.**

a. By Co-Conspirator (20Feb)

Admission of a co-conspirator is a statement that is made **during** the declarant was participating in furtherance of a conspiracy.

✔ Cocaine 판매상이 모든 구매자 이름과 income and expenses를 기록한 notes

It was made to further the conspiracy's goal.

It was for the efficiency and effectiveness of the overall operation.

⇒ **in furtherance** of a conspiracy 인정

TIP1 Admission of a co-conspirator 여부는 ① conspiracy와 ② in furtherance of conspiracy에 대해 analysis하여 판단한다.

TIP2 주어진 statement가 admission exception by co-conspirator에 해당하는 경우, Confrontation Clause에 위배되는지 그 여부를 판단한다.

b. By Employee

A statement made by employee is admissible as a statement of opponent party only when:

ⅰ. An employee's statement was made **during the employment;**

ⅱ. It describes a matter **within the scope of the employment;** and

ⅲ. **Employee's negligence** is the basis for employer's liability.

[FRE]

A statement made by employee is admissible as a statement of opponent party only when:

ⅰ. An employee's statement was made **during the employment;** and

ⅱ. It describes a matter **within the scope of the employment.**

3. Spontaneous Statement (18July)

★A spontaneous statement (the FRE excited utterance) is a statement **relating to a startling** event, made while the declarant was **under the** stress or excitement that it cause.

4. Contemporaneous Statement (18July)

★Under the CEC (the FRE present sense impression), statements that is describing the **declarant's own conduct** and while the **declarant engaged** in that conduct are admissible.

[FRE—Present Sense Impression]

★Statements are under the present sense impression exception, when the statements are describing an event or condition made **while or immediately after** the declaration perceived it.

5. Medical Diagnosis or Treatment (17Feb)

A statement made **by a child abuse victim** to obtain medical diagnosis or treatment is admissible as a hearsay exception.

The **cause** of the condition is admissible, but the statements of **fault** are inadmissible.

[FRE]

A statement made by any person **to obtain medical diagnosis or treatment** is admissible as a hearsay exception.

6. Present Condition (16Feb, 17Feb)

• Present condition = Present state of mind

A statement of **present (then-existing)** mental, emotional, or physical condition is admissible as a hearsay exception. A statement of the declarant's state of mind or emotion is also called as **present state of mind.**

✔ 응급실에 간 환자가 의사에게 "머리가 깨질 듯이 아파요"라고 언급한 문장 — present physical condition (admissible)

✔ 응급실에 간 환자가 의사에게 "머리를 기둥에 부딪혔어요"라고 언급한 문장 — reason for condition (inadmissible)

> **TIP1** 화자(declarant)가 여러 문장을 일시에 언급한 경우, 각 문장의 hearsay exception 여부는 별도로 analysis하는 것이 고득점 포인트다.

> **TIP2** Present condition에 해당하는 statement는 medical diagnosis/ treatment, spontaneous statement와 contemporaneous statement 여부에 대해서도 analysis한다.

7. Business Record (14July, 17Feb, 20Feb)

Under the business records exception, a record of **events or condition** is admissible if it is:

ⅰ. **Made at or near** the time of the recorded event;

ⅱ. By a person with **personal knowledge** of the event; and

ⅲ. Making of the record must occur **in the course of a regular business activity** (foundation).

[FRE]

Under the business records exception, a record of <u>events, condition, opinion, or diagnoses</u> is admissible if three requirements are met.

8. When Declarant is Unavailable

a. Dying Declaration

A dying declaration is a statement that is regarding the cause of death, made while a declarant believes his death was imminent.

Under the CEC, a dying declaration regarding the **cause of action, <u>in all civil and criminal cases</u>**, is admissible only when the <u>declarant is actually dead</u>.

[FRE]

Under the FRE, a dying declaration is admissible **only in civil and criminal homicide cases.**

Declarant need not be dead, but need to be **unavailable.**

b. Statement against Interest (16Feb)

The testimony of a now **unavailable declarant** may be admissible if the statement was **against** declarant's pecuniary^{금전적}, penal^{형사상의}, or social interest **when it was made.**

[FRE]

The testimony of a now **unavailable declarant** may be admissible if the statement was **against** the declarant's pecuniary^{금전적}, or penal^{형사상의} interest **when it was made.**

c. Statement of Infliction of Violence (CEC) (18July)

이는 CEC에서만 인정하는 rule로서, 화자(declarant)가 신체적 피해 또는 위협을 겪은 후 얼마 지나지 않은 시점에 이에 대해 언급한 statement는 서면으로 작성된 경우에 한해 hearsay exception으로 인정된다. 간호사, 의사와 같이 응급상황의 사람들에게 언급된 statement는 서면으로 작성되지 않았다하더라도 예외적으로 hearsay exception으로 인정된다. 본 hearsay exception은 FRE상의 present physical condition에 대한 rule과 비교하여 화자의 현재 신체적 피해에 대해 언급한 statement를 exception으로 인정한다는 점에서 유사하다. 다만, CEC에서는 화자가 반드시 unavailable할 것을 요구하나 FRE에서는 화자의 availability와 무관하게 exception을 인정한다. 또한 CEC에서는 writing 요건이 있으나, FRE에서는 writing 요건이 없으며 해당 statement가 의사에게 언급될 필요도 없다.

Under the CEC, a statement made by an **unavailable** witness is admissible as a hearsay exception if the statement:

　ⅰ. Is made to narrate, describe, or explain the **infliction or threat of physical injury** upon the declarant;

　ⅱ. Was made **at or near the time** of the infliction or threat of physical injury;

　ⅲ. Was made under circumstances indicating **trustworthiness;** and

　ⅳ. Was made **in writing,** was electronically recorded, or **made to emergency personnel** (e.g., physician, nurse, paramedic, or a law enforcement official).

[FRE — Present Physical Condition]

Under the FRE 803(3), statements as to **present bodily condition** are admissible as an hearsay exception. The rule is applicable even when the statement was not made to a physician.

E. Confrontation Clause (18July, 20Feb)

1. General Rule

★Under the Confrontation Clause of the Sixth Amendment, defendants have the **right to confront witnesses against them.**

A use of an **out-of-court statement** violates the right of confrontation, even if the statement falls within the hearsay exception, when it is:

　ⅰ. **Testimonial;**

　ⅱ. Made by an **unavailable witness;** and

　ⅲ. the defendant had **no opportunity to cross-examine** the statement.

2. Testimonial

When the statements were made to the police with the primary purpose to enable police to meet an **ongoing emergency,** these are **not** testimonial.

When the statements were made to the police with the primary purpose to **establish past events** which is relevant to a criminal prosecution, these are **not** testimonial.

✔ Co-defendant가 자신의 범행에 관한 내용을 적은 notes → non-testimonial → Confrontation Clause 적용 × → 해당 note가 hearsay exception에 해당하는 한 admissible.

✔ 엄마가 강도에게 구타당하고 있었고, 아이가 식탁에 숨어 구타장면을 목격하면서 경찰에 신고한 경우 → 해당 statement는 emergency was ongoing 상태에서 진술된 statement이다. → non-testimonial → Confrontation Clause 적용 ×

✔ 경찰이 출동한 후, 강도가 수갑이 채워진 채로 경찰차에 타고 있는 상태에서 엄마가 경찰에게 구타 당시의 상황을 설명한 경우 → 해당 statement는 응급상황에서 언급된 것이 아니고, 과거 사건(past event)에 대한 진술일 뿐이다. → non-testimonial → Confrontation Clause 적용 ×

TIP1 Confrontation Clause 적용여부를 판단하는 경우, "testimonial" statement 의미에 대해 상세히 analysis하는 것이 중요하다.

TIP2 주어진 statement가 ① defendant에게 불리한 증거이거나 ② admission exception(hearsay exception 유형 중 하나)인 경우, Confrontation Clause에 위배되는지 그 여부를 판단한다.
Hearsay의 admissibility는 ① hearsay에 적용되는 rule(hearsay exception 등)과 ② Confrontation Clause를 통해 판단한다.

V. Character Evidence (18July)

특정인의 과거 행위, 특히 범죄 행위가 증거로 제출되는 경우 증거사용 목적에 따라 ① character evidence 및 ② impeachment by crime conviction으로 인정된다. 만약 특정인의 도덕적으로 옳지 못한 행위 또는 convicted되지 않는 범죄행위가 impeachment 목적으로 사용되었다면 impeachment by bad acts로 인정된다. Character evidence가 특정인이 '예전에 행동한 것처럼 이번 사건에서도 자신의 성향대로 행동했을 것임'을 증명하고자 제출된다면 (character purpose) 편견을 야기할 수 있으므로 증거에서 배제되고, 해당인의 동기(motive), 의도(intent) 등을 증명하고자 하는 경우에 한해 증거로 채택될 수 있다.

1. General Rule

★Evidence of a person's character is not admissible **to prove that on** a particular occasion the person acted in accordance with the character trait.

Proposition 8 does not apply to character evidence rules (CEC).

2. In Criminal Cases

a. Open the Door

In a criminal case, the defendant must **open the door** and the **prosecution may rebut.** In other words, evidence of a defendant's character is inadmissible in a prosecution's case in chief.

b. Exceptions

Prosecution can offer evidence of defendant's character before the defendant open the door, when:

   ⅰ. In sexual assault, child molestation, <u>or domestic</u>^{가정의} <u>violence case</u>; or

   ⅱ. The defendant offers evidence of the victim's **violent character** and the prosecution wants to prove defendant's <u>violent character</u>.

[FRE]

Prosecution can offer evidence of defendant's character before the defendant open the door, when:

   ⅰ. In sexual assault or child molestation case; or

ⅱ. The defendant offers evidence of the victim's character and the prosecution wants to prove defendant has **same character.**

c. Methods

CEE에 따르면 피고인이 '자신'의 성격을 증명하고자 하는 경우, 이를 증명하는 피고인과 피고인의 주장을 반박하는 검사는 reputation 및 opinion(R/O) 방법만을 이용할 수 있으며, 피고인의 특정 행위(specific acts)에 대한 증거는 제출불가하다. 한편, 피고인이 '피해자'의 성격을 증명하고자 하는 경우에는 이를 증명하는 피고인과 피고인의 주장을 반박하는 검사는 R/O와 specific acts 방법 모두 사용가능하다. 강간 및 성범죄에 관한 사건에서는 상기 두 경우와는 다른 별도의 rule이 적용되는 바, 피해자의 과거 성행위에 대한 증거제출이 원칙적으로 금지된다. 다만, 특정한 경우에 한해 specific acts 방법을 이용한 증거제출이 예외적으로 허용된다.

ⅰ. Defendant's Character
① Defendant open the door — R/O
② Prosecutor rebuts — R/O (S는 Prop. 8에 의거하여 불가)

ⅱ. Victim's Character
① Defendant Open the Door — R/O + S
② Prosecutor Rebuts — R/O + S

ⅲ. Rape and Sexual Cases
Victim's past sexual behavior is inadmissible.
① R/O 항상 불가
② S 허용 only when it is used to prove that:
    (a) Third party is the source of semen or injury to the victim;
    (b) Prior acts of consensual intercourse with the defendant;
    (c) It is constitutionally required; or
    (d) It is used to prove that defendant **reasonably believed** the victim's consent.

[FRE]

ⅰ. Defendant's Character

① Defendant Open the Door — R/O

② Prosecutor Rebuts — R/O + <u>S (but extrinsic evidence 불가)</u>

ⅱ. Victim's Character

① Defendant Open the Door — R/O

② Prosecutor Rebuts — R/O + <u>S (but victim's first aggressor임을 주장하는 경우는 불가)</u>

When the defendant argues that victim is the first aggressor, prosecutor cannot use specific acts conducted by victim.

ⅲ. Rape and Sexual Cases

Victim's past sexual behavior is inadmissible.

① R/O 항상 불가

② S 허용 only when it is used to prove that:

(a) Third party is the source of semen or injury to the victim;

(b) Prior acts of consensual intercourse with the defendant; or

(c) It is constitutionally required.

[표 11-4]

	CEC	FRE
△성격에 대한 P의 반박	R/O	R/O, S
Victim 성격에 대한 △의 주장	R/O, S	R/O
Victim 성격에 대한 P의 반박	R/O, S	R/O, S 모두 가능 (다만, △가 'victim이 최초 공격자임'을 증명하고자 하였다면 S 사용불가)
Rape and sexual cases에서 S 허용되는 예외	to prove that defendant reasonably believed the victim's consent	—

3. In Civil Cases

a. General Rule

In civil cases, character evidence is inadmissible unless the evidence **is in issue.**

- ✔ Defamation — in issue (admissible)
- ✔ Negligent hiring — in issue (admissible)
- ✔ Wrongful death — in issue (admissible)
- ✔ Child molestation^{추행} and sexual assault — FRE에서는 in issue하다고 인정하나, CEC에서는 인정하지 않는다.

b. Rape Shield Provision

Under the rape shield provision, defendant cannot offer evidence as to the **victim's prior sexual conduct.**

In civil cases, the only evidence the defendant can offer is the **victim's prior sexual conduct with the defendant.**

[FRE]

Under the rape shield provision, defendant cannot offer evidence as to the victim's prior sexual conduct.

In civil cases, the defendant can offer **victim's reputation** only when its probative value substantially outweighs the danger of harm to the victim.

4. Non-Character Purpose

"MIMIC" — Motive, Intent, absence of Mistake, Identity, Common scheme

★The evidence of defendant's past acts may be admissible for another **non-character purpose,** such as proving **motive, intent, absence of mistake, identity, common scheme.**

[표 11-5] CEC v. FRE

		CEC	FRE
Legal relevance		CEC 352	FRE 403
Proposition 8		적용 ○ (only in criminal case)	적용 ×
Public policy exceptions	Subsequent remedial measures	inadmissible ① to prove negligence; or ② culpable conduct	inadmissible ① to prove negligence; ② culpable conduct; or ③ a defect in a product or its design
	Offers for medical expenses	admissions of fact → public policy rule 적용 ○ → **not** adm.	admissions of fact → public policy rule 적용 × → adm.
	Disputed settlement offers	적용 ○	—
	Expressions of sympathy	적용 ○	—
	Plea negotiations	Prop 8 적용 ○ & exception 적용 × → adm.	적용 ○ → **not** adm.
Documentary evidence	용어	secondary evidence rule	best evidence rule (BER)
	"duplicate"	photocopy carbon copy handwritten copy	photocopy carbon copy
Lay witness 요건		① based on firsthand knowledge; and ② helpful to jury	① based on firsthand knowledge; ② helpful to jury; and ③ not based on scientific, technical, or other specialized knowledge
Criminal conviction (impeachment)	time limit	time limit 없음	time limit 있음
	convictions for moral turpitude 외의 범죄	사용 불가	사용 가능 (요건 有)

		CEC	FRE
Bad acts (impeachment)		civil/crim. case 구분 (criminal case에서만 가능)	civil/crim. case 구분 ×
		요건: CEC 352	요건: ① not extrinsic ② in good-faith ③ FRE 403
Spousal immunity		civil case + crim. case	crim. case
Attorney-Client privilege		client는 eavesdropper의 증언도 막을 수 있다.	—
Work product privilege		변호사가 작성한 문서와 비변호사가 작성한 문서 구분	구분 ×
		변호사 문서: absolute privilege 그 외: qualified privilege	소송준비과정에서 작성한 문서에는 모두 동일하게 qualified privilege 적용
Hearsay	용어	multiple hearsay = layered hearsay	double hearsay
		outer layer	the first layer
		inner layer	the second layer
	구별기준	① non-hearsay ② hearsay ③ hearsay exception	① non-hearsay ② hearsay ③ officially non-hearsay ④ hearsay exception
	Prior inconsistent statement (PIS)	oath여부 무관	under oath 要
	Party admission	hearsay exception으로 구분	officially non-hearsay로 구분
	Party admission by employee	요건 ① during the employment; ② w/i the scope of the employment; and ③ employee's negligence	요건 ① during the employment; and ② w/i the scope of the employment

		CEC	FRE
Contempo-raneous Statement (hearsay exception)	용어	contemporaneous statement	present sense impression
	요건	① declarant's own conduct; and ② declarant engaged	① declarant perceive
	의미	좁은 의미(화자가 관여한 자신의 행위만을 뜻함)	넓은 의미(perceive한 모든 것을 포함)
Medical diagnosis or treatment (hearsay exception)		요건: made by a child abuse victim	무관
Business record (hearsay exception)		= a record of event, opinion	= a record of event, opinion, diagnoses
Dying declaration (hearsay exception)		요건: ① All cases ② declarant is actually dead	요건: ① civil + homicide case ② declarant is unavailable
Statement against Interest (hearsay exception)		interest 의미: against a person's pecuniary, penal, or social interest	interest 의미: against a person's pecuniary, penal
Statement of infliction of violence (hearsay exception)		적용 O	—
Open door exception (character evidence)		① sexual assault, child molestation, or domestic violence 사건; or ② to prove Δ's violent 성격	① sexual assault, child molestation 사건; or ② to prove victim과 동일한 Δ's violent 성격
Prior inconsistent statement	substantive (hearsay)	under oath 여부와 무관	under oath 要
	impeachment		under oath와 무관

	CEC	FRE
Counselor – victim of sexual assault/domestic violence (privilege)	적용 O	—
Clergy–penitent privilege	적용 O	—
News reporters privilege	적용 O	—
Doctor patient privilege	요건: ① only to communication ② for medical diagnosis/treatment	—
Character evidence civil action에서 admissible한 경우	① Defamation ② Negligent hiring ③ Wrongful death	① Defamation ② Negligent hiring ③ Wrongful death ④ Child molestation/ sexual assault
Rape shield provision civil action에서 admissible한 victim에 관한 증거	victim's prior sexual conduct with the defendant	victim's reputation (only when P>>D)
Bolstering W's credibility	허용 O	허용 X
Declarant's unavailable 상황 중 "unable to remember"	= total memory loss	
Ancient document authentication	30 years old	20 years old
"self–authenticating" document	signature of notary	-business record -trade inscriptions
Judicial notice	the court **must** compel	the court **may** compel ⇒ civil: Jury **must** accept criminal: Jury **may** accept

12장

Criminal Law and Criminal Procedure

//

본 장은 크게 Criminal Law와 Criminal Procedure 파트로 구분된다. Criminal Law는 범죄 구성요건 및 defenses에 관해 논하며, 캘리포니아 에세이 시험(CEE)에서는 피고인에게 특정 죄책 또는 특정 defense가 인정될 수 있는지 그 여부를 판단하는 문제가 출제된다. 한편, Criminal Procedure는 수정헌법 4조, 5조 그리고 6조를 중심으로 형사소송에 있어 용의자 및 피고인에게 보장되는 다양한 헌법적 권리들에 대해 논한다. 수정헌법 4조는 정부의 unreasonable seizure 및 search를 금하며, 수정헌법 5조는 강요에 의한 자백을 금하는 바, 본 권리로부터 파생되어 미란다원칙이 확립되었다. 수정헌법 6조는 변호사 선임권리 및 Confrontation Clause 등에 대해 명시하고 있다. 정부(검사, 경찰 등)가 용의자 및 피고인의 본 권리들을 침해하면서 수집한 증거는 inadmissible하다.

☑ 글쓰기 Tips

1. Criminal law보다는 criminal procedure, 특히 수정헌법 4조(unreasonable seizure and search)에 관한 문제가 자주 출제되었으나, 최근 기출문제는 criminal law와 criminal procedure를 같이 출제하는 경향이 있다.
2. Criminal procedure: 특정 증거가 채택되는 과정에서 위헌적인 요소가 있는지 그 여부를 판단하는 문제가 출제된다.
   Q: How should the court rule on the motions to suppress [the cocaine] under [the Fourth Amendment]?
   Q: How should the court rule on the motions to suppress [the statement] under [the Miranda]?
   ⇒ 주어진 헌법적 권리 침해여부를 기준으로 증거의 admissibility를 판단한다.
3. Criminal law: 특정 범죄 적용가능성 여부 및 특정 defense의 적용가능성 여부를 판단하는 문제가 출제된다.
   Q: Is 갑 guilty of [robbery]?

> ⇒ 피고인의 act, intent와 causation 그리고 피고인이 주장가능한 defenses에 대해 analysis한다.
> Q: Is 갑 likely to prevail on a defense of [entrapment] at trial?

Part One. Criminal Procedure

- Suspect: 용의자
- Prosecute: 형사소송 과정이 시작되다.
- Accuse: 혐의를 제기하다.
- Charge: 기소(n.), 검사가 기소하다(v.)

  "Being charged" with a crime means the prosecutor filed charges.
- Indictment: Grand jury가 기소함(n.)

  An indictment means the grand jury filed charges against the defendant.
- Be convicted: 선고가 내려지다.

  "Being convicted of a crime" means that the person has been found guilty after trial. A person convicted of a crime is, by law, guilty.

I. The Fourth Amendment

수정헌법 4조는 seizures와 searches에 관한 조항으로서, 국가 공권력에 의한 부당한 체포 및 수색으로부터 개인을 보호한다.

A. General Rule

★The Fourth Amendment provides that people should be free from unreasonable searches and seizures. It is applicable to the state or local governments through the Due Process Clause of the Fourteenth Amendment.

The lawful enforcement must have a **valid search warrant,** unless warrant exception is applicable.

B. Seizure (14July)

★A person has been **seized,** if a **reasonable** person would have believed that he was **not free to leave,** in light of all of the circumstances. In other words, when a reasonable person would have believed that the police uses his authority to restrain his movement, the person has been seized.

1. Arrest

PC, W 불필요

★A person has been arrested, if the person is **into custody against her will.**

The arrest should be based on probable cause and warrant is generally not required.

2. Investigatory Detention (Terry Stop)

RS, W 불필요

★The police may stop and frisk (Terry stop) an individual when it was for a **short period of time** and the police have a **reasonable articulable suspicion that the person is armed.**

✔ 경찰이 여름에 긴 패딩을 입은 행인 갑을 stop and search한 경우, 행인 갑이 be armed라고 의심하기에는 다소 어려움이 있으므로 행인 갑을 stop시킨 후 pat-down하는 과정에서 발견된 증거물은 inadmissible하다.
There are no indications that 갑 was actually armed, and the search was unreasonable.

C. Search (18Feb, 19July)

1. General Rule

★Search occurs when the police violates an individuals **reasonable expectation of privacy** or **intrudes** on the person's person or property.

2. Governmental Action

The Fourth Amendment applies to **the governmental conduct.** The conducts by a **publicly paid police** or a person **acting in the direction of the police** are governmental actions.

3. Expectation of Privacy (Standing)

a. General Rule

★A person can allege the Fourth Amendment violation only when he has **standing** to challenge it. A person has standing when he has a **reasonable expectation of privacy** in an object or premises^{장소}.

No expectancy of privacy when there is no way to control.

b. Premises

A person has a reasonable expectation of privacy when:

ⅰ. He is an **owner or a possessor** of the premises; or

ⅱ. He is an **overnight guest** at the premises.

✔ Private residence (home) — 有 E.P.(warrant 필요)

A person has reasonable expectation of privacy in his home.

✔ Open fields — no E.P.

A person does not have a reasonable expectation of privacy **in open fields.**

✔ Curtilage — 有 E.P.

✔ Porch and front door — 有 E.P.

✔ Conversation in a public telephone booth which is **enclosed.** — 有 E.P.

✔ Conversation made by a person who attempted to keep the conversation **private.** — 有 E.P.

4. Use of Technology (15July, 19July)

경찰이 장비(technology device)를 이용하여 얻은 증거는 admissible한가. 만일 장비를 이용하여 증거를 얻는 과정이 search로 인정된다면 warrant 가 발부된 상태에서 진행된 경우에 한해 해당 증거의 admissibility가 인정 되는 바, 본 챕터에서는 장비를 이용하여 증거를 얻는 과정을 search로 인 정할 수 있는지 그 여부를 판단하는 기준에 대해 논한다.

법원은 두 가지의 판단기준에 입각해 technology device를 통한 조사를 search로 인정하는 바, 이들은 Kyllo 판례로부터 정립되었다. 첫째로, 법원 은 physical intrusion 없이 관찰하기 어려운 사실을 장비(technology device)를 통해 알아낸 경우는 search로 인정한다. 둘째로, 사회에서 만연 하게 사용되지 않는 device를 사용한 관찰은 search로 인정한다.

When technology device is used to discover information about **interior of a private home** that would be known **otherwise** only by a **physical intrusion,** it is a **search.**

The use of device which is **not in general public use** is a **search.**

Generally, when the police use **sensory enhancing technology,** it is a **search.** When the police use technology that merely **supplements** sensory faculties, it is **not a search.**

✔ Thermal imaging/Heat imaging(열 영상기) → search ○ → warrant 필요(Kyllo case)
✔ Binoculars^{쌍안경}, telescopes^{망원경}, flashlight → widely available to the public → search × → warrant 불필요
✔ Eavesdropping → search ○
✔ Listening through walls → physical intrusion 없이도 충분히 감각적 으로 얻을 수 있는 증거임. → search ×

[Kyllo v. United States, 533 U.S. 27 (2001)]

Case brief: 경찰이 마리화나를 재배한다는 익명의 제보를 받고 용의자 Kyllo의 집 내부를 관찰하였다. 마리화나를 재배하기 위해서는 보통의 집 온도보다 높은 온도를 유지해야 하기 때문에 경찰은 thermal heat detector를 사용하여 Kyllo의 집 온도를 측정하였다. 경찰은 Kyllo 집 맞은편에 차를 세워두고 조수석에 앉아 집 온도를 측정하였고, 이웃집보다 높은 내부온도임을 확인하였다. 익명의 제보와 thermal imaging을 근거로 search warrant가 발부되었고, Kyllo의 집 내부를 search하는 과정에서 발견한 마리화나가 재판 중 증거로 제출되었다. 이에 Kyllo는 해당 증거에 대해 motion to suppress를 주장하였다.

Held: 법원은 '집 내부'에 대한 정보를 얻는데 있어 physical intrusion 없이 관찰하기 어려운 사실을 technology device를 통해 알아냈다면, 이 또한 search에 해당한다고 판시하였다. 즉, 집 내부에 대한 용의자의 expectation of privacy가 침해되었다고 본 것이다. 본 사안에서 경찰은 집 맞은편에서 직접 들어가지 않고는 관찰하기 어려운 집 내부 온도를 thermal heat detector를 사용하여 알아내었으므로, 이는 search에 해당한다. 경찰이 직접 physical intrusion을 하지 않았다 하더라도 search가 인정될 수 있는 것이다. 또한 법원은 사회에서 만연하게 사용되지 않는 device를 사용한 관찰은 search라고 보았다. Thermal heat detector는 사회에서 만연하게 사용되지 않는 device이므로, 경찰의 행위는 warrantless search로서 위헌이다.

⇒ ① When technology device is used to discover information about **interior of a private home** that would be known otherwise only by a **physical intrusion,** it is a **search.** This is because the private home is a place where society reasonably have an expectation of privacy. ② The use of device which is **not in general public use** is a **search. Thermal imaging technology** is not in general public use and it is unreasonable to search without a warrant.

5. Warrant

a. General Rule

To be a valid warrant, a warrant must:

ⅰ. Be supported by **probable cause;**

ii. **Particularly** state **place and items** to be seized; and

iii. Be approved by a **neutral magistrate.**

b. Probable Cause

　i. General Rule

Probable cause is established when it is reasonable to believe that the place or item to be searched is related to the crime. Probable cause can be established based on information, but such information should be obtained from a **reliable and credible source.**

　ii. Anonymous Tip

The officer may establish probable cause relying on information provided by others. The probable cause may be established by **anonymous tip** as long as it is **reasonable to believe** the commitment of the crime with the tip.

✔ The police observed through their own five senses. — PC 형성가능

✔ Hunch^{예감} — no PC

✔ 정보제공자의 identification이 밝혀지지 않은 경우(익명의 제보자인 경우) — 정보제공자의 ID는 PC 형성여부와 무관하다. 즉, 해당 정보 내용이 특정 장소 또는 사물이 범죄와 관련이 있다는 점을 믿기에 충분한 경우라면 익명의 정보도 PC를 형성할 수 있다.

The identification of the informant does not need to be revealed to establish probable cause.

⇒ Arguable point: 피고인은 익명의 제보자가 정보를 제공하였으므로 PC를 형성할 수 없다고 주장할 것이나, 제보자의 신원은 PC형성여부와 무관하다.

The defendant may argue that anonymous information cannot establish probable cause. However, the identification of the informant does not need to be revealed to establish probable cause and reliable information from the anonymous informant can establish probable cause.

✔ 예전부터 경찰에게 도움을 많이 준 자가 제공한 information (information from the reliable person) — PC 형성가능

6. Warrantless Search (15July, 17Feb, 18Feb)

본 챕터는 warrant 없이 합헌적으로 진행할 수 있는 search에 대해 논하는 바, 이는 warrant 요건의 예외적 상황이라 할 수 있겠다. 그러한 예외적인 상황에는 용의자가 동의(consent)한 경우, 경찰이 우연히 범죄에 관한 증거물을 발견한 경우(plain view), 합헌적인 체포 후 수색을 진행한 경우(search incidental to lawful arrest) 등이 있다.

a. Consent

The police may search without warrant if the police have **voluntary consent** to do so.

b. Plain View

Under the plain view doctrine, the police may [seize/search] evidence without a warrant if:

ⅰ. The police was **lawfully present** in a position;

ⅱ. The evidence is observed **in plain view;** and

ⅲ. The **illegality** of the evidence is **readily apparent** (enough to establishe **probable cause** of its illegality).

✔ 불법으로 침입한 house를 둘러보다 plain view로 발견한 cocaine → The police was not lawfully present in the house. → plain view doctrine 적용 불가 → warrant 필요

c. Exigent Circumstances

The police may make a warrantless search when there is an

emergency or a hot pursuit of a felon.

The scope of the search is limited to the search **for resolving of the exigent circumstance.**

✔ Kidnapping이 의심되는 상황에서 경찰이 용의자의 집을 warrantless search하는 경우 exigent circumstance가 인정되는 바, 용의자 집 내부 중 '사람이 숨겨져 있을 만한 곳'에 한해 수색가능하다.

d. Search Incidental to Lawful Arrest

The police may search incident to an arrest without warrant as long as it was made on **probable cause.**

The arrest should be a constitutional seizure under the Fourth Amendment. In other words, the search incident to the arrest is improper when there is no valid arrest because of no existence of the crime.

답안요령	Search

Q: <u>Should the court suppress the [cocaine] based on the Fourth Amendment?</u>
<u>경찰 갑이 을이 마약을 소지하고 있다는 익명의 제보를 받고 을의 집을 관찰하였다. 갑은 집 맞은편에서 쌍안경을 통해 을의 침실 내부에 있는 cocaine을 발견하였다. Cocaine은 admissible한가?</u>

---

1. 수정헌법 4조
2. Government action
   + analysis
3. Technology device
   + analysis (Kyllo case★)
4. E.P. 존재여부
   + analysis
5. Valid warrant (PC 존재여부)
   + analysis
6. Warrantless search 해당여부
   + analysis

There are no facts indicating that warrantless search is allowed in this case.

모범답안 040

1. The cocaine

Reasonable search under the Fourth Amendment

Under the Fourth Amendment, people should be free from unreasonable searches and seizures. It is applicable to the state or local governments through the Due Process Clause of the Fourteenth Amendment. Search occurs when the police violates an individuals reasonable expectation of privacy or intrudes on the person's person or property.

Governmental conduct

The Fourth Amendment applies to the governmental conduct. The conducts by a publicly paid police or a person acting in the direction of the police are governmental actions.

(ANALYSIS: In this case, 갑 is a state police and his conduct constitutes governmental conduct.)

Use of technology

When technology device is used to discover information about interior of a private home that would be known otherwise only by a physical intrusion, it is a search. The use of device which is not in general public use is a search. In Kyllo case, the court said that using a thermal imaging is a search.

(ANALYSIS: In this case, police 갑 used binocular. 갑 could argue that binocular is widely available to the public and his action does not constitute a search. However, 갑 used the binocular to peer into a bedroom window and saw cocaine. This case is similar with Kyllo case in which a police used technology devise to discover information about interior of a private home that would be known otherwise only by a physical intrusion. Thus, his action constitutes search.)

Expectation of privacy (house)

Only a person who has standing can allege the Fourth Amendment violation. A person has standing when he has a reasonable expectation of privacy in an object or premises. A person has a reasonable expectation of privacy when: (1) he is an owner or a possessor of the premises; or (2) he is an overnight guest at the premises.

(ANALYSIS: In this case, 을's house was searched and 을 has reasonable personal expectation of privacy in his own house. Thus, 을 can allege the violation of the Fourth Amendment.)

Probable cause (anonymous tip)

A valid warrant is required for a constitutional search. To be a valid warrant, a warrant: (1) must be supported by probable cause; (2) particularly state place and items to be seized; and (3) must be approved by a neutral magistrate. Probable cause can be established based on information, but such information should be obtained from a reliable and credible source.

(ANALYSIS: In this case, 갑 obtained information that 을 possesses cocaine from anonymous informant. 을 could argue that anonymous tip cannot establish probable cause. However, the informant in this case had provided reliable information and probable cause can be established.)

Warrant

Generally, a search warrant is required for a constitutional search.

(ANALYSIS: In this case, there is no fact indicating 갑 had a search warrant and indicating applicable warrantless search circumstances. Thus, the search is unconstitutional.)

Conclusion

In conclusion, the use of binocular was a search but there are no probable cause and valid search warrant. Thus, the court should suppress the cocaine on the Fourth Amendment.

D. The Fruit of the Poisonous Tree Doctrine (15July, 17Feb, 18Feb)

1. General Rule

★Under the fruit of the poisonous tree doctrine, the evidence is invalid if the seizures or searches violated the Fourth Amendment rights.

2. Exceptions

★A tainted evidence (fruit of poisonous tree) is admissible when the prosecution can show that:

ⅰ. The evidence is obtained from an **independent source;**

ⅱ. The evidence is **inevitably** discoverable; and

ⅲ. The illegality is **attenuated**^{희석된} by the defendant's intervening act of free will (intervening acts broke the causal chain between the illegal conduct and the evidence).

3. Statement and Search (19July)

특정 statement가 수정헌법 4조에 위배되는지 그 여부를 판단하는 문제가 출제된 경우, statement는 seizure의 대상도 될 수 없으며 search의 대상도 될 수 없으므로 이 문제는 statement가 unlawful seizure or unlawful search를 통해 얻어진 fruit of poisonous tree인지 판단토록 요구하는 문제이다. 따라서 criminal procedure에서의 증거 admissibility는 우선 제출된 증거가 어떤 유형의 '증거'인지 파악하고, 문제에서 주어진 '헌법조항'에 근거하여 증거의 admissibility를 판단하는 것이 중요하다.

답안요령 | **Statement & Search**

Q: <u>How should the court rule on the motion to suppress the 갑's statement based on the Fourth Amendment?</u>

> 1. Seizure/Search에 대한 rule
>   ① 수정헌법 4조
>   ② Seizure 정의
>   ③ Arrest/Terry stop에 관한 rule
> 또는
>   ① 수정헌법 4조
>   ② Government action
>   ③ E.P. 존재여부
>   ④ Valid warrant (PC 존재여부)
>   ⑤ Warrantless search 해당여부
> 2. Fruit of poisonous tree doctrine
> 3. (Fruit of poisonous tree doctrine 예외)

TIP1 생각 route: statement 이전에 search/seizure가 존재함. → search/seizure의 합법성 여부 판단 → 수정헌법 4조를 근거로 판단 → 수정헌법 4조에 위배되는 경우, statement는 tainted evidence (fruit of poisonous tree) → doctrine의 예외에 해당하는지 확인

TIP2 Statement의 증거력(admissibility)에 관한 헌법조항은 the Fourth Amendment와 Miranda right가 있다. The Fourth Amendment를 근거로 판단하는 경우, 타 증거의 불법적인 수집과정(search/seizure)을 우선 파악해야 한다.

TIP3 Unreasonable search 및 seizure인 경우, fruit of poisonous tree doctrine의 예외를 analysis한다.

모범답안 041

Q: How should the court rule on the motion to suppress the 을's statement based on the Fourth Amendment?
한여름, 주(州) 경찰 갑이 롱코트를 입고 지나가는 을을 stop and frisk하였다. 그 과정에서 하얀 가루가 담긴 비닐봉투가 발견되었고, 을은 "그것은 cocaine이다."라고 말하였다. 수정헌법 4조상 을 진술의 admissibility가 인정되는가?

1. 을's statement

Reasonable seizure under the Fourth Amendment

Under the Fourth Amendment, people should be free from unreasonable searches and seizures. It is applicable to the state or local governments through the Due Process Clause of the Fourteenth Amendment. A person has been seized, if a reasonable person would have believed that he was not free to leave, in light of all of the circumstances.

Governmental conduct

The Fourth Amendment applies to the governmental conduct. It occurs when a publicly paid police or a person acting in the direction of the police conducts an action.

(ANALYSIS: In this case, police 갑 is a state police and his conduct constitutes governmental conduct.)

Detention (Terry stop)

The police may stop and search an individual when the search was for a short period of time and the police have a reasonable articulable suspicion that the person is armed.

(ANALYSIS: In this case, 갑 stopped and search 을 for a short period of time. 갑 could argue that he had a reasonable suspicion since 을 was wearing a long coat in summer. However, wearing a long cost in summer does not indicate that 을 is armed. Thus, the detention was unreasonable.)

Fruit of poisonous tree doctrine

Under the fruit of the poisonous tree doctrine, the evidence is invalid if the seizures or searches violated the Fourth Amendment rights.

(ANALYSIS: In this case, 을's statement was obtained in the course of unreasonable seizure. Thus, it is a fruit of poisonous tree and it is inadmissible.)

Exception

However, a tainted evidence is admissible when the prosecution can show that (1) the evidence is obtained from an independent source; (2) the evidence is inevitably discoverable; and (3) the illegality is attenuated by the defendant's intervening act of free will.

(ANALYSIS: In this case, there are no facts indicating that the exception is applicable. Thus, the statement is the fruit of poisonous tree and inadmissible.)

Conclusion

In conclusion, 을's statement is a fruit of poisonous tree since it is obtained from unreasonable seizure. Thus, the court should not suppress the 을's statement based on the Fourth Amendment.

II. The Fifth Amendment (14July, 17Feb)

수정헌법 5조에 따르면 누구도 자신에게 불리한 진술(self-incrimination)을 강요받을 수 없다. 즉, 경찰의 강요에 의해 언급된 자백은 증거로서 효력이 인정되지 않는 바, 자백의 admissibility는 right against self-incrimination의 침해여부를 기준으로 판단된다. 본 법리는 Miranda v. Arizona, 384 U.S. 436

(1966) 판례를 통해 보다 구체화되었다. 법원은 in-custody interrogation 상황에 처한 용의자가 자백을 하기 전 미란다 원칙을 고지해야 하는 의무가 경찰에게 있음을 명시하였다. In-custody 상황이 용의자에게 심적 부담으로 작용하여 자백을 할 수 밖에 없으며 그렇게 언급된 자백은 강요에 의한 자백과 다름없기 때문에 미란다 원칙을 고지해야 한다는 것이다. 경찰은 용의자에게 묵비권을 행사하고 변호사를 선임할 수 있다는 점을 사전에 고지하여 자발적인 자백을 얻어야 한다.

미란다 원칙의 내용은 다음과 같다.

1. 진술을 거부할 수 있는 권리
2. 모든 진술이 법정에서 불리하게 작용할 수 있다는 점
3. 변호인을 선임할 수 있는 권리
4. 변호인을 선임할 수 없는 상황인 경우 국선변호사를 선임할 수 있는 권리

Under the Fifth Amendment, the lawful enforcement officer must inform Miranda rights to anyone who is in custody prior to interrogation. Miranda Warnings must include four things that:

1. You have the right to remain silent.
2. Anything you say can and will be used against you in a court of law.
3. You have the right to an attorney.
4. If you cannot afford an attorney, one will be appointed for you.

상기 내용 중 진술을 거부할 수 있는 권리(right to remain silent)와 변호인을 선임할 수 있는 권리(right to counsel)를 통틀어 "Miranda rights"라 일컫는다. 즉, Miranda rights는 수정헌법 5조 상의 right against self-incrimination으로부터 파생된 권리로서, 명확히 구분하자면 Miranda rights와 right against self-incrimination은 별개의 개념이나 혼용해서 사용하기도 한다. 한편, 경찰이 in-custody 용의자에게 미란다 원칙을 고지하면 용의자는 Miranda rights에 따라 가만히 있거나, 진술을 거부하거나, 변호사를 선임하거나 또는 Miranda rights를 포기(waive)할 수 있다. 그중 진술을 거부하는 것은 진술을 거부할 수 있는 권리(right to remain silent)에 따른 행위이고, 변호사를 선임하는 것

은 변호인을 선임할 수 있는 권리(right to counsel)에 따른 행위이다. 양 권리 모두 용의자가 권리를 행사(invoke)하고자 함을 명시(unambiguously)한 순간 부터 인정되는 바, 경찰은 본 권리를 행사하지 않은 피고인에게 자백을 유도 하는 질문을 계속할 수 있다. Miranda rights에 대한 포기(waive)는 용의자가 포기(waiver)의 의미를 충분히 인지한 상태에서(knowingly) 자발적으로 (voluntarily) 행한 경우에 한해 인정된다. 한편, 미란다 원칙에서 파생된 변호 사 선임권리는 수정헌법 5조로부터 파생된 권리인 바, 수정헌법 6조로부터 파생된 변호사 선임권리와는 다소 차이가 있다. 본 내용은 이후 「Ⅲ. Sixth Amendment」에서 자세히 논하도록 한다.

A. Right against Self-Incrimination

Under the right against self-incrimination of the Fifth Amendment, suspects should **not be compelled** to make self-incrimination statements. **It is applicable to the state or local governments through the Due Process Clause of the Fourteenth Amendment.**

B. Miranda Rights

1. General Rule

★The government are required to read Miranda warnings to a suspect when the suspect is subject to an **in-custody interrogation.**

Once an officer has read the suspect his Miranda rights, the suspect may unambiguously invoke his rights (right to remain silent and right to counsel) and it must be strictly honored by the officers.

a. In-Custody

Custody is a substantial seizure and is defined as either a formal arrest. In other words, a person is in custody when he **reasonably** would **not feel free to leave.**

b. Interrogation

Interrogation is not only a **questioning** initiated by law enforcement but also any words that are reasonably likely to **elicit an** incriminating response from the suspect.

2. Right to Remain Silent

Whenever the suspect wishes to remain silent, he may invoke his right **unambiguously.** Once the suspect invokes his right, the police should stop questioning as to the **particular** crime.

3. Right to Counsel

To invoke the right to counsel, a suspect must request it **unambiguously.** Once the suspect invokes his right, the police should stop **all questioning.**

4. Waiver of Rights

To be a valid waiver of Miranda rights, it must be **voluntary and knowing.**

a. Voluntarily

★"Voluntarily" means that the waiver is made **without coercive conduct which** is **sufficient to overcome** the will of the suspect.

b. Knowingly

★The waver is made knowingly, when an individual made the waiver by **understanding the consequence** of the waiver.

✔ No telling attorney's presence outside → the right to counsel에 위배되지 않는다. 밖에 변호사가 와있다는 사실에 대한 인지는 용의자가 자신의 right to counsel을 이해하는데 있어 어떠한 영항도 끼치지 않기 때문이다.

⇒ Arguable point: 피고인은 자신이 waive the right하기 전, 경찰이 밖에 변호사가 와있다는 사실을 알려주지 않았으므로 자신의 자백은 inadmissible하다고 주장할 것이다. 하지만 밖에 변호사가 와 있다는 사실에 대한 인지는 용의자가 자신의 right to counsel을 이해하는데 있어 어떠한 영항도 끼치지 않기 때문에, 그의 자백은

the right to counsel에 위배되지 않는다.

The defendant may argue that the police did not tell him the attorney's presence outside and, therefore, his confession is inadmissible. However, knowing of the attorney's presence does not have effect on understanding the consequence of the waiver. Thus, there is no violation of the right to counsel and the confession is admissible.

III. The Sixth Amendment

A. Right to Counsel

본 챕터는 수정헌법 6조에 따른 right to counsel에 관해 논하는 바, 이는 앞서 언급한 수정헌법 5조에 따른 right to counsel(Miranda right)과는 다소 차이가 있다. 수정헌법 5조와 6조 모두 용의자가 자신의 권리를 행사한다는 점을 표명해야만 비로소 해당 권리가 인정된다는 점과 용의자 및 피고인이 해당 권리를 포기한다는 것이 어떤 것인지 충분히 인지한 상태에서 (knowingly) 자발적으로(voluntarily) 포기(waive)해야 한다는 점을 명시하고 있다. 다만, 수정헌법 5조에 따른 right to counsel은 해당 용의자의 '모든' 혐의에 대해 적용되는 반면, 수정헌법 6조에 따른 right to counsel은 해당 용의자의 '특정' 혐의에 한해 적용된다. 예컨대, 경찰 갑이 용의자 을을 상대로 강도에 대해 수사하고 있었고, 을은 강도 외에도 살인 혐의도 있었다. 을이 right to counsel under the Fifth Amendment를 행사하였다면 갑은 을의 변호인이 동석하기 전까지 일체의 질문이 금지된다. 반면, 을이 right to counsel under the Sixth Amendment를 행사하였다면 갑은 을의 변호인이 동석하기 전까지 강도혐의에 관한 질문이 금지될 뿐, 살인 혐의에 관한 질문은 가능하다.

[표 12-1]

	Fifth Amendment	Sixth Amendment
Invoke	unambiguously	
Waiver	voluntarily + knowingly	
When	after reading the Miranda rights	in all critical stages of a criminal prosecution
Scope	all questions	specific crimes

1. General Rule

★Under the Sixth Amendment, all criminal defendants have **right to counsel** in all **critical stages** of a criminal prosecution. **The Sixth Amendment applies to the states through the Fourteenth Amendment.** To invoke the right, a defendant must request **unambiguously.**

2. Offense Specific

The right to counsel under the Sixth Amendment is **offense specific.** The right does not guarantee counsel for unrelated offenses.

3. Waiver of Right

a. General Rule

To be a valid waiver of Miranda rights, it must be **voluntary and knowing.**

The waver is made voluntarily, when the waiver is made **without coercion.**

The waver is made knowingly, when an individual made the waiver by **understanding the consequence** of the waiver.

b. Right of Self-Representation (14July)

피고인은 자신을 스스로 변론할 수 있는 권리(right of self-representation)를 가지고 있는 바, 변호사를 선임할 권리를 포기할 수 있다. 다만,

right of self-representation은 피고인이 소송과정 및 그 결과를 이해할 수 있는 competent한 상태인 경우에 한해 인정된다. 그렇다면 피고인이 right of self-representation을 주장하며 위증을 하려고 하는 경우 변호사는 어떻게 해야 하는가. 이는 피고인의 헌법적 권리와 위증을 방지해야 할 변호사 윤리와 충돌하는 문제이다. ABA에 따르면 변호사는 반드시 사퇴(withdraw)해야 한다. California Rules of Professional Conduct에서는 이에 대한 명확한 기준을 제시하고 있지는 않으나, "to mislead the judge, judicial officer, or jury by an artifice or false statement of fact or law"를 금지하고 있다 [Rules Prof. Conduct, rule 5-200].

The defendant may waive their right to counsel as they have a **right of self-representation** when they are **competent.**

To be competent, a defendant must understand **the nature of the proceedings** against him and be aware of the **consequences** of the proceedings.

c. Professional Ethical Obligation

When a defendant invokes his right of self-representation but intends to perjure^{위증하다} himself, the attorney **must withdraw from the representation** under the ABA authorities.

This is because the attorney cannot prevent the client from represent himself.

Part Two. Criminal Law

본 파트는 형법에 대해 논하는 바, 지난 7년간 캘리포니아 에세이 시험(CEE)에 출제되었던 죄책을 중심으로 설명하였다.

답안요령

> 1. Crime 정의
> 2. Specific intent/General intent 구분★
> 3. Analysis
>   ① Act
>   ② Intent
>   ③ Causation
> 4. Defenses★

TIP1   출제된 범죄의 정의뿐만 아니라 해당 범죄의 '유형'도 작성하는 것이 고득점 포인트다.

TIP2   특정 범죄에 대한 피고인의 죄책유무를 판단하는 경우, 별도의 문제가 출제되지 않더라도 피고인이 주장가능한 defenses에 대해 analysis하는 것이 고득점 포인트다. 마찬가지로 Contracts에 관한 문제에서도 피고의 defenses에 대해 analysis하는 것이 고득점 포인트다.

Ⅰ. General Concepts

To be guilty of crime, actus reus (act), mens rea (mental state), and causation should be proved.

1. Mental State (Mens Rea)

There are four types of crime: specific intent crime, general intent crime, crime requiring malice, and crime requiring no intent (strict liability).

a. General Intent Crime

General intent is an **awareness** of all circumstances constituting the crime. General intent can be inferred by **mere doing of the act.**

b. Specific Intent Crime

Specific intent crimes require defendant's specific intent at the time of the commitment.

c. Malice

Malice exists when the defendant **recklessly disregard** a substantial and unjustifiable risk that the particular harmful result would occur.

d. Strict Liability

For the strict liability crimes, the mental state of the defendant is **not** required.

[표 12-2]

Specific Intent	General Intent	Malice	Strict Liability
Solicitation Attempt Conspiracy First degree murder Assault (attempted battery) Larceny Robbery Burglary Forgery False Pretenses Embezzlement	Kidnapping False imprisonment Battery Rape	CL murder Arson	Statutory rape Selling liquor to minors Bigamy (in some jurisdictions)

II. Crimes

A. Attempt (18Feb)

Attempt is an overt act that went **beyond mere preparation.**

Attempt is a **specific intent crime** and defendant must act with the specific intent to commit the crime.

In some states, a defendant is guilty of attempt when he takes a **substantial step** in committing the crime. In other states, a defendant is guilty of attempt when his action is **dangerously proximate** to the crime.

✔ Attempted kidnapping → intent to kidnap another person
✔ Attempted robbery → intent to permanently deprive another's personal property

B. Accomplice

Accomplice는 방조죄를 뜻하며, 방조한 자에게는 정범(principal)을 방조한다(assist 또는 encourage)는 고의와 정범이 그 범죄행위를 실행할 것을 원하는 고의가 모두 있어야 하는 이중의 고의(dual intent)가 요구된다. 여기서 종범(accomplice)의 두 번째 intent는 정범의 범죄에 대한 mens rea가 종범에게도 동일하게 존재한 경우 인정된다. 예컨대, 정범(갑)이 robbery하는 과정에서 을이 robber를 실행하고자 하는 고의와 갑을 assist하고자 하는 고의를 가지고 행동한 경우 이중의 고의가 인정된다. 한편, 정범(principal)과 종범(accomplice)의 구분은 modern law와 common law에서 달리한다. Modern law의 경우 범죄를 실행한 자를 principal 그리고 principal을 방조한 자는 accomplice로 구별하고, accomplice는 다시 principal을 도운 시점을 기준으로 범행 과정에 방조한 자인 accomplice와 범행이 모두 완료된 시점에 방조한 자인 accomplice after the fact로 구분된다. 한편, common law는 범죄를 실행한 자는 principal in the first degree로 규정하고, principal을 방조한 자는 principal in the second degree, accomplice before the fact 그리고 accomplice after the fact를 포함한다. Principal in the second degree는 범행 과정에서 방조한 자 중 범행 현장에서 직접 방조한 자를 뜻하고, accomplice before the fact는 범행 현장에는 나타나지 않은 자를 뜻한다. Accomplice after the fact는 modern law와 마찬가지로 범행을 완료한 principal을 방조한 자를 의미하는 바, prosecution, investigator 등을 방해하는 crime 죄책을 진다. 즉, 수사권방해(obstruction of justice) 죄책이 인정된다.

1. Common Law

   a. Principal in the First Degree

   A principal in the first degree is a person who **actually engage** in the act (or omission) that causes the criminal offense.

   b. Principal in the Second Degree

   A principal in the second degree is a person who **aids, commands, or encourages** the principal **at the** crime.

   c. Accessory Before the Fact

   An accessory before the fact is a person who **aids, commands, or encourages** the principal, but is **not present** at the crime.

   d. Accessory After the Fact

   An accessory after the fact is a person who assists another **to help another escape arrest, trial, or conviction** after the crime. He is charged **with obstruction of justice.**

2. Modern Law

   a. Principal

   A principal is a person who **actually engage** in the act (or omission) that causes the criminal offense.

   b. Accomplice

   An accomplice is a person who **aids, commands, or encourages** the principal **before or during** the commission of the crime with the dual intent (**intent to assist** the primary party and intent **for primary party to commit** the offense charged).

   c. Accessory After the Fact

   An accessory after the fact is a person who assists another **to help another escape arrest, trial, or conviction** after the crime. He is charged **with obstruction of justice.**

[표 12-3]

	Modern Law	Common Law
Actually engage	principal	principal in the first degree
Aids, commands, or encourages	accomplice	(at crime) principal in the second degree
		(not at crime) accomplice before the fact
	accomplice after the fact	accomplice after the fact

C. Solicitation (17Feb)

Solicitation is an inciting^{선동}, commanding^{지시}, advising^{권고}, or inducing^{유도} **another** to commit a crime with the intent that the **solicited person commit** the crime.

Solicitation is a **specific intent crime.**

D. Conspiracy

Conspiracy is an agreement between **two or more** persons with the **intent** to enter into an **agreement** and an **intent to commit the crime.** In most jurisdictions, **overt act** is also required.

Conspiracy is a **specific intent crime.**

E. Robbery (19July)

Robbery is an aggravated form of larceny which is defined as a **taking** of personal property of another **by force or threats** with the **intent to deprive the victim of it.**

It is a **specific intent crime.**

[Larceny]

Larceny is a **taking and carrying away** of the personal property of another without his consent with the intent to permanently deprive the victim of his interest of it.

It is a **specific intent crime.**

F. Homicide (17Feb)

[도표 12-1]

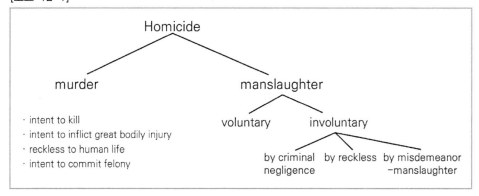

1. Murder

Murder is the unlawful killing of another with malice aforethought. There are four types of malice aforethought: intent to kill, intent to commit great bodily injury, intent to commit felony, and reckless to human life.

2. Manslaughter

Murder charge may be reduced to manslaughter. There are two types of manslaughter: voluntary and involuntary manslaughter.

a. Voluntary Manslaughter

ⅰ. Adequate Provocation

A defendant is guilty of voluntary manslaughter when:

① There was a provocation that would make a **reasonable person** in the heat of passion;

② The defendant was provoked **in fact;** and

③ There was **no sufficient time to cool-off** between the provocation and the killing;

④ The defendant **in fact did not cool off.**

ii. Imperfect Self-Defense

Under the imperfect self-defense doctrine, a defendant who killed another is guilty of voluntary manslaughter when he made imperfect self-defense.

The doctrine is applicable even when:

① The defendant **started the fight;** or

② The defendant actually but **unreasonably believed** that he was in imminent danger of death of great bodily injury.

b. Involuntary Manslaughter

i. By Criminal Negligence

Criminal negligence는 'negligence'에 중점을 둔 표현으로서, 피고인의 행위가 보통의 사람이라면 했을 행동과 편차가 큰 경우의 과실을 뜻한다. 피고인의 criminal negligence에 의한 살인이 인정되면 involuntary manslaughter가 인정된다. 따라서 피고인이 행위 당시 자신의 행동이 타인의 심각한 부상 및 죽음을 초래할 수 있다는 것을 스스로 인지하지 못했다는 사실은 involuntary manslaughter by criminal negligence의 성립여부와 무관하다.

When the defendant acted with **"criminal" negligence,** which is greater than ordinary negligence, he is guilty for involuntary manslaughter.

The defendant would be guilty if an **ordinary person** in the defendant's situation would have been aware that her conduct created an unreasonable risk of death or serious bodily injury. Thus, the unawareness of the risk by the defendant is irrelevant.

ii. By Recklessness

Reckless는 행위 할 당시 결과를 충분히 인지했음에도 불구하고 이를 무시하고 행동하는 것을 뜻하는 바, 피고인이 특정 행위를 할 당시 자신의 행동이 타인에게 '심각한 부상 및 죽음'을 초래할 수 있다는 것을 인지했음에도 불구하고 이를 무시하고 행동했다면

voluntary manslaughter가 인정된다. Reckless는 criminal negligence 와 달리, 그 판단기준이 일반인이 아니라 '행위자'이다. 즉, 합리적 인 사람의 경우 피고인 행위에 대한 위험성을 충분히 인지할 수 있 었다는 사실은 voluntary manslaughter by recklessness를 판단하 는데 있어 무관하나, 피고인이 행위 할 당시 자신의 행동에 대한 위험성을 인지했다는 사실(aware of the risk)은 고려되어야 하는 요소이다.

When a defendant killed another by acting recklessly, he is guilty of involuntary manslaughter.

Recklessness is defined as conscious disregard of a known risk.

iii. **By Misdemeanor-Manslaughter**

Involuntary manslaughter is recognized when a defendant killed another **during the commission of misdemeanor.**

✔ Violate the traffic laws (high speed driving) — misdemeanor

TIP Criminal Negligence v. Recklessness

1. Criminal negligence를 판단하는 기준은 '합리적인 사람(ordinary/ reasonable person)'이고, recklessness의 판단 기준은 '행위자'의 부주의함이다.

2. 피고인의 criminal negligence를 판단하는데 있어 '피고인 스스로 자신의 행동이 타인의 심각한 부상 및 죽음을 초래할 수 있다는 것을 인지하지 못했다는 사실'은 무관하다.

Even if the **defendant was unaware** of the risk, the defendant could be found guilty if an **ordinary person** in the defendant's situation would have been aware that her conduct created an unreasonable risk of death or serious bodily injury.

3. 피고인의 recklessness를 주장하는 검사는 '피고인은 해당 행위를 할 당시 자신의 행위가 타인의 심각한 부상 및 죽음을 초래할 수 있음을 알고 있었다(have known the risk)'고 주장할 것이다.

3. Statutory Murder

a. First Degree Murder

First degree murder is recognized when the prosecution proves: **deliberate and premeditated** killing or felony murder.

b. Second Degree Murder

Second degree murder is any murder other than first degree murder.

G. Kidnapping (18Feb)

Kidnapping is the act of confining another person **with some movement** of the person or with concealment^{숨김} of the person in a secret place.

Kidnapping is a **general intent crime.** General intent is an **awareness** of all circumstances constituting the crime. General intent can be inferred by **mere doing of the act.**

H. Receipt of Stolen Property

Receipt of stolen property is a **specific intent crime,** and it is:

i. Receiving possession and control;

ii. Of **stolen** personal property;

iii. **Knowing** that the personal property has been obtained **in committing a criminal offense** by another person; and

iv. With the **intent to permanently deprive** the owner of his interest in the property.

Ⅲ. Defenses

There are several defenses applicable to the crime: insanity, self-defense, intoxication, necessity, and entrapment.

1. Self-Defense

A defendant is not liable for harm to the plaintiff if he:

i . **Reasonably believed** that the plaintiff is in danger of immediate bodily harm; and

ii . Used **reasonable force** that was **necessary** to protect himself or another.

2. Insanity

A defendant is not liable, if there was abnormal mental condition **at the time of the crime.**

a. M' Naghten Test

Under the M'Naghten test, a defendant must show that:

i . Severe mental disease or defect;

ii . Caused a defect of reason^{생각}; and

iii. As a result of such severe mental disease or defect, defendant:

① Did not know the **wrongfulness** of his actions; or

② Did not understand the **nature and quality** of his actions.

b. MPC

Under the MPC, a defendant must show that:

i . Severe mental disease or defect;

ii . Caused a lack of substantial capacity to either:

① **Appreciate the wrongfulness** of his conduct; or

② **Conform his conduct** to the requirements of law.

3. Intoxication

There are two types of intoxication: voluntary and involuntary intoxication.

a. Voluntary Intoxication

Intoxication is voluntary when a defendant **intentionally** became intoxicated without duress.

Voluntary intoxication can be a defense only against a **specific intent crimes and first degree murder.**

b. Involuntary Intoxication

Intoxication is involuntary when the defendant becomes intoxicated:

ⅰ. **Without knowledge on the nature** of the substance;

ⅱ. Under the **duress;** or

ⅲ. Based on **medical advice** without awareness of the substance's intoxicating effect.

4. Necessity

A defendant is not liable, if his action was necessary to protect some actor's or public interest.

5. Entrapment

• Entrapment^{함정수사} = Sting operation = Trapping

A defendant may argue the defense of entrapment by showing that:

ⅰ. There was **pressure** by the government in the defendant's commission of the crime; and

ⅱ. The defendant would not have committed the crime **but for** the government's actions.

✔ When the defendant had already taken the major step to the commission of the crime — 위 ⅱ요건 미충족

✔ When the defendant had specific plan — 위 ⅱ요건 미충족

TIP ① 위 ⅰ요건은 경찰의 '압박'에 대한 요건으로서, 경찰의 force에 의한 범행인지 피고인이 경찰의 의견에 대해 자발적으로 agree 하여 행한 범행인지를 중심으로 analysis한다.

② 위 ⅱ요건은 범행에 대한 '의지(intent)'에 대한 요건으로서, 피

고인이 아닌 경찰에게 범행을 행할 의지가 있었던 경우 본 요건
은 충족된다.

Appendix

Understanding of CEE

1. 본 서는 캘리포니아 에세이 시험(CEE) 대비를 위한 책으로서, 지난 7년간의 기출문제를 바탕으로 작성되었다. Materials are reprinted "Courtesy of The State Bar of California."

2. CEE는 주어진 사안에 대한 문제를 논리적으로 작성하는 시험으로서, 시험 범위는 12 과목이다. 한 시험당 총 5개의 사안이 주어지며, 각 사안에 대한 답안 작성 시간은 1시간이 주어진다. 한 개의 사안에 대해 적게는 한 문제에서 많게는 여섯 문제가 출제되고, 각 사안이 어떤 과목에 해당하는지는 알 수 없다.

3. 각 문제에 대한 기본점수는 40점~100점이며, 기본 rule을 적어야만 40점이 주어지고 그렇지 않은 경우에는 0점이다. 하나의 답안에 대해 두 번의 채점이 이루어지고 그 평균점수(operant grade)가 최종점수이지만, 두 점수간 차이가 10점을 초과하는 경우에는 세 번째 채점점수가 최종점수가 된다. 모든 점수는 scaled score로 변환되어 계산되고, 에세이, PT, 객관식의 scaled score 총 합계가 1390점 이상 되어야 합격이다(2020년 10월 시험부터 적용).

4. 시험을 칠 때는 문제를 먼저 읽고 주어진 본문(사안)을 읽는다. 문제를 읽으면서 12개의 과목 중 어느 과목에 대한 사안인지, 어떤 issue에 대한 문제인지 파악해야 하며, 이는 본문(사안)을 읽을 때 analysis에 필요한 fact를 빨리 파악하는데 도움이 된다.

5. 에세이 답안의 기본 format는 CRAC 또는 IRAC이다. CEE는 IRAC을 선호하나 MEE만큼 strict한 format를 추구하지는 않고 있어, CEE 답안은 IRAC이라는 큰 틀 안에서 자유롭게 작성하면 된다. 다만, CEE는 한 문제에 1시간이 주어지는 만큼 풍부한 내용의 답안이 요구되는 바, 수험자가 작성하고자 하는 내용이 무엇인지 채점자의 눈에 잘 보일 수 있도록 작성하는 것이 CEE의 고득점 포인트다. 따라서 주어진 문제를 읽으면서 답안의 outline을 만들고, 그 outline을 title

화하여 작성하는 연습이 필요하다.

⇒ Analysis 부분과 conclusion 부분이 잘 드러날 수 있도록 문장의 첫 문구는 통일하는 것이 좋다.

Analysis: "In this case" "Here"

Conclusion: "In conclusion" "In sum" "Hence" "Thus"

6. 앞서 언급한 바와 같이 CEE는 풍부한 내용의 답안을 요구하는 바, 법원의 판단 및 소송당사자의 승소가능성 등에 대한 명확한 결론보다는 주어진 사안에 대해 소송당사자간 어떤 주장을 할 수 있는지, 즉 arguable point를 짚어내는 것이 CEE의 두번째 고득점 포인트다.

⇒ 작성요령:

① 특정 rule을 작성하고 해당 rule이 적용되는 경우 유리한 측(갑), 불리한 측 (을)으로 구분하여 갑 may argue that ~. In response, 을 may argue that. (요소에 해당이 된다/안 된다)

② 요건이 많은 rule의 경우, 주어진 사안에서 충족된 요소와 미충족된 요소를 구분하여 해당 rule이 적용되어야 유리한 측과 불리한 측이 may argue하는 방향으로 작성한다.

예시: request for assurance. anticipatory repudiation.

"갑이 을의 repudiation을 주장하는 경우, 갑은 만족하는 요소를 근거로 repudiation을 주장할 것이나 을은 미충족된 요소를 근거로 breach하지 않았음을 주장할 것이다."

③ 확실한 결론을 반드시 작성해야 한다는 생각을 버린다.

⇒ "Close call이나, 나의 생각에는 ~한 결론이 예상된다."

"Assuming the door is open, the court may ~" "It is a close call, but it is likely for the court to decide that~."

7. Rule을 작성 후 analysis를 하려고 할 때, 해당 rule이 적용되지 않는 case라는 것을 발견했을 경우

⇒ 이미 작성한 rule을 지우지 않고 "해당 rule은 ~한 이유로 본 사안에 적용되지 않는다."고 작성한다.

"In this case, however, the approach would not be used. This is because ~."

8. 요건이 많은 rule을 주어진 사안에 대입하여 analysis하는 경우
   ⇒ "The first prong of the Lemon test" "Under this prong, ~" "The first requirement is satisfied."

9. 하나의 rule을 반복적으로 작성해야 하는 경우
   ⇒ "앞서 언급한 rule에 따르면, ~"
   "As noted above, ~" "See rule above." "As metioned above, ~"

10. Rule에 대한 exception이 있으나, exception이 주어진 문제의 초점이 아닌 경우
    ⇒ "주어진 사안은 exception에 해당하지 않는다."는 점을 간단히 명시하면 족하다.
    "None of these exceptions apply." "There are no facts indicating ~"

11. 아래는 익혀두면 유용한 표현들이다.
    • 모든 상황을 종합적으로 고려해보면: "In light of all of the circumstances, ~" "~ considers totality of cricumstances."
    • ~에 관해: "relating to" "regarding to" "as to" "with regard to"
    • 판례가 나뉜다.
      "There are cases going various ways on this issue."
      "There are cases going both ways ~"
    • "This factor weighs in favor of 갑." "The balancing test favors 갑."
    • "This is not the case here."
    • ~에 관한 정보가 없다: "There are no facts indicating that ~."
    • ~ 여부를 판단하는 데 있어: "In determining whether ~."

	Biz. Assoc.	Civil Procedure	C.P.	Con. Law	Contracts	Criminal	Evidence	P. R.	Real Property	Remedies	Torts	Wills and Trusts
2020 Feb	o				o		o	o			o	
2019 July		o		o	o	o		o		o		
2019 Feb		o	o				o	o	o		o	o
2018 July			o	o	o		o	o				
2018 Feb		o	o	o	o	o		o	o			o
2017 July			o				o	o				
2017 Feb	o				o	o	o	o		o	o	o
2016 July		o	o	o	o			o	o			o
2016 Feb					o		o	o		o	o	
2015 July	o	o	o	o		o		o	o	o		o
2015 Feb	o	o			o				o	o		
2014 July	o		o		o	o	o	o		o	o	o
2014 Feb		o	o	o					o	o		
출제빈도	5	7	8	6	9	5	7	11	6	7	5	6

기출문제 01. 17July Torts

QUESTION 5

Concerned about the dangers of texting while driving, the Legislature recently enacted the following section of the Motor Vehicle Code:

> No person shall operate a motor vehicle upon a public road while using a mobile telephone to send or receive a text message while such vehicle is in motion.

Doug was driving down a busy street while texting on his cell phone. Doug lost control of his car, slipped off the road, and hit Electric Company's utility pole. The pole crashed to the ground, and the fallen wires sent sparks flying everywhere. One spark landed on a piece of newspaper, setting the paper on fire. The burning paper blew down the street, landing on the roof of Harry's house. The house caught fire and burned down.

A technological advance, the Wire Blitz Fuse (WBF), had made it possible to string electrical wires that would not spark if downed. Nevertheless, Electric Company had retained an old wiring system that it and other utility companies had used for years. Electric Company believed that adoption of the WBF system would require a significant increase in electrical rates, and that the WBF system had yet to gain widespread acceptance in the industry. Studies showed that utility companies that replaced their old wiring systems with a WBF system experience vastly increased safety and reliability.

Harry has sued both Doug and Electric Company.

1. What claims may Harry reasonably raise against Doug, what defenses may Doug reasonably assert, and what is the likely outcome? Discuss.

2. What claims may Harry reasonably raise against Electric Company, what defenses may Electric Company reasonably assert, and what is the likely outcome? Discuss.

3. If Harry prevails against Doug and Electric Company, how should damages be apportioned? Discuss.

QUESTION 5: SELECTED ANSWER A

H v. D

Harry (H) can bring a negligence claim against Doug (D)

Negligence

A negligence claim consists of duty, breach, causation, and damages. All elements must be present for a plaintiff to recover.

Duty

A person does not generally owe a duty to act. However, if a person acts, they owe a duty to act as prudently as the reasonable man would and is liable for harms that come to foreseeable plaintiffs for the failure to act with reasonable care. In the majority *Cardozo* view, a foreseeable plaintiff is anyone who is in the zone of danger. Under the minority, *Andrews* view, a foreseeable plaintiff is anyone who is harmed if the defendant could have foreseen harming anyone, even if the person harmed was not the type of plaintiff the defendant foresaw harming.

Standard of Care

Generally, people owe a duty to act with the care a reasonably prudent man would take. There are different standards for landlords or other special relationships.

In this case, D was driving. A reasonably prudent man would have foreseen that bystanders or property could be harmed by inattention to driving. H can argue that D could foresee that texting while driving could have caused him to crash into a person's property. It was foreseeable that he would have run into H's mailbox. Therefore, it was foreseeable that H was in the zone of danger. The fact that D did not in fact run into H's mailbox but instead hit the utility pole which caused a fire is not too remote. D could have crashed into the utility pole that snapped and fell directly into H's house, rather than sparked and caught fire. H will argue that under *Cardozo* he was a foreseeable plaintiff in the zone of danger because a driver should have foreseen that distraction would cause him to crash into a person's property. D will argue that this is too attenuated. While H may have been in the zone of danger for his mailbox being smashed, H was not a foreseeable plaintiff for having his house burned down. The key question, however, is not whether D could foresee the type or extent of harm, but rather could D foresee H as a plaintiff. As long as H's house was on the road, H was a foreseeable plaintiff in the zone of danger.

D will argue H was not foreseeable because the burning paper "blew down the street," implying that the crash occurred far from where he texted. However, H was in the zone of danger because he was on the street where D was driving and texting. It will be a close call, and many courts will not find H was a foreseeable plaintiff in the zone of danger under the *Cardozo* view. Under the *Andrews* view, H will certainly be a plaintiff D owes a duty of care to, because D could have foreseen his texting while driving would injure someone.

Breach

Assuming D owes H a duty of care, there must be a breach. A driver owes a duty to others to drive responsibly and not be distracted. A reasonably prudent man would not text and drive. Therefore, H will successfully argue that D breached his duty of care.

Negligence Per Se

H can also argue D breached his duty of care under a negligence per se theory. Under negligence per se, a defendant has breached his duty if he violated a 1) statute addressed at the behavior 2) the statute was designed to protect against a specific type of harm 3) the statute protected a specific class of people, and the plaintiff harmed is in that class of people in a way the statute was designed to protect against. Defendants can argue that in the situation it was more reasonable to not follow the statute, because the statute was vague and overbroad, or it would have been more dangerous to follow the statute than to violate it.

In this case, none of the defenses apply. D violated a statute that addressed his behavior. It said that no one should operate a motor vehicle upon a public road while using a mobile telephone and to send or receive a text message while the vehicle is in motion. D was driving the car. He was texting on his cell phone while driving down the street. Because he texted while he was driving, he lost control of his car and hit the utility pole. D will argue that the danger the legislature was trying to avoid was running over people. H will argue that it was to protect against people being run over and against property damage. D will rebut that even if it protected against property damage, the plaintiff it sought to protect would be the owner of the property. It is too much of a stretch to say the legislature intended to pass the statute to establish that a person who crashed while texting is responsible for a burning house down the street. It is simply too attenuated from the likely purpose of the legislature. Therefore, his negligence per se claim will not be successful.

Causation
For a negligence claim to succeed, there must be both actual (but-for) and legal (proximate) causation.

But for (actual)
But for causation means that but for the defendant's action, the plaintiff would not have been harmed. In this case, but for D crashing into the pole, the pole would not have crashed to the ground. But for the pole crashing into the ground, the wires would not have sent sparks up, and the burning paper

would not have landed on the roof of H's house. There is but for causation.

Proximate (legal)

The breach must also be the proximate cause of damage. Proximate cause are foreseeable causes. There can be intervening events between D's breach and H's harm as long as D's breach was still a substantial factor in causing D's harm. However, superseding events breach the chain of causation. Superseding events are unforeseeable events such as a criminal act or act of god.

In this case, H will argue that it was foreseeable that Doug texting while driving could result in his house being damaged. As stated above, he will argue it is foreseeable that a distracted driver will drive into another person's property. Even though H's property was damaged in a different way, D could have still foreseen that his actions would lead to this result. However, D will argue that the burning paper is an unforeseeable event, more similar to an act of God. The odds that he would hit the pole just right, the wires would spark, and the wind would take the burning paper down the street onto H's roof is unforeseeable. This is a close case, and different courts might come out differently on it. Under the Andrew's perspective, there would be proximate cause. However, under the *Cardozo* perspective, this would be similar to the explosion in the train station -- the harm is too attenuated from the breach.

Damages

The damages must have been caused by D's breach. If there was causation, then the court will find there are damages. H was damaged by D's breach of care. His house burned down because of D's action.

Defenses

Contributory Negligence

D can argue that H was contributorily negligent. Good roofs will not catch fire if a sheet of burning paper lands on top of it. Roofs are treated to ensure fire cannot spread. If H's house can be burned so easily, it may be because H did not build to code or maintain his roof as he ought to. D might be successful in arguing H was contributorily negligent. That will reduce his damages but not prevent him from paying, unless they are in a contributory negligence jurisdiction.

Abnormally Dangerous Activity

H could also bring an abnormally dangerous activity claim against D. This claim would be unsuccessful. Abnormally dangerous activities are those that 1) present a substantial risk of bodily harm or death 2) are uncommon to the area and 3) cannot be mitigated by sufficient care. In this case, driving is a common activity. Texting while driving, even if a stupid decision, is a common activity in the area. It can be mitigated by only texting while stopped or in other ways.

2. H v. EC

Abnormally Dangerous Activity

H could bring an abnormally dangerous activity claim against EC. This claim would be unsuccessful. Abnormally dangerous activities are those that 1) present a substantial risk of bodily harm or death 2) are uncommon to the area and 3) cannot be mitigated by sufficient care. The courts often look to whether the value to society of conducting the activity outweighs the risk and probability of harm. In addition, courts do not hold utility companies strictly liable for activities they are engaged in that makes them public utility companies. This is a matter of public policy.

In this case, utility poles are common to the area. While transmitting electricity can present a substantial risk of bodily harm or death, it can be mitigated by sufficient care. In addition, the value to society outweighs imposing strict liability for any damages that arise from running the pole. The wires are also a part of the activity that makes the utility company a public entity: transferring of electricity in the community.

Negligence

H can bring a negligence claim against EC. He has a greater likelihood of success than against D.

Duty

See above.

Standard of Care

See above. That of a reasonably prudent man.

EC owes a duty to all foreseeable plaintiffs to conduct its activities with the same prudence a reasonable man would have. H is a foreseeable plaintiff, because it is foreseeable that wires can break, causing sparks that create fire. Under both the *Cardozo* and *Andrews* view, it is foreseeable that a plaintiff's house may be burned down by such a spark. Thus, H is a foreseeable plaintiff.

Breach

H will argue that it has not breached its duty of care because it is using the same wiring system that other utility companies use. Defendants can look to industry standards to show that they have not violated the duty of care. However, industry standards are not dispositive. H can argue that WBF would have prevented the fire, it was not reasonable to rely on old writing systems, and EC should have anticipated its wires sparking. EC will argue that WBF has not gained widespread acceptance among the industry and installing WBF would require significant increase in electrical rates. Ultimately, a court will have to apply Hand's theory to determine whether there was a breach. Hand's theory compares the burden against the probability and the risk. It will look at the expense of installing WBF and compare it to the risk of its wires being defective (and the cost of the resulting damage) against the probability that the wires would break. If the court finds installing WBF or something similar is less than the risk of the old wires causing a fire x the probability of the wires causing a fire, then EC will have breached its duty of care.

Causation

But For

See above. But for not updating the wire system, the wires would not have sparked and caused the fire that burned down Henry's house.

Proximate

See above. It was foreseeable that old wires could break and send sparks. It was foreseeable that sparks could catch fire and spread, causing property damage. EC can argue that the wind was a superseding cause. However, it is foreseeable that the wind would catch a spark and carry it.

Damages

The breach in the duty of care caused the spark to land on H's house which resulted in real property damage.

Defenses

Contributory Negligence

D can argue that H was contributorily negligent. Good roofs will not catch fire if a sheet of burning paper lands on top of it. Roofs are treated to ensure fire cannot spread. If H's house can be burned so easily, it may be because H did not build to code or maintain his roof as he ought to. D might be successful in arguing H was contributorily negligent. That will reduce his damages but not prevent him from paying, unless they are in a contributory negligence jurisdiction.

Defective Product

H can sue for a defective product. Products can be defective in design, manufacture, or label. For a company to be strictly liable, it must be a part of the distributor chain. It could be a manufacturer, distributor, or retail. Companies that do not regularly sell products cannot be held strictly liable.

In this case, EC does not sell its wires. It sells electricity, but that is not a product. Therefore, H's suit will be unsuccessful.

Warranty

N can sue for the breach of warranty of merchantability of fitness for the defective wires. However, to sue for breach of contract there must be privity or N must be a member of the household.

3. Damages

In the majority of states, plaintiff can recover from defendants in joint and several liability. That means he can recover all of the damages from either of the defendants. However, he cannot "double dip" and recover anything more than 100% of his damages. A jury will apportion the fault. If the jury assigns 70% of fault to A and 30% of fault to D, and plaintiff recovers 100% from A, A can demand D reimburse him 30%. In the minority of states, plaintiff can only recover in several liability. That means he can only recover damages from the defendants in proportion to the fault they were liable for.

If the court does find that D and EC are both liable, then a jury should determine the fault. The jury may reasonably decide that the majority of the damages should be apportioned to D because without his negligence the pole would not have fallen down. His actions set it in motion.

QUESTION 5: SELECTED ANSWER B

1. H's claims against D and D's defenses

Harry (H) will file a claim for negligence against Doug (D)

Negligence

To successfully assert a negligence claim, the plaintiff must show that the defendant (i) had a duty, (ii) breached that duty, (iii) the breach of that duty was the actual and proximate cause of the plaintiff's injuries, and (iv) that the plaintiff suffered damages.

Duty

All defendants owe a duty of reasonable care to all foreseeable plaintiffs. The majority (Cardozo) view is that all plaintiffs are foreseeable if they are in the zone of danger. The minority (Andrews view) is that all plaintiffs are foreseeable.

Here, D was driving down a busy street, and therefore owed a duty of care to all foreseeable plaintiffs. H will argue that he is a foreseeable plaintiff because his house is on the street, and houses on a street are within the zone of danger if someone is not driving carefully.

Breach

A defendant breaches a duty of care if the defendant does not act as a reasonably prudent person would in carrying out an activity. Here, H will argue that a reasonable person would not text while driving on a busy street. H will argue that reasonable people know that texting is distracting, and driving a vehicle while distracted is dangerous, and a reasonably prudent person would not drive while distracted. On the other hand, D will argue that

that many people text while driving, and since many people do it, he did not act unreasonably while texting. D's argument will probably fail, and D will be considered to have breached his duty.

Negligence Per Se

Negligence per se is a doctrine that replaces the standard duty of care with a statute. If the legislator has enacted a statute with criminal penalties, and the statute is designed to protect against the harm caused, and the injured plaintiff is of the class that the statute was intended to protect, then the statute replaces the duty of care standard. If the defendant breaches the statute, then the majority view is that that conclusively proves that the defendant had a duty and the defendant breached that duty.

Here, the legislator recently passed a section of the motor vehicle code that stated that no person shall operate a motor vehicle upon a public road while using a mobile phone to text while the vehicle was in motion. Here, D was driving down a busy street, which was presumably public, while texting. Therefore, H violated the statute.

The statute will only replace the duty if H can prove that it was intended to protect against the harm caused and that H was part of the class of people intended to be protected by the statute. The legislator passed the law because they were concerned about the dangers of texting while driving. Presumably, the dangers of texting while driving include the distracted driver hitting a pedestrian, or hitting something and causing property damage. H will try to argue that D hit the pole, which then caused the fire, and this was within the property damage the legislator intended to protect. However, D will argue that although the statute was probably intended to protect property damage such as hitting the pole, it was not enacted to protect against fires caused by faulty wiring of a pole. D's argument will probably prevail because it was not likely that the legislator intended to protect homeowners from fires when they enacted the statute.

Even if H could prove that the fire to his home was the type of damage the legislator intended to protect, he also needs to prove that he was of the class of people the statute was designed to protect. H will argue that as a homeowner on a busy street, he is of the protected class because the statute was designed to protect against property damage by distracted drivers. On the other hand, D will argue that the statute is designed to protect pedestrians who might be hit, or maybe owners or passengers of vehicles struck by distracted drivers. Again, D will probably prevail on this point, because the statute was probably not designed to protect homeowners.

Therefore, H will not be able to establish negligence per se. However, as discussed above, even without negligence per se, H can prove that D had a duty and breached the duty.

Actual Cause

A defendant is the actual cause of a plaintiff's actions if but for the defendant's conduct, the plaintiff would not have suffered the harm. Here, D was the actual cause of H's damage. If D had not been distracted while driving, he would not have hit the utility pole, and the wires would not have sparked when they hit the ground, and the paper would not have lit on fire and therefore H's house would not have lit on fire.

Proximate Cause

A defendant is liable for all foreseeable incidents of his actions. If a defendant's actions combine with another force and then cause the damage, the defendant's action is only the proximate cause of the result if the intervening force was foreseeable. A dependent intervening force is a force that is foreseeable. For example, it is foreseeable that injury invites rescue, and therefore it is a dependent intervening force if someone tries to rescue someone injured by the defendant. On the other hand, an independent intervening force is one that is not foreseeable, and it cuts off liability of the defendant because the defendant was not the proximate cause of the injury.

Here, D will argue that Electric Company (EC)'s utility pole had old wiring, and that old wiring is not safe, and it was the old wiring that caused the fire. D will argue that the old wiring should be considered an independent intervening force, because it is not foreseeable that a company would use old wiring that would sent sparks flying everywhere when it fell. He will argue that it is not foreseeable that the sparks would then light a piece of paper on fire, and then that paper would land on Harry's roof. However, D's argument will probably fail. H will argue that it is foreseeable that if you drive distracted and hit an electric company's pole that sparks would fly. H will point to the fact that the new Wire Blitz Fuse (WBF) systems have yet to gain widespread acceptance in the industry, and therefore most electric poles probably have old wiring. Further, H will argue that D was on a busy street, so it was likely that if D hit the pole and there were sparks, it was likely something would catch fire. H is likely to win this argument and therefore D's distracted driving will be considered proximate cause of H's injuries.

Damages
H will be able to show damages because his house caught fire and burned down as a result of D's actions.

Conclusion
H will be able to successfully assert a negligence claim against D, and all of D's objections will fail.

2. H's claims against EC and EC's defenses
H will assert a negligence claim and a strict liability claim against EC.

Negligence
To successfully assert a negligence claim, the plaintiff must show that the defendant (i) had a duty, (ii) breached that duty, (iii) the breach of that duty was the actual and proximate cause of the plaintiff's injuries, and (iv) that the plaintiff suffered damages.

Duty

All defendants owe a duty of reasonable care to all foreseeable plaintiffs. The majority (Cardozo) view is that all plaintiffs are foreseeable if they are in the zone of danger. The minority (Andrews view) is that all plaintiffs are foreseeable.

Here, EC has a duty to provide and maintain utility poles as a reasonably prudent electrical company would do.

Breach

H will argue that EC breached their duty in not using the new WBF technology, which made it possible to string electrical wires that would not spark if drowned. H will point to the fact that studies showed that utility companies that replaced their old wiring systems with a WBF system experienced vastly increased safety and reliability. H will argue that a reasonably prudent electrical company would have replaced their wiring with WBF since it is safer and more reliable, and because EC did not, they breached their duty.

On the other hand, EC will argue that they did not breach their duty. They will argue that many other utility companies had used the old wiring for years, and the WBF system had yet to gain widespread acceptance in the industry. Although evidence of other companies' actions and industry customs can be used to determine whether a duty has been breached, it is not dispositive. The court will apply a balancing test when deciding whether a company breached its duty in not implementing new technology. The court will look at the cost of the new technology, the amount the new technology would decrease the risk of harm to potential plaintiffs, and the magnitude of the harm suffered by potential plaintiffs. EC will argue that adopting the WBF systems would be expensive and therefore require a substantial increase in electrical rates. On the other hand, H will argue that the WBF systems would vastly increase safety and reliability, and the risk of harm by not replacing (more fires when people hit electrical poles) is great. This is a close call and the court could come out either way, although the court will probably determine that EC did breach its duty because although the WBF technology would be expensive, it would significantly increase safety.

Actual Cause

But for EC's replacement of the old wires with new WBF technology, the electrical wires would not have sparked if downed and therefore H's house would not have caught fire and burned down.

Proximate Cause

EC will argue that they were not the proximate cause of H's house burning down. They will argue that D's negligent driving is an independent intervening force, and therefore they were not the proximate cause. However, it is foreseeable that a driver would drive negligently and hit a pole. Therefore, D's negligent driving was foreseeable, and D's actions do not cut off EC's liability.

Damages

H suffered damages when his house burnt down.

Conclusion

If the court determines that EC breached their duty in not using the new WBF technology, then H will be able to successfully assert a claim for negligence against EC.

Strict Liability

H will try to claim that EC was conducting an ultrahazardous activity, and H was harmed as a result. A company is strictly liable if the company is conducting an ultrahazardous activity and a plaintiff is injured by the dangerous propensity of that activity.

Here, H will argue EC was operating an electric company, which included stringing live electrical wires on poles, and electrical wires are dangerous because they can start fires. When the pole was hit by D's car, the wires fell and sparked and started a fire. Therefore, H's injury was caused by the dangerous propensity of EC's activity.

However, H's arguments will fail because the court will determine that EC was not conducting an ultrahazardous activity. An ultrahazardous activity is one that cannot be done safely, no matter how careful anyone is in conducting the operation, and it must not be of common usage. Here, every city has electrical companies that string electrical wires on poles. Therefore, the electric company's operation will be considered common usage and not an ultrahazardous activity. Therefore, H's strict liability claim will fail.

3. How damages should be apportioned

If actions by two different defendants combine to cause injury to a plaintiff, neither of which alone would have caused the injury, the defendants will be held jointly and severally liable. If defendants are held jointly and severally liable, then the plaintiff can recover the entire amount of damages from either or both plaintiffs. (The plaintiff can only recover the damages once, but it can be from either defendant alone, or some from each defendant.) If the defendant pays more than their share of the damages, the defendant can recover that amount from the other defendant.

Here, D and EC's actions combined to cause H's injuries. H will be able to recover the damages for his burned down house from either D or EC or a combination of both. Depending on how the court rules, D and EC may be assigned different percentages of liability. D and EC will be responsible for paying the percentage of the damages proportional to their percentage of liability. If either D or EC pays H more than their share of the damages, the defendant who paid more can sue the other party for contribution.

기출문제 02. 16Feb Remedies

QUESTION 4

Pop obtained a liability insurance policy from Insurco, covering his daughter Sally and any other driver of either of his cars, a Turbo and a Voka. The policy limit was $100,000.

On the application for the policy, Pop stated that his cars were driven in Hometown, a rural community, which resulted in a lower rate than if they were driven in a city. However, Sally kept and also drove the Voka in Industry City while attending college there.

Subsequently, Pop asked Insurco to increase his coverage to $500,000; Insurco agreed if he paid a premium increase of $150; and he did so. Days later, as he was leaving for Sally's graduation, Pop received an amended policy. He failed to notice that the coverage had been increased to $250,000, not $500,000.

Unfortunately, while driving the Turbo in Industry City, Pop caused a multi-vehicle collision. At first, Insurco stated it would pay claims, but only up to $250,000. Six months later, Insurco informed Pop that it would not pay any claim at all, because of his statement on the application for the policy that both the Turbo and the Voka were located in Hometown.

Insurco filed a complaint against Pop for rescission of the policy. Pop filed a cross-complaint to reform the policy to increase coverage to $500,000.

1. What is the likelihood of success of Insurco's complaint, and what defenses can Pop reasonably raise? Discuss.
2. What is the likelihood of success of Pop's cross-complaint, and what defenses can Insurco reasonably raise? Discuss.

QUESTION 4: SELECTED ANSWER A

(1) Likelihood of Success of Insurco's Complaint for Rescission

Rescission Generally

Rescission is an equitable remedy, under which a court will invalidate a contract in its entirety, such that the parties to the contract are completely excused from continued performance under the contract. Generally, rescission is available when one party has a valid defense to the formation of the contract. Moreover, typically only the wronged party can seek rescission.

Because rescission is an equitable remedy, a court has broad discretion in deciding whether it should be awarded. The court will consider the equities of the situation, taking into account the fairness of rescission to both parties. In addition, as an equitable remedy, rescission is subject to equitable defenses, such as acquiescence, estoppel, laches, and unclean hands.

Here, Insurco seeks rescission of the insurance policy so that it will not be required to reimburse Pop for his liability.

Insurco's Likely Grounds for Rescission

Fraud/Misrepresentation

Insurco's primary grounds for rescission will likely be on the basis of fraud. A contract may be invalid on the basis of fraud where: (1) a party made a false statement of past or present fact; (2) the statement was either fraudulent or was material to the contract; and (3) the other party relied on that statement of fact in entering into the contract.

Insurco can likely make out a claim of fraud under the facts of this case. Here, in applying for the liability insurance, Pop made a misstatement of fact--i.e., that his cars were driven solely in Hometown, a rural community. This was a false statement because one of his cars was driven by his daughter, Sally, in Industry City. Moreover, Pop was driving the other car in Industry City when he was involved in the collision.

Second, this statement may be deemed fraudulent, as it can probably be shown that Pop was aware of the falsity of the statement. It is very likely that Pop knew that the car was not being used solely in Hometown, as his daughter, Sally, used the car while she was attending college in Industry. Moreover, pop certainly knew that he was driving the Turbo in Industry City when he was involved in the accident.

Even if Insurco cannot establish that the statement was fraudulent, the elements of fraud are still likely established because it is clear that this statement was material to the contract. The location of the use of the cars appears to be a key factor in determining the insurance rates, and indeed, the facts make clear that Pop received a lower rate given this false statement of fact.

For this same reason, Insurco can establish that it relied on Pop's false statement in entering into the contract. As made clear in the facts, Insurco would not have entered into the contract at that lower rate, had it been aware that the car was used in Industry City.

Notably, this original contract is not the one Pop is intending to enforce. Rather, he is attempting to enforce the amended contract, in which Pop sought to increase his coverage. Because Pop paid consideration for this increase in coverage ($150), this modification of the contract is valid under the common law. In any event, this amended contract is subject to the same claim of rescission as the original contract, as there is no indication that Pop corrected his false statement when requesting the amended contract. Thus,

Insurco's same arguments for establishing fraud discussed above apply equally with respect to the amended contract.

Accordingly, Insurco has a strong case for seeking rescission on the basis of fraud or misrepresentation.

Mistake

Insurco also may seek to rescind the contract on the basis of mistake. Under the doctrine of mutual mistake, a contract may be invalidated where both parties are mistaken about a material fact, that is, a fact that was a basic assumption of the contract. Under the doctrine of unilateral mistake, a contract may be invalidated where one party is mistaken about a material fact underlying the contract, and the other party knows or has reason to know about that mistake.

Here, to the extent Pop was unaware that Sally was using the car in Industry City, and somehow unaware that he was driving the car in Industry City when he entered into the accident, both he and Insurco were mistaken about this fact. Thus, the doctrine of mutual mistake of fact may be found to apply.

Moreover, to the extent Pop was aware of Sally's use of the car, or his use of the car in Industry City, he clearly also knew that Insurco would be mistaken as to this fact, given his false statement in applying for the insurance. Accordingly, under that scenario, the doctrine of unilateral mistake may apply. Note that unilateral mistake can serve as grounds for rescission of the contract only where the unmistaken party had actual knowledge of the other party's mistake.

However, because this situation involves a false statement of fact, this issue is more properly analyzed under the doctrine of fraud, for the reasons discussed above.

Pop's Likely Defenses

As noted above, a court will consider any equitable defenses before choosing to order rescission of a contract.

Laches

Pop will first rely on the equitable doctrine of laches. That defense applies where a claimant unreasonably delays in bringing suit, and where that suit prejudices the plaintiff.

Here, Pop will argue that Insurco's delay in bringing suit for rescission of the contract--six months after the accident, and even longer after Pop entered into the contract with Insurco--was unreasonable. The facts here are unclear as to the reasonableness of this delay, as it is not clear when Insurco became aware of Pop's misstatement. Given the fact that Pop's accident occurred in Industry City, however, there is a strong argument to be made that Insurco should have been aware of the use of Pop's cars in Industry City at the time Pop made his claim for reimbursement. Thus, Pop may be able to show the delay was unreasonable.

That said, there is no evidence that the Pop was prejudiced by the delay. Pop clearly will be prejudiced by not receiving payment for his liability, but there is no indication that the delay itself in seeking rescission caused Pop any harm. Thus, the defense of laches is likely unavailable.

Acquiescence

Pop may also rely on the equitable doctrine of acquiescence, which serves as a defense where the plaintiff has previously acquiesced to similar conduct on the part of the defendant for which the plaintiff is now seeking relief.

Here, Pop will argue that this defense is appropriate because Insurco has not previously objected to coverage on the basis of Pop's misstatement in applying for coverage, and that Insurco stated that it would pay his claims. However, Insurco will respond that it had no reason to be aware of Pop's misstatement until Pop sought reimbursement under the policy, and that this is the first time Pop has sought such reimbursement.

Insurco likely has the better argument here, given that it has never previously paid Pop under the policy in spite of the misrepresentation.

Unclean Hands

Unclean hands is an equitable defense available where the plaintiff has engaged in some wrongful or inequitable conduct with respect to the same underlying transaction for which the plaintiff is seeking relief.

Here, Pop may attempt to point to Insurco's previous statement that it would pay out on Pop's claim, and then its reversal of course. However, a court is unlikely to deem this inequitable or wrongful conduct, especially if Insurco was not aware of Pop's initial misstatement when it first agreed to pay Pop's claims.

Estoppel

Estoppel is an equitable defense available where a defendant reasonably, foreseeably, and detrimentally relied on a plaintiff's statement that the plaintiff's conduct is permissible, and where it is equitable to enforce that promise.

Pop will attempt to argue that Insurco is estopped from refusing to pay out on the claim, given its previous statement to Pop that it would reimburse him for his claim. However, there are no facts indicating that Pop relied on this promise to his detriment. Rather, the only harm Pop appears to have suffered is the fact that Insurco refuses to pay out on his claim. The facts do not indicate that Pop changed his position in any way in reasonable reliance on Insurco's promise itself.

Thus, this defense is unlikely to succeed.

(2) Likelihood of Success of Pop's Cross−Complaint for Reformation

Reformation Generally

Like rescission, reformation is also an equitable remedy. However, under the doctrine of reformation, a court will not invalidate the contract in its entirety, but rather will rewrite the contract to conform it to the parties' original intent. Moreover, like rescission, reformation is typically only available to the wronged party.

Again, because reformation is an equitable remedy, a court has broad discretion in deciding whether it should be awarded, taking account all of the equities. Reformation too is subject to equitable defenses, such as acquiescence, estoppel, laches, and unclean hands.

Pop's Likely Grounds for Reformation

Mistake

Pop will likely seek rescission on the doctrine of mutual mistake. As discussed above, that doctrine applies where both parties are mistaken about a material fact--i.e., a fact that was a basic assumption of the contract.

Here, the elements of that doctrine appear to apply. It seems that both parties intended that the amended contract increase the coverage limit to $500,000, as opposed to $250,000. In reducing the contract to writing, it appears that a clerical error was made, and that the contract was mistakenly written to state that the limit is $250,000. This appears to have been a mutual mistake, as the facts indicate that both parties initially intended that the limit be $500,000. Moreover, the mistake clearly regards a basic assumption of the contract, as a liability limit is one of the key elements of an insurance contract.

The doctrine does not apply where the party seeking to reform the contract assumed the risk of the mistake. That exception does not apply here, however, as it was Insurco, not Pop, who drafted the contract.

Accordingly, Pop has likely made out a prima facie case for mistake, and a court will likely reform the contract to make it consistent with the parties' intent that the liability limit be $500,000.

Insurco's Likely Defenses

Parol Evidence

Insurco may first rely on the parol evidence rule, which generally holds that where a contract is integrated (intended by the parties to be a final agreement), a party may not admit evidence of a prior agreement that is inconsistent with the contract's terms.

However, there is an exception to the parol evidence rule where a party seeks to provide evidence of mistake or clerical errors in reducing the contract to writing. This exception will apply here.

Unclean Hands

As noted above, the equitable defense of unclean hands applies where the plaintiff has engaged in some wrongful or inequitable conduct with respect to the same underlying transaction for which the plaintiff is seeking relief.

Here, Insurco has strong arguments for application of this defense, given that it can likely show that Pop fraudulently induced the contract. For the reasons discussed above, this claim will likely succeed. Accordingly, Pop's wrongful conduct in inducing the contract will likely serve as a defense to any claim for reformation.

Acquiescence and Laches

Insurco may also assert the defense of acquiescence and laches, the elements of which are discussed above.

With respect to both of these defenses, Insurco will argue Pop did not seek to reform the contract until many months after the amended policy went into effect, thus prejudicing Insurco. Insurco will focus on the fact that Pop had the policy in his possession at this time, and easily could have become aware of the mistake and sought reformation at an earlier time.

However, this argument is unlikely to be successful. A court will likely note that Insurco had a greater ability to have found the mistake, given that it was the party that reduced the contract to writing. Moreover, there do not appear to be facts indicating that Insurco was prejudiced by Pop's delay in seeking rescission.

QUESTION 4: SELECTED ANSWER B

1. INSURCO'S COMPLAINT

APPLICABLE LAW

The contract at issue is an insurance contract. UCC Article 2 governs sale of goods. All other contracts are governed by the common law. Accordingly, the common law would control.

RESCISSION

The issue in Insurco's complaint is whether it is entitled to rescission of the contract. The remedy of rescission allows the party asserting rescission to avoid its obligations under the contract. Rescission is allowed if there is a valid basis for rescission and there are no valid defenses. The remedy of rescission is meant to cure a problem that occurred during contract formation. Typical bases for rescission include: mutual mistake; unilateral mistake; fraudulent misrepresentation; misrepresentation of a material fact (even if not fraudulent); and ambiguous terms in the contract that neither party understood. The applicable bases for rescission in this case will be discussed in turn below.

A. Misrepresentation

Misrepresentation occurs when one party: (i) states a fact to the other party; (ii) the fact turns out to be false; (iii) the other party relied on the false statement when agreeing to enter the contract; and (iv) the party making the false statement either did so fraudulently, or the statement involved a material part of the contract (i.e., even if the statement was not made fraudulently, if it involved a material fact, that is still enough to make out a claim of misrepresentation).

Here, Insurco will argue that Pop made either a fraudulent or material misrepresentation in his application for insurance. In the application, Pop stated that his cars were driven in Hometown, which is a rural community that presumably has less traffic and less risk of accident than an urban center. In reality, however, one of the cars to be insured, the Voka, was also driven in Industry City by daughter while attending college. This made a difference to Insurco, as evidenced by its later refusal to pay once it realized that the application had only listed Hometown as the location of the cars, when in actuality the Voka was located much of the time in Industry City. The issue, however, is whether that discrepancy in the application was either fraudulently represented or material to the contract.

Fraud

There is no indication in the facts regarding whether Pop acted in good faith when he listed Hometown as the location of both cars. It is possible that Pop thought because the Turbo was always located in Hometown, and the Voka was only located in Industry City when college was in session, that he only needed to list Hometown. Pop would argue that Hometown was really the Voka's homebase, and that the car was only temporarily in Industry City for periods of time when college was in session.

Insurco would argue that Pop fraudulently listed only Hometown. Insurco would argue that anyone who drives a car knows that insurance rates go up in urban centers and will be lower in rural areas.

Based on the limited facts, Pop will likely prevail on the issue of fraud. Pop may still be on the hook for misrepresentation, however, if the fact at issue was material.

Materiality

A material fact is one that both parties needed to agree on for the contract to be valid--it is a term that cuts to the heart of what the contract is about. Here, the fact of where both cars were located most likely would be considered a material term. It would be considered a material term because the price of car insurance is affected greatly by where a car is driven. In urban centers the rates may be considerably higher than in rural areas. Accordingly, the fact of where the cars were located likely would be considered material.

Pop may argue it was an innocent mistake that he did not include Industry City in his application. Nonetheless, this is not a defense to mutual misrepresentation of a material fact. It does not matter whether the person who made the statement intended to defraud, it only matters whether they made an untrue statement of material fact.

Pop would further argue that he did not make an untrue statement. His statement that the cars were driven in Hometown was true, although incomplete. Although a party to a contract does not have a duty to disclose facts he is not asked about, he is not allowed to conceal facts or fail to disclose facts he is asked about. Here, Pop was asked in the application where the cars were located. By failing to answer the question completely, it is more likely a court would consider this a misrepresentation or concealment as opposed to a mere failure to disclose. Accordingly, Insurco can likely establish that the location of the cars was material.

Other Elements

In addition, Insurco can likely establish that Pop made a statement that turned out to be false regarding the location of the cars and that Insurco relied on that information when entering into the contract. As discussed above, Pop's intent is not what is at issue, it is only whether his answer turned out to be false. Here, the answer did turn out to be false because the Voka was also driven in Industry City.

Finally, Insurco also relied on the fact when it entered the contract. Insurco's rates were tied to the location of the cars. The fact that Insurco later refused to pay out the claim based on the location of the cars is evidence that it relied on the fact when entering into the contract.

Based on the above, Insurco can likely make out a claim of misrepresentation of a material fact. Thus, Insurco would be entitled to rescission unless Pop raises a valid defense.

B. Mutual Mistake

Mutual mistake occurs when both parties to a contract made a mistake regarding a material term of the contract on which the contract was based. For a party to successfully assert mutual mistake, that party must not have assumed the risk of the mistake occurring. A classic example of mutual mistake was the case involving the sale of a cow that both parties believed was barren, but that later turned out to be able to have children. In that case the two parties made a contract for the sale of a barren cow. The fact that the cow was barren was a mistake that involved a material issue that the contract was based on. In that case, if the seller could have easily had the cow examined to find out whether it was actually barren, then the seller assumed the risk and would not be able to assert mutual mistake.

Here, Insurco would argue that even if it cannot establish the misrepresentation discussed above, it can establish mutual mistake. The mutual mistake would be the fact of where the cars were driven. It was a mistake from Pop's end because he mistakenly forgot to include the fact that the Voka was driven in Industry City. It was a mistake from Insurco's end because it mistakenly thought the cars were driven only in Hometown even though the Voka was also driven in Industry City.

This argument is weaker than the misrepresentation argument. Here, Insurco's mistake was not really based on the terms in the offer or acceptance, but instead was based on Pop failing to disclose information. Mutual mistake usually applies in situations where a fact in the offer or acceptance turns out to be different than both parties thought. Here,
Pop knew the Voka was driven in Industry City, and Insurco did not know because Pop failed to disclose that information. Accordingly, mutual mistake is not as strong an argument for Insurco as misrepresentation.

C. Unilateral Mistake

Unilateral mistake can serve as a basis for rescission when one party made a mistake in the contract formation that the other party knew or should have known about. The typical example arises when many subcontractors are bidding for a construction contract and one subcontractor's bid is so low that the general contractor should know that the subcontractor made an error in its bid. In such a situation, the subcontractor who made the error can rescind the contract based on unilateral mistake because the general contractor knew or should have known of the mistake. In unilateral mistake, the negligence of the party that made the mistake is not a defense to rescission of the contract.

Here, Insurco would argue that it made a unilateral mistake in issuing the insurance policy under rates applicable only to Hometown. Further, Pop knew or should have known of the error. It appears Pop reviewed the initial policy because he requested an increase in coverage. Accordingly, Pop should have known that there was a mistake in the initial policy based on Insurco's misunderstanding of where the cars were located.

Unilateral mistake is a difficult claim to make out, and Insurco would likely not succeed in this argument. The doctrine would be more applicable if Insurco made a mistake in information it provided to Pop. Here, the real issue is information Pop provided to Insurco. Accordingly, misrepresentation is a stronger basis for Insurco's argument.

D. Ambiguity

If a term in contract formation is ambiguous, such that it is open to multiple interpretations, then one of the parties to the contract can later avoid the contract based on that ambiguity. The classic example of ambiguity is the case of the Peerless, where one party thought the shipment referred to the November Peerless, and the other party thought the shipment referred to the December Peerless. In that case, because the term Peerless was open to multiple meanings, it was considered ambiguous, and the party was able to avoid the contract as a result. However, if one party knows that the ambiguous term could refer to multiple interpretations, then that party is charged with knowledge and the unknowing party can enforce the contract based on what it believed the ambiguous term to mean.

Here, Insurco would argue that the term regarding where the cars were driven was ambiguous. The term was ambiguous because Pop understood the term to refer only to where the cars were located much of the time, whereas Insurco believed the term to refer to where the cars were located all of the time. Under such an argument, Insurco would claim that because Pop had reason to know that the Voka was driven in Industry City as well, Pop was the party with knowledge, and the contract should be construed against Pop to Insurco's benefit.

This argument is also a difficult one. Usually ambiguous terms refer to the word itself. Here, the word "Hometown" was not ambiguous. What was ambiguous was the question on the application of where the cars were located. If Insurco can establish that the question was ambiguous to the point it led to miscommunication, then it may be able to succeed in its argument. Still, the stronger claim for Insurco is misrepresentation.

E. Defenses

Rescission is an equitable remedy, so equitable defenses apply. The defenses of unclean hands and laches are the most common. Unclean hands refers to the plaintiff taking inequitable actions regarding the contract itself. Laches refers to an unreasonable delay in bringing a claim that prejudices the defendant.

Laches

Here, Pop would argue that the claim for rescission is barred by laches. After the accident, Insurco agreed to pay out the $250,000. Only six months later, did Insurco inform Pop it would not pay the claim at all. Pop would argue the six month delay was unreasonable. After the accident occurred, Insurco had all the information it needed to make its decision about paying the claim. If Insurco intended not to pay out the claim, it should have made that clear right away after the accident. By waiting six months, Pop and Sally were prejudiced by the delay. They likely incurred many costs associated with the accident, and were depending on the insurance payout to be able to cover those costs.

Insurco would counter that it was unable to ascertain the fact that the Voka was located in Industry City until doing in-depth investigation. The facts do not state how Insurco ultimately learned the Voka had been located in Industry City. If it is true that that information was difficult to find out, then Insurco has a good argument for the delay. If, however, it was easily ascertainable that the car was located in Industry City, Insurco's argument is weaker.

Because rescission is an extreme remedy here given the damage in the accident and also given that the most Insurco is willing to pay out is only $250,000 and not $500,000, the court would likely not find rescission to be the appropriate remedy.

2. POP'S CROSS−COMPLAINT

Pop's cross−complaint asserts a claim to reform the contract to allow for the full $500,000 in coverage. For reformation to be available, there must be a valid contract, grounds for reformation, and no valid defense. Reformation is typically ordered in situations where both parties agreed to certain terms of the contract, and those terms did not end up in the finalized contract due to an error such as a scrivener's error.

Here, Pop will argue that he and Insurco made a valid contract modification to increase the coverage of the insurance policy from $100,000 to $500,000. For a contract modification to be valid, there must be consideration for the modification. Here, there was $150 in consideration paid, and as a result, both Pop and Insurco agreed that the coverage would be increased to $500,000. Here, Pop paid the additional $150, and at that point the agreement was complete and the modification should have been for coverage of $500,000.

Pop will further argue that even though there was a valid modification, the increase was only to $250,000. Pop will claim this must have been due to a scrivener's error or some other error, because the agreement he had made with Insurco before receiving the amended policy was clear.

Based on the facts, Pop has a strong argument for reformation of the contract because it appears that the clear intent of the parties was to modify the contract for $500,000 coverage, and Pop complied with his end of the bargain by paying the $150.

Defenses

Lack of Initial Contract

Insurco can argue that reformation is not permitted because there was never a valid contract in the first place. For reformation to be a possible remedy, there first must have been a valid contract. Insurco would assert the same arguments discussed above regarding contract formation (i.e., mistake, misrepresentation, ambiguity) to argue there never was a valid contract in the first place, and therefore reformation is not allowed.

Parol Evidence

Insurco would also argue that the oral agreement between Pop and Insurco regarding the increase in coverage is inadmissible under the parol evidence rule. Under the parol evidence rule, if there is a final, fully integrated contract, then any communications regarding the contract terms that contradict or supplement the contract either before or contemporaneous with the contract being finalized are inadmissible.

Here, Insurco would argue that the amended policy was a final integration of the contract, and that any evidence of what happened leading up to the amendment is inadmissible parol evidence.

Pop would counter that because the agreement served as the basis for the contract itself, it would not be considered parol evidence, but rather was the basis for the entire modification. Based on the facts, however, it appears the amended policy was a final integrated contract. Accordingly, Pop's arguments would likely fail.

Unclean Hands

Finally, Insurco could assert a defense of unclean hands. Insurco would argue that Pop intentionally misled Insurco into believing the two cars were located solely in Hometown, when in reality the Voka was located in Industry City. Insurco would make similar arguments as discussed above in its claim for rescission. Ultimately Pop would probably prevail on this argument, because there is no evidence he acted in bad faith.

Conclusion

The court would probably not grant Pop's claim for reformation of the contract because of the parol evidence rule. However, they could probably also not grant Insurco's claim for rescission. Acting in equity, the court would most likely find that the contract for $250,000 of coverage controlled.

QUESTION 4: SUMMARY

Equitable restitution

Q: <u>What is the likelihood of success of 갑's complaint for [rescission]?</u>

---

1. Rescission에 관한 기본 rule
2. Rescission 주장의 근거
   + analysis
3. Defenses★
   (+ analysis — parol evidence rule)
   + analysis — laches, unclean hands

TIP1 위 2번: 소송당사자가 주장하는 'remedy에 대한 근거(들)'를 title화
한다.

TIP2 Equitable remedy에 대한 근거 중 fraud(misrepresentation) 또는
mistake가 자주 출제되는데, 이들은 소송당사자간 arguable points
가 많은 close call로서 특정 사안에 대해 각 소송당사자가 주장/반
박할 수 있는 내용을 서술하는 것이 고득점 포인트다.

"갑 may argue that ……. 을 may argue that ……."

"It is a close call, but it is likely for the court to decide that ……."

⇒ Arguable point ①

갑(원고)은 을(피고)의 진술이 계약에 있어 material fact에 대한 내
용이라고 주장할 것이나, 이에 대해 을은 단순히 부수적인 fact에
대한 진술일 뿐이라고 반박할 것이다.

갑 **may argue** that the statement is **material,** [since the parking
lot was the key factor in determining the price]. 을 **may argue**
that the location is **collateral** to the purchase, and therefore
there is no misrepresentation of material fact. **The court is likely
to view** the parking lot material.

⇒ Arguable point ②

갑(원고)은 을이 해당 사안을 알면서도 알리지 않은 것은 misre-presentation에 해당한다고 주장할 것이다. 이에 을(피고)은 자신은 해당 사안에 대해 갑에게 어떠한 언급도 하지 않았으므로 misrepresentation은 발생하지 않았다고 주장할 것이다. 부작위에 의한 misrepresentation이 인정되는 바, 법원은 을의 misrepresentation을 인정할 것이다.

갑 **may argue** that 을 made a misrepresentation because he knew that parking lot was unavailable but he did not notice to 갑.

을 **may argue** that he did not mention any statement regarding the parking lot and therefore there is no misrepresentation. Failure to disclose could be a misrepresentation based on omission, and the court **is likely to recognize** the misrepresentation.

TIP3   별도의 질문이 없다 하더라도 remedy에 관한 문제에서 defenses에 대해 서술하는 것이 고득점 포인트다.

QUESTION 4: 백변 ANSWER

1. Likelihood of success of Insurco's complaint for [rescission] and Pop's defences

Rescission

Rescission is an equitable remedy. It is the court's order to make a contract invalid and make the parties left as a contract had never been made. Generally, it is available when a party has a valid defense to the formation, such as fraud, mistake, illegality, and unconscionability. The court has broad discretion in deciding the award of an equitable remedy. The court will consider the equities of the situation, considering the fairness of the remedy to both parties. Rescission is subject to equitable defenses, such as laches, acquiescence, unclean hands, and estoppel.

Grounds for rescission

Fraud

Rescission may be allowed based on fraud, which occurs when a party: (1) made a misrepresentation of material fact; (2) with the intent to make the other party rely on the misrepresentation; (3) the other party in fact relied on the misrepresentation; and (4) the other party suffered damages.

(1) Misrepresentation of material fact

In this case, Pop made a false statement that his cars were driven in Hometown, a rural community. Insurco may argue that the statement is material, since the location resulted in a lower rate. Pop may argue that the location is collateral to the purchase, and therefore there is no misrepresentation of material fact. Pop would fail. Thus, the first requirement is satisfied.

(2) With the intent

Insurco may argue that Pop knew the fact and had an intent to defraud him. Pop may argue that he did not know whether his daughter, Sally, drove the Voka in Industry City while attending college there. However, the possibility a father did not know whether his daughter drives the car in Hometown is very low. Thus, the second requirement is satisfied.

(3) Reliance

Insurco amended policy in relying on Pop's false statement. Thus, the third requirement is satisfied.

(4) Damages

Insurco would have received higher amount if Pop had not made the misrepresentation. Thus, the fourth requirement is satisfied.

Conclusion

In conclusion, it is a close call, but it is likely for the court to decide that Pop made misrepresentation. Rescission may be allowed based on fraud.

Mistake

Rescission may be allowed based on either mutual mistake or unilateral mistake.

(1) Mutual mistake

Mutual mistake occurs when: (1) both parties have a mistaken belief about material fact; and (2) Both parties did not assume the risk of the mistake.
In this case, both Insurco and Pop had a mistaken belief that Sally was driving the car only in Hometown. As mentioned above, the location is material fact in this case. Moreover, there is no fact indicating that both parties assumed the risk of the mistake. Thus, Insurco may seek rescission based on mutual mistake.

(2) Unilateral mistake

Unilateral mistake occurs when: (1) one party has a mistaken belief about material fact; (2) the mistaken party did not bear the risk of that mistake; and (3) the other party knew/had reason to know of that mistake.

Insurco may argue that only Insurco had a mistaken belief because Pop knew Sally uses the car in Industry City. Insurco did not bear the risk of the mistake. Thus, Insurco may seek rescission based on unilateral mistake.

Conclusion

In conclusion, it is a close call, but rescission may be allowed based on either mutual mistake or unilateral mistake.

Defenses

Rescission is an equitable remedy and equitable defenses are applicable.

Laches

Laches defense arises when a party delays in bringing an equitable action and the delay causes prejudice on the defendant. If the delay did not cause any harm to the defendant, laches defense is unavailable.

In this case, Pop may argue that Insurco recognized Pop's misrepresentation or mistake when the accident is occurred and Insurco delayed in bringing a complaint for rescission. However, Pop suffered no damages caused by the delay. Thus, laches defense is unavailable.

Unclean hands

The unclean hands defense arises when the party seeking equitable remedies is engaged in wrongdoing related to the contract.

In this case, there is no wrongdoing Insurco engaged in. Thus, unclean hands is unavailable.

Parol evidence rule

Under the parol evidence rule, the parties cannot provide extrinsic evidence of prior agreements that is inconsistent with the contract terms when there is a written contract which is finally expressed and is a complete integration. However, such evidence is allowed when it is to prove mistake, clerical errors, or fraud.

In this case, Pop may argue that the statement that his cars were driven in Hometown, a rural community, is inadmissible under the parol evidence rule, since the contract between Pop and Insurco is a written contract. However, Insurco uses the statement to prove fraud made by Pop and it is admissible under the exception rule. Thus, Pop's defense under the parol evidence rule is unavailable.

Conclusion

In conclusion, there are no defenses applicable in this case.

Conclusion

In conclusion, Insurco's complaint for rescission based on fraud would be successful, since there are no defenses applicable in this case.

2. Likelihood of success of Pop's complaint for [reformation] and Insurco's defences

Reformation

Reformation is the court's order to rewrite a contract reflecting the true agreement of the parties.

Grounds for reformation

Mistake

(1) Mutual mistake

Mutual mistake occurs when: (1) both parties have a mistaken belief about material fact; and (2) Both parties did not assume the risk of the mistake.

In this case, both Insurco and Pop intended to increase Pop's coverage to

$500,000. However, the coverage had been increased to $250,000, and they had a mistaken belief. The policy limit is a material fact in insurance contract. Thus, Pop may seek reformation based on mutual mistake.

(2) Unilateral mistake

Unilateral mistake occurs when: (1) one party has a mistaken belief about material fact; (2) the mistaken party did not bear the risk of that mistake; and (3) the other party knew/had reason to know of that mistake.

Insurco may argue that the mistake was a clerical error and it had no knowledge on it. However, Pop may argue that only Pop had a mistaken belief, since Insurco drafted the contract and should have known the mistake. Thus, Pop may seek reformation based on unilateral mistake.

Conclusion

In conclusion, it is a close call, but reformation may be allowed based on either mutual or unilateral mistake.

Defenses

Reformation is an equitable remedy and equitable defenses are applicable.

Laches

Laches defense arises when a party delays in bringing an equitable action and the delay causes prejudice on the defendant. If the delay did not cause any harm to the defendant, laches defense is unavailable.

In this case, Insurco may argue that Pop recognized Insurco's mistake, at least, when he caused the multi-vehicle collision, but Pop delayed in bringing a complaint for rescission and more than six months have been passed. However, there is no fact indicating that Insurco suffered damages caused by the delay. Thus, laches defense is inapplicable.

Unclean hands

The unclean hands defense arises when the party seeking equitable remedies is engaged in wrongdoing related to the contract.

In this case, Insurco may argue that Pop made misrepresentation in making the contract. As mentioned above, the court is likely to recognize the misrepresentation. Thus, unclean hands defense is available.

Parol evidence rule

See rule above.

In this case, Insurco may argue that Pop's statement asking Insurco to increase his coverage to $50,000 is inadmissible, since the contract between Pop and Insurco is written and is a complete integration. However, Pop may argue that he uses the statement to prove the clerical error made by Insurco and it is admissible under the exception rule. Thus, Insurco's defense under the parol evidence rule is unavailable.

Conclusion

In conclusion, unclean hands defense is applicable in this case.

Conclusion

In conclusion, Pop's complaint for reformation based on mistake would fail, since unclean hands defenses is applicable in this case.

*총 단어 수: 1,296 words

기출문제 03. 14July Trusts/C.P.

Question 5

Henry and Wynn married in 2000. During the first ten years of their marriage, Henry and Wynn lived in a non-community property state. Henry worked on writing a novel. Wynn worked as a history professor. Wynn kept all her earnings in a separate account.

Eventually, Henry gave up on the novel, and he and Wynn moved to California. Wynn then set up an irrevocable trust with the $100,000 she had saved from her earnings during the marriage. She named Sis as trustee and Henry as co-trustee. She directed that one-half the trust income was to be paid to her for life, and that the other one-half was to be paid to Charity, to be spent only for disaster relief, and that, at her death, all remaining assets were to go to Charity.

Wynn invested all assets in XYZ stock, which paid substantial dividends, but decreased in value by 10%. Charity spent all the income it received from the trust for administrative expenses, not disaster relief.

Later, Sis sold all the XYZ stock and invested the proceeds in a new house, in which she lived rent-free. The house increased in value by 20%.

Henry has sued Sis for breach of trust, and has sued Charity for return of the income it spent on administrative costs.

1. What is the likely result of Henry's suit against Sis? Discuss.
2. What is the likely result of Henry's suit against Charity? Discuss.

3. What rights, if any, does Henry have in the trust assets? Discuss. Answer according to California law.

QUESTION 5: SELECTED ANSWER A

1. Henry v. Sis

As discussed in #3, Henry does not currently have a personal interest in the trust assets. However, he is the co-trustee of the trust, and this may be sufficient to give him standing as trustee to bring an action against Sis for breach of her fiduciary duty as trustee.

Trust creation

To be valid, an express private trust must have a settlor, an ascertainable beneficiary, res, a valid purpose, and a trustee. However, the court will appoint a trustee if one is not provided for, or the elected trustee declines to serve. Here, Wynn is the settlor, and she has designated herself and Charity as lifetime beneficiaries, and Charity as the remainder beneficiary. Any natural person, entity or government can be a beneficiary of an express private trust. Both are ascertainable beneficiaries because they are either persons or entities expressly named in the trust instrument. The res can be any property or present interest. Here it is the $100,000 from Wynn's separate account. The trust appears to have two purposes: to provide lifetime income to Wynn; and to contribute to disaster relief via Charity. To be valid, a trust purpose must be able to be determined from the trust document, and must not be illegal. Neither of the purposes are illegal and are clear from the trust document. Wynn has designated Sis as trustee and Henry as co-trustee, and from the facts it does not appear that either declined to serve. They must be competent but there is no indication of incompetency in the facts.

Charitable trusts differ in that they must have a charitable purpose: something that contributes to societal good, such as abating hunger, education generally, religion, or the like. The beneficiaries of the trust must be indefinite, not a specific person. Here, because Wynn is a specific person, this could not be a charitable trust.

A valid express private trust was created.

Trustee powers

A trustee has the powers expressly granted in the trust document itself, and those implied in order to effect the purpose of the trust. Here, the trust instrument directed Sis to pay one-half of the income to Wynn, and the other half to Charity. This expressly gave her the power to make these distributions.

Trustee duties

A trustee has the duty of loyalty, to act for the benefit of the beneficiaries solely, and not in her own self-interest or that of third parties. This duty requires the trustee to be impartial as to multiple beneficiaries. Here, Sis has a duty to treat Wynn and Charity impartially. If this were a revocable trust, she would have a primary duty during Wynn's lifetime to Wynn as the settlor, but the trust is irrevocable.

As part of the duty of loyalty, a trustee has a duty not to self deal. Sis is living in the house owned by the trust, rent-free. Thus she is reaping personal benefit from her position as trustee. She has violated her duty of loyalty.

The trustee has a duty of care as well, which requires her to act as a prudent person would in handling their own affairs. This includes the duty to account regularly to the beneficiaries, and not commingle trust assets with her own.

As part of the duty of care, a trustee has a duty to invest the trust res as a reasonably prudent investor would. Under the traditional view, this limited the holdings of the trust to things such as blue chip stock, 1st trust deeds on real estate, government bonds and other conservative and safe investments. Each separate investment was considered separately in determining this. Modernly, the investments are looked at as a whole, and factors such as the need for income, tax consequences, and particular trust purposes are considered. Thus, the court will need to look at how Sis invested the trust res in light of whether the trust was intended more for lifetime income sources, or as a gift to Charity at Wynn's death, at how the income would affect taxes, at what was reasonable as an investment in light of what was available to invest, at what reasonable investors were doing at the time.

Wynn originally invested the trust assets in XYZ stock, which provided substantial dividend income but lost value overall. This would seem to indicate a preference for lifetime income over growth of the principal.

Henry will need to be able to show that a reasonably prudent investor would not have sold the XYZ stock and invested it in a house. The sale of the stock itself may have been prudent given the loss in value. However, a trustee also has a duty to diversify in order to reduce the risk of loss and enhance income/growth opportunity, as would a reasonable investor. While the duty to diversify may have called for Sis to sell some or all of the XYZ stock, that same duty would generally preclude sinking all of the proceeds into one property. The trust res is then subject to any decline in real estate in the market, and will not benefit from any gains in other potential investments. Sis has probably violated her duty of prudent investment, and has certainly violated her duty to diversify.

The duty to make the res productive requires that Sis put the assets to work for the benefit of the beneficiaries. When she lived in the house rent-free, she violated this duty. The rental income from the house is to be distributed to Wynn and Charity, not retained for her benefit.

Sis has a duty to effect the purpose of the trust, by ensuring that income is maximized, based on the express and apparent intent of the settlor. She has not done so by selling the income stock and buying a house that currently provides no income to the trust.

Because Henry is currently subject to these same duties as co-trustee, he is obligated to prevent the wrongdoing of the other trustee. Thus he has standing to bring an action against Sis for her violations of duty, as a trustee of the trust.

Remedies available

The remedies available against a trustee who has violated their duties includes removal, surcharge for lost income/profits, disgorgement of any benefit wrongfully taken by the trustee. This benefit does not run to Henry, who is acting solely for the trust beneficiaries' benefit.

Henry will seek an accounting for the rent that should have been paid by Sis while living in the house owned by the trust. These funds must be paid personally by Sis. Additionally, he will seek surcharge for the lost income from the XYZ stock or similar investment that would have maximized lifetime income. Sis will have to make up the shortfall in income from her own funds.

Finally, Henry will seek removal of Sis as trustee. The court may then allow Henry to act as sole trustee or may appoint someone else.

Given Sis's breach of duty, the apparent purpose of the trust, the court will allow all of these remedies.

2. Charitable trusts are enforced by the attorney general, rather than by private action. If Charity is a charitable trust, Henry will not have standing to bring an action.

Assuming Henry has standing as the co-trustee of Wynn's trust, he can seek a constructive trust by tracing the funds from the trust to Charity as used for admin purposes. This will mean that Charity's sole duty as trustee of the constructive trust is to use the funds as directed.

3. California is a community property (CP) state. All property acquired during marriage while domiciled in CA or another CP state is presumed to be CP. All property acquired prior to marriage, or after separation, is presumed to be separate property. Additionally, all property acquired at any time by gift, descent, devise or bequest is presumed to be CP.

All property acquired during marriage while domiciled in a non-CP state that would be CP if domiciled in CA, is presumed to be quasi-CP (QCP). At termination of the marriage, to determine the character of property, a court will look at the source of the funds used to acquire property, any applicable presumptions, and any actions by the spouses that may change the character of the assets. A mere change in form does not alter the character of the asset.

Source:
Here, the source of the funds for the house, which is the sole trust asset, can be traced back to the XYZ stock and further, back to Wynn's earnings as a history professor. Because all earnings by community labor are CP, these earnings would be CP if the spouses had been domiciled in CA at the time they were earned. Thus, by definition, they are QCP (defined supra). During marriage, QCP remains the SP of the owning spouse. At divorce or death of a spouse, the character as QCP affects the property determination.

Presumptions:
All assets acquired during marriage are presumed to be CP. However, as noted, the source of the house is earnings that are Wynn's SP until termination of the marriage. Spouses can also take title in ways that raise a presumption, such as a gift to the community, which arises on death of a spouse under Lucas. However, Wynn kept the funds in a separate account, and then created an irrevocable trust with the funds, so no alteration in the

title is shown in the facts.

Actions of the spouses

Spouses can by transmutation or other actions alter the character of their own SP. Henry may argue that the change from Wynn's separate account to a trust is such a transmutation. However, a transmutation, to be valid, must be in writing, signed by the adversely affected spouse and clearly express the intent to transmute. This is not evident here, so no transmutation has taken place.

Distribution of assets

At divorce, QCP is treated as CP, and this would entitle Henry to half of the QCP. Death also impacts the character, depending on which spouse dies. If the SP owner (Wynn) predeceases the non-owning spouse, the non-owning spouse may choose their forced share (take against the will) in order to get to QCP assets. However if the non-owning spouse dies first, they have no right to devise the QCP that belongs to the other spouse.

As a result, Henry has no immediate right in the trust assets. In the event of divorce or death of Wynn, he would acquire such rights as are discussed above.

QUESTION 5: SELECTED ANSWER B

1. What is the likely result of Henry's suit against Sis

A trustee owes fiduciary duties of loyalty and care to the beneficiaries of a trust. A trustee may bring suit against a co-trustee for breaching the fiduciary duties, and move to have the violating trustee removed from their position.

A. Duty of Care

Generally, a trustee owes a duty of care to the beneficiaries to act as a reasonably prudent person under similar circumstances. This includes the duty to prudently invest trust property in a manner that will create the greatest return for the benefit of the trust.

ⅰ. Prudent investment

A trustee has a duty to prudently invest trust funds so as to increase the benefits from investments for the trust beneficiaries. Here, Sis sold all of the XYZ stock in the trust and used the proceeds to pay for a house. Sis will argue that this is a prudent investment because XYZ stock had decreased in value by 10%, whereas the value of the house has appreciated 20%. This increased the value of the trust property. However, Henry will likely argue that to tie up all of the trust assets in one piece of property which potentially can fluctuate wildly in the real estate market is not a prudent investment. Instead he will argue that Sis should have diversified to different stock from other companies other than XYZ in order to keep a more stable and broad base for the trust property.

Based on these arguments, it is likely that Henry will prevail against Sis in arguing that exchanging all of the stock into one parcel of real property is not a prudent investment.

ii. Duty to diversify

A trustee also has a duty to diversify the stock held by the trust. Here, as discussed above, the trust initially only held XYZ stock. Henry will argue that Sis had a duty to diversify the stock to include stocks from other corporations, and that consolidating the trust assets into one piece of property which is less liquid and potentially subject to market fluctuations in price and value violated the duty to diversify.

A. Duty of loyalty

A trustee is a fiduciary and owes a duty of loyalty to the beneficiaries and the trustor of the trust. Therefore, Sis has a fiduciary duty of loyalty to act solely in the best interest for the trust.

i. Duty to avoid self-dealing

A trustee has a duty to avoid self-dealing with respect to trust assets. The trustee must obtain court approval before the sale of any property which benefits the trustee personally. Here, Sis sold all of the trust assets and used the proceeds from the sale to purchase a house in which she lives in rent-free. She is therefore using trust assets for her own personal benefit, which is impermissible absent court authorization. She has a duty to pay fair market rent to the trust for use of the property in order to avoid a claim of self-dealing.

Therefore Sis has arguably violated her duty to avoid self-dealing

ii. Fairness to all beneficiaries

A trustee also has a duty to act impartially and fairly towards both the income and the principal beneficiaries. The trustee cannot favor one beneficiary over another in terms of their investments or distributions. Here, whereas Wynn and Charity are both income beneficiaries of the trust currently, Charity is the only principal beneficiary after Wynn's death.

(a) "Income"

Income beneficiaries are entitled to cash dividends from stocks, and rents from property held by the trust. Initially XYZ stock issued substantial dividends which are considered income to the trust and distributed to the income beneficiaries. Therefore Wynn and Charity were sharing the substantial income beneficiary. However, as noted above, the stock declined in value and therefore was worth 10% less, therefore reducing the future value for the principal beneficiary.

However, upon changing the stocks for the house, the principal beneficiary would obtain a 20% increase in value of the property. However, Sis is not paying any rent for the property, and therefore Wynn is no longer getting an income from the trust as a result of this change. This change, coupled with the lack of rental payments by Sis, means that Henry will likely be successful in arguing that Sis has violated her duty to act fairly and impartially towards both income and principal beneficiaries.

D. Conclusion

Because of the aforementioned breaches in duty, it is likely that Henry will prevail against Sis in claiming a breach of trust. The trust would likely be entitled to a constructive trust for the unpaid rent that was due on the propety, and Henry may have Sis removed as trustee for breaching her duties of care and loyalty.

2. What is the likely result of Henry's suit against Charity for return of the income

A. Purpose of a charitable gift

A trust must have a valid purpose in order to be properly formed. Here, part of the trust's express purpose at the time of formation was for income from the trust to be delivered to Charity but only go towards disaster relief. Charitiable contributions and trusts are considered valid purposes and therefore the trust is permissible.

B. Violation of a condition by a beneficiary

However, a violation by a beneficiary of an express condition of the trust violates the trust purpose. The court will look at the totality of the circumstances to determine whether the language was intended to merely express a wish on the party of the trustor, or rather if it is an express condition for receipt and use of funds. Here, the trust had an express condition that the share of income given from the trust to Charity was only to be used for disaster relief. However, the beneficiary here instead used the funds for administrative expenses, not disaster relief. The Charity will likely argue that it was only a general wish because they would receive the full benefit of the property upon Wynn's death and therefore should be able to use and dispose of trust income in any manner that benefits the charity. However, Henry will likley argue that the express terms of the trust are explicit in requiring that the funds only be spent on disaster relief. Therefore the beneficiary has violated an express term of the trust.

C. Remedy for violation by a beneficiary

If a beneficiary violates an express term of a trust, the trustee can sue for return of the income used in violation of the trust terms. Therefore Henry would likely prevail in a suit against Charity for return of the income.

3. What rights does Henry have in the trust assets?

All property acquired during marriage in CA is presumed community property (CP). However, property acquired by (1) gift or inheritance; (2) expenditure of separate property funds, (3) the rents, profits, or income derived from separate property; or (4) acquired before the marriage are presumed to be separate property (SP) of the acquiring spouse.

A. Quasi-Community Property

If a married couple acquires property in a non-community property state that would have been community property had the couple been residents of a community property state, such items are considered "quasi-community property" (QCP) and are potentially subject to community property laws if the couple later moves to a community property state. During the marriage, the QCP is treated as SP of the acquiring spouse. However, upon divorce or death of the acquiring spouse, the QCP will be treated as CP and divided equally between the spouses. Upon the death of the non-acquiring spouse, the property will remain the SP of the acquiring spouse.

B. Wages earned during marriage

Wages, earnings, and pensions earned during marriage are considered CP, absent an agreement between the spouses agreeing otherwise. Here, Wynn earned a salary working as a history professor while living out of CA. Regardless of whether she kept the earnings in a separate account, in CA the earnings would be considered CP. The facts do not show that Wynn and Henry had any agreements changing the character of the property. Therefore upon moving to CA, Wynn's earnings are presumed to be QCP. However, as noted above, they retain their SP characterization until death or divorce.

C. The trust assets

Wynn and Henry are still married at the time that Wynn sets up the trust fund with $100,000 of her earnings. Even though these funds are earmarked as potential QCP, during the marriage they are still considered the SP of the spouse who earned them. Therefore at this time, Henry does not have any interest in the trust assets because of the ongoing marriage. Henry will not have any possible rights to the trust assets until death or divorce.

QUESTION 5: SUMMARY

#2번 문제

> 답안요령

---

1. Trust validity★
2. Express conditions에 대한 기본 rule
3. Wish v. Condition
   + analysis★
4. 결론(remedy)

TIP1   Trust에 관한 답안은 'trust validity'에 대한 내용으로 시작되어야 한다.

TIP2   Arguable point: Beneficiary는 trust상 문구가 단순히 settlor's wish에 불과하다고 주장할 것이나, 이에 대해 trustee는 express condition임을 주장하여 beneficiary에게 수익반환을 요구할 것이다.

TIP3   Settlor 사망 후 모든 trust property가 한 명의 beneficiary에게 지급되는 경우, 해당 beneficiary는 express condition이 아닌 settlor's wish임을 주장할 것이다.

#3번 문제

> 생각 route

---

1. Presumption: 혼인생활 중 취득한 자산은 CP이다.
2. Source tracing (commingled source): 돈의 흐름
3. Contribution/Improvement: 명의변경, 가치 증가 등
4. Special rules
5. Transmutation
6. Distribution (at divorce/at death)

QUESTION 5: 백변 ANSWER

Trust validity

A trust is fiduciary relationship where the settlor gives legal title the trustee as to certain property. The trustee is subject to fiduciary duties to certain beneficiaries, who have equitable rights in the property. A valid express trust requires: (1) a definitive beneficiary; (2) trust property; (3) a valid trust purpose; (4) an intent to create a trust; and (5) a settlor with capacity.

In this case, Wynn and Charity are beneficiaries and the house is trust property. There is no fact indicating invalid trust purpose and Wynn had an intent to create his trust with capacity. Thus, the trust is valid.

1. What is the likely result of Henry's suit against Sis?

Fiduciary duty

A trustee owes fiduciary duties to the beneficiaries of a trust. A beneficiary or a trustee (co-trustee) may bring a suit against a trustee who breaches the fiduciary duties, and may remove the trustee from his position.

In this case, Henry and Sis are co-trustee and Henry may bring a suit against Sis for her breach of fiduciary duty.

Duty to investigate and duty to diversify

Under the duty of care, a trustee must act as a reasonable prudent person when he deals with trust affairs. A trustee owes duty to investigate any investment and duty to diversify investments.

In this case, Sis sold all stock and invested the proceeds in a new house. It is unreasonable to exchange all of the stock into one property, a house. Thus, Sis violated duty to investigate any investment and duty to diversify investments.

Duty to avoid self-dealing

A trustee owes duty of loyalty to act in the best interest of beneficiaries. A trustee cannot engage in self-dealing. A trustee should not use the trust asset for his own benefits. Any trust beneficiary can cause a self-dealing purchase by a trustee to be set aside (rescind the contract) or obtain a damages award. In this case, Sis purchased the new house, in which she lived rent-free. Sis used the trust asset for his own benefits. Thus, Sis violated the duty to avoid self-dealing.

Duty to act fairly

A trustee should act fairly and impartially towards all beneficiaries. The trustee should not favor one beneficiary in investment or distribution. If a duty to act fairly is breached, a constructive trust is allowed for the interest of beneficiary. In this case, Wynn and Charity are beneficiaries of the trust and Sis should act fairly towards them. Sis sold all the XYZ stock and invested the proceeds in a new house. Since Sis lived rent-free, there is no rent, trust income. Thus, Wynn has no right from the trust anymore. In contrast, Charity is entitled to all trust assets after Wynn's death and the interest of Charity remains. Thus, Sis violated the duty to act fairly.

Conclusion

In conclusion, Sis violated fiduciary duties and Henry may be successful to bring a suit against Sis.

2. What is likely result of Henry's suit against Charity?

Express conditions

A settlor may make an express conditions for distribution of trust interest.
In this case, the settlor, Wynn expressly directed that the trust income to be paid to Charity, to be spent only for disaster relief.

Wish v. Condition

In determining whether the terms of a trust is merely showing settlor's wish or is an express condition of distribution, the court considers totality of the circumstances.

In this case, Charity may argue that the terms of the trust is merely a general wish of Wynn. At Wynn's death, Charity may receive all trust principal and income and she is entitled to use the funds as she wants according to the trust terms. However, trustee Henry may argue that the terms of the trust expressly limit the use of funds. In sum, the court likely determines that the terms of the trust is an express condition of distribution and Charity violated the condition.

Conclusion

In conclusion, Charity violated the condition and the trustee Henry can sue Charity for return of the income used in violation of the trust terms.

3. What rights, if any, does Henry have in the trust assets?

Community property law

California is a community property (CP) state. Under the community property law, all property acquired from the date of the marriage until separation is generally presumed to be CP. On the other hand, property that is acquired before marriage, after the separation, or by gift, bequest, or devise is presumed to be separate property (SP). Quasi-community property (QCP) a property obtained by the spouses during marriage while they lives in a non-community property state, but it would have been considered community property if obtained in California.

Presumption

A property acquired during the marriage is presumptively community property.

In this case, the new house is the trust asset. The house is bought through the proceeds of XYZ stock and the stock is traced back to the $100,000 which Wynn had saved from her earnings during the marriage. Even though it is saved in a separate account, it is presumed as community property in California. However, Henry and Wynn lived in a non-community property state. Thus, the trust asset is quasi-community property.

Distribution

Prior to the death of acquiring spouse or dissolution of marriage, the property is treated as separate property of the acquiring spouse. If owner (Wynn) predeceased non-owning spouse (Henry), the non-owning spouse chooses whether to take a share under the will or to take a share under the community property law. At divorce, QCP is treated as community property and Henry has half of the new house under the community property law.

Conclusion

In conclusion, Henry has no right in the trust assets until the divorce or death of Wynn.

*총 단어 수: 971 words

기출문제 04. 19July Prof. Resp.

QUESTION 4

Larry is an associate lawyer at the ABC Firm (ABC). Larry has been defending Jones Manufacturing, Inc. (Jones) in a suit brought by Smith Tools, Inc. (Smith) for failure to properly manufacture tools ordered by Smith. XYZ Firm (XYZ) represents Smith. Larry has prepared Jones' responses to Smith's discovery requests.

Peter is the partner supervising Larry at ABC in the <u>Smith v. Jones</u> case. Peter has instructed Larry to file a motion to compel discovery of documents that Smith claimed contains its trade secrets. Larry researched the matter and told Peter that he thought that the motion would be denied and may give rise to sanctions. Peter, who had more experience with trade secrets, told Larry to file the motion.

Larry also told Peter about a damaging document that Larry found in the Jones file that would be very helpful to Smith's case. Larry knows that the document has not been produced in discovery. The document falls into a class of papers that have been requested by Smith. Larry knows of no basis to refuse the production of the document. Peter told Larry to interpose hearsay, trade secrets, and overbreadth objections and not to produce the document.

Larry recently received an attractive job offer from XYZ.

1. May Larry ethically follow Peter's instructions to file the motion? Discuss.
2. What are Larry's obligations in relation to the damaging document? Discuss.

3. What ethical obligations must Larry respect with regard to XYZ's job offer? Discuss.

Answer according to California and ABA authorities.

QUESTION 4: SELECTED ANSWER A

An attorney owes his clients the duty of loyalty, confidentiality, competence, and financial responsibility. A lawyer also owes third parties, the public, and the court the duties of fairness, dignity, and candor.

I. FOLLOWING PETER'S INSTRUCTIONS TO FILE THE MOTION

FILING THE MOTION

The issue here is whether Larry, who is an associate lawyer at ABC, must follow the supervising partner Peter's instructions to file a motion to compel discovery of documents that Smith claims contains trade secrets. The second issue is whether there is a questionable issue of law as to whether it is proper to file the motion to compel.

A lawyer owes the duty to supervise attorneys and staff that work under the lawyer and ensure they do not commit any ethical violations. A lawyer who is being supervised still must follow the ethical rules despite being told otherwise from supervising attorneys. If there is an arguable question of law/duty regarding the ethical violation, then the lawyer may rely on supervising attorneys for advice and instruction. If there is no questionable issue of law or duty, the attorney must adhere to the ethical rules of the ABA and California, even if it goes against what the partner says. If the attorney violates the rules, both the associate lawyer and the partner will have committed ethical violations. Here, Peter has instructed Larry to file a motion to compel discovery of documents that Smith believes contains trade secrets. Larry believes that the motion would be denied and may give rise to sanctions. It appears that Larry is less experienced in trade secrets than Peter, who is a partner and has likely been a practicing attorney longer than Larry. Thus, there appears to be a questionable issue of law; therefore, Larry can rely on Peter's advice as a supervising attorney and file the motion to compel. If Larry does further research and discovers that there are no grounds to file the motion, and therefore no questionable issue of law, then Larry must not file the motion to compel despite Peter's instructions. If Larry does further research and learns that there are no grounds to file the motion to compel, he will be violating the duty of competence to Jones. The duty of competence requires an attorney to act with the legal knowledge and skill necessary to perform for the client. In California, the duty of competence is looked at under a reckless standard; a lawyer will not violate the rules for a single issue that breaches the duty of competence. Here, if Larry knows the motion to compel should not be filed, and files it anyway because of Peter's instructions, he is violating his duty of competence to Jones. He is also violating the duty of fairness to Smith, the opposing party, and the duty of candor and dignity to the court.

Because there likely is a questionable issue of law, Larry may rely on Peter as the supervising attorney and file the motion. However, if Larry further learns that the motion to compel discovery is unwarranted and may give rise to sanctions, then he cannot rely on Peter's instructions and must not file the motion; if he does, he will have committed an ethical violation.

RESEARCHING TRADE SECRETS

There is a possibility that Larry has violated the duty of competence for failing to familiarize himself with trade secret law adequate enough to represent Jones. The duty of loyalty requires an attorney to act with the legal skill and knowledge necessary to represent the client. If the area of law is unfamiliar to the attorney, they have a duty to familiarize themselves with the area of law in order to adequately represent the client. Though Larry is an associate, he still must familiarize himself with trade secret law in order to competently represent Jones, or must associate with a lawyer who has sufficient experience in trade secret law. Here, Peter appears to have adequate knowledge of trade secret law to assist Larry. However, Larry may need to speak with someone else at the firm or conduct further research to ensure that the trade secret law is properly followed in relation to filing the motion to compel. Under California rules, Larry likely has not violated the duty of competency since California follows a reckless standard and does not punish for a single isolated event of incompetency.

Additionally, there is a possibility that Larry will violate his duty of competency if he files the motion, knowing that sanctions are likely, and the court imposes trade secrets, thus hurting his client Jones. This may give rise to reckless behavior. As such, Larry could violate the duty of competency under both ABA and California rules for filing a motion he thinks will bring sanctions.

II. LARRY'S OBLIGATIONS IN RELATION TO DAMAGING DOCUMENTS: PRODUCING DAMAGING DOCUMENTS

Here, the issue is whether Larry will commit an ethical violation if he fails to produce the damaging document he has discovered.

A lawyer owes a duty of fairness, dignity, and candor to the court and opposing party. Simultaneously, a lawyer owes the duty of confidentiality and loyalty to their client. A lawyer has a duty to follow court orders, including discovery request, and to not assert frivolous litigation claims or defenses. Here, Larry has found a damaging document that has not been produced in discovery. The document is damaging to Larry's client, Jones. However, the document falls into a class of papers that have been requested by Smith. Larry has a duty to turn over the document to Smith because it has been requested by Smith. This does not violate the duty of loyalty to Jones because the duty of loyalty does not ask an attorney to withhold evidence from a proper discovery request. Additionally, while the duty of competency requires attorneys to fight zealously for their clients, it does not allow an attorney to assert false, misleading or frivolous defenses. Here, there does not seem to be a reason for Larry to claim hearsay, trade secrets, or any other defense to keep the document from being produced to Smith. Thus, Larry has a duty to turn over the document to Smith. If Larry were to assert these frivolous claims to try and avoid turning over the document, Larry will be violating his duties of candor, fairness and dignity to the court and Smith. Additionally, asserting a false claim is likely considered reckless, as it could lead to sanctions on Larry, Peter, ABC, and Jones. As such, Larry will likely be violating his duty of competence to Jones if he asserts a frivolous and false defense to try and protect the document. Therefore, Larry must turn over the document.

As explained above, if there is a questionable issue of law, an attorney may rely on a supervising partner to determine how to proceed. Here, Larry knows of no basis to refuse the production of the damaging document. Even though his supervising attorney, Peter, is ordering Larry to refuse to produce the document, Larry must go against Peter's wishes and produce the document in order to avoid committing an ethical violation.

DUTY REPORT VIOLATIONS OF OTHER LAWYERS

The issue here is whether Larry must report Peter's ethical violation to the bar. The ABA rules require that an attorney report any ethical violations of another attorney or judge to the bar. Here Peter has committed an ethical violation by refusing to produce the document and making up frivolous and meritless defenses to avoid producing the document. Therefore, Peter has breached his duties of fairness, candor, and dignity to the court and to Smith. Thus, Larry must report Peter's actions to the bar. California does not follow the same rule, so Larry will not need to report Peter's violations to the California bar. However California has a duty to self-report violations, malpractice claims, or other ethical violations/cases that may arise. Larry may need to self-report if he commits any ethical violations under California rules.

III. XYZ'S JOB OFFER

At issue here is whether Larry must disclose his job offer from XYZ to Jones in order to avoid committing any ethical violations.

CONFLICT OF INTEREST — DUTY OF LOYALTY

A lawyer owes their current clients the duty of loyalty. A conflict of interest may give rise to breaching the duty of loyalty. A conflict of interest exists when a lawyer represents two clients in the same suit as adverse parties or when there is a significant risk that the lawyer's personal life, duties to current clients, or duties to former clients may materially limit the attorney's ability to act in the best interests of his client. If there is a conflict of interest, an attorney may still represent the client if the attorney reasonably believes he can still represent the client without breaching any duties and acting in the client's best interests and the client is aware of the conflict and gives informed, written consent. The attorney cannot represent the adverse clients in the same case in a tribunal, and the representation cannot be prohibited by law. In California, the client's consent must be in writing.

Here, Larry is representing Jones in a suit against Smith. Larry works for ABC, who is representing Jones, and Smith is represented by the firm XYZ. Larry has received a job offer from the law firm XYZ, which is directly adverse to his client Jones in a current case. This creates a conflict of interest for Larry. Even if Larry decides not to take the job from XYZ, he still must disclose the job offer to Jones, as it gives rise to a conflict of interest. Here, a conflict of interest has occurred because there is a significant risk that Larry's personal life will impact his duty of loyalty to Jones. (Additionally, there is the potential that, should Larry accept the job with XYZ, it could impact his duty of confidentiality to Jones.) Larry may reasonably believe that he can still represent Jones competently and diligently without violating his duties of loyalty and confidentiality despite the job offer from XYZ. Even if he reasonably believes this to be the case, Larry must still disclose the conflict of interest to Jones. He must get Jones' informed, written consent before proceeding with the representation. Additionally, in California, the disclosure must be in writing and the client must confirm in writing that they are consenting to the representation. It is unlikely this conflict of interest would be prohibited by law. If Larry does not reasonably believe that he can continue representing Jones due to the job offer, even if he does not take the job offer, then he must cease representing Jones and allow another attorney at his firm to take over the case. He will likely need to be screened off from the case, and not share in a portion of fees earned from the Jones v Smith case. In California, an attorney must disclose, in writing, to his client any personal relationship the attorney may have with another party, witness or lawyer in the case. Here, Larry has created a personal relationship with XYZ because of the job offer. Because of this personal relationship, he must disclose, in writing, the relationship to Jones.

CONFLICT OF INTEREST – DUTIES TO FORMER CLIENTS

At issue here is what duties Larry will breach if he accepts the job offer from XYZ. If Larry leaves ABC and goes to XYZ, he will now be adverse to former client Jones and ABC. This gives rise to a conflict of interest. A lawyer owes the continuing duty of confidentiality to former clients. A lawyer's conflict may be imputed to the firm if it is not personal in interest. Here, if Larry took the job, Larry's conflict with Jones at his new firm XYZ would not be personal and would therefore be imputed to the firm since he worked significantly and substantially on the case Jones v. Smith. Larry has learned significant confidential information from Jones about the case. If Larry were to go to XYZ, then he must be screened off from the case, not share in any fees earned from the case, and XYZ must give notice to ABC. Under the ABA rules, Larry may be allowed to take the job if he is properly screened, shares no fees from the Jones v Smith case, and does not give any confidential information about Jones to XYZ or Smith; additionally, notice must be given to Jones. In California, if an attorney has worked on the same matter in a substantial way, the conflict cannot be cured from screening off the client. Therefore, in California, Larry would likely not be able to take the job because XYZ would have to stop representing Smith, since Larry's conflict would be imputed to the firm.

QUESTION 4: SELECTED ANSWER B

May Larry Ethically Follow Peter's instructions to file the motion

Associate attorney's duties with regard to following a supervising attorney's instructions

Under both the ABA Model Rules (MR) and the California Rules of Professional Conduct (RPC), an attorney that is working under the supervision of a partner or other attorney has a duty to abide by the instructions that the supervising attorney gives, while still maintaining her duty to maintain independent professional judgment and to avoid committing a clear ethical violation.

Here, it could be argued that, by filing this motion to compel, L is bringing a frivolous claim in violation of the MR and RPC.

Duty to avoid frivolous claims

Under both the MR and the RPC, an attorney must not bring a cause of action or claim that has no basis in law or fact, or where the attorney has no good faith argument for an extension of existing law or a change in existing law. Here, Peter (P) is instructing Larry (L) to file a motion to compel discovery documents that Smith (S) claimed contain trade secrets. It could be argued that if L files this motion after doing the research and believing that the motion will be denied, filing that motion would constitute a frivolous claim and would thus violate both the MR and the RPC.

However, on the other hand, L could argue that he only "thought" that the motion would be denied and "may give rise to sanctions", not that it absolutely would be denied. He could note that, because it wasn't absolutely clear that this would be denied, there is a basis in law for obtaining the discovery and that the claim is therefore not frivolous. He can further note that P is much more experienced with trade secrets, and he told L to file the motion. Note that the efficacy of following P's instructions in this instance is discussed in more detail below.

On balance, a court is likely to find that this is not a frivolous claim because there is some basis in law for making the request.

Duty with regard to following P's instructions

This balance between following the instructions of the supervising attorney and maintaining that independent professional judgment turns on whether the action sought by the supervising attorney is clearly an ethical violation or whether it is a reasonable question of law or fact. If the reasonable minds of attorneys would differ as to whether the action ordered by the supervising attorney would constitute a violation of an ethical duty, then the attorney must abide by the supervising attorney's instructions and will not be liable for an ethics violation. If no reasonable minds would differ as to the propriety of an action, or if it is clearly a request for a violation of an ethical rule or law, then the associate attorney must refuse to take the action.

Here, Larry (L) has been instructed to follow through with filing this motion to compel. As noted above, this may constitute a violation of the duty to avoid frivolous claims.

However, L has an argument that reasonable minds could differ as to whether this is a frivolous claim, as well as whether this request could lead to sanctions. Furthermore, he could note that, because reasonable minds could differ, in this instance, he was under a duty to follow his supervising attorney's instructions.

Conclusion

On balance, a court is likely to agree that this is an arguable question of law in which reasonable minds could differ, and L therefore did not violate any ethical duties by following P's instructions and filing the motion to compel.

Duty to report ethical violations

Under the MR, an attorney has a duty to report any ethical violations that they know another attorney has committed. The RPC does not have a corresponding duty to report ethical violations of others, but it does impose a duty on attorneys to self-report when they know that they have committed ethical violations.

Duty to report others under MR

Here, it could be argued that L violated MR's duty to report by not reporting P for ordering him to file this motion to compel, a possible frivolous claim. However, as discussed above, this is likely not a frivolous claim, and if it is, he did not know it with a certainty, so he is not under a duty to report.

Duty to self-report under RPC

Furthermore, under the RPC, it could be argued that L has a duty to self-report after filing the possibly frivolous claim. However, again, this is a close call, and likely not a frivolous claim, so L was not under a duty to report. As such, L has not violated his duty to report ethical violations under the MR or under CA.

Larry's obligations in relation to the damaging document

Duty of Confidentiality

Generally speaking, under both the MR and the CA, an attorney must not disclose any information relating to the representation of a client unless authorized by the express written consent (informed written consent in CA, informed consent confirmed in writing under the MR), or unless impliedly authorized in order to carry out the representation.

Here, L has discovered a document that contains information relating to the representation of Jones. However, this information has likely been legitimately requested in discovery, and one situation in which an attorney is impliedly authorized to disclose such information in order to carry out the representation is in response to a discovery request.

Therefore, L would not be violating his duty of confidentiality to Jones by turning this document over in disclosure.

Duty of Diligence

Under both the MR and CA RPC, an attorney owes a client a duty to provide reasonably diligent and prompt representation. Under the RPC, an attorney must be committed and dedicated to their client's cause. However, this duty does not require an attorney to press for every available advantage. And as discussed below, an attorney must not violate the duty of fairness in an effort to zealously advocate for their client.

Here, L may need to balance the need to protect his client's interests against disclosing this information. He must be dedicated to protecting his client's interests. However, this duty may give way to the duty of fairness to opposing counsel, as discussed more below.

Duty of Fairness

The duty of fairness requires that an attorney act with fairness to opposing counsel during the courts of litigation. This requires that an attorney not knowingly obstruct another party's access to evidence, nor alter, conceal, or destroy evidence, or counsel or instruct another to obstruct access to evidence, or conceal, alter, or destroy evidence in the course of litigation.

Here, L has discovered a damaging document in the Jones file. He knows that the document has not been produced in discovery, but he also knows that it falls into the class of papers that have been requested by Smith, and he knows of no basis for refusing to produce the document. It could therefore be argued that, by failing to disclose this document, and by "interposing hearsay, trade secrets, and overbreadth objections" in order to not produce the document, he is intentionally and knowingly obstructing Smith's access to evidence. Although L could argue that P told him to do this and that he should trust P's judgment on this issue, it should also be noted that L himself "knows of no basis to refuse the production of the document."

A court is therefore likely to find that L has violated his duty of fairness by obstructing Smith's access to the evidence.

Duties following a supervising attorney's instructions

See rule above.

Here, claiming hearsay, trade secrets, and overbreadth with regard to this document could be a frivolous claim. L can only avoid liability for violating an ethical duty if this is a question of law in which reasonable minds would differ. If they would not, then L has a duty to avoid committing the ethical violation.

Duty to avoid frivolous claims

See rule above.

Here, L clearly "knows of no basis to refuse the production of the document." When P instructed L to "interpose hearsay, trade secrets, and overbreadth," L likely should have executed some research to determine whether this would be an adequate basis for claiming that they should not be required to turn over the document. If not, then no reasonable minds could differ as to whether or not they had an obligation to do so.

Following P's instructions in this instance would constitute making a frivolous claim, and therefore violating both the MR and CA RPC.

For this reason, L must either turn over the document or refuse to offer those objections.

Duty of candor

Under both the CA RPC and MR, an attorney owes a duty of candor to the court, and must not knowingly make a false statement of law or fact to the court. If such a false statement is made and the attorney learns of it, an attorney must promptly correct such false statements.

Here, if L files these objections, or raises them in opposition of a motion to compel, then it is possible that he is violating his duty of candor to the court. This would be the case if the documents do not legitimately contain hearsay, trade secrets, or if the request for the document is not overbroad. In such a case, making those claims would be false statements of law and fact, and L will have violated his duty of candor to the court.

For this reason, L should exercise great caution in ensuring that he does not violate his duty of candor.

Duty to report

See MR and RPC rules above.

MR duty to report

Under the MR, L may have a duty to report P if L refuses to file those objections and P follows through with them, because they may constitute a violation of the duty of candor and the duty of fairness.

CA duty to self- report

Under the RPC, L will not be under a duty to report P if P files such objections, but L would be under a duty to self-report if he does so.

Larry's ethical obligations with regard to XYZ's job offer

Duty of loyalty

Under both the MR and the RPC, an attorney owes all clients, past and present, a duty of loyalty and independent professional judgment. When there is a substantial risk that the attorney's representation will be materially limited due to their own interests, or the interests of past or present clients, then a conflict of interest may exist that could hinder the attorney's ability to provide competent and diligent representation. If a conflict of interest exists, then the attorney may be in breach of their duty of loyalty.

Duties of loyalty and confidentiality of past clients

An attorney owes continuing duties of both loyalty and confidentiality to past clients, even after the representation of those clients has ceased. The duty of confidentiality to past clients means that an attorney may not reveal information relating to the representation of that client, regardless of the source, unless authorized by the express written consent of the client. The duty of loyalty to past clients means that the attorney may not participate in an action against that client, or use information relating to the representation of the client, unless under the MR, the client provides informed consent confirmed in writing, or under the CA RPC, the client provides informed written consent.

Here, L has been in the process of representing Jones in a suit between Jones and

Smith. L is now entertaining an offer to join XYZ, the firm that is currently representing Smith in the same suit against Jones. Regardless of whether L takes on the case or works on it personally, L is under an absolute duty not to use or disclose any information relating to his representation of Jones.

Conflict of Interest-When moving to new firms Past and Present Client Conflicts

Under both the MR and the RPC, where an attorney has worked on the same or substantially similar matter for one client, and then moves to a new firm that is working on the same or substantially similar matter for the adverse party of that representation, a conflict of interest exists. That conflict of interest is imputed onto the other attorneys in the firm, and the firm must not take on the case, regardless of who works on it, unless (1) the former client gives informed written consent (under CA) or informed consent confirmed in writing (under the MR), or (2) the new attorney is properly screened.

Informed Written Consent/Informed Consent Confirmed in Writing

Note while informed consent confirmed in writing only requires an attorney give full disclosure orally before the client provides written notice of consent, informed written consent requires that the disclosure of the conflict is in writing, and the client's consent is also in writing.

Screening procedure

An alternative for the firm exists where the new attorney is properly screened. This requires that the new attorney with the conflict does not work on the case in any way, does not have access to the case files nor discuss the case with any of the parties working on the case, and is not apportioned any fee for that case. Additionally, the firm must provide notice of the decision to screen and the screening procedures put in place to the former client, and must certify compliance with those screening procedures if requested by the former client.

Here, if L wants to take the job at XYZ, he should let them know that this is a likely consequence of taking the new work. The firm will either need to inform Jones of the new conflict or implement appropriate screening procedures. However, as discussed in more detail below, this will not work under the CA RPC.

California exception for personal and substantial work

Under the CA RPC, a new lawyer's conflict is imputed into the entire firm, and the entire firm may not take on or continue a case, even with appropriate screening procedures or informed written consent, if the new and conflicted attorney worked substantially and personally on the same matter for the other client.

Here, it could be argued that L worked personally and substantially on the

Jones v. Smith case. Although just an associate, "he has been defendant Jones" and prepared Jones's responses to Smith's discovery requests. He has consulted significantly with P, the partner, on issues involving sensitive materials.

It is therefore likely that L's conflict will be imputed to XYZ, and he should inform XYZ that this could cause problems with their representation. The best course of action would be to seek a delay in hiring until after the conclusion of the case.

Duty of confidentiality

See rule above. The duty of confidentiality applies to past clients as well as present ones.

Therefore, L will have a continuing duty to maintain confidentiality to Jones, even if he is able to take on the new work at XYZ.

기출문제 05. 19Feb Prof. Resp.

QUESTION 5

Attorney Anne shared a law practice with Kelly representing professional athletes. In the past Kelly represented professional athlete Player, but Kelly was disbarred several months ago. Kelly immediately resigned from the firm, and was re-hired by Anne as a litigation support clerk. Anne now represents Player.

Player is currently involved in a dispute with the professional team that employs him. Despite a valid and enforceable contract, Player refused to play because he wanted to re-negotiate his salary. The team obtained a preliminary injunction requiring Player to play under the terms of his current contract. Player sent Kelly an email asking for advice as to his next move.

Kelly referred Player to Anne who told Player to ignore the court order and to continue to refuse to play. To put pressure on the team to re-negotiate Player's contract, Anne also called the team owner, and implied that she could file a discrimination complaint against the team with a federal administrative agency that handles civil rights matters. Anne and Kelly agreed that there wasn't really a basis to file this complaint.

After the team refused to re-negotiate Player's contract, Anne filed a counterclaim drafted primarily by Kelly so as to "get the team owner's attention" for "tortious interference with contractual relations."

As part of the civil lawsuit, the team owner (Owner) was deposed. Before the deposition, Kelly drafted questions for Anne to ask Owner. During the deposition, Kelly sat next to Anne and passed her notes with further suggested questions for Owner.

What ethical violations, if any, has Anne committed? Discuss.

Answer according to California and ABA authorities.

QUESTION 5: SELECTED ANSWER A

The issue is whether Anne committed any ethical violations. Based on the facts, Anne has in fact committed several violations.

Hiring and Use of Kelly's Services

Under both the ABA and California rules, a lawyer may not assist another in the unauthorized practice of law. This rule extends to the hiring and employment of disbarred attorneys. Here, Anne engaged in several activities involving Kelly, who was disbarred several months ago. Thus, these actions must be examined to determine whether Anne violated any ethical obligations.

Hiring of Kelly.

A lawyer may employ a disbarred lawyer as a clerk or paralegal to assist in certain activities that do not involve the practice of law, However, the lawyer must take care to prevent the disbarred attorney from conducting activities that constitute the unauthorized practice of law. For example, a disbarred attorney can conduct research, draft documents reviewed and supervised by the lawyer, and conduct other administrative tasks such as communicating with the client concerning billing. The disbarred lawyer may not engage in counseling of the client, appear before any tribunal, or communicate with the client or adversaries concerning substantive matters that constitute the practice of law.

Here, Kelly previously shared a law practice with Anne but, after being disbarred, Kelly resigned from the firm (as required). Anne hired Kelly as a litigation support clerk. There is nothing inherently improper about Anne's hiring of Kelly. However, under the California rules, where a lawyer retains a disbarred attorney as an employee, the lawyer must notify the state bar of the employment, as well as the client. Here, there are no facts indicating that Anne notified the bar that Kelly was employed by Anne, or disclosed to Player that Anne had retained a disbarred attorney to perform clerical duties. To the contrary, Player appears to have believed that Kelly was still a lawyer because he emailed Kelly for advice regarding the preliminary injunction. Anne should not have permitted Kelly to communicate with Player directly about substantive legal advice, although it appears that Kelly properly referred Player to Anne to answer his question. Nevertheless, Anne should have made it clear to Player that Kelly was disbarred and that all substantive communications should be directed to Anne.

Therefore, although Anne's retention of Kelly did not itself constitute an ethical violation, Anne failed to notify the bar and the client of Kelly's involvement. This constituted an ethical violation under California law.

Filing of Counterclaim Drafted by Kelly

After the team refused to renegotiate Player's contract, Anne filed a counterclaim that was drafted primarily by Kelly. As a disbarred attorney, Kelly cannot engage in activities that constitute the unauthorized practice of law.

As stated above, a lawyer may allow a disbarred attorney to draft documents so long as the attorney properly reviews, supervises, and takes ownership of the activity. Here, it appears that Kelly primarily drafted the counterclaim, but it is not clear whether Anne provided appropriate supervision and review of Kelly's work. If Kelly was the sole drafter and Anne did not review or supervise her work, which is possible given that they were formerly partners and/or co-workers, then Anne will have committed an ethical violation by allowing Kelly to engage in the unauthorized practice of law. If, however, Anne closely reviewed, edited, and supervised Kelly's work, and had the ultimate authority over the filing of the counterclaim, she will not likely have committed any ethical violations by permitting Kelly to engage in the drafting.

Based on the facts, it appears that Anne may have also committed an ethical violation if Kelly was primarily responsible for the filing.

Kelly's presence at deposition

As part of the civil lawsuit between Player and the professional team that employs him, the team owner (Owner) was deposed. Kelly assisted Anne in preparing for the deposition by preparing draft questions for Anne to ask Owner during the deposition. Here, Kelly's assistance in drafting deposition questions may have violated the ABA and California rules depending on the level of supervision and management by Anne, similar to the drafting of the counterclaim. A lawyer may use a non-lawyer (including a disbarred lawyer) to draft documents and conduct research. However, the disbarred lawyer may not engage in activities that constitute the practice of law. Drafting deposition questions requires legal skill and judgment and would likely constitute the unauthorized practice of law unless Anne merely used Kelly's work for reference and supervised and edited her work. However, it is not clear from the facts the extent to which Anne played a part.

Kelly also attended the deposition, and sat next to Anne and passed her notes with further suggested questions for Owner. This likely constituted an ethical violation under the ABA and California rules because Kelly was participating in the deposition, even though she was not directly asking questions. Depositions are typically limited to counsel, the witness, and the court reporter; the parties also typically make their appearance on the record, and the opposing side would have understood Kelly to be second-chairing the deposition on the facts. Therefore, Kelly's appearance at – and passing of notes to Anne during – the deposition likely constituted an ethical violation. Even though she was not directly asking questions, Kelly's feeding of questions to Anne and serving as the second chair would likely be deemed to be the unauthorized practice of law.

In short, it is likely that Anne did not violate any ethical duties in using Kelly to prepare for the deposition, but her presence and assistance at the deposition likely constituted an ethical violation.

Filing of Counterclaim

A lawyer may not assert a legal claim for the purpose of harassing another party or gaining an unfair litigation advantage. Here, after the team refused to re-negotiate her client's contract, Anne filed a counterclaim with the purpose of "get[ting] the team owner's attention" for "tortious interference with contractual relations."

Accordingly, because the purpose of the claim was solely to get the team's attention, Anne likely committed a violation when she filed the counterclaim for tortious interference with contractual relations.

Advising Player to Ignore the Court Order

Here, after the team obtained a preliminary injunction requiring Player to play under the terms of his current contract, Anne told Player to ignore the court order and to continue to refuse to play. This likely constituted a violation of both the ABA and California rules.

A lawyer must not counsel a client to violate a court order. Although Anne could have counseled Player to push back on his contractual obligations if she had a good faith basis for doing so, here the court had imposed a preliminary injunction requiring Player to perform under the contract. Thus, Anne directly advised her client to violate the court order without any good faith basis for doing so.

In addition to breaching her duty to the tribunal, this likely constituted a breach of her duty of competence owed to Player because a reasonably prudent lawyer would not counsel their client to disregard a court order that is likely to subject them to contempt charges.

Accordingly, Anne likely committed an ethical violation when she advised

Player to ignore the court order.

Threatening to file a discrimination complaint

In order to put pressure on the team to re-negotiate Player's contract, Anne called Owner and implied that she could file a discrimination complaint against the team with a federal administrative agency that handles civil rights matters. Anne knew that there was not a legal basis to file the complaint but made the threat in order to put pressure on the team.

Under California rules, a lawyer may not threaten to report another person for disciplinary purposes in order to gain an advantage in a litigation. Where the lawyer has a good faith belief that a violation has occurred, the lawyer may advise the party that they might file a complaint. But the lawyer must not do so in order to gain a litigation advantage.

Here, Anne knew that there was no basis to file a discrimination complaint, yet made the complaint in order to put pressure on the team. This constituted a violation of the California rules because Anne lacked any good faith basis for making the complaint and did so solely in order to advance her client's position in the contractual negotiations.

QUESTION 5: SELECTED ANSWER B

Anne (A) has committed several ethical violations, as discussed below.

Disbarred Attorney/Resigning

A disbarred attorney must resign from their law firm and cannot associate with that firm as an attorney.

Here, A and K shared a law practice. Thereafter, K was disbarred and immediately resigned from the firm. Assuming that the firm name was changed to recognize that K was no longer associated with the firm then A did violate the ABA or CA RPC.

Employing Disbarred Attorney

The issue is whether it is permissible to hire a disbarred attorney to work in one's law firm. In CA, a disbarred attorney can be hired to work as a litigation support clerk or in a similar support. The disbarred attorney can only work in this limited capacity; moreover, the CA State Bar must be notified if an attorney seeks to hire a disbarred attorney.
Additionally, the disbarred attorney is prohibited from interacting with clients in a manner that would reasonably lead the client to believe the disbarred attorney was an attorney. Therefore, their client contact must be minimal.

Here, A hired K to work as a litigation support clerk. A did not notify the CA bar that she had hired K, who was a disbarred attorney. A was required to notify the CA State Bar, but failed to do so. Therefore, she violated her duties under the Cal RPC.

Also, the facts indicate that K's former clients may have still been contacting her for legal advice. As a disbarred attorney, K is prohibited from providing legal advice and can only interact with clients in an administrative capacity. Because K referred Player to A after he emailed her, this conduct would likely not create separate grounds for an ethical violation.

Telling Client to Ignore Court Order

A lawyer has a duty to the court and the profession to act with integrity, in good-faith, and ethically. Failure to do is a violation of both the CA and ABA RPC.

Here, A told Player that he should ignore the court order that required him to play under the terms of his current contract. This advice by A was in direct contravention to a legitimate court order. There are no facts – such as a stay of the court's order – that indicate that Player was bound by the court order and obligated to comply with. The fact that he disagreed with what it required, or that A may have believed that his noncompliance would create leverage in the negotiation of his contract are not sufficient bases for not complying with a lawful court order. Moreover, a litigant is liable to be held in contempt for failing to comply with a preliminary injunction. Therefore, A's legal advice to Player was to ignore a court order, the consequences of which could result in her client being ordered to jail or to pay a fine until he begins to comply with the order. Consequently, A did not act with integrity because she told her client to ignore the court's order without a legitimate basis for doing so.

This conduct by A violated both the ABA and CA RPC.

A lawyer also has a duty of competence. A lawyer must act with the knowledge and skill reasonably necessary to provide competent and diligent legal services. Under the ABA, the standard for a breach of this duty is reasonableness. In CA, a lawyer breaches their duty of competence if they act intentionally, recklessly, or with gross negligence.

Based on the above facts, A acted intentionally when she told Player not to comply with the order. Because failure to comply with a lawful order of a preliminary injunction has the consequences of contempt, it seems grossly negligent by A to give her client legal advice that would result in him violating the law.

As a result, A breached her duty of competence under both the ABA and CA RPC.

Calling and Threatening Team Owner

A lawyer cannot have contact with an opposing party that the lawyer knows is represented by counsel, unless opposing counsel consents.

Here, A called Team Owner and spoke with him without his lawyer present. A likely knew that Team Owner had retained counsel since he was engaged in a contract dispute with Player. There are also no facts that show that Team Owner's counsel consented to this call without him.

A also threatened Team Owner that she would file a civil rights complaint against him. The purpose of this threat was to create leverage in her dispute with Team Owner, as A and K "agreed there wasn't really any basis for the complaint." A lawyer must not threaten to bring an administrative complaint against a lawyer or non-lawyer absent a good-faith basis for filing the complaint. It is unethical to threaten or pursue such a complaint purely for the purposes of harassing the subject of the complaint.

As a result, A violated her ethical duties under both ABA and CA RPC by talking with an opposing party who has counsel and also by threatening someone with filing an administrative complaint against solely as a means of negotiating.

Duty of Good-faith/Candor re Counter Claim

A lawyer must have a reasonable, good-faith basis for pursing a legal claim. In other words, they must have a reasonable belief in the merits of the claim and they must be pursuing the litigation for a legitimate basis (i.e., remedying a legal right and not to harass)

Here, A filed a counter claim against Team Owner. Presumably, this counter claim was filed as part of strategy by A and K to be in a better position to negotiate Player's contract dispute. Generally, such a counter claim would be permissible and not constitute an ethics violation. However, it is not clear that A believed the claims asserted had merit. The fact that the court ruled in the PI in Team Owner's favor weighs against a finding that this counter claim had merit. Moreover, if the only purpose for bringing the claim was to "get the team owner's attention", then it seems likely that A's motivation was not to necessarily vindicate Player's contract rights, but to impermissibly harass and create leverage in negotiating a better contract for Player. In sum, it is not clear that A had a good faith basis in prosecuting this action.

Therefore, A may have committed an ethical violation if she filed this counter claim with a good faith based as to the merits of the case. If it was done purely to harass, then A committed an ethical violation under both the ABA and CA RPC.

Duty to Supervise

A lawyer may delegate tasks to their nonlawyer employees. However, the lawyer must closely supervise the nonlawyer's work and the lawyer remains ultimately responsible for the work product.

- Drafting Complaint

Here, K was primarily responsible for drafting the complaint. For the reasons discussed above, the filing of this counter claim could be the basis for a violation of the ABA and CA RPC. If so, then A clearly failed to supervise K. If she had done so, they would have thoroughly discussed the theory of the counter claim and whether the facts support that theory. A should not have filed the counter claim if this was not satisfied. Moreover, because an attorney is ultimately responsible for the work delegated to a nonlawyer, A can argue as a defense that K was "primarily responsible."'

Therefore, A may have breached her duty to supervise her nonlawyer employee.

- Drafting deposition questions

Here, A's nonlawyer employee K drafted questions for A to ask during the depositions. The facts do not indicate how closely, or whether at all, A supervised K in this process. It is likely that A provided limited oversight over K in this process since she probably reasoned that this was something that K had experience doing and could be trusted. It is not impermissible for the nonlawyer to provide a draft of deposition questions to the attorney. A likely exercised supervision by using her discretion as to which questions drafted by K she chose to ask. However, if A did not do this and simply followed K's deposition outline without exercising her own independent judgment and, as a result, she asked impermissible questions, there could be a basis for finding that A breached her duty to supervise. Moreover, although K is a disbarred attorney, this type of conduct is not impermissible for a disbarred attorney. A litigation support clerk, under the supervision of an attorney, can draft deposition questions to help the attorney prepare for a deposition.

Therefore, it was likely permissible for A to allow her non-lawyer employee to draft the deposition questions.

K's participation in the Depo

A lawyer is liable for ethical violations of their employees. Moreover, as discussed above, a disbarred attorney is limited in the type of employment that they may engage in as it relates to working for a law firm.

Here, A and K jointly participated in the deposition of Team Owner. K is carrying on in the capacity as a licensed attorney would during a deposition –

actively participating and thinking of additional questions to ask the deponent. This type of conduct would lead a reasonable person to believe that K was an attorney. However, it is not clear that a nonlawyer cannot participate and assist during a deposition.

As a result, this conduct may have violated the CA RPC because the CA state bar was not notified that a disbarred attorney was being employed by A and A allowed her to work in a capacity greater than administrative.

기출문제 06. 18July Prof. Resp.

QUESTION 3

Betty and Sheila, who have been friends for a long time, were charged with armed robbery, allegedly committed in a convenience store. They decided to hire Betty's uncle, Lou, as their lawyer. Lou is an estate planning attorney and has never represented defendants in criminal cases before.

Both Betty and Sheila met with Lou together. In that meeting, both of them emphatically denied that they robbed anyone. Lou agreed to represent them in their criminal cases and gave them a retainer agreement, which states:

> **Scope of representation.** Lawyer agrees to represent Clients through any settlement or trial.
>
> **No conflicts of interest.** From time to time, Lawyer may represent someone whose interests may not align with that of Clients. Lawyer will make every effort to inform Clients of any potentially conflicting representations.
>
> **Fees and expenses.** Lawyer will advance the costs of prosecuting or defending a claim or action or otherwise protecting or promoting Clients' interests, but Clients are ultimately responsible for repaying Lawyer for all costs that Lawyer advances. If Clients are unsuccessful at trial, Clients will owe only costs advanced by Lawyer and zero fees. If Clients are successful either before or at trial, Lawyer will be paid $10,000 plus any costs incurred.

Betty and Sheila each signed the retainer agreement.

Two days later, Lou represented both defendants at the joint arraignment. He angered the court during the arraignment because of his unfamiliarity with criminal procedure, and the court relieved Lou and appointed new counsel for Betty and Sheila. Betty and Sheila agreed to new counsel.

Although Lou had not incurred any costs by that point, Lou asked Betty and Sheila to pay him a total of $2,000, divided up however they wanted, to reimburse him for his time spent on the case.

What, if any, ethical violations has Lou committed? Discuss.

Answer according to California and ABA authorities.

QUESTION 3: SELECTED ANSWER A

Lou (L) has committed a number of ethical violations that would subject him to discipline under both the CA and the ABA rules.

Duty of Loyalty

The first issue is L's breaches of the duty of loyalty. A lawyer has a duty to act in the best interests of their client, which means avoiding potential and actual conflicts of interest.

Potential Conflicts of Interest

L's representation raises a potential conflict of interest by representing two criminal co-defendants.

Representing two co-defendants raises the significant possibility that their interests will become adverse to each other in the future.

Under the ABA and CA rules, an attorney may represent two clients with a potential conflict of interest if he (1) reasonably believes that the representation of either client, the lawyer's own personal interests, or the interests of his family will not materially limit his duties to the other; (2) informs the client in understandable language of the conflict; and (3) obtains written consent. Under the CA rules, the belief that representation won't be materially limited doesn't have to be objectively reasonable (it can be subjectively reasonable based on what the attorney knew).

So under the ABA rules, an attorney must advise a client of any conflict of interest, and obtain consent, memorialized in writing (if the client consent was initially oral). CA requires written consent to all conflicts of interest. Additionally, CA requires the lawyer to advise on all potential and actual conflicts, and obtain additional consent if a conflict actualizes.

Here, L was representing two co-defendants in a criminal case. Even if both maintain innocence now, there's a strong possibility that one might want to testify against the other in exchange for favorable sentencing, or to mitigate their own culpability as compared to the co-defendant. A disciplinary board might view that as making representation unreasonable. L might point to the fact that Betty (B) and Sheila (S) have been friends for a long time, and both emphatically deny guilt, so they are less likely to become adverse. But that argument is weak, since L has a duty to convey to each client the best possible legal course of action, and it's very likely that B and S will have conflicting interests. Under the CA rule, L probably has a stronger argument that he subjectively believed it was possible, given his knowledge of B and S, and the defenses they were making.

More information about the strength of their relative cases might be useful here. But on the whole, under the ABA standard, it's probably a close call but representation is likely unreasonable, and under the CA rule, L can probably prevail under the subjective test.

But, L likely failed to adequately warn of conflicts. L's retainer contains general language about conflicts of interest. But he doesn't specifically warn B and S about the risk that his representation would be limited. Nor does he inform them that information between them won't be protected by attorney-client privilege if he represents both, so there's a real risk their statements to him would be used against them.

Because his retainer is wholly inadequate at advising B and S about the risk, the fact that they signed the retainer likely doesn't constitute consent. Therefore, L would likely be subject to discipline under both the ABA and CA rules for failing to get adequate consent to a potential conflict of interest.

Actual Conflicts of Interest

The next issue is that L failed to reveal an actual conflict of interest, because he has a personal conflict.

An actual conflict of interest is treated under the same standard as above. But under the CA rules an attorney just needs to advise a client of a personal conflict in writing. They don't need written consent.

Here, L is Betty's uncle, so they are close family. That raises an actual personal conflict of interest. L is much more likely to favor B's representation; he is likely to be uncomfortable with taking action that will harm B's position, and he likely faces family pressure to ensure that B gets the best possible outcome. He doesn't face similar pressure with S.

So that's an actual personal conflict of interest.

L failed to advise either client of that risk, let alone in writing, because the retainer is completely silent on that issue.

Therefore, L would also be subject to discipline under both ABA and CA authorities for failing to adequately disclose an actual, personal conflict of interest.

Duty of Confidentiality

L's representation also raises an issue with the duty of confidentiality.

A lawyer has an obligation to keep all of a client's non-public information private, and not to use that information against them. There are limited exceptions for: (1) when legally required to do so by a statute, ethical rule, or court order, when the client consents, when the representation is at issue (i.e. in a fee or malpractice dispute); when necessary to prevent death or serious bodily injury; or under the ABA to prevent your services from being used to commit a financial crime or fraud.

When an attorney represents co-clients, attorney client privilege and confidentiality is waived as between them. So B and S would be able to use the confidential information of the other against each other. An attorney may represent co-defendants, but must advise them of the risk from losing confidentiality, and obtain written consent.

Here, L made no mention of confidentiality. There's no indication, though, that L has yet disclosed any information, so this is probably more a violation of the duty of loyalty, than a direct violation of the duty of confidentiality: L failed to warn his clients about the risk, and adequately protect their confidentiality, and act in their best interests.

Therefore, L would likely be subject to discipline under the ABA and CA rules for failing to receive informed consent for this part of the arrangement as well.

Financial Duties

A lawyer also owes a client a number of financial duties. Here L would likely be subject to discipline for violations of these as well.

Improper Fee Agreement

The issue here is whether L entered into an improper fee arrangement, and made the appropriate disclosures, under the ABA and CA rules.

The ABA prohibits contingent fees in criminal and domestic cases. CA prohibits contingent fees in criminal cases, or in a domestic case where the contingent fee "promotes the dissolution of a savable marriage."

A contingent fee is a fee where payment depends on the outcome. Usually the lawyer is only paid upon the resolution of a favorable result.

Here, L entered into a fee agreement where he was only paid if they were successful at trial. L might argue that he wasn't recovering a percentage, just a flat fee for certain results. But since this is a criminal case, making the fee contingent on the outcome of the case seems like the only way to enter into such an arrangement. So the ABA and CA disciplinary boards would probably find this was a contingent fee.

Therefore, L entered into an impermissible contingent fee arrangement in a criminal case.

The next issue is whether L complied with the formal requirements for a fee arrangement. CA requires all fee agreements to be in writing, unless the client is a corporation, the fee is less than $1000, or the fee is for routine work for a regular client.

None of these exceptions apply, so the fee would have to be in writing signed by the client, with informed consent. Here, that information is contained in the retainer, and it was signed by B and S. But there is still a potential issue with the informed consent. It's unclear whether L went over the fee arrangement, and it's not clear the retainer is in sufficiently plain language.

So in all, the retainer could satisfy the writing requirement, but more information about the nature of the fee meeting would probably be necessary.

Next, both the ABA and CA require certain information in a contingent fee arrangement. The ABA requires the attorney's percentage of recovery; whether it's taken out before or after expenses; and who pays for which expenses. CA also requires the lawyer to advise the client how work not paid for under the contingency will be compensated.

Here, L arguably meets neither requirement. Specifically, he does not explain how work outside the contingency will be paid for. For example, the agreement is completely silent about how L will be compensated in the event that one of the clients pleads guilty. It's unclear whether that would be counted as success at trial, or whether L would recover nothing. That information would be highly relevant to the clients in determining the veracity of L's advice. Under the ABA, by analogy to a civil case, it's like L is only explaining what his percentage would be with the best and worst possible outcomes. Under the CA rules, he's failing to explain how work outside the contingency will be compensated.

Therefore, L is likely subject to discipline under both these rules as well.

Excessive Fee

The size of L's fee also raises an issue. Under the ABA rules a lawyer's fee must be reasonable in light of the experience of the lawyer, time and preparation required, nature of the case, and the result achieved. Under the CA rules the fee must not be unconscionable.

Here, a board might argue that L was unqualified for the case, and didn't plan on doing much work, $10000 is unreasonable. On the other hand L might argue that this is a complex robbery case, where he represents 2 defendants, and he is charging a flat fee, so $10,000 makes sense through trial. The outcome likely depends on more facts. Under the higher CA standard that's obviously a harder argument. But the board would likely look to the fees for similar work to see if this is unreasonable/unconscionable.

So this might be grounds for discipline depending on additional facts.

Request for Payment After Discharge

L also requested payment for $2000 for the work already performed. Generally, when a lawyer is discharged by a client they represent on contingency, they may recover through quantum meruit for the work already done. Here though, L appears to have added almost no value to B and S's case. Additionally, if a lawyer is discharged by the court they may not be able to recover. Finally, this was an unethical fee arrangement, so it's unlikely the court would enforce a portion of it to compensate L.

Therefore, although a lawyer might ordinarily be entitled to quantum meruit, L probably isn't entitled to the $2000, and demanding that payment is unreasonable.

Duty of Competence

Finally, L has violated his duty of competence. A lawyer has an obligation to competently represent his clients.

Under the ABA rules, a client must employ the time, preparation, skill, expertise, knowledge, and experience necessary to reasonably represent the client. If a client does not have those factors, he must learn the relevant material if possible without undue delay or associate with a competent attorney.

CA looks to a similar standard, but will only discipline a lawyer for repeated or reckless violations of the duty of competence.

Here, L was an estate lawyer, with no criminal experience. There's no indication he associated with a competent attorney. And it seems unlikely that he took time to prepare since the court was so frustrated with him they dismissed him as counsel. Under the ABA standard then, it's very likely that L failed to employ the requisite experience, skill, knowledge, time, and preparation in the case.

Therefore under the ABA rules, it's highly likely that L would be subject to discipline. Under the CA rules it's unclear whether this is L's first violation, so he might argue that his conduct is not repeated. But there's a strong argument he acted recklessly. An armed robbery prosecution has a potential to seriously and permanently harm the interests of the lawyer's client(s). Failing to act competently at any stage could waive issues on appeal, or cause a host of problems that lead to long-term incarceration, and a felony conviction. That risk would be apparent to any attorney undertaking a serious criminal case. Taking on such a case without apparently any preparation, or association when you have no prior background in that area is arguably disregarding a substantial and known risk.

Therefore, even under CA's standard, L probably not only violated the duty of competence, but would be subject to discipline for reckless conduct.

Duty of Decorum in the Court

A lawyer also owes duties to the court.

Among others, a lawyer has a duty to uphold decorum in the court, and behave professionally and appropriately at all times. They should act in a way that builds the confidence in the legal profession. Arriving at an arraignment with such serious lack of preparation that the court was forced to appoint alternative counsel, and discharge the lawyer arguably violates those duties. The lack of preparation is clearly disruptive to the court proceedings, and inconveniences the court and the parties, so it violates the duty to uphold decorum in the court. Such flagrant lack of preparation also undermines public confidence in the judicial system, by appearing to undermine the integrity of counsel. That's particularly important in a criminal prosecution, where there's a strong interest in ensuring adequate representation on both sides.

Therefore, L may be subject to discipline for violating (some of) his duties to the court as well.

In all, under both the ABA and CA rules, L is likely subject to discipline for violations of the duty of loyalty, the duty of confidentiality, financial duties, duty of competence, and duty of decorum in the court.

QUESTION 3: SELECTED ANSWER B

Duty of loyalty

A lawyer has a duty of loyalty to his clients. The duty of loyalty prohibits a lawyer from representing an individual with interests that are adverse to that of a current or former client. A lawyer may nevertheless represent parties with conflicting interests if he reasonably believes that he can provide adequate representation despite the conflict, if he can inform both clients of the conflict without breaching his duty of confidentiality, and if he obtains the consent of both clients to proceed. In California, the lawyer needs only a subjective belief that he can provide adequate representation. Additionally, California requires that the lawyer obtain written consent from the clients. Moreover, the California rules require a lawyer to get the consent of the clients when the potential is merely a potential conflict and again when the conflict ripens into an existing conflict.

Here, a potential conflict exists between the clients because they are co-defendants. During the course of the criminal trial, it is possible for the interests of Betty and Sheila to become adverse to each other. For example, Betty and Sheila might not agree on a defense to assert or they might not agree on plea deal. Because there is a potential conflict of interest, Lou is required to inform the clients of the conflict of interest and to get their written consent before proceeding. There is nothing in the facts to indicate that the clients consented to the potential conflict of interest. However, under the ABA rules, Lou has not breached his ethical duties because the conflict is merely a potential and not an existing conflict.

Therefore, it is likely that Lou breached his ethical duty in CA by not obtaining written consent from the clients. However, it does not appear that he has breached his duties under the ABA rules.

Personal conflicts of interest.

The duty of loyalty also requires that the lawyer disclose his clients of personal conflicts that he has. In California, personal conflicts simply require disclosure and not consent and personal conflicts are not imputed to other lawyers at the attorney's firm.

Here, Lou likely has a personal conflict of interest because Lou is Betty's uncle. The fact that Lou is Betty's uncle indicates that he might tend to act more in Betty's best interest rather than acting in the best interest of Sheila. This is purely a personal conflict of interest. In California, Lou is simply required to disclose the conflict to Sheila. Under the ABA rules, however, Sheila is required to consent to the conflict and the consent must be memorialized in writing. The facts here do not indicate that there has been disclosure and do not indicate that Sheila has consented to the conflict.

Therefore, Lou has breached his ethical duty by not disclosing her personal relationship to Betty to Sheila.

Lou's retainer agreement

The facts here indicate that L will make every effort to inform clients of potentially conflicting representations. This disclaimer is not enough to satisfy the consent requirement for a conflict of interest and does not relieve Lou of any liability for not receiving consent for conflicts of interest. This disclaimer has no effect on Lou's duty of loyalty to Betty and Sheila.

Moreover, the agreement states that the lawyer will make every effort to inform clients of any potentially conflicting representations. According to the CA rules, this is not sufficient and Lou must obtain written consent from the clients for any potential conflicts of interest.

Duty of competence

A lawyer has a duty of competence which requires him to provide competent representation to his clients by using the appropriate skills, knowledge, and thoroughness. A lawyer who is not competent in a particular area may nevertheless take a case in that area if he can either 1) become competent before trial through research and familiarizing himself with the area of law or 2) associating with a lawyer who is competent in the area. Additionally, in an emergency, a lawyer may act in an area in which he is not competent, as long as he stops the representation when the emergency is over. In California, a lawyer breaches his duty of competence only if he intentionally, recklessly, or repeatedly acts without competence.

Here, Lou is an estate planning attorney who has never represented defendants in a criminal case before. Lou has not breached his duty of competence merely by taking the case because he can potentially become competent in the area or he can associate with an attorney who is competent in the area. The facts, however, do not indicate the Lou has done either of these things. Lou clearly has not familiarized himself with the area of law because the court was angered during the arraignment with Lou's unfamiliarity with criminal procedure. Additionally, there is nothing in the facts that indicates that Lou has associated with a competent attorney. Therefore, under the ABA rules, it is likely that Lou has breached his duty of competence.

Under the CA rules, a lawyer breaches his duty of competence only if he acts incompetently intentionally, recklessly, or repeatedly. In this instance, Lou has not repeatedly acted without competence because there is no indication that it was Lou's normal practice to accept representation for clients in areas in which he is not competent. There is a strong argument that Lou has intentionally or recklessly acted without competence. If Lou has not made any effort to familiarize himself with the area of law, then he has intentionally acted incompetently. However, if Lou truly made an effort to become competent but nevertheless was unable to become competent, it is unlikely that he acted intentionally or recklessly.

Therefore, Lou has clearly breached the ABA rules by acting incompetently. His actions preceding the arraignment would indicate whether or not he has breached his duty under the CA rules by intentionally or recklessly acting incompetently.

Fee agreement

Contingent fees

In a contingent case, the lawyer must give the client a written fee agreement that states 1) the lawyers % of the recovery, 2) expenses to be paid out of the recovery, 3) whether the lawyer's fee will be taken before or after expenses are taken out, 4) other expenses that the client will be required to pay. Additionally, under both the ABA and CA rules, contingent fee agreements are not permitted in criminal cases.

Here, Lou clearly has a contingent fee agreement because his payment is contingent on whether or not the clients are successful either before or after trial. Additionally, this is a criminal case because Betty and Sheila were charged with armed robbery. Therefore, it was not proper under either the ABA or the CA rules for Lou to enter into a contingency agreement with Betty and Sheila because of the criminal nature of their case. Moreover, even if it were proper for Lou to enter into a contingency agreement with his clients in this instance, the contingency agreement would not meet the requirements under the ABA and CA rules because the agreement states that Lou will be paid $10,000, which is not a percentage of the recovery.

<u>Non-contingent fees</u>

If this is not a contingent agreement but rather is a fee agreement, certain requirements must be met. The agreement must state how the lawyer's fee is calculated, what the duties of the clients and the lawyer are, and what expenses will be paid out of the fee. In California, the agreement is required to be in writing unless it is for 1) less than $1000, 2) a corporation, 3) regularly performed services for a regular client, 4) it is impracticable, or 5) there is an emergency.

Here, the fee agreement does not indicate how L's fee is calculated: it merely states what the fee is, $10,000, and when the fee is incurred: if the client is successful in their case. Although the fee agreement is in writing in this instance as it was contained in the retainer agreement, it does not meet all the requirements for a fee agreement because it does not provide enough details about how the fee is calculated and it does not provide information about the lawyer's and client's duties.

Therefore, Lou has breached his ethical duties because he has used a contingent agreement in a criminal case. Even if the agreement were not contingent, he has breached his ethical duties because he did not include enough information about how the fee is calculated to satisfy the CA and ABA rules.

Fee amount

<u>The $10,000 flat fee</u>

Under the ABA, the fees that a lawyer charges must be reasonable. Under the ABA, a lawyer's fees cannot be unconscionably high. Some factors used to determine whether a lawyer's fees are reasonable are the time he spends on the case, his expertise and experience, the difficulty and novelty of the matter, and the result obtained.

Here, it is difficult to determine whether Lou's fee of $10,000 is unconscionable or unreasonable. Given that the fee is obtained only if the client is successful at trial, it could be considered reasonable. However given that it is a flat fee instead of a percentage of the client's recovery indicates that it might not be reasonable or conscionable, depending on what the client actually recovers at trial. Additionally, the fee does not take into account how much work that Lou puts in the case. Under the agreement, it is possible for Lou to get the $10,000 fee if the case is dismissed early on in the proceeding before Lou has performed any work.

Given all these facts, it is likely that the $10,000 flat fee is not reasonable or conscionable under the CA and ABA rules.

The $2,000 charge

The $2,000 charge that Lou eventually charged to Betty and Sheila likely is not reasonable or conscionable since he had not yet incurred any costs. Additionally, the arraignment was only 2 days after Betty and Sheila came to Lou for help. This means that Lou is seeking to be paid $1,000 per day. This fee is definitely unreasonable and unconscionable, especially given that Lou apparently made no effort to learn criminal procedure or criminal law since the judge was angered during the arraignment due to Lou's unfamiliarity with criminal procedure.

Therefore, Lou violated his ethical duty by asking Betty and Sheila to pay him $2,000 for a mere 2 days of incompetent work.

Loans to clients

Under the ABA rules, a lawyer is prohibited from making loans to his client unless 1) the loan is an advance of litigation costs to an indigent client or 2) the loan is an advance of litigation fees in a contingent case. Under the CA rules, a lawyer is allowed to make a loan to his client for any reason so long as the client and the lawyer enter into a written loan agreement. Additionally, in CA, a lawyer is prohibited from promising to pay a client's debts in order to persuade the client to agree to have the lawyer represent them.

Here, Lou has promised to advance the costs of prosecuting or defending a claim or action or otherwise protecting or promoting the client's interest. The facts here do not indicate that either Betty or Sheila are indigent, so this agreement would not be permitted on this grounds. However, the fee arrangement here is appears to be a contingent fee basis since Lou will recover only if the clients are successful at trial. Therefore, the lawyer could appropriately advance the litigation costs in this instance under the ABA rules.

This agreement is likely valid under the CA rules because the clients have entered into a written loan agreement with Lou. The agreement is written because it is contained in the retained agreement, which was signed by both Betty and Sheila.

Therefore, Lou has not breached his ethical duties under the CA rules because he has entered into a written loan agreement with the clients. Additionally, he has not breached his duties under the ABA rules if this agreement can validly be classified as a contingent fee agreement.

Withdrawal

A lawyer is required to withdraw from a case when he is fired or when continuing representation would violate a law or ethical duty. Upon withdrawal, the lawyer must return all materials related to the representation to the clients. In CA, the lawyer is prohibited from keeping the materials in order to persuade the client to pay the lawyer any fees owed.

In this instance, Lou has been removed from the case by the judge. This is likely akin to being fired. If this act is not alone enough to constitute Lou being fired, it is likely that the clients agreeing to representation by new counsel is enough for Lou to be considered fired, thus requiring that he withdraw from the case. The fact that Lou's retainer agreement states that the Lawyer agrees to represent Clients through any settlement or trial does not affect his ability to withdraw from or to be fired in the case. Here, Lou contends that Betty and Sheila owe him $2000 to reimburse Lou for the time that he spent on the case. Under the CA rules, Lou would not be permitted to hold the materials of the clients hostage while he waits for them to pay this amount. Under both the ABA and CA rules, Lou is required to give the materials related to the representation back to the clients.

Therefore, it is not clear that Lou has breached an ethical duty yet. But it is possible for him to breach an ethical duty by not withdrawing or by not promptly returning the clients' materials.

QUESTION 3: 백변 ANSWER

1. Duty to avoid conflicts of interest

A lawyer owes a duty of loyalty to his clients to zealously advocate on their behalf. Thus, a lawyer is required to avoid any conflicts of interest that could materially affect their ability. That duty begins when an attorney-client relationship is formed or, at very least, at the execution of a retainer agreement. If a client reasonably believes he was being represented by the lawyer, an attorney-client relationship is formed.

In this case, Betty and Sheila signed the retainer agreement. Moreover, Betty and Sheila decided to hire Lou and they reasonably believed they were being represented by Lou. Thus, an attorney-client relationship is formed and Lou owes a duty of loyalty and duty to avoid conflicts of interest to Betty and Sheila.

(1) Conflicts of interest (between clients)

A lawyer owes duty to avoid all conflicts of interest with his client. Duty of loyalty is breached when a lawyer represents a client with interests adverse to the interest of the lawyer, other clients, or third party. Under the ABA rules, a lawyer should not represent a client when there is actual conflict. In California, a lawyer should not represent a client when there is actual conflict or potential conflict.

In this case, Lou is representing co-defendants, Betty and Sheila, and potential conflict exists. This is because both defendants may become adverse each other in the future trial process. Thus, there is breach of duty of loyalty in California, but no breach under the ABA rules.

Exceptions

ABA rules

Under the ABA rules, a lawyer can represent a client when: (1) he reasonably believes that he can provide competent and diligent representation to affected client; (2) affected client gives informed consent, confirmed in writing; and (3) the representation is not prohibited by law.

In this case, there is no breach of the duty of loyalty and the exception rule is not applicable.

California rules

In California, even though there is potential conflicts of interest, a lawyer can represent a client when: (1) affected client gives informed consent in writing; and (2) the representation is not prohibited by law.

In this case, the retainer agreement states that lawyer will make every effort to inform clients of any potentially conflicting representations. However, it does not state the potential conflicts of interest between Betty and Sheila specifically. Moreover, there is no fact indicating that Lou informed about it. Thus, exception rule is inapplicable and Lou breached the duty of loyalty.

Conclusion

In conclusion, Lou breached the duty of loyalty under the California rules. However, there is no breach under the ABA rules.

(2) Conflicts of interest (personal interests)

Duty of loyalty is breached when a lawyer represents a client with interests adverse to his own interests. Under the ABA rules, same exception rule above is applied. In California, a lawyer can represent the client with written disclosure and written consent is not required.

In this case, Lou is Betty's uncle. Lou has interest to act in Betty's best interest as Betty's uncle. The interest conflicts with the interest of Sheila's interest. However, Lou did not make both written disclosure and written consent to the defendants. Thus, Lou breaches the duty of loyalty under the both ABA rules and California rules.

Conclusion

In conclusion, Lou breaches the duty of loyalty under the both ABA rules and California rules.

2. Duty of confidentiality

Under the duty of confidentiality, a lawyer should not disclose any information relating to the representation. A lawyer may disclose confidential information when: (1) there is an express written consent by a client; (2) there is an implied authorization; (3) it is necessary to prevent death or serious bodily injury; (4) a lawyer reasonably believes that disclosure is necessary to avoid imminent bodily harm to a third party; or (5) the fact has become generally known to the world.

In this case, Betty and Sheila are co-defendants and the duty of confidentiality is waived between them when co-defendants are represented by a lawyer. However, an attorney must tell the defendants regarding the risk of losing confidentiality and get written consent. There is no fact indicating Lou got written consent from Betty and Sheila.

Conclusion

In conclusion, Lou breached the duty of confidentiality.

3. Duty of competence

A lawyer has a duty of competence, requiring a lawyer to act with the legal knowledge and skill necessary to represent the client. ABA uses reasonable lawyer standard, requiring a lawyer to act with the knowledge and skill reasonably necessary to provide competent and diligent legal services. In California, reckless standard is used, requiring a lawyer not to act intentionally, recklessly, or with gross negligence.

In this case, Lou is an estate planning attorney and he is representing Betty and Sheila in a criminal case. The fact that an estate planning attorney represents a criminal case does not mean the breach of duty of competence. However, there is no fact that indicating Lou tried to be competent in the criminal case. A reasonable lawyer may associate with competent lawyer or try to be competent in other ways. Thus, under the ABA rules, Lou breached the duty of competence. Under the California rules, Lou did not breach the duty of competence, since there is no fact indicating that he intentionally become unfamiliar with criminal procedure.

Conclusion

In conclusion, under the ABA rules, Lou breached the duty of competence, but no breach of the duty under the California rules.

4. Contingent fee agreement

Under the both ABA rules and California rules, contingent fees are prohibited in criminal cases.

In this case, Lou will be paid $10,000 plus any costs incurred if clients are successful. Thus, the agreement between Beety and Sheila, and Lou is a contingent fee agreement. However, the case is a criminal case and the agreement is improper under the both ABA rules and California rules.

Conclusion

In conclusion, the agreement is improper under the both ABA rules and California rules.

5. Duty of decorum to the tribunal

A lawyer has duty of decorum to the tribunal not to influence jurors or judges or disrupt proceedings.

In this case, Lou angered the court during the arraignment because of his unfamiliarity with criminal procedure. His lack of preparation disrupts the proceeding and he breached the duty of decorum to the tribunal.

Conclusion

In conclusion, Lou breached the duty of decorum to the tribunal.

6. $2,000

When a lawyer withdraws or is discharged, he is entitled to the amount for his work already done. Under the ABA rules, retainer fee should be reasonable. In California, retainer fee should not be illegal or unconscionable.

In this case, Lou asked Betty and Sheila to pay him a total of $2,000 to reimburse him for his time spent on the case. However, Lou represented both defendants only for two days and he is discharged by the defendants with the court order. Thus, asking both defendants $2,000 is unreasonable and unconscionable for Lou's work.

Conclusion

In conclusion, $2,000 is unreasonable and unconscionable.

*총 단어 수: 1,166 words

기출문제 07. 17July C.P.

QUESTION 1

Wanda, a successful accountant, and Hal, an art teacher, who are California residents, married in 2008. After their marriage, Wanda and Hal deposited their earnings into a joint bank account they opened at Main Street Bank from which Wanda managed the couple's finances. Each month, Wanda also deposited some of her earnings into an individual account she opened in her name at A1 Bank without telling Hal.

In 2010, Hal inherited $10,000 and a condo from an uncle. Hal used the $10,000 as a down payment on a $20,000 motorcycle, borrowing the $10,000 balance from Lender who relied on Hal's good credit. Hal took title to the motorcycle in his name alone. The loan was paid off from the joint bank account during the marriage.

At Wanda's insistence, Hal transferred title to the condo, worth $250,000, into joint tenancy with Wanda to avoid probate. The condo increased in value during the marriage.

On Hal's 40th birthday, Wanda took him to Dealer and bought him a used camper van for $20,000, paid out of their joint bank account, titled in Hal's name. Hal used the camper van for summer fishing trips with his friends.

In 2016, Wanda and Hal permanently separated, and Hal filed for dissolution. Just before the final hearing on the dissolution, Hal happened to discover Wanda's individual account, which contained $50,000.

What are Hal's and Wanda's rights and liabilities, if any, regarding:

1. The condo? Discuss.

2. The motorcycle? Discuss.

3. The camper van? Discuss.

4. The A1 Bank account? Discuss.

Answer according to California Law.

QUESTION 1: SELECTED ANSWER A

California is a community property state. Unless the parties have agreed otherwise in writing, all property acquired during the course of marriage is presumed to be community property (CP). Property acquired before marriage and after the marital economic community has ended is presumed to be separate property (SP). In addition, property acquired by gift, devise, or descent is presumed to be SP as well. To determine the characteristic of an asset, courts generally trace the property to the assets that were purchased.

At divorce, all CP is equally divided between the parties unless they have otherwise agreed in writing, orally stipulated to in open court, or an exception applies to the general rule of equal division of CP at divorce. A spouse's SP remains his or her SP at divorce. With these general principles in mind, each property will be assessed individually.

The Condo

At issue is whether the condo is completely part of Hal's (H) SP or whether the community estate has an interest in the condo. As stated above, property acquired by gift or devise, such as an inheritance, is presumed to be SP of the spouse receiving the gift/inheritance. Here, H's uncle left him the condo and Hal inherited it. Therefore, unless H and Wanda (W) expressly agreed in writing that it was to change from SP to CP, H owned it as SP alone. However, the facts indicate that H transferred the title to the condo to W into a joint tenancy with W to avoid probate. Therefore, at issue is whether this vested the community estate with an interest in the apartment.

In California, property that is held in joint form is presumed to be CP.

Therefore, when H transferred his interest in the Condo to W as joint tenants, the law will presume that he intended to gift the condo to the CP and for each to hold as joint tenants with right of survivorship. When property that is held in joint form is to be divided at divorce, two statutes apply. First, in order for the transferring spouse to have an interest of ownership it must establish that there was either a written agreement that he was to hold it as SP or that the deed itself contains language that the property is only to be SP. Here, no such written agreement exists. On the contrary, W and H agreed to transfer the condo to W and H as joint tenants. However, a spouse who "gifts" SP to CP is entitled to reimbursements for down payment, principal payments for the mortgage, and for improvements made to the property. Here, H essentially paid the price of the condo $250k when he transferred it from his SP to CP. Therefore, he will be entitled to receive a $250k return on the apartment's value if it is deemed to be CP. The remainder of the condo's apartment will be CP.

However, H can argue that the transaction should be set aside because it is presumptively obtained through undue influence and, therefore, void. In the course of dealing with one another, spouses owe the same duties as those who are in confidential relationships. This duty imposes upon them the highest duty of good faith and fair dealing when the spouses enter into transactions with each other during their marriage. If one spouse gained an unfair advantage over the other in a transaction, the court will presume that the transaction was obtained via undue influence and, thus, invalidate it. The spouse who obtained the advantage will have the burden to prove that the transaction was entered into by the other spouse freely and voluntarily with full knowledge of all the facts relevant to the transaction and the basic effect of the transaction.

Here, H will argue that W insisted that he transfer the property into both of their names as joint tenants to avoid probate. H will argue that because W was an accountant, he believed her word and relied on her professional experience to believe that the best move for the couple was indeed to hold it as joint tenants. Furthermore, he will argue that as an art teacher who knows nothing about estates and marital property, he relied on her word and did not know that holding as joint tenants will deprive him of full interest in the condo if they were to divorce. W has the burden here. She will have to show that she explained everything to H and that she indeed told him of the basic effect of the transaction. However, this does not appear to be the case. It appears that all W did was insist that H transfer it to avoid probate, but did not inform him of any other consequences that such a transfer may have. Therefore, H has a good argument to void the transfer to W as joint tenants for the condo because W gained an unfair advantage over him.

If H is successful in arguing that the presumption that property held in joint form is CP, W may argue that the transfer constituted a valid transmutation. A transmutation is an agreement by the parties that changes the form of ownership from CP to SP, or SP to CP, or one's SP to the other's SP. However, to be valid, there must be a written agreement signed by the party whose interest is adversely affected and expressly state that a change of ownership is to occur. Here, this is not the case.

The Camper Van

At issue is whether the camper van is H's SP due to a gift from W or it remains as CP. During their marriage, the parties can enter into agreement to change the character of any particular property by transmutation. As stated above, transmutation is when the parties change CP to SP, or SP to CP, or one's SP to the other's SP. However, for a transmutation to be valid, it must be in writing, signed by the party whose interest is adversely affected and expressly states that a change in ownership is to take place. The general exceptions to writing requirements do not apply here. The only exception is when a spouse gives a gift of a tangible item of personal property to the other spouse. However, this personal gift exception only applies to gifts of low value and does not apply to those with substantial value.

Here, the wife purchased a camper van for $20,000 on H's 40th birthday using money paid from their joint bank account, titled in H's name. Title alone does not establish the characteristic of property for community law purposes. Rather what is more important is the funds that were used to acquire the property. Here, the funds were used from a joint bank account. The joint bank account is indeed community property because both of them were depositing money into it from the income they earned from their respective jobs. Therefore, the camper van purchased with CP is presumed to be CP unless there was a valid transmutation or other exception. Here, there was no valid transmutation. When W gifted the camper van to H, it was not accompanied by any written agreement, signed by W, that stated that H was to own the property as his SP and that W was gifting it to him outright. The issue then is whether the personal gift exception applies here. It does not. Generally, the personal gift exception applies to gifts of personal property with low value (such as a piece of jewelry that was inherited by a spouse). A $20,000 camper purchased with CP will not be presumed to be a personal gift from one spouse to the other for community property law purposes. The subjective intent of the spouses does not matter.

In conclusion, the camper van is CP subject to be divided 50/50 between H and W because it was acquired with CP property and no exception applies to change its characterization.

The Motorcycle

To determine whether property is CP or SP, the courts will trace the funds used to acquire to purchase the property. Here, H used an initial down payment of $10,000 to purchase the motorcycle. This $10,000 was his SP because he had inherited it from his uncle and, as stated above, gifts acquired via inheritance are presumed to be SP. However, H then paid off the remainder of the 10k from a loan borrowed from a lender. Thus, the issue is whether then $10,000 credit to purchase the motorcycle was CP or SP. Each spouse has an equal right of management over CP and, therefore, has the right to individually enter into agreements to purchase property on credit without the approval of the other. Determining whether a property purchased with a credit from a lender hinges on the primary intent of the lender and where he was looking for assurances before giving out the credit. For example, if the purchasing spouse used his own SP for collateral for the credit purchase, then it would be presumed to be SP because the lender's primary purpose for giving the loan was due to the collateral. However, where the lender relies on the purchasing spouse's good credit, the property purchased with that credit is presumed to be SP. This is because one's good credit or reputation as having good credit is community property.

Therefore, because the lender relied on H's good credit in giving out the $10,000 loan for the purchase of the motorcycle, the $10,000 is presumed to be CP. As a result, H owns a 50% SP interest in the motorcycle because he used $10k to purchase the property (50% of the purchase price) and shares the other half of the value of the motorcycle as CP with W. To conclude, H owns 50% of the motorcycle as SP and both H and W own the other half of the motorcycle as CP.

Additionally, even if the court determines that the lender's primary intent was based on H's SP and, therefore, the motorcycle was not presumed to be SP, the community estate will still have a 50% interest due to the principal debt reduction method. Where a spouse has acquired property before the marriage or acquired property through inheritance and then CP funds are used to pay for the principal of the property, the community estate obtains a pro rata interest in the property based off of the principal debt reduction due to funds paid from the CP. Here, the remaining $10k of the motorcycle's balance was paid off with the joint bank account during the marriage, which is indeed CP. Therefore, the community estate would be entitled to a principal debt reduction of 50%, meaning it would have an interest of 50% of the total value of the motorcycle.

The A1 Bank Account

As stated above, all property acquired during the course of marriage is presumed to be CP, regardless of who holds title to the property. Here, W owned an individual bank account at A1 Bank without telling Hank and deposited some of her earnings into it. Earnings by each spouse are deemed to be community property when earned during the course of the marriage. It does not matter where the spouse transfers the earnings or what type of account she transfers it into. The fact remains that the funds that she deposited in the A1 Bank were CP and she was not entitled from hiding CP or depriving H of his rights to the CP. The fact that she held the bank account solely in her name is not determinative here. Where the A1 Bank account would matter is if third party creditors of H's debts were seeking payment from him, they would not be able to attack this bank account because W expressly held the Bank account in her name, H did not have any rights of withdrawal and there was no commingling. However, at divorce, the bank account is subject to equal division as it was funded by W's earnings. Thus, H and W own 50% interest each in the bank account.

At issue is whether H may argue for an exception to the equal division of assets to apply here because W misappropriated CP. Although the general rule is that CP is to be divided 50-50 on divorce, a spouse who misappropriated community funds may not be entitled to receive an equal share due to her wrongful acts. H will argue that W misappropriated community funds here because she secretly opened up a bank account without informing H and deposited only her earnings in there. H will argue that because each spouse's earnings are CP he was entitled to those funds during the course of their marriage as it was supposed to be part of the community estate rather than W's private funds. Due to this misappropriation, H will argue that W should be forced to forfeit her interest in the A1 Bank and that he be entitled to take the 50k in full. Ultimately, this is a decision for the judge to make when he is ordering the divorce decree.

Additionally, H may argue that W again breached her duty of good faith and fair dealing by hiding the funds from him. He will argue that W had assumed control over the couple's finances and used that power to obtain an unfair advantage over H by hiding funds from him. He will argue that the agreement to allow her to control the couple's finances imposed a duty on W to use the duty of the highest good faith and fair dealing when she managed the finances and that she breached it by failing to disclose all the funds to H. W will have to overcome the presumption of undue influence by showing that H knew of all the facts constituting the transaction. However, because H did not have any idea about the secret bank account it will be impossible for W to overcome this burden.

Therefore, H has a strong argument for having the court strip W's interest in the A1 Bank account funds and reward the full 50k to H for breaching her fiduciary duties as a spouse and for misappropriation of community funds. However, it is important to note that H's and W's marital economic community ended in 2016. The marital economic community ends when there is a permanent separation by the parties and an intent by one of the spouses to not resolve the marriage. The filing for a marriage dissolution is determinative evidence of such intent. Therefore, the marital economic community ended in 2016. From that time, any money that W deposited into the A1 Bank Account will be presumed to be her SP since the marital economic community has ended.

QUESTION 1: SELECTED ANSWER B

General Presumptions

California is a community property state (CP) all property acquired from the date of the marriage until separation is presumed to be CP – owned by the spouses equally 50/50. All wages earned from the time or labor of a spouse during marriage are CP. Property acquired before marriage or after separation is presumed to be Separate Property (SP) of the acquiring spouse. Property received by gift, bequest, or devise is also the separate property of the receiving spouse, as are the rents, issues and profits produced by SP. The character of the property may not be changed simply by changing the manner in which the property is held, the property will be traced to its source and characterized according to the source used to acquire the property. Upon divorce, spouses are entitled to in kind 50/50 distribution of all property.

Transmutation

One spouse may not gift themselves community property. In order to change the character of property from CP to SP or SP to CP, there must be an agreement in writing signed by the spouse whose interest is adversely affected explicitly stating that the spouse intends and understands that she is altering the character of the property. Oral agreements will not be a valid transmutation.

1. THE CONDO

The general presumption is that property acquired during the marriage is CP. Hal acquired the condo in 2010 which was during his marriage to Wanda. However, by law, property acquired through inheritance is the separate property of the inheriting spouse. Since Hal acquired this property from his uncle through inheritance, the condo was Hal's SP. The issue is that Hal, at

Wanda's insistence, titled the property in Joint tenancy with Wanda.

Title in Joint Form

A married couple who takes title in joint form when it is inconsistent with the nature of the funds used to acquire the property will be presumed to have intended the property as CP. Taking title in joint form with no indication that a spouse wanted to reserve a separate property interest creates the presumption of CP. Here, Hal and Wanda took title in joint form and Hal did not reserve any separate property interest, there also is no other writing that evidences an agreement between Hal and Wanda for Hal to keep a separate interest so the court will presume that because they took title in a joint form that they intended the property to be CP.

Transmutation by Deed

In order for spouses to change the character of property from SP to CP as in the case with the condo being Hal's SP and then later conveying to CP, there must be a valid transmutation. The issue is whether the deed from Hal to Hal and Wanda will be a valid transmutation of his interest. Typically, a deed satisfies the writing requirement for the transmutation if signed by the party adversely affected, in this case Hal. However, Hal may not have intended for interest in the property to be adversely affected. The facts indicate that he only agreed to put the condo in joint tenancy after Wanda's insistence that he do so in order to avoid probate. It is likely that Hal being an artist relied on Wanda's assertion because Wanda was a successful accountant who would have known the consequences of such decisions as titling property in a particular manner. The courts have been unclear in whether or not they consider a deed by one spouse to other spouses to be a valid transmutation. Assuming that that the deed from Hal to Wanda is a valid transmutation, then at most Hal would be allowed reimbursement for his SP that was used to acquire the condo by the community. The reimbursement will be allowed without interest or apportionment of increase in value to the items. A court would likely use the value of the property at the time it became CP which for the condo was $250,0000, Hal would be reimbursed for the $250k at divorce and the remaining value of the condo would be divided in kind 50/50 between Hal and Wanda.

Fiduciary Duties of Spouses

Spouses owe one another the highest duty of care and are fiduciaries to one another. If one spouse breaches her fiduciary duty to the other and takes advantage of that spouse by gaining an interest financially or in an asset, then the non-breaching spouse may be able to set aside the conveyance on those grounds. Here, Wanda was a successful accountant and Hal was an art teacher, there is a strong possibility that but for Wanda's insistence that Hal put the condo in joint form that he would not have done so. By insisting that the condo be in joint title, Wanda gained a financial interest in property that she would have otherwise had no rights to because it was received by Hal through inheritance. If Hal can show that Wanda breached her duty to him in convincing him to put the condo in joint form only to benefit herself, Hal may be able to have the conveyance set aside.

Equal Rt of Mgmt

Each spouse has an equal right to manage the assets of the community and keep the other spouse reasonably informed as to the financial situation. Here the facts indicate that Wanda managed the couple's finances and that she also kept a secret bank account without Hal's knowledge. By doing this she breached the duty to share management with Hal and used it to her advantage to try to hide $50k – Hal will also be able to use this to bolster his case that Wanda breached her fiduciary duty to him and should not be allowed to take an interest in the condo.

Conclusion as to the Condo: Hal will likely be entitled to reimbursement for his contribution of SP to CP – in this case the condo was valued at $250k at the time he conveyed to Joint Tenancy so he will have a right to reimbursement of the $250k and the remaining value will be CP. However if the court finds that the deed was not a valid transmutation from Hal's SP to CP then the condo would remain Hal's SP.

2. THE MOTORCYCLE

One spouse may not appropriate CP to themselves by simply taking title to the property in their name alone. When both SP and CP are used for the purchase of an asset the funds used to acquire the property will be traced to their source and the property will be characterized in accordance with funds used for acquisition.

Down Payment

Property that was initially SP will continue to be SP even if the SP is exchanged or sold and the form changes. Hal inherited $10k from his Uncle – inheritance is an area of SP. Hal then took his $10k of SP and used it for a down payment on a motorcycle that he took title to in his name alone. Had the motorcycle cost only $10k, there would be no issue here because the $10k used to purchase the motorcycle could be traced directly to the inheritance which was Hal's SP making the motorcycle then SP as well. The motorcycle cost $20k, though, so it must be determined where the other $10k came from and whether the additional $10k can be traced to other SP or to CP.

Credit – Intent of the Lender

The credit, good will and reputation of a spouse belong to the Community during the marriage, this also includes credit scores. A loan taken out during the marriage is a community debt unless it can be shown that the lender in determining whether to loan one spouse the money relied solely on the borrowing spouse's separate property for repayment. The fact that a lender "relied" on one spouse's good credit is not the determining factor because good credit of one spouse belongs to both spouses as community property. When Hal borrowed the additional $10k from the lender, the lender, relied on Hals good credit – Hal's good credit belongs to the community and so therefore, the loan for the motorcycle was a community debt. If there were other facts that indicated that the lender relied on Hal's separate property interest – such as the condo – for repayment then the debt could belong to Hal alone, but based on the facts present that the lender relied on credit of Hal the debt was community debt.

Repayment of Loan w Joint Acct $

Wages and earning of a spouse are community property if earned during the marriage. Here Wanda and Hal were putting their earnings into a joint checking acct which was used to pay off the motorcycle loan. Because CP was used to pay off half of the motorcycle loan, the community owns a 1/2 interest in the motorcycle.

Conclusion as to the motorcycle: Hal owns the motorcycle as 50% SP because half of the purchase price can be traced to his SP inheritance, the community owns the other 50% interest because community property was used to obtain the loan and pay off the loan.

3. CAMPER VAN

When one spouse uses CP to buy a gift for the other spouse and puts title into that spouse's name alone, it is presumed to be a gift. While one spouse may not appropriate CP, one spouse may make a gift of interest in CP to the other spouse as SP. In this case, Hal will argue that Wanda taking him out for his 40th birthday and buying the camper van was her gifting her interest in the CP to Hal as his SP. On the other side, Wanda will argue that she did not intend to make a gift to Hal as SP, but instead intended to retain a CP interest in the van and that there was no valid transmutation from CP to Hal SP.

Gift Exception to Transmutation

There is an exception to the requirement that all transmutation be in writing. The exception is for gifts given to one spouse that are for that spouse's personal use and that are not substantial in value. Here Hal may argue that the van would also fall into the gift exception even if there was no writing that evidenced Wanda's intent to may a gift. Hal did use the camper van for fishing and summer trips with his friends. There is no mention of Wanda participating in these trips which would indicate that the van was for her personal use. However the gift must also not be substantial in nature and the van cost $20k; whether or not this is of substantial value would be considered in light of Hal and Wanda's station in life – their assets etc. While this may be an arguable issue, courts have typically found that cars are not items that are personal enough in nature to fall within the exception.

Conclusion as to the Van: If a court finds that by purchasing the van and titling it in Hal's name alone that Wanda intended a gift of her CP to Hal SP, then the van will be considered Hal's SP at divorce. Otherwise by tracing the funds to the CP checking account the van will be deemed cp.

4. A1 BANK

Wages earned by either spouse's time, labor, or skill during the marriage belong to the community. Here Wanda took her earnings during the marriage which are CP and deposited them into a secret acct w/o Hal's knowledge or name. Regardless of the fact that Hal's name is not on the account, Wanda's wages still belong to the community and, therefore all of the money in the account ($50k) is CP. A court may continue to have jurisdiction over the proceedings and assets until they are all disbursed. Just because in this case Hal did not discover the $50k until right before the final hearing will not affect his rights – and if Wanda purposely hid the money or failed to inform the court of its existence then she may be denied interest in the money to the extent that justice and fairness require.

Conclusion: The $50k in the A1 acct is CP subject to in kind division upon divorce.

QUESTION 1: SUMMARY

생각 route

1. Presumption: 혼인생활 중 취득한 자산은 CP이다.
2. Source tracing (commingled source): 돈의 흐름
3. Contribution/Improvement: 명의변경, 가치 증가 등
4. Special rules
5. Transmutation
6. Distribution (at divorce/at death)

Bibliography

1. 국내서

곽윤직, 김재형, 민법총칙(제9판)(박영사, 2013)

김준호, 민법강의(제22판)(법문사, 2016)

김흥수, 한 철, 김원규, 상법강의(제4판)(세창출판사, 2016)

류병운, 미국계약법(제3판)(홍익대학교출판부, 2013)

백희영, 미국변호사법 Essay편(박영사, 2020)

서철원, 미국 계약법(법원사, 2015)

서철원, 미국 민사소송법(법원사, 2005)

서철원, 미국 불법행위법(법원사, 2005)

서철원, 미국 형법(법원사, 2005)

서철원, 미국 형사소송법(법원사, 2005)

성낙인, 헌법학(제19판)(법문사, 2019)

신호진, 형법요론(2017년판)(문형사, 2017)

이영종, 이재열, 황태정, 송인호, 이세주, 법학입문(제2판)(집현재, 2016)

이시윤, 新民事訴訟法(제11판)(박영사, 2017)

토이 예거 파인, 미국법제도 입문(제2판)(진원사, 2016)

홍정선, 행정법특강(제15판)(박영사, 2016)

2. 외국서

AmeriBar Bar Review. MBE Released Questions. AmeriBar Bar Review. 2008

Barbri. The Conviser Mini Review: New York—July 2015/February 2016. Barbri, Inc. 2015

Barbri. Outlines for Multistate—July 2015/February 2016. Barbri, Inc. 2015

Barbri. Outlines for MEE—July 2016/February 2017. Barbri, Inc. 2016

California Bar Tutors. 2020 California Bar Exam Total Preparation Book. QuestBarReview. 2019

Gordon Brown, Scott Myers. Administration of Wills, Trusts, and Estates; 4th Edition. Delmar Cengage Learning. 2008

J.Scott Harr, Kären M. Hess, Christine H. Orthmann, Jonathon Kingsbury. Constitutional Law and the Criminal Justice System; 7th Edition. Cengage Learning. 2017

Kaplan. MBE Practice Questions & Answers. Kaplan, Inc. 2014

Kaplan. MEE Bar Points. Kaplan, Inc. 2014

Kenneth W. Clarkson, Roger LeRoy Miller, Frank B. Cross. Business Law: Text and Cases; 13th Edition. Cengage Learning. 2015

Mary Basick, Tina Schindler. Essay Exam Writing for the California Bar Exam; 4th Edition. Wolters Kluwer. 2018

SmartBarPrep. Essay Prep Outline. SmartBarPrep. 2017

Steven Emanuel. Constitutional Law; 7th Edition. Wolters Kluwer. 2019

Steven L. Emanuel. Steve Emanuel's Bootcamp for the MBE: Contracts. Aspen Publishers. 2010

3. 판례

Ashcroft v. Iqbal, 129 S. Ct. 1937 (2009)

Bell Atlantic Corp. v. Twombly, 550 U.S. 544 (2007)

Byrne v. Boadle, Court of Exchequer England (1863)

Erie Railroad Co. v. Tompkins, 304 U.S. 64 (1938)

Euclid v. Ambler Realty Co., 272 U.S. 365, 47 S. Ct. 114 (1926)

Garratt v. Dailey, Wash. 279P.2d 1091 (1955)

Hess v. Pawloski, 274 U.S. 352 (1927)

International Shoe Co. v. Washington, 326 U.S. 310 (1945)

Kelo v. New London, 545 U.S. 469 (2005)

Kyllo v. United States, 533 U.S. 27 (2001)

Los Angeles v. Lyons, 461 U.S. 95, 103 S. Ct. 1660 (1983)

Lucas v. South Carolina Coastal Council, 505 U.S. 1003 (1992)

Mathis v. United States, 391 U.S. 1 (1968)

Miranda v. Arizona, 384 U.S. 436 (1966)

Palsgraf v. Long Island Railroad, 248 N.Y. 339 (1928)

Penn Central Transportation Co. v. New York City, 438 U.S. 104 (1978)

Taylor v. Standard Gas & Elec. Co., 306 U.S. 307 (1939)

Troxel v. Granville, 530 U.S. 57 (2000)

Walker v. Armco Steel Corp., 446 U.S. 740 (1980)

Index

저자약력

백 희 영

서울 출생
중국KISQ고등학교 졸업
미국미주리주립대 경영학과 졸업
미국변호사(워싱턴DC)
경영학, 법학, 컴퓨터공학 전공
현 중국법무법인 신화그룹 파트너 변호사

저 서
「미국변호사법 — Essay편」

미국변호사 CEE편

초판발행	2021년 5월 10일
지은이	백희영
펴낸이	안종만 · 안상준
편 집	장유나
기획/마케팅	장규식
표지디자인	이미연
제 작	고철민 · 조영환
펴낸곳	(주) **박영사**
	서울특별시 금천구 가산디지털2로 53, 210호(가산동, 한라시그마밸리)
	등록 1959. 3. 11. 제300-1959-1호(倫)
전 화	02)733-6771
f a x	02)736-4818
e-mail	pys@pybook.co.kr
homepage	www.pybook.co.kr
ISBN	979-11-303-3898-9 13360

* 파본은 구입하신 곳에서 교환해 드립니다. 본서의 무단복제행위를 금합니다.
* 저자와 협의하여 인지첩부를 생략합니다.

정 가   39,000원